ATTP 3-34.23 (FM 5-71-100, 5-100-15, 5-116)

ENGINEER OPERATIONS–ECHELONS ABOVE BRIGADE COMBAT TEAM

July 2010

HEADQUARTERS, DEPARTMENT OF THE ARMY

Published by Books Express Publishing
Books Express Publishing, 2011
ISBN 978-1-78039-979-9

Books Express publications are available from all good retail and online booksellers. For
publishing proposals and direct ordering please contact us at: info@books-express.com

Army Tactics, Techniques, and Procedures
No. 3-34.23 (FM 5-71-100, 5-100-15, 5-116)

Headquarters
Department of the Army
Washington, DC, 8 July 2010

Engineer Operations–Echelons Above Brigade Combat Team

Contents

Distribution Restriction: Approved for public release; distribution is unlimited.

*This publication supersedes FM 5-71-100, 22 April 1993; FM 5-100-15, 6 June 1995; and FM 5-116, 9 February 1999.

Figures

Tables

Preface

Army Tactics, Techniques, and Procedures (ATTP) 3-34.23 describes engineer operations at echelons above brigade (EAB) combat team level. It is the engineer doctrinal manual for engineer support to division, corps, and theater army echelons. The manual is an extension of Field Manual (FM) 3-34, and is linked to joint and Army doctrine to ensure its usefulness for operational-level commanders and staff. This manual serves as a guide for the application of engineer combat power and employment of engineer forces in support of full spectrum operations primarily at higher echelons and within a joint framework.

ATTP 3-34.23 consolidates doctrine previously published in three separate manuals: FM 5-71-100, FM 5-100-15, and FM 5-116. The consolidated doctrine has been updated and revised to align with revisions to FM 3-34 and other Army and joint doctrine. This revision has been driven by major changes to Army and joint doctrine, including—

- Revision of our Army's capstone manual, FM 3-0.
- Revision of Joint Publication (JP) 3-34.
- Revision of the engineer keystone manual FM 3-34.
- Lessons learned from experience fighting the war on terrorism.
- Conversion of the Army to a brigade combat team (BCT)-based, modular force that is joint and expeditionary.
- Organization of the Engineer Regiment as the modular engineer force.
- Change from maintaining readiness within the "band of excellence" to achieving readiness through the force pool progression dictated by Army forces generation model.

The manual is organized into seven chapters plus numerous appendixes to provide additional details on selected operational topics. The first three chapters follow the flow of FM 3-34 and generally describe engineer operations at higher echelons. The next three chapters focus on operations at each of the higher echelons and operational configurations. The final chapter discusses sustainment support to the engineer forces operating at these echelons. A brief description of each of the chapters is provided below:

- Chapter 1 describes the engineer view of the operational environment (OE) as it pertains to operations at echelons above BCT. It discusses the challenges and opportunities that translate to requirements for engineer capabilities and combat power. It describes the forces and capabilities available including joint, interagency, and multinational forces. It concludes with a discussion of categorizing capabilities within the engineer functions and synchronizing their application through the warfighting functions.
- Chapter 2 discusses implications of the modular force organization for operations at higher echelons. It includes a discussion of the modular engineer force implications and the implications of the modular force headquarters at each higher echelon. It also addresses tailoring engineer force pool capabilities in support of engineer operations.
- Chapter 3 lays the foundations for engineer operations at EAB. It focuses on integration at each echelon and throughout the entire operations process. It includes a discussion of the engineer coordinator (ENCOORD). It also describes command and support relationships as the critical linkage for engineer integration throughout the force.
- Chapter 4 describes engineer operations at the theater echelon. It includes a discussion on integration in theater operational design, force-tailoring considerations, and operational themes at this echelon. It also includes a focused discussion on engineer support in each of the operational configurations described for a theater army headquarters.
- Chapter 5 describes engineer operations at the corps echelon. It includes a discussion on integration in corps operations processes, force-tailoring considerations, and full spectrum operations at this echelon. It also includes a focused discussion on engineer support in each of the operational configurations described for a corps headquarters.

- Chapter 6 describes engineer operations at the division echelon. It includes a discussion on integration in division operations processes, force-tailoring considerations, and full spectrum operations at this echelon. It also includes a focused discussion on engineer support in each of the operational configurations described for a division headquarters.
- Chapter 7 discusses sustainment of engineer capabilities. Successful engineer operations include effective incorporation of sustainment support. This chapter describes the integrated sustainment effort required to support engineer operations.

ATTP 3-34.23 provides operational guidance for engineer commanders and trainers at all higher echelons and forms the foundation for established curriculum within the engineer portions of the Army's education system. Information contained in this manual will assist multinational forces and other Services and branches of the Army to plan and integrate engineer capabilities. This doctrine also will assist Army branch schools in teaching the integration of engineer capabilities into Army and joint operations.

Terms that have joint or Army definitions are identified in both the glossary and the text. Glossary references: The glossary lists most terms used in ATTP 3-34.23 that have joint or Army definitions. Terms with an asterisk in the glossary indicate that this manual is the proponent FM (the authority). Text references: Definitions printed in boldface in the text indicate that this manual is the proponent. These terms and their definitions will be incorporated into the next revision of FM 1-02/Marine Corps Reference Publication (MCRP) 5-12A. For other definitions in the text, the term is italicized, and the number of the proponent FM follows the definition.

This publication applies to the Active Army, the Army National Guard (ARNG)/Army National Guard of the United States (ARNGUS), and the United States Army Reserve (USAR) unless otherwise stated.

The proponent for this publication is the United States Army Training and Doctrine Command (TRADOC). Send comments and recommendations on Department of the Army (DA) Form 2028 (*Recommended Changes to Publications and Blank Forms*) directly to Commandant, United States Army Engineer School (USAES), ATTN: ATZT-TDD-E, 320 MANSCEN Loop, Suite 270, Fort Leonard Wood, Missouri 65473-8929. Submit an electronic DA Form 2028 or comments and recommendations in the DA Form 2028 format by e-mail to <leon.mdottddengdoc@conus.army.mil>.

Unless this publication states otherwise, masculine nouns and pronouns do not refer exclusively to men.

Introduction

ATTP 3-34.23 provides engineer doctrine for operating at EAB in support of full spectrum operations. It is linked to the keystone doctrinal manual for engineer operations, FM 3-34, and is linked to joint and Army doctrine to ensure its usefulness for commanders and staff at higher echelons. Like FM 3-34, this manual describes engineer operations integrated through the warfighting functions in a combined arms application of combat power. This manual, however, provides greater detail for commanders and staff at EAB to ensure synchronization of engineer capabilities throughout the operations process and across the spectrum of conflict and applied operational themes. ATTP 3-34.23 answers the question, "How to?" for EAB engineers.

While the nature of war remains constant throughout history, the conduct of war is continually changing in response to new concepts, technologies, and requirements. Just as Army transformation has flattened higher-echelon structure into modular, scalable capabilities, this manual flattens the associated engineer doctrine for these echelons for greater effectiveness and efficiency. This edition describes an engineer view of the OE that captures challenges and opportunities impacting full spectrum operations at the tactical, operational, and strategic levels. It describes the engineer capabilities available to Army and joint commanders at every level, and implications of force-tailoring these capabilities at higher echelons. It also discusses the foundations of engineer operations to ensure integration at each echelon. Finally, the manual develops considerations for engineer operations within the operations process, tailored organization, operational themes, and headquarters configuration unique to the division, corps, and theater army echelons.

ATTP 3-34.23 is built directly on the new and revised concepts of FM 3-0, FM 3-07, FM 3-34, FM 3-90, and FM 4-0. It is synchronized with the key doctrine in JP 2-03, JP 3-15, and JP 3-34 to ensure that Army elements of a joint force use all engineer assets to their fullest extent.

Like FM 3-34 and FM 3-0, this manual emphasizes simultaneous combinations of offensive, defensive, and stability or civil support operations during all operations. It describes engineer support to Army forces conducting full spectrum operations within the framework of joint operations. The manual also more extensively addresses the engineer roles and functions within multinational operations, under potentially multinational or interagency leadership, and within diverse command relationships. One constant that is unchanged in this edition is that engineer operations continue to rely on the engineer Soldier to provide the leadership and flexibility required to integrate the application of engineer combat power within combined arms operations.

ATTP 3-34.23 not only consolidates FM 5-71-100, FM 5-100-15, and FM 5-116 but also provides a significant revision from the manuals and has been driven by changes in the OE, structure of the Army, availability of technologies, and a number of changes in Army and joint doctrine. Changes not already mentioned above that have directly affected this manual includes—

- Replacing the battlefield operating systems with the warfighting functions and the subsequent splitting of the mobility, countermobility, survivability battlefield operating system between the movement and maneuver and protection warfighting functions.
- Restructuring the engineer force to support the need for modularity in Army and joint operations, development of multifunctional battalion and brigade-level structures with significant engineer capabilities, and creation of the maneuver enhancement brigade (MEB) and its implications.
- Eliminating the term *battlespace* and the subsequent change from *engineer battlespace functions* to simply the engineer functions of *combat, general, and geospatial engineering*.
- Revising the joint definitions for combat, general, and geospatial engineering.
- Eliminating the term *force protection* except as it applies to force protection conditions as a part of the antiterrorism element of the protection warfighting function.

- Acknowledging the range engineer reconnaissance and its role and relationship to infrastructure reconnaissance. Staff proponency for infrastructure reconnaissance can be an additional requirement placed on the staff engineer similar to other staff integration responsibilities such as environmental considerations.
- Revising and renaming the civil engineering support plan to simply the engineer support plan (ESP).
- Readjusting the contingency construction standards.
- Eliminating the terms *combat, combat support*, and *combat service support* to describe categories for forces, functions, and capabilities.
- Converting the engineer command to the theater engineer command (TEC) structure and its implications.

The foundations of engineer operations provided in this manual, together with related engineer doctrine, will support the actions and decisions of engineer commanders at all levels. However, like FM 3-34 and FM 3-0, the manual is not meant to be a substitute for thought and initiative among engineer leaders. No matter how robust the doctrine or how advanced the new engineer capabilities and systems, it is the engineer Soldier who must understand the OE, recognize shortfalls, and adapt to the situation on the ground. It is the adaptable and professional engineer Soldiers of the Regiment who are most important to our future and who must be able to successfully perform their basic skills and accomplish the mission with or without the assistance of technology.

Chapter 1

Engineer View of the Operational Environment

Make no mistake—combat engineering, tactical warfighting expertise, and our Sapper-Warrior spirit are still paramount, and the hallmark of our Regiment. But today's operational environment of persistent conflict requires a more balanced engineer capability that can more effectively deliver combat, general, and geospatial engineering effects in order to expertly support full spectrum operations.

From "Join the Campaign: Engineer Leader Technical Competency" by Colonel Jerry C. Meyer and Brigadier General Gregg F. Martin

Today's OEs require responsive Army forces tailored to individual combatant commander's (CCDR's) needs. BCTs, modular support brigades, and functional brigades are now pooled for use as part of expeditionary force packages that enhance flexibility and responsiveness. The combined arms BCTs have become the centerpiece for Army maneuver. They and other brigades from the pool are attached to a higher-echelon headquarters—a division, corps, or theater army—as part of a force-tailored formation based on operational requirements. Engineers assigned to these higher-echelon headquarters provide critical roles in full spectrum operations. They provide engineer expertise contributing to a broader and deeper understanding of the OE and assist in defining the CCDR's needs. Engineers participate along with other leaders and staff specialists in an analysis of the OE. As is true for each leader and specialty, the individual's background and expertise will result in a unique understanding of the OE which adds scope and depth to the overall understanding. In a second critical role, engineers at each higher echelon coordinate the application of lethal and nonlethal engineer combat power available through employment of force-tailored formations and from other sources. This chapter proceeds from an examination of the engineer view of the OE into discussing the broad array of engineer capabilities that must be considered and how these capabilities are integrated in unified action. Engineer operations at EAB begin with an understanding of the OE that includes unique challenges and opportunities calling for the coordinated application of engineer combat power.

CHALLENGES AND OPPORTUNITIES

1-1. An engineer view of the OE is in addition to the common understanding gained through the application of analytical tools by other specialists and leaders. The engineer view shares a common general understanding of the OE while adding a degree of focus on those aspects within the purview of an engineering background (see figure 1-1, page 1-2). Guided by the common general understanding, the engineer view seeks to identify potential challenges and opportunities associated with operational variables of the OE. Within each critical variable of the framework being employed, the engineer view shares a common level of understanding while seeking the added specialty view.

Figure 1-1. Engineer view of the OE

SPECTRUM OF REQUIREMENTS

1-2.   The United States employs its joint military capabilities at home and abroad in support of its national security goals in a variety of ways. These operations vary in size, purpose, and combat intensity. The spectrum of conflict is the backdrop for Army operations. It places levels of violence on an ascending scale marked by graduated steps. The spectrum of conflict spans from stable peace to general war. The four primary descriptors (stable peace, unstable peace, insurgency, and general war) along the spectrum are not static points, and they are not exclusive. The levels of conflict and corresponding politically motivated violence may vary in different areas of the world and within a theater. It is common to conduct operations at different points along the spectrum within a theater or even within an area of operations (AO).

1-3.   An engineer view of the OE is not limited to any one point on the spectrum of conflict. The engineer view, including a shared general understanding and an added degree of focus on those aspects within the purview of an engineering background, seeks to identify potential challenges and opportunities across the spectrum of conflict. While the magnitude of violence varies over a spectrum of conflict, the magnitude of challenges and opportunities from an engineer view of the OE may remain consistently high (see figure 1-2). This spectrum of engineer requirements provides a menu of actions available in support of desired military operations.

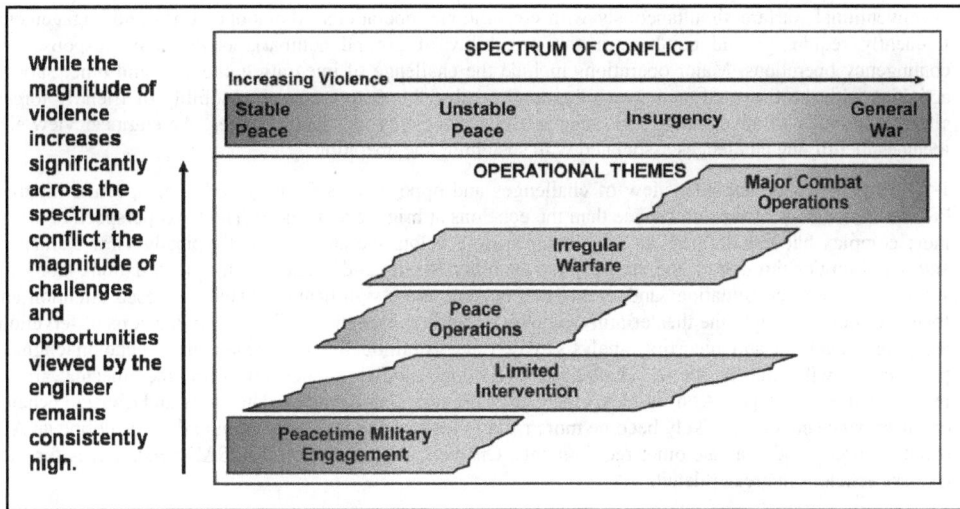

Figure 1-2. Challenges and opportunities from the engineer view

1-4. Stable peace is an ideal situation characterized by little or no violence. Peaceful interaction may include competition, cooperation, and assistance. Engineer activities may include geospatial engineering support to provide a clear understanding of the physical environment. Military engagement, security cooperation, and deterrence activities sometimes require large numbers of forces. These forces will need infrastructure, facilities, lines of communications (LOCs), and bases to support their sustainment. Even in areas with well-developed existing infrastructure, significant engineer effort will often be required to plan, design, construct, acquire, operate, maintain, or repair it to support operations. Assistance in response to disaster and humanitarian relief usually includes significant engineering challenges and opportunities to immediately and positively impact the situation.

1-5. Stable peace may degenerate into unstable peace. Unstable peace may also result when violence levels decrease after violent conflict. In some cases, outside powers may apply force to limit conflict. Preventing a return to violent conflict may require peace operations. If stable peace is not immediately achievable, the goal of conflict termination is establishing conditions in which peace operations can prevent conflict from recurring. Doing this allows the other instruments of national power to work toward stable peace. Opportunities to improve stability might be available through infrastructure development, building or improving host nation (HN) technological capacity, or other engineering projects. Opportunities may also include providing specialized engineer support to other agencies as necessary. Operational challenges may include access through ports and airfields, establishing a sustainment base, or support for intermediate staging bases (ISBs).

1-6. Violence increases along the spectrum toward insurgency, but short of large-scale operations by conventional forces. Most common military operations here are either counterinsurgency (see FM 3-24) or support to insurgencies, termed unconventional warfare. The engineer view will seek to identify challenges to the commander's ability to move and maneuver freely, protect the forces employed, and sustain the operation. Opportunities include directly impacting the adversaries' freedom of action and a variety of constructive actions aimed at improving stability.

1-7. At the far end of the spectrum is general war. In general war, conventional and unconventional forces vie for military supremacy, and major combat operations predominate. Major combat operations aim to defeat or destroy the enemy's armed forces and seize terrain. Commanders do this primarily through offensive and defensive operations accompanied by stability operations. These stability operations primarily shape the OE to assure order and security in the areas controlled by friendly forces and to prepare for postconflict operations. Commanders reduce the level of conflict to smaller, less coordinated actions by gradually decreasing numbers of disaffected parties. These actions move the situation down the spectrum of conflict until achieving stable peace. Major combat operations normally include insurgency or unconventional warfare simultaneously with conventional operations. Major operations and engagements frequently require ground combat (or the possibility of ground combat), as do crisis response and contingency operations. Major operations include the challenge of integrating engineer and other support activities with the fires and maneuver of ground combat forces to assure the mobility of friendly forces, alter the mobility of adversaries, and enhance the survivability of friendly forces. An engineer view also includes identifying challenges associated with sustaining the operation.

1-8.   In general, the engineer view of challenges and opportunities from the EAB perspective involves broader dimensions of time and space than the echelons at brigade and below. The EAB perspective is also more complex but less defined. At the theater army echelon, the engineer will typically view challenges and opportunities throughout the area of responsibility (AOR) and consider multiple situations along the spectrum of conflict. Situations and events that become more significant demand increased attention and focus. Routinely though, the theater army echelon engineer perspective includes simultaneous observations along the spectrum and recurring analysis over time. Additionally, the theater army echelon engineer perspective will include those challenges and opportunities associated with the theater army's responsibilities to support Army forces, other Services, and other agencies. The corps and division echelon engineer perspectives will likely become more rigid in time and space as operational designs define an AO, estimate forces, and evaluate other requirements. Chapters 4 through 6 discuss EAB perspectives for each of these echelons in greater detail.

ANALYTICAL FRAMEWORK

1-9.   Engineers will be challenged to understand the OE they face and apply their knowledge and background to add to the overall understanding. Their analysis must share a common general understanding of the OE while adding a degree of focus on those aspects within the purview of an engineering background. They identify potential challenges and opportunities associated with the variables analyzed in the OE. The engineer view must be consistent with the shared framework and variables employed to analyze the OE. Army doctrine describes an OE in terms of eight operational variables: political, military, economic, social, information, infrastructure, physical environment and time (PMESII-PT). Discussion of engineer considerations for each variable is provided in FM 3-34.

1-10. Analysis of the OE in terms of operational variables provides the relevant information (RI) that commanders can use to frame operational problems. When commanders receive a mission, they require a mission analysis focused on their specific situation. The Army uses mission variables—mission, enemy, terrain and weather, troops and support available, time available, civil considerations (METT-TC—as a framework for this mission analysis. When used together, mission and operational variables help commanders visualize their situation. The RI required for consideration of the METT–TC variables during mission analysis can be drawn from the ongoing analysis of the operational variables (PMESII-PT).

1-11. Engineers review the OE using operational variables to add to the shared common understanding by identifying potential challenges to and opportunities within the operation before and during mission execution. While the engineer view of the OE is not limited to considerations within the OE that may result in engineer functional missions, it is organized by engineer functions and linked to the common overall understanding through warfighting functions.

1-12. Combat power is the way Army leaders conceptualize capabilities. For Army and United States Marine Corps (USMC) forces, the joint functions—intelligence, fires, movement and maneuver, protection, sustainment, and command and control (C2)—become the six warfighting functions. To these six warfighting functions the Army adds two elements, leadership and information, which tie together and multiply the effects of the other six. These eight are the elements of combat power. The Army employs combat power through combined arms. Combined arms are organized through tailoring and task organizing Army forces to optimize the elements of combat power for a particular mission. The engineer view of the OE, and engineer operations broadly, are synchronized to support combined arms using the warfighting functions.

THE MILITARY VARIABLE

1-13. The military variable explores the military capabilities of all relevant actors in a given OE. Engineer capabilities can be a significant and relevant component within the military variable. Chapter 2 provides a summary discussion of modular engineer force capabilities, while FM 3-34 provides a more detailed discussion including Army, joint, interagency, and multinational capabilities. Recent significant changes impacting the military variable can be summarized by—

- A complex, noncontiguous AO, where boundaries will not be clearly defined.
- A threat scenario in which potential adversaries are not readily identifiable.
- Simultaneous, geographically dispersed operations that will result in extremely long and potentially unsecured LOCs.
- Increased coordination of organizations and functions to achieve appreciable gains.
- The prevalence of joint organizations at the operational level and single-Service organizations operating in a collaborative or interdependent joint environment at the tactical level.
- A significant degree of joint and single-Service interaction with other government and nongovernmental organizations (NGOs), multinational forces, and contractors.

1-14. Understanding the theater structure commonly used to array military capabilities enables an understanding of engineer capabilities within the context of the OE. A theater is a geographical area for which a geographic combatant commander (GCC) is assigned military responsibility. The command views a theater from a strategic perspective and assesses the level of international military cooperation available with the degree of dedicated United States (U.S.) military resources necessary. These factors influence prospective Army operations in each theater or GCC AOR.

1-15. To conduct operations, the GCC may designate a specific area within his AOR as a theater of war, theater of operations, or a joint operations area (JOA). Commanders may use these terms independently or in conjunction with one another, depending on the needs of the operation. If used in conjunction, the theater of war would encompass the larger area comprising smaller theaters of operation and JOAs. JP 3-0 describes the criteria for each designation in more detail. This manual uses the more generic term AO to refer to any area where engineer capabilities may deploy to conduct operations. The GCC (or subordinate unified commander) maintains responsibility for the operations of U.S. forces in an AOR or designates a joint task force (JTF) to command forces in a designated area. The Army Service component command (ASCC) provides Army forces to the joint force commander (JFC) and JTF to support those operations.

UNIFIED ACTION

1-16. Unified action describes the wide scope of actions (including synchronizing activities with governmental and nongovernmental agencies) taking place within unified commands, subordinate unified commands, or JTFs under the overall direction of the commanders of those commands. Under unified action, commanders integrate joint, single-Service, special, and supporting operations with interagency, nongovernmental, and multinational operations (see JP 1). Multinational, interagency, and nonmilitary forces work with the CCDR through cooperation and coordination. EAB engineers coordinate and employ joint, multinational, and other engineer and construction capabilities to support the strategic and operational objectives. The aim is to achieve unity of engineer effort among many diverse agencies in a complex OE. Subordinate echelon engineers synchronize the efforts of subordinate military engineer forces and coordinate with the efforts of other engineer capabilities to achieve the same goal.

1-17. Engineering and construction constitute a significant portion of those diverse activities taking place within and impacting the JOA. Increasingly at higher echelons, engineers on the staff provide coordinating links which assist the commander in integrating engineer operations with related interagency, nongovernmental, and multinational operations. The higher-echelon engineer staff may have established linkages or may rely on supporting engineer headquarters and United States Army Corps of Engineers (USACE) elements or other Service equivalent organizations to develop and coordinate activities.

CHAIN OF COMMAND

1-18. The typical operational chain of command extends from the CCDR through a JTF commander to the functional component commander. Often Army forces are under operational control (OPCON) of the joint force land component commander (JFLCC), a functional component commander given control of all Army and Marine forces. When the CCDR retains command directly, the combatant command is the joint force headquarters and there may not be a JTF headquarters. In this case, the ASCC may become the land component C2 Army and other land forces, in addition to its Service responsibilities.

1-19. The ASCC may also function as an Army forces, or there may be an Army force subordinate to it. An *Army force (ARFOR)* is the Army Service component headquarters for a JTF or a joint and multinational force. (FM 3-0) The Secretary of the Army directs the flow of administrative control (ADCON). ADCON for most Title 10 functions flows through the ASCC, then through the ARFOR to assigned or attached units. However, ADCON is not tied directly to the operational chain of command. ADCON responsibilities may include recruiting, organizing, supplying, equipping, training, servicing, mobilizing, demobilizing, and administering forces; maintaining, outfitting, and repairing of military equipment; constructing, maintaining, and repairing of buildings, structures, and utilities; and acquiring real property. The ASCC provides administrative and logistic services to assigned ARFOR and serves as executive agent for other Services when required. When appropriate, the ASCC may delegate authority for support tasks to a single theater support command (TSC) or another subordinate Army headquarters, such as the TEC or the medical command (MEDCOM), when the focus of support suggests this as the best solution. USACE is often involved with supporting the ASCC as well, and will generally operate through the TEC, if one is present.

JOINT AND OTHER CAPABILITIES

1-20. In full spectrum operations, Army engineers operate as part of a joint force and often within a multinational and interagency environment. Each Service has core engineering units and capabilities that stem from their traditional roles and associations to meet specific operational needs and to support accomplishing a variety of mission requirements in any OE. An understanding of the Services' engineering capabilities and limitations and the increasing interdependence among Service engineers in joint operations allow the JFC and the joint force engineer to tailor the engineer force to effectively and efficiently accomplish the mission. The JFC should understand multinational, interagency, NGO, and intergovernmental organization engineer capabilities to better coordinate coherent activity, develop viable courses of action (COAs) and, when appropriate, to properly integrate them into the joint operation. The joint force engineer is responsible for providing comprehensive recommendations to the JFC on the effective employment of all engineer capabilities in support of joint operations. Recommendations are developed in collaboration with identified engineer unit commanders tailored to support the operation as soon as that collaboration is feasible. The JFC, with the assistance of the joint force engineer, analyzes mission requirements to tailor optimal engineer force packages. The engineering capabilities of each Service component may provide engineering support to the other components to meet joint force requirements. See JP 3-34, JP 3-08, and Standardization Agreement (STANAG) (NATO) 2394E (Allied Tactical Publication [ATP]-52(B)) for further discussion of engineer participation in joint, interagency, and multinational (allied) operations.

1-21. Joint integration does not require joint commands at all echelons; it does require understanding joint synergy at all levels of command. Joint synergy extends the principles of combined arms to operations conducted by two or more Service components. The strengths of each Service or functional component combine to overcome the limitations or reinforce the effects of the other components. The combination of multiple and diverse joint force capabilities generates combat power more potent than the sum of its parts. Integrating the variety and special capabilities of engineer organizations requires an understanding of the various capabilities and limitations of the engineer assets available for any given mission. Integration also requires a common understanding of the C2 structure and processes in place to employ the engineer capabilities in unified action.

1-22. A brief summary of Service engineer capabilities is provided in FM 3-34. Of note is that some capabilities that are categorized as engineering by other Services reside in other branches of the Army (such as explosive ordnance disposal [EOD] and chemical, biological, radiological, and nuclear [CBRN] defense capabilities).

Other Engineering Capabilities

1-23. In addition to U.S. military engineer forces including USACE and other Service equivalent organizations, multinational engineers can provide valuable capabilities. Multinational military units and civilian contractors, in addition to providing labor, material, infrastructure, and services, may possess certain engineering capabilities specifically adapted to the local environment. There are other benefits to the use of multinational military units and civilian contractors, but these need to be weighed against their potential limitations. This mixture of capabilities may change during the phases of an operation and may require management across Service lines to ensure that the JFC has appropriate forces in place.

1-24. The Department of State (DOS), United States Agency for International Development (USAID), and other interagency partners may deploy capabilities in-theater which integrate engineer efforts within the context of their diplomatic and development missions. DOS may establish an Office of the Coordinator for Reconstruction and Stability with a substantive or lead role in the development and execution of certain security sector reform programs. USAID may participate in the establishment of provincial reconstruction teams (PRTs) as interim civil-military organizations to develop local institutional capacity for the provision of basic services and other governmental functions. These agency capabilities, along with the nongovernmental development agency efforts they coordinate, offer both challenges and opportunities for engineers at EAB to achieve a unity of engineer effort in a complex OE.

1-25. HN engineer capabilities may be available if adequate technical capacity and infrastructure exist. Potentially, this could include a wide array of civil and public works organizations. It is also increasingly common to contract for a wide range of engineer services with local or third-party national organizations and civilian contractors. These assets are typically used to free up military construction assets and minimize the military footprint in-theater when requirements exceed military capabilities or when the engineer operations and requirements are to be conducted in areas that are relatively safe from active combat. Consideration must be given to providing adequate contractor oversight when this option is employed. Additionally, emphasis should be placed on using local construction techniques whenever feasible and local contractors are employed. This emphasis typically will assist in building local technical capacity.

Application of Other Engineering Capabilities

1st Cavalry Division established a contract with Baghdad University during Operation Iraqi Freedom (OIF) II to employ engineering students to conduct quality assurance inspections on contracted construction projects, especially in areas that U.S. forces did not routinely enter.

Civil Augmentation Program

1-26. Civil augmentation programs, such as the Army's logistics civil augmentation program (LOGCAP), the Navy's global contingency construction and contingency service contract programs, and the United States Air Force (USAF) contract augmentation program (AFCAP), also play a significant role in mission accomplishment by providing the JFC and joint force engineer with additional options and flexibility in general engineering and logistic support. Construction may be within the scope of any of these types of contract services. EAB engineers recommend construction under a civil augmentation program option whenever analysis of the mission variables dictates that this is the most effective option—for example, if limited military construction assets are required for other missions in less permissive areas. Even when this option is selected, EAB engineers (units and staffs) continue to have a significant role in optimizing the delivery of construction by appropriately mixing troop construction, LOGCAP, and other contracted construction support to meet commanders' needs.

Domestic Capabilities

1-27. The Department of Homeland Security (DHS) is the primary federal agency in charge of reducing the vulnerability of the United States to domestic incidents, emergencies, and disasters. State (ARNG and others), local (first responders as well as private organizations), and federal responders are all coordinated by DHS in a federal response that may include civil support operations. The DHS is responsible for two primary documents describing national policy and procedures for effective, coordinated, multiple-organization incident response operations. The National Incident Management System (NIMS) contains the initial guidance required for establishing multiorganization command and management structures (these are somewhat comparable to a military headquarters structure) for a disaster response, from the local to federal level. It provides the primary core concepts, principles, and terminology that enable all organizations, from the local to federal level, to work together effectively. The primary command and management structure and terminology described within NIMS serve as a "base foundation" for the additional guidance and procedures contained within the National Response Framework (NRF). The additional guidance and procedures in the NRF include what organizations are involved based on the type of incident and level of required response. The NRF gives guidance on "who does what" from the local to federal level, including private, nongovernment, volunteer, and government organizations. Engineers at EAB must be familiar with the fundamentals of the NIMS and NRF. The degree of familiarity required depends on the anticipated level of required coordination. A general understanding of the NIMS and NRF helps ensure unity of effort across all organizations when planning for and conducting civil support operations.

ENGINEER FUNCTIONS

1-28. The JFC and joint force engineer must understand the Services' engineering capabilities and limitations to effectively and efficiently tailor the engineer force. Three categories of related engineer capabilities and activities, the engineer functions, are designed and used to relate specific Service capabilities to joint capability areas and actual requirements. Services use the engineer functions to categorize forces and assets based on their primary function (combat engineering, general engineering, and geospatial engineering). Forces can sometimes perform tasks from other functions, but engineer forces and assets are not interchangeable. Planners must be careful to accurately identify the capabilities required for an operation and the forces that have those capabilities.

1-29. *Engineer functions* are defined as categories of related engineer capabilities and activities grouped together to help JFCs integrate, synchronize, and direct engineer operations. The three engineer functions are combat engineering, general engineering, and geospatial engineering. (FM 3-34) See figure 1-3. Engineer reconnaissance, though not a separate engineer function, is a critical part of each one. See FM 3-34.170 for additional discussion of engineer reconnaissance.

Combat Engineering	General Engineering		Geospatial Engineering
Conduct Reconnaissance Employ Demolitions Provide Engineer Advice Fight as: Engineers or Infantry	Conduct Assessment Provide Engineer Advice Harden Facilities Horizontal Construction Hauling Port Construction Underwater Construction Pipeline Construction Produce Asphalt Prime Power Survey/Design Environmental Protection	Support M/C/M/S Fight as Engineers Vertical Construction Bridging Utilities Firefighting Dig Wells Quarry Aggregate Produce Concrete Construction Management Facilities Management Real Estate	Geospatial Planning Data Generation Analysis Dissemination
Mobility Breach Obstacles Construct Combat Roads Assault Bridge Clear Explosive Hazards Forward Aviation Combat Engineering			
Countermobility Place Mines or Munitions Construct Obstacles			
Survivability Construct Field Forts Construct Positions			

Note: The capabilities listed are illustrative and should not be considered all inclusive.

Figure 1-3. Engineer functions

Combat Engineering

1-30. Combat engineering includes those capabilities organic to and augmenting the BCTs. Combat engineering provides tactical-level engineer support to combat (offensive and defensive), stability, or civil support operations. In combat operations it is typically (though not always) focused on the support of close combat. Combat engineer units have the capability of fighting as engineers, or, if required, as infantry. Augmentation will typically be required for engineers to fight as infantry; see chapter 3 for additional discussion. Combat engineering capabilities may be augmented at times with general engineering support but retain a focus on the integrated application of engineer capabilities to support the combined arms team's freedom of maneuver (mobility and countermobility) and protection (survivability).

1-31. Since combat engineering focuses primarily on tactical-level engineer support, adequate tailoring of these capabilities relies on the level of detail available in understanding tactical-level requirements and ultimately the tactical-level plan. At the higher-echelon headquarters, engineer analysis and planning perspectives tend to consider the broad operational-level requirements and operational design and must collaborate with subordinate tactical echelons to fill in the detail. The operational-echelon engineer planners may initially have only a broad outline of combat engineering capabilities required to provide tactical-level support. These requirements are then refined as tactical-level planning occurs. Chapters 4, 5, and 6 include additional discussion on force-tailoring considerations for each higher-echelon headquarters.

General Engineering

1-32. General engineering capabilities are not organic to the BCTs, and although they may be performed in support of combat engineering and combat operations, general engineering capabilities are not typically associated with close combat. Tactical-level perspectives may include uncertainty in distinguishing purely combat engineering from general engineering capabilities but will in most cases identify requirements for both. More distinguishable at the operational level, general engineering capabilities are applied to establish and maintain the infrastructure necessary for sustaining military operations in-theater. At times, the military operation may extend general engineering support to restore or develop facilities, power, and life-support systems within the infrastructure of the AO or build technical capacity of the HN. This effort aids in the recovery and the transition to preconflict conditions or may be the objective of stability or civil support operations. For more information on general engineering, see FM 3-34.400.

1-33. General engineering is the most diverse of the three engineer functions and is typically the largest percentage of all engineer support provided to an operation. General engineering tasks—

- May include construction or repair of existing logistics-support facilities, LOC and other supply routes (including bridging and roads), airfields, ports, water wells, power generation and distribution, water and fuel pipelines, and base camps or force beddown. Firefighting and engineer dive operations are two aspects that may be critical enablers to these tasks.
- May include coordination with local or national-level government agencies or ministries that maintain or control infrastructure associated with essential services.
- May emphasize development of local technical and engineering capacity, both civilian and military.
- May be performed by modular units or through the use of commercial contract construction management assets such as USACE, Naval Facilities Engineering Command (NAVFAC), the Air Force Civil Engineer Support Agency (AFCESA), or multinational, HN, and other agencies.
- May also be performed by a combination of joint engineer units, civilian contractors, and HN forces, or multinational engineer capabilities.
- Incorporate field force engineering (FFE) to leverage all capabilities throughout the Engineer Regiment. This includes the linkages that facilitate engineer reachback.
- May require various types of reconnaissance and assessments to be performed before, or early on in, a particular mission (see FM 3-34.170).
- Include disaster preparedness planning, response, and support to consequence management.
- Include the acquisition and disposal of real estate and real property.
- Include those survivability planning and construction tasks that are not considered under combat engineering.
- May include camouflage, concealment, and deception tasks (see FM 20-3).
- May include the performance of environmental support engineering missions.
- May include base or area denial missions.
- May require large amounts of construction materials, which must be planned and provided for in a timely manner.
- May include the production of construction materials.
- Require the integration of environmental considerations.

Geospatial Engineering

1-34. Geospatial engineering is generating, managing, analyzing, and disseminating positionally accurate terrain information that is tied to some portion of the earth's surface. These actions provide mission-tailored data, tactical decision aids, and visualization products that define the character of the zone for the maneuver commander. Key aspects of the geospatial engineering mission are databases, analysis, digital products, visualization, and printed maps. Both organic and augmenting geospatial engineer capabilities at the theater, corps, division, and brigade levels are responsible for geospatial engineering.

1-35. The geospatial engineer uses analysis and visualization capabilities to integrate people, processes, and tools, using multiple information sources and collaborative analysis to build a shared knowledge of the physical environment. Whether it is using one of the examples indicated above, or through some other special product, the geospatial engineer, in combination with other engineers and staff officers, provides support to the unit's mission and commander's intent. FM 3-34.230, FM 2-0, and JP 2-03 are the primary references for geospatial engineering.

FULL SPECTRUM OPERATIONS

1-36. Engineer capabilities are a significant force multiplier in full spectrum operations, facilitating the freedom of action necessary to meet mission objectives. Engineer operations modify, maintain, provide understanding of, and protect the physical environment. In doing so, they enable the mobility of friendly forces, alter the mobility of adversaries, enhance the survivability and enable the sustainment of friendly forces, contribute to a clear understanding of the physical environment, and provide support to noncombatants, other nations, and civilian authorities and agencies. Table 1-1 lists the elements of full spectrum operations, the primary tasks associated with them, and the purposes of each element. Each primary task has numerous associated subordinate tasks.

Table 1-1. Elements of full spectrum operations

Offense	*Defense*
Primary Tasks • Movement to contact • Attack • Exploitation • Pursuit **Purposes** • Dislocate, isolate, disrupt, and destroy enemy forces • Seize key terrain • Deprive the enemy of resources • Develop intelligence • Deceive and divert the enemy • Create a secure environment for stability operations	**Primary Tasks** • Mobile defense • Area defense • Retrograde **Purposes** • Deter or defeat enemy offensive operations • Gain time • Achieve economy of force • Retain key terrain • Protect the populace, critical assets, and infrastructure • Develop intelligence
Stability	*Civil Support*
Primary Tasks • Civil security • Civil control • Restore essential services • Support to governance • Support to economic and infrastructure development **Purposes** • Provide a secure environment • Secure land areas • Meet the critical needs (including infrastructure) of the populace • Develop local capacity for security, economy, and the rule of law • Gain support for host nation governance • Shape the environment for interagency and host nation success	**Primary Tasks** • Provide support in response to disaster • Support civil law enforcement • Provide other support as required **Purposes** • Save lives • Restore essential services • Maintain or restore law and order • Protect infrastructure and property • Maintain or restore local government • Shape the environment for interagency success

1-37. Commanders plan for the concurrent conduct of the elements of full spectrum operations in weighted combinations. Within broader combinations of full spectrum operations, ARFOR conduct multiple component operations simultaneously. Simultaneity requires the ability to conduct operations in depth. Commanders consider the full depths of their AOs, the enemy, the information environment, and civil considerations and act in the times and places necessary to achieve their objectives. Army forces increase the depth of their operations through combined arms, advanced information systems, and joint capabilities. Because Army forces conduct operations across large areas, enemies face many potential friendly actions. Depth is equally important in stability operations to preclude threats from operating outside of the reach of friendly forces, where they can affect the operation. In civil support operations, depth gives the Army its ability to reach all the citizens in an affected area, bringing relief and hope.

1-38. There is an inherent complementary relationship between the use of lethal force and the application of military capabilities for nonlethal purposes. Though each situation requires a different mix of violence and restraint, lethal and nonlethal actions used together complement each other and create dilemmas for the opponent. Lethal means remain at the heart of offensive and defensive actions; however, nonlethal means are becoming increasingly important. Today's threat no longer fights "around" populations, but "among" them. Unavoidable collateral damage may significantly impact mission accomplishment, since many times that mission includes gaining and maintaining support of the local populace. Commanders consider nonlethal applications when the effects achieved from them support the mission as well as other lethal methods, hence mitigating the risk of adverse effects if collateral damage results. Nonlethal, constructive actions can persuade the local populace to withhold support for adversaries, and provide intelligence to friendly forces. This can force the enemy to choose between abandoning an area and exposing his forces to lethal combat. Commanders analyze the mission variables to achieve a balance between lethal and nonlethal actions. Engineer operations contribute significant combat power, both lethal and nonlethal in nature, linked to the commander's objective through warfighting functions.

WARFIGHTING FUNCTIONS

1-39. Full spectrum operations require the continuous generation and application of combat power, often for protracted periods. Combat power is the actual application of force—the conversion of fighting potential into effective action. It includes the unit's constructive and information capabilities and its disruptive or destructive force. Engineer operations—the application of engineer combat power—are linked to full spectrum operations through the six warfighting functions.

1-40. Every unit—regardless of type—generates combat power and contributes to the operation. A variety of engineer capabilities and unit types are available to contribute combat power. Engineer functions are the categories of related engineer capabilities and activities grouped together to help JFCs integrate, synchronize, and direct engineer operations. These engineer functions are each generally aligned in support of specific warfighting functions (see figure 1-4), though they have impact in and across the others (for example, survivability support may be provided with linkages to the fires warfighting function). Combat engineering is aligned primarily with the movement and maneuver and the protection warfighting functions; general engineering aligns to focus its support on the sustainment, protection warfighting functions, and reinforcement of combat engineering outside of close combat; and geospatial engineering is primarily aligned with the C2 and intelligence warfighting functions.

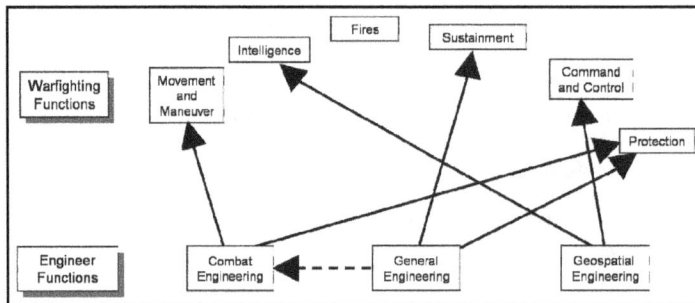

Figure 1-4. Primary relationships of engineer functions to the warfighting functions

MOVEMENT AND MANEUVER

1-41. Combat engineer support applied through the movement and maneuver warfighting function includes mobility operations (see FM 3-34.2) and countermobility operations (see FM 90-7 and FM 5-102). Combat engineers are at the vanguard because they fight alongside maneuver units with a focus on close combat. When conducting combat operations, they must be prepared to fight and employ their combat skills, using fire and maneuver to accomplish their engineer mission.

1-42. General engineering support to movement and maneuver accomplishes tasks exceeding the capability of the combat engineer force and more extensive upgrades or new construction of lines of communications and intermediate staging bases (see FM 3-34.400). General engineering support is typically applied through the sustainment warfighting function but may include many of the following tasks that also cross over to support movement and maneuver:

- Construct and repair combat roads and trails exceeding the capability of combat engineer assets.
- Provide forward aviation combat engineering (FACE) exceeding the capabilities of combat engineer assets, to include the repair of paved, asphalt, and concrete runways and airfields.
- Install assets that prevent foreign object damage to rotary-wing aircraft.
- Construct tactical, support, and LOC bridging.
- Conduct area damage control (ADC) missions that support the mobility of the maneuver force.
- Ensure theater access through the construction and upgrade of ports; airfields; and reception, staging, onward movement, and integration (RSOI) facilities.

INTELLIGENCE

1-43. The intelligence warfighting function comprises the related tasks and systems that facilitate understanding of the OE. Intelligence is a continuous process that involves analyzing information from all sources and conducting operations to develop the situation. Commanders make decisions and direct actions based on their situational understanding. They keep their situational understanding current by continuously assessing the situation and stating the information they need in commander's critical information requirements (CCIR). The required information is obtained through various detection methods and systematic observation, reconnaissance, and surveillance. Engineer capabilities can be employed during key activities in the operations process to add to the commander's situational understanding. Geospatial support improves understanding of the physical environment. Engineer reconnaissance can provide data that contributes to answering the CCIR.

Geospatial Engineering Operations and Functions

Note. See FM 3-34.230 for more information on geospatial engineering.

1-44. The term *geospatial intelligence (GEOINT)* is defined as the exploitation and analysis of imagery and geospatial information to describe, assess, and visually depict physical features and geographically referenced activities on the Earth. Geospatial intelligence consists of imagery, imagery intelligence, and geospatial information. (JP 2-03) GEOINT was created to describe and encompass both the standard and the advanced (integrated) capabilities of all three of these. The full power of GEOINT comes from the integration and analysis of all three capabilities, which results in more comprehensive, tailored intelligence products for a wider scope of problems and customers. Imagery, imagery intelligence, and geospatial information are now considered to be three complementary elements of GEOINT, rather than separate entities. Advances in technology and the use of geospatial data have created the ability to integrate and combine elements of any or all of the areas.

1-45. The GEOINT discipline encompasses all activities involved in the planning, collection, processing, analysis, exploitation, and dissemination of spatial information to gain intelligence about the OE, visually depict this knowledge, and fuse the acquired knowledge with other information through analysis and visualization processes.

1-46. The geospatial engineering contribution to GEOINT includes the standards, processes, Soldiers, and equipment required to generate, manage, analyze, and disseminate the geospatial information necessary to assemble the best view of the OE for the command. Geospatial engineers manage the enterprise geospatial database compiled from all sources—including the National Geospatial–Intelligence Agency (NGA), Topographic Engineering Center, other Services, other federal agencies, and multinational partners—and exploiting new collection and production from deployed Soldiers and sensors. Geospatial engineers manage the geospatial foundation of the common operational picture (COP)—synchronizing hard and soft copy products that are necessary components of all source intelligence and C2. See FM 2-0 and JP 2-03 for additional discussion of GEOINT.

Engineer Reconnaissance

Note. See FM 3-34.170 for more information on engineer reconnaissance.

1-47. The responsibility for conducting reconnaissance does not reside solely with specifically organized units. Every unit has an implied mission to report information about the terrain, civilian activities, and friendly and enemy dispositions—regardless of its location within the AO and primary function. Though all units conduct the implied reconnaissance mission, the commander typically focuses specifically organized reconnaissance units on the highest priority requirements.

1-48. Though reconnaissance primarily relies on the human dynamic rather than technical means, the situation may require the collection of a higher degree of technical information than nonspecialized units possess. An area with suspected contamination by toxic industrial materials, for example, must be targeted for reconnaissance by assets equipped to determine the type and level of contaminants present and protected from the contamination. Supporting units such as engineers, CBRN, EOD, military police (MP), and others have specialized capabilities to collect technical information that complements the force's overall reconnaissance effort. The engineer functions provide a menu of reconnaissance capabilities varying in linkages to warfighting functions and varying in type and degree of tactical or technical expertise and effort applied to the assigned mission and tasks. It is this collection of necessary tactical and technical information that defines the range of engineer reconnaissance capabilities (see FM 3-34.170).

1-49. General engineers provide a range of technical reconnaissance capabilities. At the tactical level, engineer reconnaissance tends to occur as an integral component of the continuous tactical reconnaissance effort. General engineers working at the operational level will conduct reconnaissance to identify requirements for construction or other engineering projects. Technical reconnaissance capabilities are typically conducted by general engineering assessment or survey teams to gather the technical information required for—

- Maintenance and upgrade of ground LOCs.
- Bridge construction or repair.
- Support of airfields and heliports.
- Support of seaports.
- Support of survivability.
- Real estate and real property maintenance activities.
- Procurement or production of construction materials.
- Support of base camps and support areas.
- Power generation and distribution.
- Petroleum pipeline and storage facilities.
- Water supply and well drilling.
- Underwater and other specialized construction support.
- Infrastructure survey.
- Assessment of HN capacity.
- Environmental baseline assessment or survey.
- Environmental remediation survey and assessment.

1-50. Technical capabilities include robust support from joint Service, multiagency, contractor, HN and reachback elements. FFE provides a broad range of primarily generating force activities linked through the general engineering element on the ground to apply a higher degree of technical expertise to the assessment or survey mission.

SUSTAINMENT

1-51. Sustainment is the provision of logistics, personnel services, and health service support (HSS) necessary to maintain and prolong operations until mission accomplishment. General engineering applications are primarily linked through, and provide a major category of tasks under, providing logistics support in the sustainment warfighting function. As already discussed, general engineering capabilities can also be applied in support of combat engineer applications and will have linkages across both the movement and maneuver and the protection warfighting functions. Provision of general engineering support (see FM 3-34.400) includes—

- Restoring damaged areas.
- Constructing and maintaining sustainment LOCs.
  - Constructing and maintaining roads and highways.
  - Constructing and maintaining over-the-shore facilities.
  - Constructing and maintaining ports.
  - Constructing and maintaining railroad facilities.
  - Constructing and expanding airfield facilities.
  - Constructing and maintaining pipelines and tank farms.
  - Constructing and maintaining standard and nonstandard fixed bridges.
- Providing engineer construction support.
- Supplying mobile electric power.
- Providing facilities engineering support.
  - Providing waste management.
  - Acquiring, managing, and disposing of real estate.
  - Providing firefighting support.
  - Constructing, managing, and maintaining bases and installations.

1-52. In stability or civil support operations, sustainment support may shift to the establishment of services that support civilian agencies in addition to the normal support of U.S. forces. Stability operations tend to be of longer duration than the other elements in full spectrum operations. As such, the general engineering level of effort, including FFE support from USACE, is very high at the onset and gradually decreases as the theater matures. As the operation matures, the general engineering effort may transfer to theater or external support contracts such as LOGCAP, AFCAP, or the Navy's Global Contingency Construction Contract.

COMMAND AND CONTROL

1-53. Whether a subordinate or supporting unit, engineer unit commanders and their staffs must understand and exercise the art and science of C2 as described in FM 3-0 (see also FM 5-0 and FM 6-0). As modular units and headquarters elements are tailored and allocated to division, corps, and Army headquarters, those unit commanders and staff must recognize and integrate within the respective C2 structure. The engineer headquarters elements provide C2 for the conduct of engineer operations but also add depth to the engineer staff capabilities within the supported or gaining headquarters. Similarly, task-organized units face challenges in quickly recognizing and integrating into the distinct character of their "new unit." Thorough understanding of and practice with the C2 function and the operations process that it drives enable the flexibility necessary for modular engineer forces to plug into supported units. In unique cases in which an engineer headquarters serves as the base around which a task force or JTF is formed, as in a disaster relief operation, it becomes even more critical that the C2 function and the operations process it drives adheres closely to the ideal described in the referenced FMs (and applicable joint doctrine when operating as a JTF).

1-54. Finding ways to accomplish the mission with an appropriate mix of lethal and nonlethal force is a paramount consideration for every Army commander. Through synchronization, commanders mass the lethal and nonlethal effects of combat power at the decisive place and time to overwhelm an enemy or dominate the situation. Engineer leaders and staff planners at each echelon play a pivotal role in ensuring the synchronization of the variety of engineer capabilities that are available to conduct or support full spectrum operations. Engineer leaders and staff synchronize the application of engineer functions through the warfighting function framework by integrating into the operations process.

PROTECTION

1-55. The protection warfighting function facilitates the ability of the commander to maintain the integrity and combat power of the deploying force. Within the AO, the application of the protection warfighting function integrates protection capabilities within the force to safeguard bases, secure routes, and protect forces. The protection warfighting function focuses on several tasks:

- Employ air and missile defense (AMD).
- Conduct personnel recovery operations.
- Conduct information protection.
- Perform fratricide avoidance.
- Conduct operational area security.
- Conduct antiterrorism activities.
- Conduct survivability operations.
- Conduct force health protection.
- Conduct CBRN operations.
- Employ safety techniques.
- Implement operations security.
- Provide EOD protection support.

1-56. Engineers have unique equipment and personnel capabilities that can be used to support survivability efforts. Combat engineers, supported by general engineering capabilities when required, provide selected survivability operations (see FM 5-103) through the protection warfighting function. Survivability operations also include camouflage, concealment, and deception support to tactical ground maneuver forces. Combat engineers typically provide the basic hardening and camouflage, concealment, and deception support while general engineering support is focused on longer-term survivability efforts. General engineering support is also applied through the protection warfighting function to control pollution and hazardous materials and to harden facilities.

1-57. When conducting stability operations or civil support operations, survivability remains a key concern. Though the likelihood of combat operations is reduced, key resources and personnel remain vulnerable to other types of hostile action or attack. Commanders must consider protecting vital resources such as fuel sites, sustainment convoys, forward operating bases (FOBs), and logistics support areas since the entire AO has an equal potential for enemy attack. Therefore, priority of work for construction assets will be much more focused on protecting these types of resources than constructing fighting positions for combat vehicles or crew-served weapons. Vital resources requiring survivability may also include facilities critical to the civilian infrastructure such as key industrial sites, pipelines, water treatment plants, and government buildings. Engineers also employ protective obstacles as a key tool in protecting these important assets and locations. Protective obstacles range from tetrahedrons and concrete barriers to networked munitions. Physical barriers provide relatively inexpensive, though relatively inflexible, survivability capability. Networked munitions, with their built-in sensor capabilities and central control over nonlethal and lethal fields, provide a flexible intrusion detection and denial system.

COMBAT POWER

1-58. Commanders ensure that deployed Army forces have enough combat power to conduct necessary combinations of full spectrum operations appropriate to the situation. Commanders balance the ability to mass the effects of lethal and nonlethal systems with the requirements to deploy and sustain the units that employ those systems. Sustaining combat power throughout the operation is important to success. Tailored force packages maximize the capability of initial-entry forces consistent with the mission and the requirement to project, employ, and sustain the force. Follow-on forces increase the entire force's endurance and ability to operate in depth—employing reserves, focusing joint support, arranging rest for committed forces, and staging sustainment assets to preserve momentum and synchronization. All these assist in applying combat power effectively over time and space.

1-59. Combined arms is the synchronized and simultaneous application of several arms—such as infantry, armor, field artillery, and engineers—into the warfighting functions to achieve an effect that is greater than using each arm and function separately or in sequence. The warfighting functions provide engineers a common framework within which to link the required engineer capabilities to the synchronized application of combined arms (see figure 1-5, page 1-18).

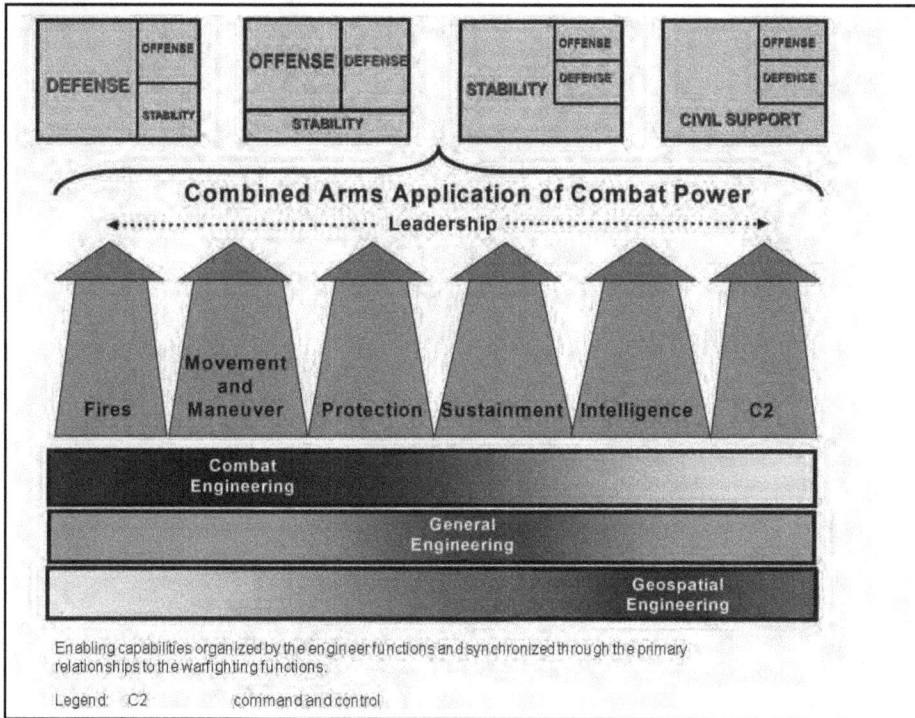

Figure 1-5. Application of engineer combat power

1-60. The Army employs combat power through combined arms. Combined arms are organized through tailoring and task-organizing Army forces to optimize the elements of combat power for a particular mission. Chapter 2 describes the modular force organization of Army engineer capabilities and higher-echelon headquarters. It also discusses implications for force-tailoring engineer forces at EAB.

This page intentionally left blank.

Chapter 2

Modular Force Organization

The (7th Engineer) Brigade units occupied various locations in tactical assembly area (TAA) Juno in advance of VII Corps. We immediately began sustainment operations which provided life support and protection for arriving units. These missions included constructing unit-sized protective berms, airfields, helipads, hospitals, roads, ammunition storage areas, and a petroleum storage area and applying dust palliative. The brigade also executed projects in support of the corps trainup for offensive operations. Several tank gunnery ranges were built in division areas and the 176th Engineer Group constructed a replica of the Iraqi barrier system to rehearse combined arms breaching operations. The engineers participated in this breach training as an integral part of the team, which culminated in a live-fire exercise using the mine-clearing line charge (MICLIC).

From the 7th Engineer Brigade Command Report–Operations Desert Shield and Desert
Storm, dated 9 April 1991, Colonel Samuel C. Raines, Commanding

Modular Army forces are tailored to meet CCDRs' needs. No single, large fixed formation can support the diverse requirements of full spectrum operations. To meet joint requirements, the Army reorganized its operational forces to provide for a mix of land combat power that can be tailored for any combination of offensive, defensive, and stability or civil support operations as part of an interdependent joint force. While BCTs become the centerpiece for Army maneuver, the modular division, corps, and theater army provide a mix of tactical and operational headquarters able to function as land force, joint, multinational, and component command headquarters. Similarly, Army engineer forces are being reorganized from larger fixed formations into modular capabilities with scalable functional and multifunctional headquarters. The modular engineer capabilities are a significant force multiplier in full spectrum operations, while facilitating greater responsiveness to meet needs. This chapter describes the engineer capabilities available to the modular division, corps, and theater army headquarters. It then discusses the primary operational configurations for each echelon and engineer considerations within that organization and role. Finally, the chapter discusses general considerations for force-tailoring EAB engineer formations.

ENGINEER FORCE CAPABILITIES

2-1.   FM 3-0 emphasizes the integral role of Army forces in unified actions—joint, multinational, and interagency undertakings that execute campaigns and major operations. Army commanders, especially at EAB, will require significant engineering support in the conduct of operations, and much of that support may be from joint, multinational, interagency, and contract capabilities as briefly described in chapter 1. Army engineer forces will, however, continue to provide an essential capability readily available for the application of combat power. Army engineers also provide a vital coordinating link for the application of those other capabilities in unified action. FM 3-34 discusses in some detail both the Army engineer capabilities available to Army and joint commanders, and a variety of other—joint, multinational, interagency, and contract—engineering resources that are of interest. This section focuses on those Army modular engineer forces of greatest interest at EAB.

"Modular" Engineer Capabilities in Operation Iraqi Freedom

In December 2002, V Corps and the 130th Engineer Brigade were ordered to deploy to Kuwait and prepare for possible combat operations. The brigade deployed in January and February 2003 and in late February finalized the initial echelons above division (EAD) engineer task organization to support V Corps's initial maneuver elements, which included the 3d United States Infantry Division (3ID) (V Corps main effort) and the 11th Attack Helicopter Regiment (V Corps supporting effort.)

The engineer plan maximized the support forward to the divisions and accepted risk in the corps rear area. The early-arriving EAD engineer units went to support 3ID. The 130th Engineer Brigade initially detached its organic 94th Engineer Battalion (combat)(Heavy) and 54th Engineer Battalion (combat), along with several multirole bridge companies and the 937th Engineer Group, to reinforce the 3ID division engineer brigade and its organic units—the 10th, 11th, and 317th Engineer Battalions (combat).

Shortly before the attack, the 130th controlled just a single combat heavy company until follow-on EAD engineer units from Forts Lewis, Carson, and Drum arrived and were able to cross the line of departure. This decision was made to ensure that 3ID was properly weighted with EAD units and set for success.

Because there were not enough engineers to provide the needed engineer support for all the 3ID BCTs on a continuous basis, the 3ID engineer brigade in coordination with the 130th Engineer Brigade created engineer force packages. The force packages or modules were developed to perform specific tasks in support of a particular 3ID BCT, and once those tasks were completed, the force packages were transferred on the move to another BCT to perform another set of tasks. These engineer modules were continuously moved among the divisions' BCTs throughout the offensive phase of Operation Iraqi Freedom (OIF). For example, during the initial attack to seize the airfield at Tallil, the 317th Engineer Battalion supporting the 3d BCT was task-organized with an engineer module that consisted of a general engineering team that was specifically organized to clear and repair Tallil airfield in order to place it back in operation as quickly as possible. Additionally, this engineer module had extra horizontal construction assets to dig survivability positions and a multirole bridge company to execute river crossings on the Euphrates River, as necessary. As soon as these missions were complete, the general engineering team was moved north under division control to support other engineer assets building a contingency airfield. The bridge company was task-organized to support the 1st Marine Expeditionary Force (MEF) to conduct river crossings with Marines also moving north.

The V Corps and 3ID continued to create engineer modules using EAD assets and move them among the divisional engineer brigade and engineer battalions supporting the BCTs up through the fall of Baghdad. The movement of the modules required significant planning and coordination on the part of ENCOORDs at corps, division, and each of the BCTs. In many instances, in addition to the planning and coordination, the engineer battalions supporting each BCT were used to physically link up with the modules to ensure that they were appropriately integrated into and out of the BCT AO.

Operating throughout Iraq (after) the end of the ground offensive, the V Corps engineer brigade (130th Engineer Brigade) then grew substantially. In addition to the missions reinforcing divisional engineer requirements, the 130th Engineer Brigade executed more than 3,000 missions, focused on V Corps and Coalition Joint Task Force–7 (CJTF–7) priorities, while backstopping each major subordinate on a wide variety of their missions.

These experiences during the combat phase of OIF illustrate that the concept of modularity is not new and demonstrate the use of engineer modules to compensate for a lack of adequate engineer forces available to task-organize at every echelon and unit where they are required. It also illustrates that robust coordination and C2 at all echelons are required to integrate the application of these engineer capabilities.

2-2.   The Engineer Regiment represents the Army's engineer capabilities in both the operational Army and the generating force. The Regiment includes USACE and military engineer units. The Regiment supports the conduct of joint operations and is experienced at interagency support and leveraging nonmilitary and nongovernmental engineer assets to support mission accomplishment. At the operational to strategic level, the Regiment is represented as shown in figure 2-1.

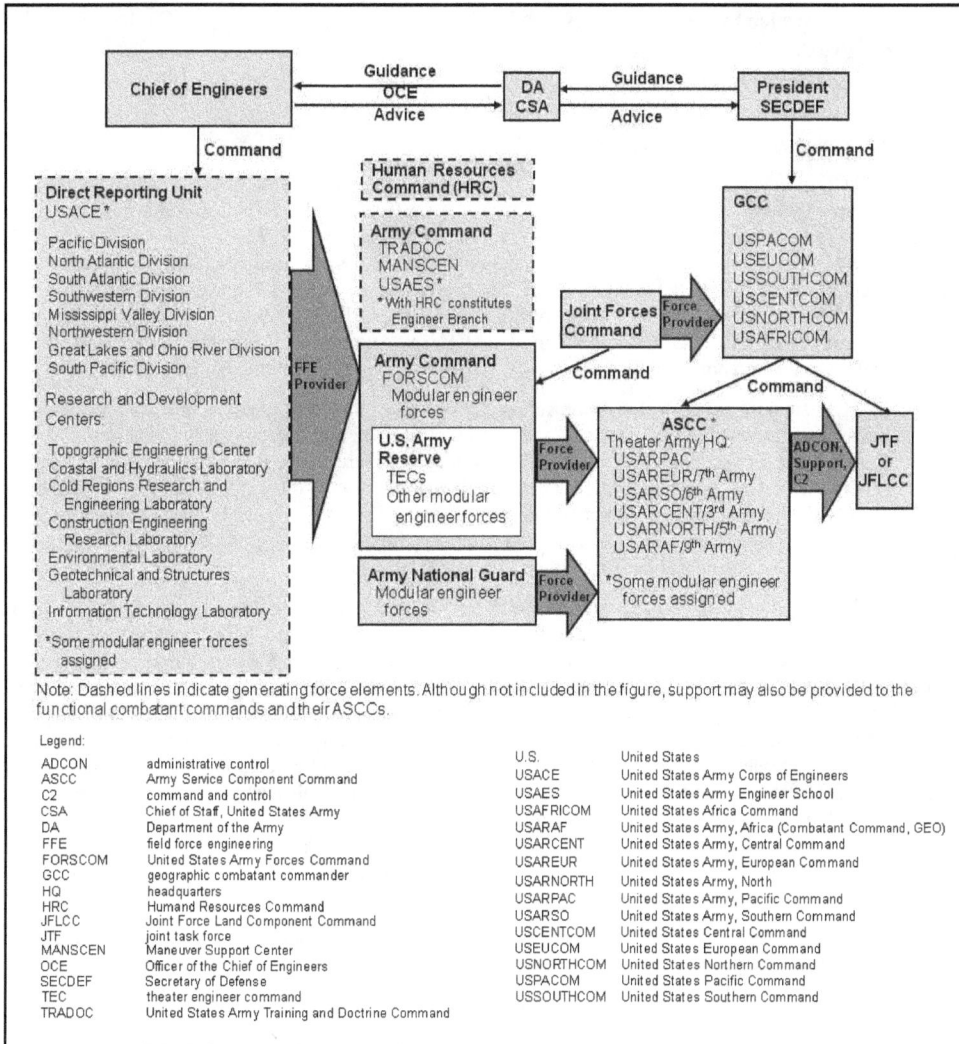

Note: Dashed lines indicate generating force elements. Although not included in the figure, support may also be provided to the functional combatant commands and their ASCCs.

Legend:

ADCON	administrative control	U.S.	United States
ASCC	Army Service Component Command	USACE	United States Army Corps of Engineers
C2	command and control	USAES	United States Army Engineer School
CSA	Chief of Staff, United States Army	USAFRICOM	United States Africa Command
DA	Department of the Army	USARAF	United States Army, Africa (Combatant Command, GEO)
FFE	field force engineering	USARCENT	United States Army, Central Command
FORSCOM	United States Army Forces Command	USAREUR	United States Army, European Command
GCC	geographic combatant commander	USARNORTH	United States Army, North
HQ	headquarters	USARPAC	United States Army, Pacific Command
HRC	Humand Resources Command	USARSO	United States Army, Southern Command
JFLCC	Joint Force Land Component Command	USCENTCOM	United States Central Command
JTF	joint task force	USEUCOM	United States European Command
MANSCEN	Maneuver Support Center	USNORTHCOM	United States Northern Command
OCE	Officer of the Chief of Engineers	USPACOM	United States Pacific Command
SECDEF	Secretary of Defense	USSOUTHCOM	United States Southern Command
TEC	theater engineer command		
TRADOC	United States Army Training and Doctrine Command		

Figure 2-1. Engineer Regiment from the strategic to operational level

UNITED STATES ARMY CORPS OF ENGINEERS

2-3.   USACE is the Army's direct reporting unit (DRU) assigned responsibility to execute Army and Department of Defense (DOD) military construction, real estate acquisition, and development of the nation's infrastructure through the civil works program. Most of its assets are part of the generating force (see FM 1-01), but selected elements are a part of the operational Army, to include selected forward engineer support teams (FESTs) and the 249th Engineer Battalion (Prime Power). USACE also operates the

United States Army Engineer Research and Development Center (ERDC), a comprehensive network of laboratories and centers of expertise, to include—

- Geotechnical and Structures Laboratory.
- Coastal and Hydraulics Laboratory.
- Environmental Laboratory.
- Information Systems Laboratory.
- Engineer Waterways Experiment Station.
- Cold Regions Research and Engineering Laboratory.
- Construction Engineering Research Laboratory.
- Topographic Engineering Center.

2-4. USACE provides technical assistance and contract support to joint forces deployed worldwide. USACE capabilities include access to the expertise of ERDC's centers and laboratories and all the resources within the divisions, districts, and other sources. Within USACE, the Chief of Engineers has aligned USACE divisions with and assigned liaison officers (LNOs) to combatant and Army commanders as they reinforce and extend the capabilities of the Regiment (see figure 2-1, page 2-3). This relationship with the CCDR and the operational force allows direct access to USACE resources to support engagement strategies and wartime operations. Within USACE, a contingency response unit provides staff augmentation to the divisions and districts as they support combatant and Army commanders.

2-5. USACE support provides for technical and contract engineering support, integrating its organic capabilities with those of other Services and other sources of engineering-related reachback support. USACE may have assets integrated within the military structure in-theater and may have established coordination with a TEC or senior engineer headquarters or already be operating under contract in-theater. Whether providing construction contract and design support in the AO or outside of the contingency area, USACE can obtain necessary data, research, and specialized expertise not present in-theater through tele-engineering and other reachback capabilities.

2-6. USACE is the primary proponent of FFE and related generating force support, which enables engineer functions within the operational Army. FFE is provided through USACE personnel and assets (deployed and participating through reachback) or through engineer Soldiers linked into reachback capabilities through tele-engineering. The USACE objective for FFE is to more effectively execute its generating force roles (engineering expertise, contract construction, real estate acquisition and disposal, and environmental engineering) in all operations and maximize use of reachback to provide technical assistance and enable the engineer functions in support of operational force engineers and the combatant or JTF commander. The contingency response unit mentioned above may also augment FFE requirements as necessary. One of the ways USACE accomplishes this is by training, equipping, and maintaining specialized deployable FESTs. Another way that USACE supports the operational force is through its infrastructure assessment planning cell. A third way that USACE supports the operational force is through its base development cells.

2-7. The FFE concept is applicable in joint and multinational operations to provide a better engineer solution that can be implemented faster and with a smaller footprint. The Air Force and Navy have similar capabilities—the Air Force uses its Geo-Reach program while the Navy has the capability to conduct engineer reconnaissance with reachback to NAVFAC.

2-8. USACE has expertise that may support the strategic, operational, or tactical levels in engineer planning and operations and can leverage reachback to technical subject matter experts in districts, divisions, laboratories and centers of expertise, other Services, and private industry in its role as part of the generating force. USACE FFE can also be employed as a means to access specialized engineer capabilities that can augment EAB engineer planning staffs. Teams can rapidly deploy to meet requirements for engineering assessments and analyses in support of the full array of engineer operations. The two types of FESTs provide support to primarily general engineering efforts through forward-deployed engineer elements that can communicate with TeleEngineering Kits and reachback to technical experts within USACE. Engineer facility detachments (EFDs) from the TECs provide a wide variety of services to forward-deployed forces in a public works capacity, including assistance in the reception and staging of troops. Infrastructure assessment and base development planning cells and teams are nondeployable capabilities available through reachback support.

- **Forward Engineer Support Team–Advance (FEST–A).** Its mission is to provide additional technical engineering planning capability to combatant command, ASCC, and other echelon engineer staffs down to brigade level. It can also deploy in support of a JTF with a limited execution capability. Its capabilities include engineer planning and design, real estate acquisition and disposal, and contracting personnel. The FEST–A may provide an initial technical infrastructure assessment or survey, technical engineer assistance, contracting support, and real estate acquisition support.

- **Forward Engineer Support Team–Main (FEST–M).** Its mission is to provide C2 for USACE teams in the AO and sustained USACE engineering execution capability within an AO. This team generally supports a JTF or the land component of a JTF. The FEST–M provides LNOs and USACE engineering planning modules to supported units, as required. It is a flexible, self-sustaining organization with a mission of providing USACE capabilities through forward presence and reachback for the following primary mission areas: infrastructure engineering planning and design, technical engineering expertise, contract construction, real estate acquisition and disposal, environmental engineering, and geospatial engineering support.

- **Engineer facility detachment.** The EFD is a 15-Soldier unit whose mission is to provide additional facility engineering planning and support to the CCDR. It supports base development including master planning, construction design and supervision, and contractor supervision. The unit can support multiple sites.

- **Infrastructure assessment planning cell.** The infrastructure assessment planning cell is a nondeployable working group that provides engineering infrastructure assessments for military deployments and civil-military operations in forward areas. Focus areas for the teams are infrastructure related to USACE missions and aspects of the AO impacting contract construction to include roads, utilities, water resources, and HN support. The cell's resources and expertise are available to support FFE teams and operational forces through the USACE reachback operations center.

- **Base development planning cell.** A base development planning cell is a nondeployable working group that can quickly provide base development engineering and planning and facilities design for staging bases, base camps, FOBs, displaced persons camps, and any similar requirement. The cell's resources and expertise are available to support FFE teams and operational forces through the USACE reachback operations center.

DEPARTMENT OF DEFENSE CONSTRUCTION AGENTS

2-9. The Secretary of Defense has designated USACE and NAVFAC as construction agents for the design and construction execution within assigned areas of responsibility for U.S. military facilities worldwide. (The Air Force is the designated DOD construction agent for military construction in the British Isles.) USACE and NAVFAC provide a significant engineering capability to be leveraged in joint operations. Both USACE and NAVFAC have the capability to support general engineering operations with technical assistance and contract support to joint forces deployed worldwide. They also maintain in-depth expertise in engineering research and development. Inherent in their mission support capabilities is a planning and engineering capability for advanced base and infrastructure development. The CCDR may use USACE and NAVFAC to provide technical engineering assistance for design and award of construction contracts to civilian companies in support of military operations.

ENGINEER OPERATIONAL FORCE CAPABILITIES

2-10. Army engineer forces of the operational force operate at the strategic, operational, and tactical levels across the spectrum of conflict. Units are organized in a scalable, modular, adaptable manner to support combat, general, and geospatial engineering requirements. Army engineer forces operate as an integral member of the combined arms team during peace and war to provide a full range of joint engineering capabilities. They execute combat engineering tasks at the tactical and operational levels of war in support of combat maneuver forces and provide general and geospatial engineering throughout the entire JOA and at all levels of war. Engineer operational force capabilities are represented by the various engineer organizations and capabilities shown in table 2-1, page 2-6.

Table 2-1. Elements of the Engineer Regiment

Engineer Element		Force Provider			
		United States Army Forces Command			
		Active Component	United States Army Reserve	Army National Guard	Other Army Service Component Command
Organic Engineer Forces	Brigade Combat Team Engineer Company	m		m	m
	Geospatial Team	m		m	m
Engineer Command and Control Forces	Engineer Battalion Headquarters	m	m	m	m
	Engineer Brigade Headquarters	m	m	m	m
	Theater Engineer Command		m		
Baseline Engineer Forces	Sapper Company	m	m	m	
	Mobility Augmentation Company	m	m	m	
	Clearance Company	m	m	m	
	Engineer Support Company	m	m	m	m
	Horizontal Construction Company	m	m	m	m
	Vertical Construction Company	m	m	m	m
	Multi-Role Bridge Company	m	m	m	
Specialized Engineer Forces	Survey and Design Team	m	m	m	*
	Concrete Section	m	m	m	
	Asphalt Team	m	m	m	
	Firefighting Team	m	m	m	
	Explosive Hazard Team or Coordination Cell	m		m	*
	Engineer Squad (Canine)	m		m	
	Diving Team	m		m	
	Topographic Company or Geospatial Planning Cell	m		m	*
	Construction Management Team	m	m	m	*
	Engineer Facility Detachment		m	m	*
	Prime Power Company				m
	Well Drilling Team			m	
	Quarry Platoon			m	
	Real Estate Team		m		*
	Forward Engineer Support Team				m

*United States Army Corps of Engineers may provide some capabilities from its generating force organization.

Organic Capabilities (Organic Engineer Units)

2-11. Each of the three types of BCTs has an organic engineer capability. Geospatial engineering capabilities are assigned at brigade level and higher staffs. These organic combat engineer units and geospatial elements provide the minimum combat and geospatial engineering capability to support BCT operations and may also perform some very limited and selected general engineering tasks. Capabilities of organic engineers include—

- Providing geospatial data management and analysis, except in the armored cavalry regiment (ACR) which does not have organic geospatial elements.
- Providing support to close combat (mobility, countermobility, and survivability).
- Providing mobility assessments.
- Supporting mobility through urban terrain.
- Providing C2 for engineer forces.

2-12. During offensive and defensive operations they will require augmentation by baseline elements to include potentially an engineer battalion headquarters. Other specialized engineer units and equipment may also provide mission-tailored engineer support when required. Explosive hazard (EH) support elements may be included in this augmentation. Mission-tailored task organization will also be required in support of stability or civil support operations. Organic engineers train with and remain an integral part of their parent BCT. Additionally, engineers are organic within the staffs of all Army command level echelons, providing engineer staff planning functions and integrating geospatial engineering support.

Force Pool Capabilities

Engineer Headquarters Unit

2-13. C2 of engineer forces is provided by three echelons of engineer headquarters units. Multifunctional units, discussed later in this chapter, at both brigade and battalion echelons may also provide C2 for engineer forces in cases where engineer support is integral to the multifunctional mission. C2 for engineer functional capabilities and missions is provided by the TEC, the engineer brigade, and the engineer battalion. The TEC may form or provide augmentation for a JTF engineer staff. Inherent within the design of both the engineer brigade and battalion headquarters is a capability to develop and conduct operations to build local technical and engineering capacity. The TEC is the only organization designed for operational command of engineer capabilities at echelons above corps (EAC) level and often will provide C2 for the JFC if an operational engineer headquarters is required. The TEC provides C2 for all assigned or attached Army engineer brigades and other engineer units and missions for the joint force land component (JFLC) or Army commander. When directed it may also provide C2 for engineers or other formations from other Service, multinational, and contract construction engineers. The TEC is focused on operational C2 of engineer operations across all three of the engineer functions and typically serves as the senior theater or land component engineer headquarters. Specific considerations for organization and employment of the TEC include—

- The TEC is a modular organization that can be tailored based on mission requirements. Each TEC can deploy its main command post (CP) and two deployable command posts (DCPs) to provide flexibility and rotational capability. The DCP can be augmented with FFE assets from USACE. Typical capabilities that may be included with this augmentation might be contracting and real estate support and interagency coordination capability.
- Both the TEC and USACE can deploy modular staff elements and organizations to support the needs of the operational commander. Together they are capable of providing a wide range of technical engineering expertise and support from USACE, other Service technical laboratories and research centers, and other potential sources of expertise in the civilian community. They are enabled by the global reachback capabilities associated with FFE.

2-14. The engineer brigade is one of the Army's functional brigades and is capable of conducting engineer missions and controlling up to five mission-tailored engineer battalions including capabilities from all three of the engineer functions. It synchronizes engineer support across multiple organizations that control an AO and may also provide C2 for other nonengineer units focused on the performance of such missions as support of a deliberate gap (river) crossing. Inherent within the engineer brigade headquarters design is a capability to conduct operations to build local technical and engineering capacity. Unlike a BCT or MEB, the functional engineer brigade is not designed to control terrain. It would require significant augmentation to accomplish such a mission. Specific considerations for organization and employment of the engineer brigade headquarters include—

- One or more engineer brigades are required in the division or corps whenever the number of engineer units or the functional nature (such as synchronization of engineer capabilities) calls for brigade-level C2 capability. The brigade's span of control exceeds the engineer functional C2 capability of the multifunctional MEB. Once deployed, engineer brigades become the focal point for apportioning and allocating mission-tailored engineer forces across the entire AO. The engineer brigade is capable of supporting a JTF commander or component commander (land, air, or sea) and providing C2 of all Service engineers and contracted engineering within an operational area. The engineer brigade has the ability to provide DCPs and staff expertise for C2 of engineer operations as required. With augmentation, it may serve as a joint engineer headquarters and may be the senior engineer headquarters deployed in a JOA if full TEC deployment is not required.
- The engineer brigade has the capability to provide two DCPs. It provides engineer-specific technical planning, design, and quality assurance and quality control during 24-hour operations. The engineer brigade provides C2 for up to five assigned engineer battalions, including preparing them for deployment in support of the brigade or other organizations.

2-15. The engineer battalion is capable of conducting engineer missions controlling any mix of up to five mission-tailored engineer companies. They are typically found within the engineer brigade, the MEB, or in support of a BCT. With the exception of the prime power battalion that performs a specific technical role, all engineer battalion headquarters are capable of providing C2 for combat, general, or mixed engineering missions when they have been task-organized to perform those roles. Selected battalion headquarters include additional capabilities such as being airborne or air assault capable. For the conduct of construction or EH clearance missions, the battalion should receive survey and design or EH teams to facilitate those missions. Inherent within the engineer battalion headquarters design is a capability to conduct operations to build local technical and engineering capacity. Specific considerations for organization and employment of the engineer battalion headquarters include the following:

- Whenever two or more engineer modules are task-organized in support of a BCT, MEB, engineer brigade, or other unit, an engineer battalion headquarters may be required for the C2 and sustainment of those modules.
- An engineer battalion may support an MEB for combat or general engineering missions. The engineer battalion provides C2 for up to five assigned engineer companies, including preparing them for deployment in support of the battalion or other organizations.
- When in support of a BCT, an engineer battalion will provide C2 of engineer operations. The battalion may be focused on a single mission such as route clearance, security construction, or cache interrogation and reduction. The engineer battalion may be organized to perform as a breach force command when the BCT is conducting a combined arms breach. During a gap (river) crossing operation the engineer battalion provides the option to be designated as the crossing site command.

Baseline Engineer Units

2-16. Baseline engineer units include both combat and general engineering units (see table 2-2). They are the primary building blocks for the organization of most engineer battalions. These units are used to augment the organic engineer capabilities of a BCT and may be task-organized under an engineer battalion headquarters to serve under any of the EAB headquarters, providing the specific tailored capabilities needed to support any particular mission requirements.

Table 2-2. Baseline engineer units

Combat Engineer Units	General Engineering Unit
Sapper company	Engineer support company
Mobility augmentation company	Horizontal construction company
Clearance company	Vertical construction company
Multirole bridge company	—

2-17. Baseline combat engineer units are focused on support to combined arms operations at the tactical level and are designed to participate in close combat as necessary. All have the capability of fighting as engineers or, if required, as infantry. An engineer battalion headquarters will typically be included to provide the necessary C2, logistics, and staff supervision for attached and assigned units when two or more are assigned to a BCT, MEB, or other organization. Combat engineer (Sapper) units may provide limited general engineering capability for construction-related tasks. The more specialized combat engineer capabilities of assault bridging, breaching, and route and area clearance are added to the organic engineer capabilities in BCTs (or to deployed baseline Sapper companies) to enable them to accomplish mission requirements.

2-18. General engineering units are composed of support and construction capabilities. The horizontal and vertical companies have a construction focus and are capable of constructing, rehabilitating, repairing, maintaining, and modifying landing strips, airfields, CPs, main supply routes (MSRs), supply installations, building structures, bridges, and other related aspects of the infrastructure. These units may also perform repairs and limited reconstruction of railroads or water and sewage facilities. The basic capabilities of these construction units can be expanded with augmentation from specialized engineer units. For example, the augmented baseline construction units can provide bituminous mixing and paving, quarrying and crushing, and major horizontal construction projects such as highways, storage facilities, and airfields. Additional augmentation could also include pipeline construction or dive support, depending on the type and scope of the construction mission.

Specialized Engineer Units

2-19. The specialized engineer units' portion of the force pool provides for general and geospatial engineering capabilities at the operational and strategic levels and for specific augmentation to the tactical level (see table 2-3). The specialized capabilities are typically lower density than the baseline engineer units. These smaller, more specialized units are designed to support technical aspects within larger engineer-related missions or to provide augmentation to selected headquarters elements.

Table 2-3. Specialized Army engineer force pool units

Explosive Hazard Support	Construction Support	Infrastructure Support	Geospatial Support	Field Force Engineering
• Explosive hazard coordination cell • Explosive hazards team • Military working dogs	• Survey and design team • Construction management team • Real estate team • Diving team • Asphalt team • Concrete section • Well drilling team • Quarry platoon	• Prime power company, platoon, or detachment • Engineer facility detachments • Firefighting team	• Topographic engineer company • Geospatial planning cell	• Forward engineer support team; advanced or main (with embedded environmental, contingency real estate, and other support teams as needed) (see paragraph 2-9)

2-20. EH support elements focus on providing C2 for specialized elements and the integration of other EH capabilities. (EH support capability is limited in scope for Army engineers and is primarily resident in the EOD specialty of the ordnance branch. Other Services include EOD capability within their engineer specialties.) Military working dogs include both specialized search dog teams and mine dog teams. These teams assist in locating firearms, ammunition, and explosives in both rural and urban environments. They may be used to augment a variety of route and area clearance capabilities found in the clearance company.

2-21. Construction support elements provide construction support for C2, management, procurement, contract support, and greater capabilities for asphalt, concrete, and haul operations. All these capabilities have a role in infrastructure support as well.

2-22. Infrastructure support elements include prime power units to generate electrical power and provide advice and technical assistance on all aspects of electrical power and distribution systems. Prime power units have a limited electrical engineering capability (design and analysis); provide electrical surveys; and operate, maintain, and perform minor repairs to other electrical power production equipment, to include HN fixed plants. EFDs support theater opening and closing, base development, construction management, contractor coordination, base operations, and master planning. Firefighting teams provide first responder support for facilities and aviation operations.

2-23. Geospatial engineer units provide terrain and digital imagery analysis and support the integration of other geospatial information (the foundation information upon which all other information about the physical environment is referenced to form the COP to the headquarters that they support. The topographic engineer companies provide geospatial support to deployed units that require augmentation. The companies provide modules tailored to support the GCC and JTF headquarters; theater army, corps, and division headquarters; sustainment brigades; other joint or multinational division- and brigade-size elements; and the Federal Emergency Management Agency (FEMA) regions with analysis, collection, generation, management, and printing capability. Geospatial planning cells have a specific mission of generating, managing, and disseminating geospatial data, information, and products in support of the theater army headquarters and GCC.

MULTIFUNCTIONAL ORGANIZATIONS

2-24. C2 for engineer functional capabilities and missions is primarily provided by the TEC, the engineer brigade, and the engineer battalion. Multifunctional units at both brigade and battalion echelons may also provide C2 for engineer forces in cases where engineer support is integral to the multifunctional mission. This section briefly describes both the brigade special troops battalion (BSTB) and the MEB. Analysis of operational variables informs the suitable tailoring of both functional and multifunctional headquarters while mission variables are analyzed to determine task organization. The division construct normally starts with an MEB and then adds a functional engineer brigade when the type (technical requirement) or size (magnitude of subordinate engineer elements) of the engineer mission or the requirement to integrate engineer capabilities across the force becomes too large for the MEB. The corps level normally starts with at least an engineer brigade and expands to other engineer brigades as necessary. In some instances, an MEB may also be required at the corps level—for example, to provide C2 of a seaport of debarkation (SPOD) or aerial port of debarkation (APOD) (both of which are terrain-focused) during early-entry operations. The MEB provides multifunctional capability with a smaller footprint and has the ability to control terrain for these types of operations.

Brigade Special Troops Battalion

2-25. The BSTB is a multifunctional battalion within the heavy brigade combat team (HBCT) and infantry brigade combat team (IBCT) which provides the BCT with military intelligence (MI) support, communications, engineer, MP, and CBRN reconnaissance capabilities. The BSTB is organized with a BSTB headquarters and headquarters company (HHC), the BCT HHC, an MI company, and a network support company. The BSTB of the IBCT and HBCT each have an engineer company although the composition varies. The BSTB HHC has command and staff sections, an MP platoon, a CBRN reconnaissance platoon, a support platoon (with medical support, maintenance, Class III, and field feeding), and a security section. See FM 3-90.61 for additional information on the BSTB.

2-26. A key to modularity is the ability to task-organize units to BCTs based on the mission variables of the operation. The BCT can use the BSTB to provide C2 for various task-organized units and related operations. In the case of engineer forces, generally the BSTB will provide adequate C2 for the addition of a baseline engineer module. If two or more modules will be task-organized to the BCT, an engineer battalion headquarters will likely also be required.

Maneuver Enhancement Brigade

2-27. BCTs are the primary organizations designed to fight tactical engagements and battles. A mix of other functional and multifunctional brigade types is available to support theater army, corps, and division commanders. The multifunctional supporting brigade types include the battlefield surveillance brigade (BFSB), combat aviation brigade (CAB), the MEB, the fires brigade, and the sustainment brigade. These brigades may be combined arms units and are designed to support BCTs and carry out specific tasks in support of EAB. A division involved in major combat operations should be supported by all five types of support brigades.

2-28. The support brigades are not fixed organizations. All support brigades except the CAB are designed around a small base of organic elements, to which a mix of additional capabilities is added based on the mission variables. The MEB is designed to receive and control forces to provide protection and mobility to prevent or mitigate the effects of hostile action against divisional forces. The MEB's mission is to preserve freedom of maneuver for operational and tactical commanders by controlling terrain and facilities and by preventing or mitigating hostile actions against the protected force. An MEB has a combined arms staff and is task-organized based on mission requirements. It has C2 capabilities that suit it for a variety of missions. They typically control combinations of several different types of battalions and separate companies, such as civil affairs (CA), CBRN, engineer, EOD (company), MP, and in special situations AMD or a tactical combat force (TCF).

2-29. The number of MEBs placed under the control of an EAB headquarters depends on the mission variables. A JFC may place an MEB in support of another Service or functional component, such as the Marine forces—to provide sustainment area security for a Marine air-ground task force (MAGTF) or joint force air component command (JFACC)—to secure an airbase. The MEB may be assigned an AO, but is not responsible for the supported echelon's unassigned areas. For example, movement control of sustainment operations in the division AO as a whole remains the division transportation officer's function even when it passes through the MEB AO. The division transportation officer coordinates those movements with the MEB.

2-30. In addition to the MEB, the supported headquarters may have been tailored with functional brigades to support the force as a whole or to carry out a particular task. The MEB may be required to provide support to these additional functional brigades. For example, in addition to an MEB, a division might receive an MP brigade to control displaced civilians and process detainees. In this case, the MEB may be tasked to provide general engineering support to the MP brigade from its assigned engineer battalion to construct detainee facilities. An engineer brigade is provided to a division or higher organization when the magnitude of functional engineer requirements and C2 calls for brigade-level C2 capability. The brigade's span of control exceeds the engineer functional C2 capability of the multifunctional MEB. Some functional capability such as an engineer battalion will likely remain under the MEB even when a functional engineer brigade is provided to the division.

THEATER ARMY ORGANIZATION

2-31. Each theater army headquarters is composed of three different units. These are the main CP with an HHC, the operational command post (OCP), and a headquarters battalion. See appendix A for discussion of the engineer staff assigned to the theater army headquarters.

2-32. Each theater army will be assigned a mix of forces to support the theater. While the type and size of the forces will vary, the theater army normally has a theater sustainment command, a signal command (theater), a medical command (deployment support), MI brigade, and a CA unit (command or brigade). The size of these subordinate elements depends on theater requirements.

2-33. Some contingencies may require the deployment of significant Army capabilities in the JOA either before or without the deployment of tactical Army forces. To meet its support responsibilities, the theater army receives additional attachments in the form of brigades and commands requisite for the campaign or missions in the AOR in addition to the assigned mix of regionally focused, supporting commands and brigades. These latter forces are not regionally focused but are drawn from the "pool" of available forces assigned to general warfighting and maintained in the continental United States (CONUS) and around the world. The situation in each theater dictates the size of these formations, that is, commands, brigades, or groups. Command relationships also vary across theaters between the theater army and supporting capabilities. In some theaters, the commands are assigned; in others, they are OPCON or aligned for planning only. When the ASCC is the JFLCC for major combat operations, a number of functional commands may augment it. These may include the TEC.

2-34. A number of functional brigades are also available to support theater-level operations. They may be task-organized under theater-level functional commands or be directly subordinate to the ASCC. When required, the ASCC may task-organize functional brigades to corps or divisions. Examples of functional brigades include the engineer brigade.

2-35. In major combat operations, the theater army normally receives one TEC (see figure 2-2). The TEC provides C2 and an organizational framework for the operational-level engineer effort within the AOR. The TEC focuses on reinforcing and augmenting tactical-level engineer efforts and developing the theater sustainment base. This focus involves conducting engineer operations supporting the operational design and coordinating engineer operations supporting the subordinate tactical echelons. The TEC supervises geospatial support, construction, real property maintenance activities, LOC sustainment, engineer logistics management, and base development. The TEC has primary responsibility for theater infrastructure repair or development as required.

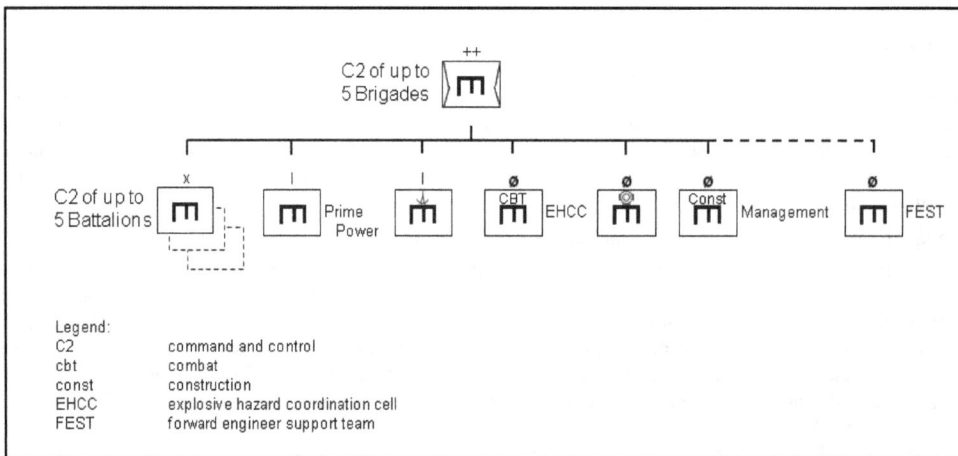

Figure 2-2. Notional theater engineer command

2-36. The TEC develops plans, procedures, and programs for engineer support for the theater army, including requirements determination, operational mobility and countermobility, general engineering, power generation, ADC, military construction, topography, engineering design, construction materiel, and real property maintenance activities. The TEC commander exercises command over those engineer (or other) units (Army and joint) task-organized to the TEC, to include commercial contract construction capability such as USACE, NAVFAC, AFCESA, multinational, HN, or other as assigned. The TEC receives policy guidance from the theater army based on the guidance of the GCC's joint force engineer. The TEC headquarters element provides staff supervision over operational-level engineer operations in the operational area and reinforces engineer support to all theater army forces. The TEC also may support joint and multinational commands and other elements according to lead Service responsibilities as directed by the supported JFC. It provides policy and technical guidance to all Army engineer units in the operational area. This headquarters maintains planning relationships with the theater army and joint force staff engineers to help establish engineer policy for the theater. It maintains required coordination links with other Service and multinational command engineering staffs. In some situations, a tailored engineer brigade may provide theater-level engineer support. The engineer brigade would provide similar expertise and capability to the theater army as the TEC, but with a reduced span.

CORPS ORGANIZATION

2-37. The corps is the Army's premier headquarters for joint operations and can rapidly transition to either a JTF or a JFLCC headquarters for contingency operations. Corps can deploy to any AOR to provide C2 for Army, joint, and multinational forces. Corps do not have any echelon-specific units other than the organic corps headquarters. They can control any mix of modular brigades and divisions and other-Service or multinational forces.

2-38. The modular corps headquarters design, combined with robust communications, gives the corps commander a flexible CP structure to meet his requirements. The corps headquarters has three command nodes—the corps mobile command group, main CP, and the tactical CP. The corps's two CPs are organized around the warfighting functions and integrating cells. See appendix A for discussion of the engineer staff assigned to the corps headquarters.

2-39. The engineer force supporting a corps is not set by rules of allocation. Rather, the force will be tailored to meet anticipated requirements based on an analysis of the situation. The corps engineer force is likely to include joint engineer elements or a joint engineer headquarters. In some situations, the corps may require a combination of engineer forces organized functionally and multifunctionally. While either battalion or brigade echelons of engineer or multifunctional headquarters may be allocated as a corps engineer headquarters, the functional engineer brigade echelon headquarters is more typical for most operations. Figure 2-3 provides a notional organization for both an engineer brigade headquarters and a joint engineer headquarters supporting a corps.

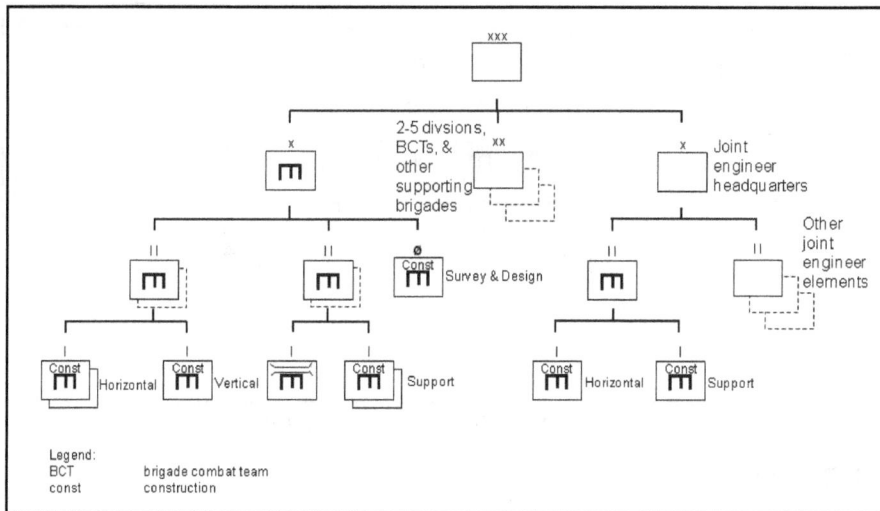

Figure 2-3. Notional corps engineer force

DIVISION ORGANIZATION

2-40. Divisions are the Army's primary tactical warfighting headquarters. Their principal task is directing subordinate brigade operations. Divisions are not fixed formations. They are completely modular entities designed to exercise C2 over any mix of brigades. Divisions do not have any organic forces beyond their headquarters elements. Their organic structure includes communications network, life support, and CP elements. With appropriate joint augmentation, a division can be the JTF or JFLCC headquarters for small contingencies. The headquarters is organized functionally. It includes an organic joint network capability and liaison teams. See appendix A for discussion of the engineer staff assigned to the division headquarters.

2-41. Divisions have no organic structure beyond the headquarters, so not all types of brigades may be present in an operation. In some operations, divisions may control more than one of a particular type of support brigade. They may also control functional groups, battalions, or separate companies; however, these are normally task-organized to a brigade. Each division is tailored for a specific operation; the composition of the division is completely variable. However, for a major combat operation, divisions should have at least one of each type of support brigade OPCON or attached.

2-42. The tailored engineer force supporting a division is not set by rules of allocation. Rather, the force will be tailored to meet anticipated requirements based on an analysis of the situation. The divisional engineer force may be organized under a multifunctional headquarters, such as the MEB, or may be organized under a functional engineer headquarters. In some situations, the division may require a combination of engineer forces organized both functionally and multifunctionally. While either battalion or brigade echelons of engineer or multifunctional headquarters may be allocated as the divisional engineer headquarters, a brigade echelon headquarters is more typical for most operations. Figure 2-4 provides a notional organization for both an engineer brigade headquarters and an MEB supporting a division.

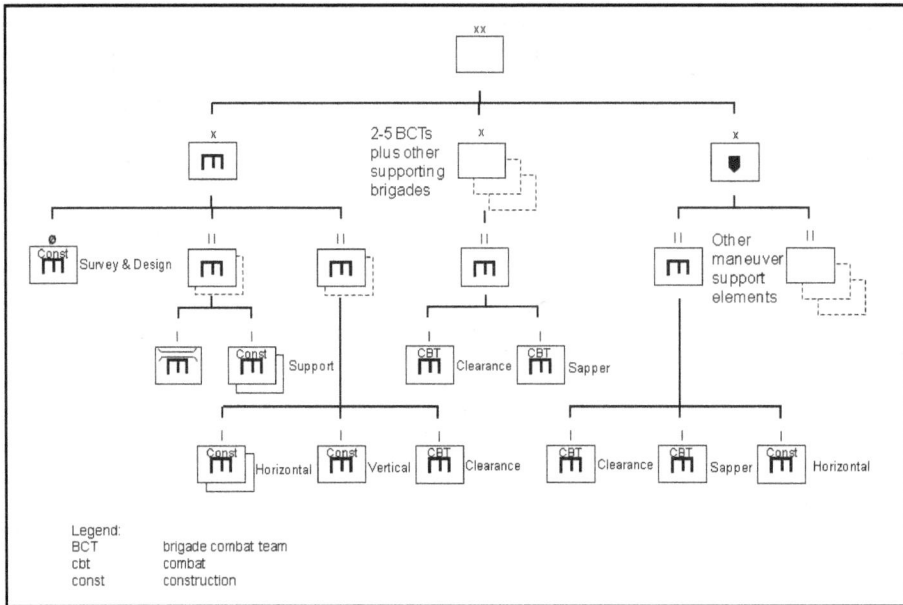

Figure 2-4. Notional division engineer force

FORCE TAILORING

2-43. In addition to the organic engineer capabilities of the BCT, the JFC is able to draw from a large force pool of baseline and modular engineer units available to be integrated into joint force units at various echelons. This structure enables independent action and allows tailoring of forces to meet changing situations. Actual requirements for forces in a campaign are seldom identical to planning figures. As a consequence, the theater army commander recommends the appropriate mix of forces and the deployment sequence for forces to meet the GCC's actual requirements. This is force tailoring (selecting forces based on a mission and recommending their deployment sequence) and may include both operating Army and generating force elements.

2-44. The tailored engineer force selection and their deployment sequence result from recommendations by engineer planners at EAB headquarters. Engineer planners at the theater army, with input from appropriate corps and division headquarters, select engineer forces based on analysis of mission variables and recommend the deployment sequence. Actual requirements for engineer forces in a campaign or major combat operation seldom match planning figures and, in fact, will more typically exceed the planning figures. Tactical-level requirements are difficult to fully define at operational levels. The engineer planners at the theater army echelon gain a broad understanding of the operational-level requirements, but must rely on subordinate echelons to assist in defining tactical-level requirements. Each echelon must understand the capabilities of modular engineer forces and their associated scalable C2 to effectively meet requirements. Engineer planners must also consider and leverage the variety of other engineer capabilities that may be available to meet or mitigate requirements.

2-45. EAB engineer planners will consider a variety of other engineer capabilities to meet operational-level requirements and, in some cases, tactical-level requirements. Each theater is supported by a designated DOD contract construction agent (CCA) (most typically USACE or NAVFAC) that may have mission support capabilities available. Planners review operational and mission variables considering the availability of local engineer resources, including HN military and civilian sources. Joint, multinational, and interagency capabilities are also considered. Despite a full accounting of contract and other resources available, operational-level engineer planners will typically identify a number of requirements for which the most effective engineer capability must be force tailored from the Regiment.

2-46. Theater army echelon engineer planners will likely understand some requirements more fully than others. Typically, the theater army echelon will comprehend clearly the various engineer support requirements for accessing the theater and establishing a sustainment base. Many of these may be translated to potential engineer missions and the related tasks. For example, theater engineer planners may know the requirements for upgrading selected SPODs and APODs with enough clarity to include tentative designs, plans, and estimates. Similarly, a selected ground LOC may require construction activities that can be clearly defined. The most well-defined requirements will tend to focus on operational-level support, and most engineer support at this level is organized in the general engineering and geospatial engineering functions.

2-47. Theater army echelon engineer force planners do not disregard tactical-level requirements. They must analyze operational and mission variables to determine and shape the engineer forces required for the tactical-level operations of subordinate echelons. These forces will include capabilities organized in the combat engineering, general, and geospatial engineering functions. Since the theater army echelon analysis may not include full resolution of tactical-level requirements, the subordinate echelon corps and division headquarters offer refinements for the engineer forces required to support their more detailed concept of operations. For example, based on an understanding of the physical environment in a potential AO and an initial design for operational maneuver, the engineer planner may identify the requirements for a number of gap crossings by subordinate tactical elements. After consideration for joint, multinational, and other capabilities, the planner may determine and shape baseline engineer forces capable of supporting the gap-crossing requirements. As corps, division, and subordinate planners add depth to the understanding of the AO and develop a scheme of maneuver, the shape of the baseline forces to support gap crossings allocated by the higher-echelon design will be impacted by decisions on timing, locations, and other factors refining the gap-crossing design.

2-48. The Engineer Regiment is organized and equipped to support full spectrum operations. A variety of engineer forces will be tailored to meet both the clearly defined engineer missions expected at the operational level and the broader, less defined tactical-level tasks. Actual requirements for engineer forces, even after accounting for other resources available, will typically exceed tailored force capabilities. Reachback is also used to expand technical engineering capabilities of tailored forces. Even with the expanded capabilities enabled through reachback, the modular engineer force units are more narrowly designed to accomplish specific types of tasks. The larger fixed formations of general purpose engineer organizations have been transformed into smaller, more task-specific modules. EAB engineer planners must consider the broadest range of capabilities required and tailor an engineer force adequate to meet those requirements.

2-49. Engineer force packages must contain the right mix of capabilities to assure timely and relevant engineer support. This mix will often need to change drastically during transitions, and the EAB engineer must anticipate and plan for these changes. For example, combat engineers often make up the majority of engineer forces in-theater during sustained combat operations, but they must be reinforced during transition to stability operations because they typically do not have the right capabilities to accomplish all the general engineering tasks required. Also, since EH support requirements during transition operations are often significantly higher than during combat operations, additional capabilities may be required. The tailored engineer force structure will be refined both in the determination of the capabilities required and in the recommended deployment sequence.

2-50. Prioritization occurs in applying the tailored engineer forces most effectively against actual requirements. EAB engineer staff and planners recommend priorities to the commander based on the continuous assessment maintained through the running estimate. EAB engineer staffs also shape the organization of the tailored forces for the conduct of engineer operations. Tailoring the engineer force should not be confused with task organizing. Tactical and operational commanders organize and reorganize groups of tailored engineer units for specific missions. This process of allocating available assets to subordinate commanders and establishing their command and support relationships is called task organizing. Considerations for the command and support relationships used in task organizing engineer units are discussed in chapter 3. Flexibility to meet evolving engineer requirements as an operation is conducted depends directly on the ability to efficiently task-organize the tailored engineer force and integrate it within the gaining or supported force. Additional discussion of engineer force-tailoring considerations at the theater army, corps, and division echelons is included in chapters 4, 5, and 6. See FM 3-34 for a discussion of some force generation considerations for modular engineer forces.

Chapter 3

Foundations of Engineer Operations

Combined arms operations are familiar to Army forces. Unified actions—those integrating the capabilities of joint forces with those of multinational military and civilian organizations—have become typical as well. This integration requires careful preparation. Training and exchange of liaison at every level are necessary for successful unified action.

FM 3-0

FM 3-0 emphasizes operations that simultaneously combine offensive, defensive, and stability or civil support operations by defining a distinct operational concept around full spectrum operations. Army forces conduct full spectrum operations within the larger framework of joint operations and unified action. The engineer capabilities described in chapter 2 are a significant force multiplier in full spectrum operations, facilitating the freedom of action necessary to meet mission objectives. This chapter describes foundational characteristics and considerations for engineer operations with a focus on EAB. At higher echelons, engineer operations are intrinsically full spectrum—simultaneously combining tasks which support offensive, defensive, and stability or civil support operations. The technical aspects of higher-echelon engineering tasks become increasingly essential to the effective application of the engineer support. Applications of engineer support efforts at EAB must, nevertheless, remain integrated within the combined arms framework. Integration enables a synchronized application of combat power, maximizing the effect of the engineering effort. Integration is a foundation of engineer operations—integration within the supported unit staff, throughout the operations process, and across the force.

STAFF INTEGRATION

3-1. The staff's primary function is to help the commander and subordinate commanders exercise control. Control functions increase in complexity at each higher echelon. As the control function becomes increasingly complex, units are typically assigned larger staffs to ensure integration through the warfighting functions and synchronization of combat power. A staff section is a grouping of staff members by area of expertise. Depending on the echelon and type of unit, engineer staff members may be assigned within an operations section (common among Army staffs), under a logistics section (more common in joint staffs), under an engineer section (more common on combined staffs), or they may be dispersed within numerous staff sections. In every case, a senior engineer staff officer is identified and must assume responsibility for coordinating the overall engineer staff effort. Regardless of where engineers are assigned on the staff, they must integrate their efforts under the overall coordination of the senior engineer staff officer (the ENCOORD).

3-2. Regardless of mission, every Army staff has common areas of expertise that determine how commanders divide duties and responsibilities. Grouping related activities by area of expertise gives commanders an effective span of control. It also facilitates unified effort by the staff. Areas of expertise may vary slightly, depending on the command echelon, mission, and environment. For example, at battalion level there is normally no resource manager and certain logistic units combine the intelligence and operations areas of expertise. Each maneuver force echelon down to brigade level has an organic engineer planner and staff element to integrate engineers into the combined arms fight. The engineer staff member is responsible for understanding the full array of engineer capabilities (combat, general, and geospatial engineering) available to the force and for synchronizing them to best meet the needs of the maneuver commander. Staff leadership may recommend or require new staff officers to have combat, general, or geospatial engineering experience at the battalion, brigade, or division level to prepare for an EAB position. As previously mentioned, the section of assignment and grouping of engineer staff varies among echelons and unit types. Organization of the assigned staff to meet the unique requirements of the headquarters and situation is ultimately determined by the theater army, corps, or division commander (see figure 3-1).

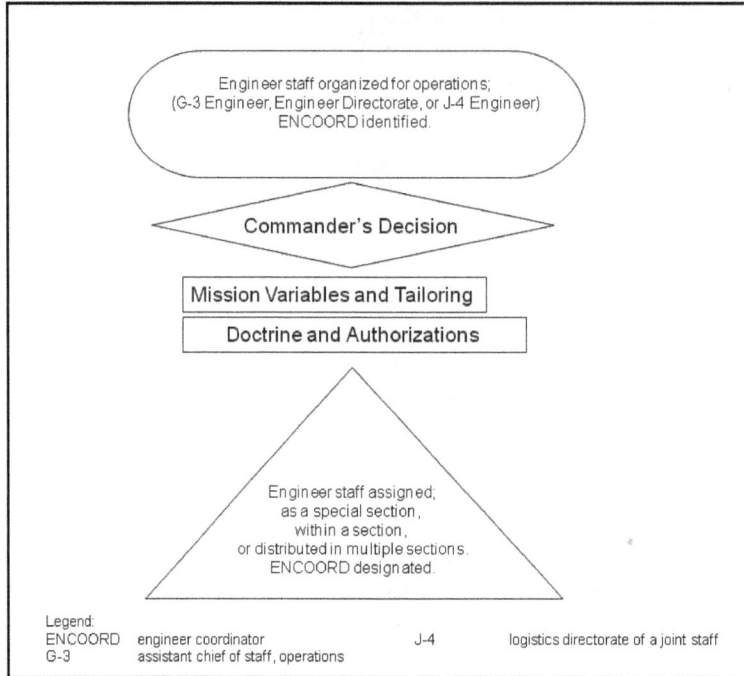

Figure 3-1. Organization of the engineer staff

3-3.   While staffs differ by echelon and unit type, all staffs include similar staff sections. The staff consists of the chief of staff or executive officer and coordinating, special, and personal staff sections. Commanders organize the staff into CPs for operations. Commanders organize their headquarters into CPs to help them exercise C2 throughout the conduct of operations. By organizing their C2 system into CPs, commanders disperse their staff and C2 capabilities in the AO. This expands the commander's ability to exercise C2 and makes the C2 system more survivable. They base the number and internal structure of CPs on available resources, planning horizons, and warfighting functions.

Commander Organizes the Staff Considering Mission Variables

"The engineer expertise on the division staff in the modular structure resides in the two tactical CPs, the division operations center, and the Division Engineer cell. By the modified table of organization and equipment (MTOE), engineers support other sections within the headquarters...." In our division, we were organized as a Division Engineer section. "The MTOE engineers assigned throughout the division headquarters worked within [our section]. The exception was the engineer planner, who remained a member of the [plans section].

The [Division Engineer section] included the engineers and several CA personnel. The figure [below] depicts the areas of [Division Engineer] responsibility. The section coordinated reconstruction efforts at the division level, as well as the traditional engineer and civil-military operations functions. Placing all of the engineer personnel within [this section] allowed the engineer section to battle-track, coordinate engineer support, provide resources to the BCTs, and execute nonstandard missions, as assigned. The [section] provided personnel to the division operations center and executed the traditional roles of maintaining situational awareness of the current fight, providing engineer input for the staff battle drills, and briefing the commander. The [section] also coordinated with the assigned engineer brigade headquarters and corps for additional engineer capability, as required for the mission or as requested by the BCTs."

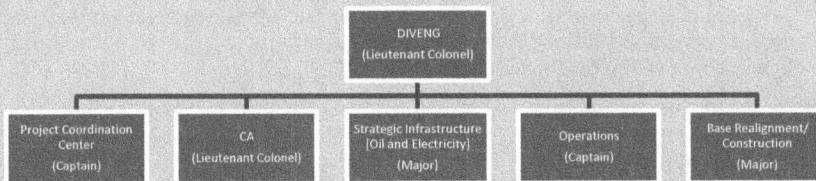

Extracted from "Modular Engineer Structure in Divisions," by Colonel Jeffrey R. Eckstein, in *Engineer, The Professional Bulletin of Army Engineers*, January-March 2008, pp. 61–62. Colonel Eckstein served as Division Engineer and assistant chief of staff, information engagement (G-7), for the 25th Infantry Division as part of Operation Iraqi Freedom.

3-4.   Doctrine and a unit's MTOE provide commanders a starting point for organizing their engineer staff. Each operation is unique based on mission variables. Just as commanders organize their entire force for an operation, they organize their staff and other control systems for effective C2. Mission variables are considered in determining the operational configuration for the headquarters, and the mission also determines which activities the operationally configured headquarters must accomplish. These activities determine how commanders organize, tailor, or adapt their staff to accomplish the mission. The mission also determines the size and composition of the staff. For example, a division headquarters may serve as the base for a JTF headquarters. Based on analysis of mission variables, the division staff would be augmented with additional staff members and C2 capabilities to accomplish the JTF mission. Because of the variance of assigned staff at each EAB headquarters, and the changes occurring to authorizations over time, a generic reference for the authorized engineer staff at each echelon is included in appendix A.

ENGINEER COORDINATOR

3-5. The senior engineer staff officer assumes the duties and responsibilities of ENCOORD. Regardless of the distribution of engineer staff or their section of assignment, the ENCOORD ensures the synchronization of the overall engineer effort. The *engineer coordinator* is the special staff officer, usually the senior engineer officer on the staff, responsible for coordinating engineer assets and operations for the command. (FM 3-34) The ENCOORD must ensure a coordinated effort among the assigned engineer staff assisting the commander in exercising control over engineer forces in the AO.

3-6. The ENCOORD may also act as the senior engineer advisor to the commander or that role may be assigned to a senior engineer force commander. Dual-hatting the senior engineer unit commander as both the engineer force commander and the senior engineer staff advisor to the supported commander is no longer the preferred option for providing C2 for engineer forces and meeting the supported commander's requirement for engineer staff advice. Ultimately, the decision on whether the senior engineer unit commander will serve both roles will be made by each supported force commander and be situationally dependent. Some specific considerations for determining the relationship of the senior engineer staff advisor and the engineer force commander include the following questions:

- What staff assets are available to support the engineer staff advisor versus the engineer unit commander? Are these elements from the same unit or are separate units resourced for each role?
- What experience level is needed for the engineer staff advisor? Should this role be resourced with a current or former commander?
- What duration of time will the augmenting engineer element, commanded by the senior engineer unit commander, be working for or with the force? Is there enough time for this engineer commander to acclimate and effectively advise the force commander?
- What working relationship is established between an existing engineer staff advisor and the force commander? Similarly, is there an existing working relationship between the engineer unit commander and this force commander?

3-7. The responsibilities and functions of Army staff are described in FM 6-0. Joint engineer staff responsibilities are discussed in JP 3-34. In general, the engineer staff at EAB or of a joint force assist their commander by furnishing engineer advice and recommendations to the commander and other staff officers; preparing those portions of plans, estimates, and orders that pertain to engineering; participating on boards and working groups as necessary; and coordinating and supervising engineer unit and other activities within the engineer staff span of control. The ENCOORD coordinates the efforts of the engineer staff to assist the commander. The ENCOORD coordinates a variety of activities throughout the operations process in the conduct of engineer operations. These include the following:

- **Plan.**
  - Assist the intelligence staff with the intelligence preparation of the battlefield (IPB), including information from the preparation of the engineer running estimate.
  - Determine and evaluate critical aspects of the engineer situation.
  - Formulate ideas for engineer support to meet the commander's intent.
  - Decide what engineer missions must be accomplished to support current and future fights.
  - Integrate the geospatial engineer team in the planning process to explain the military significance of the terrain to the commander and staff, and create geospatial products for decisionmaking.
  - Identify operational- and tactical-level engineer requirements to support the operation.
  - Make the commander aware of the capabilities, limitations, and employment considerations of supporting engineers and related assets, including Army, joint, and multinational forces; interagency and nongovernmental assets; and HN and other civilian contract capabilities.
  - Develop a scheme of engineer operations concurrent with the concept of operation.
  - Recommend the engineer priorities of effort and support, essential tasks, and acceptable mission risks to the commander.

- Recommend the engineer organization for the current operation and consider the transition to the next one.
- Visualize the future state of engineer operations in the AO.
- Integrate the engineer functions of combat, general, and geospatial engineering into future plans.

- **Prepare.**
  - Train the staff engineer cell and ensure integration within the various unit CPs.
  - Issue timely instructions and orders to subordinate engineer units through the base order to simplify preparation and integration. Develop the necessary input to orders, annexes, and engineer unit orders (as required).
  - Coordinate production and distribution of maps and terrain products.
  - Recommend intelligence requirements to the intelligence staff officer through the operations staff officer.
  - Participate in the targeting process.
  - Participate in appropriate working groups.
  - Recommend MSRs and logistics areas to the logistics staff officer based on technical information.
  - Coordinate with the logistics staff officer for additional resources to support the engineering and construction effort, such as supply Class III supplies (petroleum products) and Class IV supplies (construction and barrier materials).
  - Coordinate with the logistics staff officer to support base camp, facilities, and other sustainment-related construction requirements.
  - Advise the commander on environmental issues, coordinate with other staff members to determine the impact of operations on the environment, and help the commander integrate environmental considerations into decisionmaking.
  - Recommend when engineer diver support may facilitate specific engineer reconnaissance requirements.
  - Ensure EH support integration in the conduct of operations.

- **Execute.**
  - Alter the engineer plan using the feedback received from subordinate echelons, the supporting engineer headquarters, and other augmenting engineer units as required.
  - Provide information on the status of engineer assets on hand.
  - Make time-sensitive engineer decisions on requests for immediate support received from subordinate echelon engineers.

- **Assess.**
  - Track all templated and known obstacles, scatterable mines (SCATMINEs), the survivability status, the route status, engineer missions, and any other engineer-specific information.
  - Establish and maintain a continuous, open link among all engineer cells and supporting engineer CPs.
  - Use the running estimate and the continuous link with the supporting engineer staffs and engineer units to compute resource and force requirements and recommend engineer task organization.
  - Monitor the execution of engineer orders and instructions by tracking the current fight.
  - Use reporting from engineer unit CPs to measure and analyze engineer performance and anticipate change and unforeseen requirements.

3-8. Regardless of the decision made determining the relationship of the senior engineer staff advisor and the engineer force commander, any senior engineer commander allocated will provide significant advice to the supported commander in addition to command of assigned engineer forces. The ENCOORD must establish and maintain a collaborative relationship with the engineer force commander and his headquarters to ensure a coordinated engineer effort. The allocation of engineer headquarters units is considered in tailoring the force and will vary dependent on analysis of mission variables (see chapters 4, 5, and 6 for echelon-specific discussion of force-tailoring considerations). As previously discussed in chapter 2, the modular force includes three echelons of engineer headquarters units: the TEC, engineer brigade, and engineer battalion. Additionally, the multifunctional MEB is capable of C2 for engineer forces in cases where engineer support is integral to the multifunctional mission. Though modular engineer headquarters units do not possess the integral capability to augment supported unit engineer staff sections, the assistant corps, or division engineer sections as in legacy organizations, they will typically provide a significant contribution for the ENCOORD's conduct of engineer operations. Depending on task organization and other mission variables, they will also provide C2 for much of the tailored engineer force conducting operations.

GEOSPATIAL INTEGRATION

3-9. Geospatial capabilities are distributed at BCT, division, corps, and theater army echelons to provide geospatial engineering support. Geospatial engineering support provided to the Army and other Services varies in focus at each echelon. It is focused on geospatial data generation, geospatial data analysis, geospatial data management, and quality control at the theater army and combatant command level. At the corps and division levels, the majority of the workload is required to support database management, mission planning, and the IPB process. Below division level, geospatial engineering is increasingly focused on current operations and updating the geospatial database (database management).

3-10. The corps and division team supports the assistant chief of staff, intelligence (G-2) and assistant chief of staff, operations (G-3) planners to fuse intelligence and geospatial information into a common picture for the commander, staff, and subordinate units. The geospatial engineer team requires access to the classified tactical network to update and disseminate geospatial information and products. The geospatial engineer team organic to the corps and division collects and provides updated geospatial data and products in support of corps and division operations.

3-11. A geospatial planning cell (GPC) is assigned to each Army command to provide geospatial operational planning; generation, analysis, preparation of maps, map updates, and tactical decision aids; and coordination with other geospatial engineer elements and higher headquarters. Topographic engineer companies and GPCs are the only units with unique, dedicated geospatial data generation capability within the Army force structure. The topographic engineer company and the GPC require access to the Global Information Grid and classified tactical local area network to update and disseminate geospatial information and products.

3-12. NGA produces digital terrain and feature data which is available to users via the web or directly from NGA. The Defense Logistics Agency (DLA) distributes maps. The geospatial engineer can request imagery which can be used for spatial and temporal reasoning or multispectral analysis products that are customized to meet particular operational requirements. Imagery enhances three-dimensional and fly-through perspectives. NGA geospatial analysts may be attached to units, normally at division and above, to supplement the organic geospatial engineers and staffs.

WORKING GROUPS, CELLS, AND BOARDS

3-13. Commanders at each echelon may establish working groups, boards, or cells to manage and coordinate functional or multifunctional activities. The engineer staff will be key members on many of these and may chair construction-related groups. Working groups conduct staff coordination at the action officer level and prepare materials for decisions to be made at a board. Boards establish policies, procedures, priorities, and oversight to coordinate efficient use of resources. Cells group personnel from various sections on a headquarters authorization document to integrate key functions, such as cells focused on each warfighting function. Appendix A discusses the various boards and cells on which the staff engineer may participate.

Boards Formed to Solve Problems

"Resourcing in Iraq is requirements-based. Many of the resources required by engineers were construction materials, particularly barriers. These were justified through the Division Acquisition Review Board or the Joint Acquisition Review Board, depending on the monetary thresholds. The engineers provide input for the division-level approval, or process the requests going to corps for their action. In addition to the material requests, an engineer reviewed all construction requests and conducted a work classification to ensure compliance with statutory construction limits. Within Iraq, the LOGCAP is a source of base camp support. As part of our division-level review process, the Division Engineer [ENCOORD] validates all LOGCAP requests over $100,000."

Extracted from "Modular Engineer Structure in Divisions" by Colonel Jeffrey R. Eckstein, in *Engineer, The Professional Bulletin of Army Engineers*, January-March 2008, p. 61. Colonel Eckstein served as Division Engineer and G-7 for the 25th Infantry Division as part of Operation Iraqi Freedom.

3-14. The geospatial engineering units available to the commander may become part of the command's GEOINT cell. The GEOINT cell comprises the people and capabilities that constitute the GEOINT support, to include imagery and geospatial assets. The cell ensures GEOINT requirements are coordinated through appropriate channels as applicable and facilitates shared access of various domains. This cell may be centrally located or distributed throughout the command and connected by networks. Cell members do not have to work directly for a designated GEOINT officer; they may work for their parent unit, but coordinate efforts across staff directorates. The key to a successful process is collaboration across functional areas within the command and among the GEOINT cell, higher headquarters, and other stakeholders.

JOINT ENGINEER STAFF

3-15. A combatant command engineer staff assists the GCC by performing a variety of functions to synchronize engineer operations in the AOR. A joint force engineer serves as the principal advisor to the JFC for matters pertaining to the planning and execution of joint engineering support operations. The GCC and subordinate JFC will organize their staffs to carry out their respective assigned duties and responsibilities. When a functional component command employs forces from more than one Service, the staff should reflect each Service represented. Based on mission-specific requirements, the engineer staff may be placed within the directorate for operations (J-3), directorate for logistics (J-4), or organized as a separate staff to the JFC. The JFC may choose to organize geospatial engineers or geospatial information and services (GI&S) officers within the directorate for intelligence (J-2). Regardless of the option or combination of options used, the requirement for the staff engineer remains, and the need for constant communication, liaison, and coordination throughout the entire staff. A notional engineer staff is depicted in figure 3-2, page 3-8.

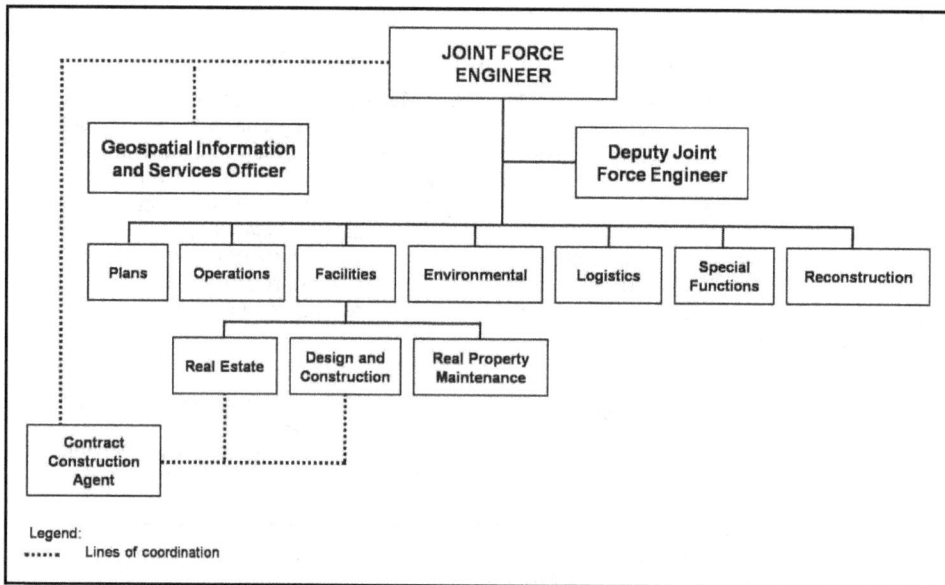

Figure 3-2. Notional joint engineer staff

3-16. Typical joint engineer responsibilities are as follows:

- Plans and coordinates theater engineering support.
- Provides recommendations on the assignment of engineering missions to subordinate commanders. Recommendation may include which subordinate commander (Service or functional component, subordinate JTF or subunified commander) will be assigned the mission, the scope of the project, and which commanders will be placed in a supporting role.
- Furnishes recommendations on the tasking of components for theater engineering missions, tasks, or projects.
- Recommends policies and priorities for construction and real estate acquisition and for Class IV supplies. Compiles a joint integrated priority list for construction projects for U.S.-funded contingency construction and for HN-funded construction.
- Furnishes advice on the effect of joint operations on the physical environment according to applicable U.S., international, and HN laws and agreements.
- Recommends construction standards.
- Identifies engineering support requirements that exceed component funding authorizations and organized engineer capabilities.
- Furnishes advice on the assessment of the risk to mission accomplishment of engineering support shortfalls.
- Furnishes advice on the feasibility, acceptability, and suitability of component engineering plans.
- Prepares, as part of the joint operation planning process, the engineer parts of operation plans (OPLANs) and operation orders (OPORDs).
- Reviews all engineer-related annexes and appendixes of OPLANs and OPORDs.
- Provides input to the theater security cooperation plan. Develops and programs construction projects to include exercise-related construction (ERC) program and humanitarian and civic assistance (HCA) program construction projects to support theater security cooperation strategies.
- Develops training and exercise programs to evaluate and improve preparedness for engineering missions.

- Plans and coordinates the procurement and distribution of Class IV supplies based on established priorities. Service components are responsible for procurement and distribution of their Class IV requirements.
- Coordinates with DOD and DOS construction agents and other engineer support agencies.
- Participates in joint engineering boards and engineer-related working groups, as required.

3-17. Key joint engineer staff functions are as follows:

- Develops and coordinates combat, general, and geospatial engineering requirements for the joint force.
- Acts as the intermediary, facilitator, and coordinator among JTF elements, including nonmilitary elements, requesting engineering services. Receives guidance and reports actions to a joint civil-military engineering board (JCMEB) if established.
- Develops and coordinates tasks for component engineer forces.
- Coordinates and facilitates the Joint Facilities Utilization Board (JFUB), JCMEB, and joint environmental management board (JEMB). Integrates actions from these boards, assigns tasking based on board recommendations, and monitors completion.
- Screens, validates, and prioritizes all engineering projects and mission assignments. Participates in management of LOGCAP, when used, to validate operations and maintenance services and construction requirements.
- Plans, programs, and controls facility use. Receives guidance and reports actions to JFUB if established.
- Prepares logistic reports on engineer resources using the Joint Operation Planning and Execution System (JOPES).
- Develops the ESP.
- Plans and coordinates the distribution of construction and barrier materials and engineer munitions based on established priorities. Participates on the joint acquisition review board to validate requests for construction equipment leases and purchases.
- Functions as the primary interface among the joint force, HN, contingency contractors, and other theater construction organizations.
- Establishes the statement-of-work, development of contracts, and employment of services.
- Plans and provides guidance for environmental considerations that impact joint operations.
- Serves as the program manager for all engineer-related functions.

INTEGRATION THROUGHOUT THE OPERATIONS PROCESS

3-18. Full spectrum operations follow a cycle of planning, preparation, execution, and continuous assessment. The operations process is the context within which engineer capabilities are integrated into combined arms application. This context gains importance because of multiple and distinct interactions throughout engineer operations with the C2 function. At every echelon from BCT to theater army and JTF, engineer leaders and staff exercise C2, participate in their supported commander's C2, and provide geospatial and other support through their supported commander's C2 warfighting function.

STAFF RUNNING ESTIMATE

3-19. The ENCOORD uses the running estimate as a logical thought process and extension of the analysis of the OE. It is conducted by the ENCOORD throughout the operations process of the supported force commander and is continually refined. This estimate allows for early integration and synchronization of engineer considerations into combined arms planning processes. In their running estimates, staff sections continuously consider the effect of new information and update assumptions, friendly force status, effects of enemy activity, civil considerations, and conclusions and recommendations. An ENCOORD's running estimate assesses the following:

- Friendly force engineer capabilities with respect to ongoing and planned operations.
- Enemy capabilities as they affect the engineer section's area of expertise for both current operations and future plans.

- Civil considerations as they affect the engineer section's area of expertise for both current operations and future plans.
- The physical environment and other operational variables' effect on current and future operations from the section's perspective.

3-20. The development and continuous maintenance of the running estimate drives the coordination among the staff engineer, supporting engineers, the supported commander, and other staff officers in the development of plans, orders, and the supporting annexes. Additionally, the allocation of engineer assets and resources assists in determining command and support relationships that will be used. Appendix B provides a tool for use in developing and maintaining the engineer running estimate.

ENGINEER PLANNING PROCESS

3-21. The levels of war are doctrinal perspectives that clarify the relationship among strategic objectives (ends), operational approach (ways), and tactical actions (means). EAB engineer planners will be primarily focused on the operational to tactical perspective. Scope, complexity, and length of planning horizons differ between operational and tactical planning. Operational-level planning involves broader dimensions of time and space than tactical-level planning. It is often more complex and less defined. Operational-level planners are often required to define an AO, estimate forces required, and evaluate the requirements for the operation. Operational planners mesh service capabilities with joint and multinational formations, interagency, and NGOs. Operational planners also program and manage multiple budget channels to receive and execute funds from outside agencies. Tactical planning has the same clarity of purpose as operational planning but has a shorter planning horizon. Tactical level planning proceeds from an existing operational design. Normally AOs are prescribed, objectives and available forces identified, and sequences of activities specified for tactical-level commanders. The plan guides subordinates as they progress through the operation. Comprehensive, continuous, and adaptive planning characterizes successful operations at the operational and tactical levels of war.

3-22. Commanders use their staffs and integrate input from subordinate commanders into their planning processes. Engineer leaders must understand and be integral participants in the planning processes impacting engineer operations at their echelon of employment. Supporting engineer unit commanders and leaders conduct parallel planning processes which provide both effective outcomes for the engineer units employed and appropriate input to the higher commander's process. Geospatial support elements and engineer staff planners integrate directly within the planning staff at each echelon to participate in the planning process.

3-23. Engineer operations are complex, resource (time, manpower, equipment, and materials) intensive, and require extensive and proactive coordination. Additionally, a successful engineering effort requires an understanding of all engineer requirements (combat, general, and geospatial) and their role in supporting the concept of operations. Planning, from the perspective of engineer operations, includes even more than the description above ascribes to it. Engineer operations must be directed and synchronized through planning as one of the critical activities in the operations process, but many engineer activities also require the critical reasoning and technical skills as well as problem solving techniques which form the base logic for the planning processes (see FM 5-0). Engineer operations will involve the use of some functionally unique analytic tools to solve construction, design, facilities, and other engineer-specific problems.

Military Decisionmaking Process

3-24. Planning is a form of decisionmaking, which is selecting a COA as the one most favorable to accomplish the mission. Planning is the means by which the commander envisions a desired outcome, lays out effective ways of achieving it, and communicates to his subordinates his vision, intent, and decisions, focusing on the results he expects to achieve (FM 3-0). Not all decisions require the same level of planning. Commanders make hundreds of decisions during operations in an environment of great uncertainty, unpredictability, and constant change. The commander makes some decisions very quickly. Other decisions are deliberate, using the military decisionmaking process (MDMP) and a complete staff to create a fully developed and written order. The MDMP is defined in detail in FM 5-0 (see figure 3-3). JP 5-0 provides the planning construct in a joint environment in much the same manner.

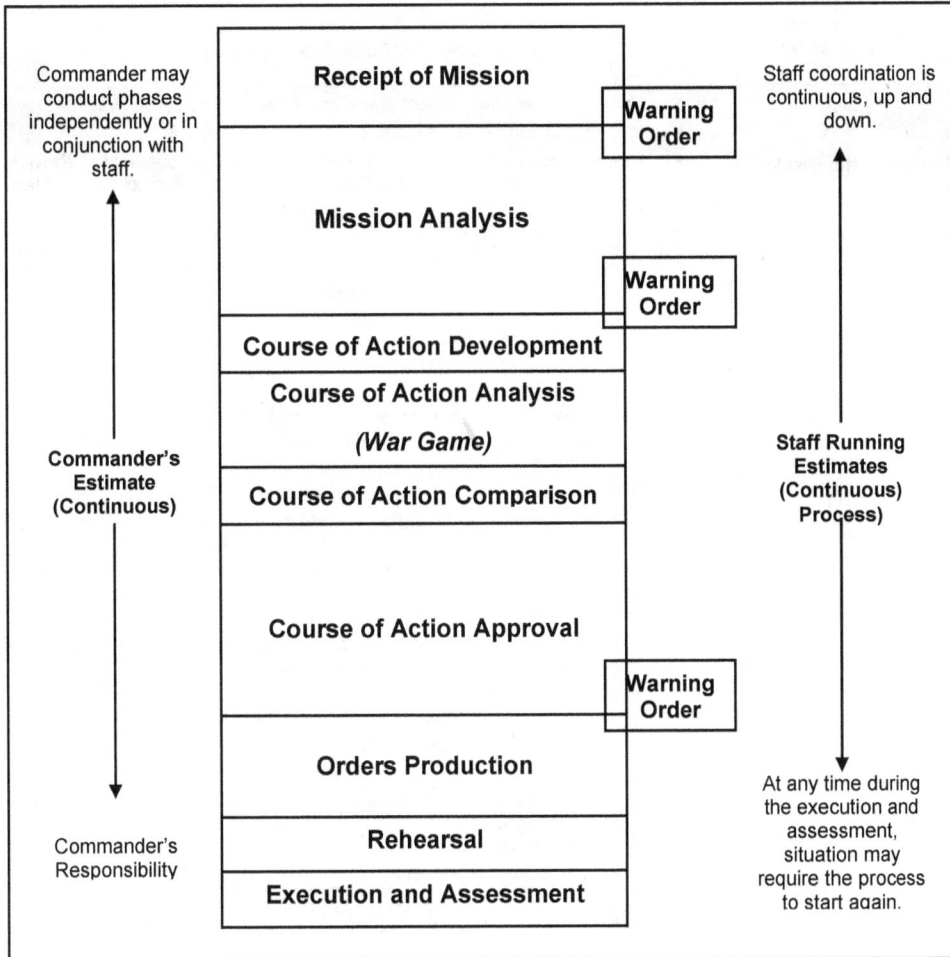

Figure 3-3. Military decisionmaking process

3-25. Engineer planning will include considerations unique to the particular situation and mission. Some considerations are more generic and can be summarized for broad reference in any application of the MDMP. Table 3-1, page 3-12, lists some of the generic engineer planning considerations as they pertain to each step of the MDMP, focused primarily at operational-level planning.

Table 3-1. Engineer considerations in the military decisionmaking process

Steps of the Military Decisionmaking Process	Engineer Considerations
Receipt of the Mission	• Receive higher headquarters plans, orders, and construction directive(s) • Understand commander's intent and time constraints • Request geospatial information about the area of operations. Provide geospatial engineer products to the staff for use during military decisionmaking process • Establish and participate on engineer-related boards
Mission Analysis	• Analyze available intelligence on existing obstacles. Evaluate terrain, weather, and threat capabilities to determine potential impact on mobility, countermobility, survivability • Conduct terrain analysis • Develop essential mobility, countermobility, survivability and other engineering tasks • Identify available information on routes and key facilities. Evaluate line of communications, aerial port of debarkation, and seaport of debarkation requirements • Determine availability of construction and other engineering materials • Review availability of engineer capabilities to include Army, joint, multinational, host nation, and contract • Determine beddown requirements for supported force. Review theater construction standards and base camp master planning documentation. Review unified facilities criteria as required • Review existing geospatial data on potential sites, conduct site reconnaissance (if possible), and determine the threat (to include environmental and explosive hazards) • Obtain necessary geologic, hydrologic, and climatic data • Determine the level of interagency cooperation required • Determine funding sources as required • Determine terrain and mobility restraints, obstacle intelligence, threat engineer capabilities, and critical infrastructure. Recommend commander's critical information requirements • Integrate reconnaissance effort
Course of Action Development	• Identify priority engineer requirements, including essential mobility/countermobility/survivability and other engineering tasks developed during mission analysis • Integrate engineer operations into course of action development • Recommend an appropriate level of survivability effort for each course of action based on the expected threat • Produce construction designs that meet the commander's intent (use Theater Construction Management System when the project is of sufficient size and scope) • Determine alternate construction location, methods, means, materials and timelines to give the commander options • Determine real property and real estate requirements
Course of Action Analysis	• War-game and refine the engineer plan • Use the critical path method to determine length of different courses of action and the ability to accelerate the project
Course of Action Comparison	• Determine the most feasible, acceptable, and suitable methods of completing the engineering effort • Determine and compare the risks of each engineering course of action

Table 3-1. Engineer considerations in the military decisionmaking process (continued)

Steps of the Military Decisionmaking Process	Engineer Considerations
Course of Action Approval	• Gain approval of the essential mobility, countermobility, survivability and other engineering tasks, construction management plan, safety plan, security plan, logistics plan, and environmental plan as required
Orders Production	• Produce construction directives as required • Provide input to the appropriate plans and orders • Ensure that all resources are properly allocated
Rehearsal	• Coordinate combined arms rehearsals as appropriate • Conduct construction prebriefings • Conduct preinspections and construction meetings • Synchronize construction plan with local and adjacent units
Execution and Assessment	• Implement survivability construction standards, including requirements for security fencing, lighting, barriers, and guard posts • Conduct quality assurance and mid-project inspections • Participate in engineer-related boards • Maintain "as-built" and "red-line" drawings • Conduct project turnover activities

Joint Engineer Planning

3-26. Joint planning is focused at the strategic and operational levels of war. While corps and below Army units normally conduct Army tactical planning, ARFOR frequently participate in or conduct joint operations planning. For example, ASCCs routinely participate in joint operation planning, to include developing plans as the joint force land component. Corps and divisions perform joint operations planning when serving as a JTF or Army forces headquarters. Corps, divisions, and brigades, directly subordinate to a JTF, participate in joint operations planning and receive joint-formatted orders. It is important that Army leaders serving in headquarters above battalion understand the joint planning process and are familiar with the joint format for plans and orders.

3-27. Joint operation planning uses two distinct methods: contingency planning and crisis action planning. For a detailed explanation of joint operation planning, see JP 5-0 and JP 3-33. The primary joint doctrinal publication for planning engineer operations is JP 3-34. Army planners should understand that the Air Force and Navy have a narrower focus for the engineering mission and consider (general) engineering to be primarily a logistics function that is executed to sustain their forces in a contingency operation. Their activities tend to focus on missions such as base camp and life support development, construction and repair of SPODs, APODs, and other facilities and sites and not focus on operational support to ground maneuver forces. The Naval construction force bridging mission in support of maneuver forces is an exception to this broad generalization of Navy focus areas.

3-28. In joint operation planning, engineers should consider the following:

- Has the JTF engineer been identified?
- Has engineering policy and guidance been received from the GCC engineer?
- Have a JCMEB and JFUB been established? How will board procedures impact engineer operations?
- Have traffic regulations, dictated by physical conditions of routes and communications, been established?
- Has engineer support in the collection and processing of information for preparation and revision of maps been identified?
- Have future engineering requirements been anticipated and planned for?
- Have requirements for real estate, use of existing facilities, interservice support, and construction been forwarded? Are procedures in place for this to occur?

- Has tasking been received for ADC missions (for example, airfield damage repair)?
- Has the JTF engineer established, issued, and executed the JTF environmental management support plan? How will the plan impact engineer operations?
- What HN engineer support is available? How will language and cultural barriers be dealt with?
- What Class IV (construction and barrier material) is available? What responsibilities does the JTF engineer have with regard to Class IV material acquisition and management?
- What are the component responsibilities for engineering support?
- Will contract construction be used? How will contract management and contractor management be conducted?

3-29. Joint engineer activities and considerations are similar during both contingency and crisis action planning processes. (For additional information about the deliberate planning and crisis action planning processes, see Chairman of the Joint Chiefs of Staff Manual [CJCSM] 3122.01A and JP 5-0.) The ESP (appendix 6, annex D of a joint OPLAN) is produced by a joint engineer staff for input to a joint OPLAN as part of the planning process. It ensures that essential engineering capabilities are identified and will be provided at the required locations and times. It is the most critical appendix for engineering in a joint OPLAN. For joint operations, the engineer prepares the ESP and provides significant input to other annexes due to their possible impact on engineer operations as shown in JP 3-34.

3-30. Engineering planning is an integral part of joint operation planning. The ESP identifies the minimum essential facilities and engineering capabilities needed to support the commitment of military forces. Based on Service component input, unified commanders are responsible for preparing the ESP. See appendix C for a sample ESP. Joint engineer planners consider the following issues when preparing input for an ESP:

- HN restrictions imposed on the use of bases and installations.
- Assumptions regarding the availability of critical HN support.
- Major construction resources to be allocated.
- Anticipated and sustainment of Class IV supplies resources. ESP should consider whether or not the Class IV items will need to be contracted locally or shipped from other sources. Consider use of LOGCAP or similar program management and contract support requirements.
- Desired standards of construction (initial or temporary).
- A provision for force withdrawal, such as base denial and movement of relocatable residual assets.

3-31. The engineer component of the Global Combat Support System (GCSS)-Engineer (EN) (formerly referred to as the joint engineer planning and execution system) is a tool used to support quantitative aspects of engineering support planning and execution. It provides the general requirements for the ESP and provides a common automated system for the joint force engineer planners to determine the appropriate amount of engineer assets and capabilities to support the selected COA. GCSS-EN is a web-based application residing on the SECRET Internet Protocol Router Network (SIPRNET). GCSS-EN assists the engineer planners in determining the correct engineer capability for the proper location, timed correctly to support the concept of operations. GCSS-EN includes a Theater Construction Management System (TCMS) module to assist with facilities planning and links into construction resource and materials planning. It also includes an environmental module. GCSS-EN is used to—

- Generate time-phased facility requirements based on the OPLAN.
- Analyze and assess engineering support by comparing facility requirements to in-theater facility assets and HN, contract, and troop engineering capability.
- Provide facility feasibility assessment, manpower, material, and nonunit cargo requirements for other processes.
- Provide infrastructure data to assist in mission analysis and COA development.
- Provide real time monitoring capability needed to track plan execution.

Force Projection

Force projection is defined as the ability to project the military instrument of national power from the United States or another theater in response to requirements for military operations. (JP 5-0) Force projection operations extend from mobilization and deployment of forces to redeployment to CONUS or home theater (see JP 3-35). FM 3-34 includes a brief discussion of engineer considerations for force projection.

3-32. Engineer force units and individual augmentees must be requested through the request for forces process to meet force projection requirements. Engineer staff at the GCC and theater army headquarters are primary points of contact to initiate a request for engineering forces as part of force tailoring. Subordinate commanders may forward requests to the theater army echelon. Once validated, the request is forwarded to the CCDR and then to United States Joint Forces Command (USJFCOM) for sourcing after final validation. For further information on the request for forces process, see JP 1-0.

Facilities and Construction Planning

3-33. EAB staff engineers must plan for the acquisition of uncontaminated land and facilities and their management and ultimate disposal to support operations, including—

- Operational facilities (such as CPs, airfields, ports).
- Logistics facilities (such as maintenance facilities, supply points, warehouses, ammunition supply points [ASPs], and APOD or SPOD for sustainment).
- Force beddown facilities (such as dining halls, billeting, religious support facilities, clinics, and hygiene facilities).
- Common-use facilities (such as roads and joint RSOI facilities).
- Facility survivability (such as site selection, proximity to potential threat areas, and sniper screening).

3-34. The JFC, with input from the appropriate EAB command, will determine what facilities are needed to satisfy operational requirements. Facilities are grouped into six broad categories that emphasize the use of existing assets over new construction. To the maximum extent possible, facilities or real estate requirements should be met from these categories in the following priority order:

- U.S.-owned, -occupied, or -leased facilities (including captured facilities).
- U.S.-owned facility substitutes pre-positioned in-theater.
- HN and multinational support where an agreement exists for the HN or other nation to provide specific types and quantities of facilities at specified times in designated locations.
- Facilities available from commercial sources.
- U.S.-owned facility substitutes stored in the United States.
- Construction of facilities that are considered shortfall after an assessment of the availability of existing assets.

3-35. The EAB and joint force engineer staff plan expeditious construction of facility requirements that are considered shortfalls (such as those facilities that cannot be sourced from existing assets). In these circumstances, the appropriate Service, HN, or multinational partner should to the extent possible perform construction during peacetime. Contracting support should be used to augment military capabilities. If time constraints place risk on the completion of new construction to meet mission requirements, the EAB and joint force engineer staff seek alternative solutions to new construction. Expedient construction such as rapid construction techniques (for example, prefabricated buildings or clamshell structures) should also be considered, as these methods can be selectively employed with minimum time, cost, and risk.

3-36. Adequate funding (see appendix D) must be available to undertake early engineer reconnaissance and acquisition of facilities to meet requirements, whether by construction or leasing. Funding constraints are a planning consideration. The JFC, with input from the appropriate EAB command, articulates funding requirements for construction and leasing of facilities by considering the missions supported and the amount of funds required. The JFC should take steps to ensure that the Service components allocate sufficient funds for facility construction, including associated contract administration services and real estate acquisition and disposal services. Facility construction planning must be routinely and repetitively accomplished to ensure that mission-essential facilities are identified well in advance of the need and, wherever possible, on-the-shelf designs are completed to expedite facility construction in time of need.

3-37. The GCC, in coordination with Service components and the Services, specifies the construction standards for facilities in-theater to optimize the engineer effort expended on any given facility while ensuring that the facilities are adequate for health, safety, and mission accomplishment. Figure 3-4 shows the beddown and basing continuum and highlights the need for early master planning efforts to help facilitate transition to more permanent facilities as an operation develops (see appendix E for a more detailed discussion of base development). While the timelines provide a standard framework, the situation may warrant deviations from them. In addition to using these guidelines when establishing initial construction standards, the JFUB should be used to periodically revalidate construction standards based on current operational issues and provide recommendations to the JFC on potential changes. Ultimately, it is the GCC who determines exact construction type based on location, materials available, and other factors. The EAB engineer staff must recommend the most feasible solutions to each requirement. Construction standards are guidelines, and the engineer staff must consider a number of other factors in their planning as well. See FM 3-34.400 and JP 3-34 for additional discussion of construction standards.

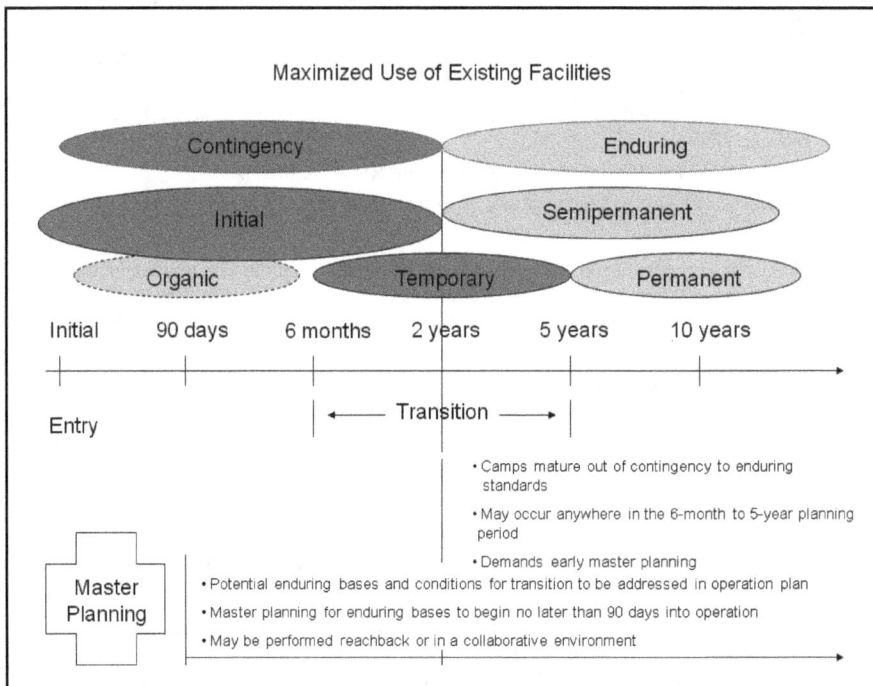

Figure 3-4. Force beddown and base development

3-38. Unified facilities criteria (UFC) provide facility planning, design, construction, operations, and maintenance criteria for all DOD components. Individual UFC are developed by a single-disciplined working group and published after careful coordination. They are jointly developed and managed by USACE, NAVFAC, and AFCESA. Though UFC are written with long-term standards in mind, planners who are executing under contingency and enduring standards for general engineering tasks will find them useful. Topics include pavement design, water supply systems, military airfields, concrete design and repair, plumbing, electrical systems, and many more.

3-39. UFC are living documents and will be periodically reviewed, updated, and made available to users as part of the Services' responsibility for providing technical criteria for military construction. UFC are effective upon issuance and are distributed only in electronic media from the following sources:

- UFC Index <http://65.204.17.188//report/doc_ufc html>.
- USACE TECHINFO Internet site <http://www hnd.usace.army mil/techinfo>.

- NAVFAC Engineering Innovation and Criteria Office Internet site <http://www.wbdg.org/references/pa_dod.php>.
- Construction Criteria Base System maintained by the National Institute of Building Sciences at Internet site <http://www.wbdg.org/ccb>.

3-40. General engineering planners must consider any and all construction standards established by GCCs and ASCCs for their AOR. Specific examples of these are the *Red Book* in the United States European Command (USEUCOM) AOR and *Sand Book* in United States Central Command (USCENTCOM). These constantly evolving guidebooks specifically establish base camp standards that consider regional requirements for troop living conditions and therefore have a major impact on projects such as base camps and utilities. Because availability of construction materials may vary greatly in various AORs, standards of construction may differ greatly among them. GCCs often also establish standards for construction in OPORDs and fragmentary orders (FRAGOs) that may take precedence over guidebooks. Planners must understand the expected life cycle of a general engineering project to apply these standards. Often the standards will be markedly different, depending on whether the construction is a contingency construction or is intended to have an enduring presence.

Project Management

3-41. Planners use the project management system described in FM 5-412 as a tool for the process of coordinating the skill and labor of personnel using machines and materials to form the materials into a desired structure. Figure 3-5, page 3-18, shows the project management process that divides the effort into the preliminary planning, detailed planning, and project execution. Today, when engineer planners are focused on general engineering tasks, they rely extensively on the TCMS to produce the products required by the project management system. These products include the design, activities list, logic network, critical path method (CPM) or Gantt chart, bill of materials, and other products. Effective products produced during the planning phases also greatly assist during the construction phase. In addition to TCMS, the engineer has various other reachback tools or organizations that can exploit resources, capabilities, and expertise that is not organic to the unit that requires them. These tools and organizations include, but are not limited to, the USAES; USACE Engineering Infrastructure and Intelligence Reachback Center and ERDC TeleEngineering Operations Center, 412th and 416th TECs; the AFCESA; and NAVFAC. See appendix D for additional information on how to access reachback support.

3-42. The project management process normally begins at the unit level with the construction directive. This gives who, what, when, where, and why of a particular project and is similar to an OPORD in its scope and purpose. Critical to the construction directive are plans, specifications, and all items essential for success of the project. Units may also receive general engineering missions as part of an OPORD, FRAGO, warning order, or verbally. When a leader analyzes a construction directive, he may need to treat it as a FRAGO in that much of the information required for a thorough mission analysis may exist in an OPORD issued for a specific contingency operation.

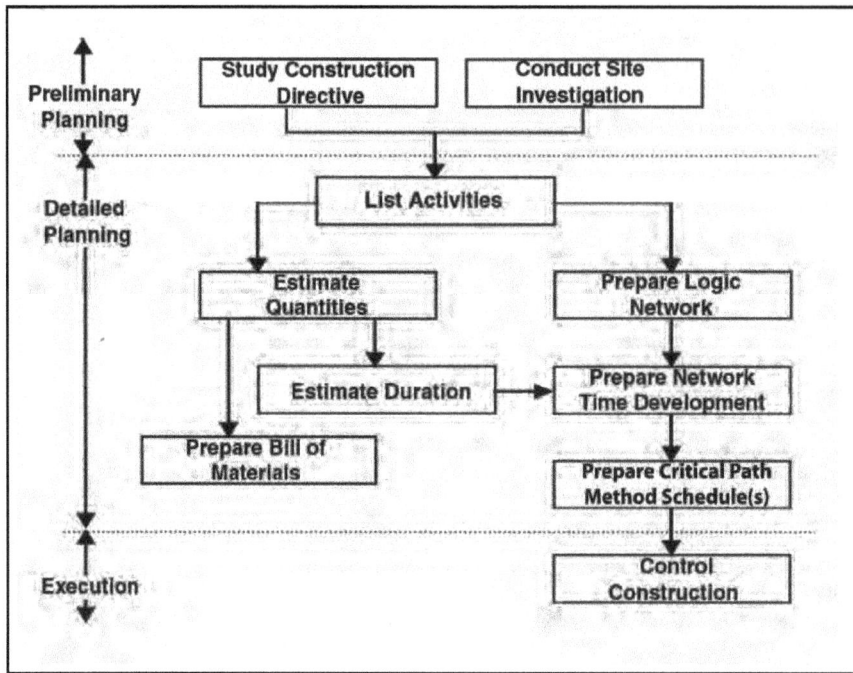

Figure 3-5. Project management process

INTEGRATION ACROSS THE FORCE

3-43. Full spectrum operations require simultaneous combinations of offensive, defensive, and stability or civil support operations. Higher-echelon engineer operations are intrinsically simultaneous—supporting combinations of operational components, occurring at every echelon, impacting each level of war, influencing the entire spectrum of conflict. Engineer operations modify, maintain, provide understanding of, and protect the physical environment. In doing so, they enable the mobility of friendly forces, alter the mobility of adversaries, enhance the survivability and enable the sustainment of friendly forces, contribute to a clear understanding of the physical environment, and provide support to noncombatants, other nations, and civilian authorities and agencies. Indeed, engineer operations may be so widespread and enveloping that they may be viewed as a standalone objective. However, engineer operations are not standalone. Engineer applications are effective within the context of the supported objective. Military engineer operations are focused on the combined arms objective. To identify and maintain that focus for the widespread application of engineer capabilities, engineer operations are integrated within the combined arms operation.

COMBINED ARMS INTEGRATION

3-44. Combat power is the actual application of force—the conversion of fighting potential into effective action. It includes the unit's constructive and information capabilities and its disruptive or destructive force. Engineer operations contribute significant combat power, both lethal and nonlethal in nature, to all the elements of full spectrum operations. Organic engineer capabilities are embedded in each of the BCTs to provide close support to the maneuver of those forces. Based on analysis of the mission variables, the BCTs will be task-organized with additional modular engineer capabilities to meet mission requirements. Other, more technically specialized engineer capabilities support the BCTs' requirements linked to the movement and maneuver, protection, and sustainment warfighting functions. These same capabilities may be employed at division, corps, and theater echelon to enable force mobility, survivability, and sustainment. Force-tailored engineer capabilities from the force pool also provide critical nonlethal capabilities to conduct or support stability or civil support operations. Geospatial capabilities, both organic and from the force pool, support all four elements by adding to a clear understanding of the physical environment.

Fighting as Engineers

3-45. Combat engineers are organized, trained, and equipped to fight and destroy the enemy, in addition to their primary responsibilities within combat engineering. Combat engineers engage in close combat to accomplish their engineer missions and to—

- Support a movement to contact or attack as a part of a maneuver formation in the movement to accomplish the formation's mission.
- Fight as the breach force during BCT combined arms breaching operations.
- Assist the supported organization to defeat an unexpected attack.
- Protect a critical demolition target that must remain passable until friendly forces are able to withdraw.
- Maintain security at a work site.
- Protect themselves in an assembly area or on the march.

3-46. General and geospatial engineering units are armed primarily with small arms and have only a limited number of crew-served weapons. They are not organized to move within combined arms formations or apply fire and maneuver. They are capable of engaging in close combat with fire and movement primarily in a defensive role.

3-47. During combat operations, combat engineer units are task-organized with maneuver units and are integrated into the combined arms formation. The engineer unit is designed to provide demolition, terrain reinforcement, breaching, and hasty gap-crossing capabilities to the combined arms team. The engineer unit can also employ direct-fire weapons systems to aid in employing demolitions and breaching assets. Regardless of the mission, armored engineer vehicles are combat vehicles and provide a significant contribution to the combat power of the entire formation. To accomplish the mission, engineers will fire and move under the direction of the formation commander, as necessary, using demolition, breaching, and gap-crossing skills when appropriate. Fire and movement techniques are based on rifle, automatic rifle, and grenadier covering fire, allowing the placement of demolition charges within striking range.

3-48. When involved in an assault, engineers will fight dismounted on the objective. However, they will focus on breaching the close-in protective obstacles and demolition tasks against positions and dug-in vehicles. Demolition charges produce significant shock and concussion effects on defenders and destroy critical positions, munitions, and combat vehicles.

3-49. Combat engineers employed on reserve demolition targets in the defense mainly execute the technical procedures necessary to ensure target destruction. However, the engineer demolition party responds to enemy contact. It assists the demolition guard in securing the target by holding it open or gaining time to ensure that it is destroyed. The engineer force may assist in target defense by installing antitank and self-destructing antipersonnel mines to support the defensive scheme.

3-50. Combat engineers must be prepared to operate or "fight" the networked munitions they emplace in support of defensive and offensive operations. These weapons systems provide rapidly emplaced, highly lethal capabilities to the combined arms team but require trained operators to engage the enemy at the appropriate time and place during the enemy attack. Therefore, when engineers are required to emplace networked munitions and then stay and fight these systems, these engineers must integrate their units into the scheme of maneuver and scheme of fires and fight as part of the combined arms team. They should also participate fully in the combined arms rehearsals to achieve the maximum effectiveness from these weapons systems.

3-51. Combat engineer units engaged in emplacing obstacle systems provide their own local security. Within their capability, they will employ close-combat techniques against attackers to ensure that the obstacle system is completed. General and geospatial engineer organizations also provide their own local security but may require support from combat units depending on where they are employed in the AO. They participate in base cluster defense as required. They install local protective obstacles and fight from perimeter defensive positions. They also form reaction forces that can repel or destroy the enemy forces that penetrate a base cluster.

Fighting as Infantry

3-52. Engineer organizations may be required to fight as infantry as a secondary mission. The combat engineer organization is capable of executing infantry tasks in conjunction with other combat units. Organizational deficiencies include the lack of organic fire support, communications equipment, and medical personnel. If an engineer battalion has been designated to fight as infantry (a maneuver unit), then it requires the same support and potentially the integration of other maneuver elements (such as armor and fire support) into its task organization to accomplish its mission. Once a decision is made to convert engineers to infantry, the unit no longer performs as an engineer unit. Any commander who commands combat engineers has the authority to employ them as infantry, unless otherwise reserved. However, a commander must carefully weigh the gain in infantry strength against the loss of engineer support. Engineers provide far more combat power in their primary mission than when configured as infantry. Stopping the engineer work may reduce the combat power of a commander's entire force.

3-53. Reorganizing engineer units as infantry requires careful consideration and is typically reserved to the operational-level command. Reorganizing involves extensive equipment and training specific to the reorganization and must be coordinated with the headquarters with ADCON responsibilities. Employing engineers merely implies the gaining commander is using the engineers for a short period of time. On the other hand, reorganization requires resources, time, and training.

COMMAND AND CONTROL

3-54. Command and control are interrelated. Command resides with commanders. It consists of authority, decisionmaking, and leadership. Control is how commanders execute command. It resides with both commanders and staffs. Commanders cannot exercise command effectively without control. Conversely, control has no purpose without command to focus it. C2 of engineer operations consists of two distinct but interrelated functions: C2 of engineer forces conducting operations and engineer staff participation in a supported commander's C2. All engineer units must execute C2 and the operations process activities required to conduct unit operations, and many engineer units will also interact with the C2 activities and conduct of supported unit operations. The interaction may be primarily through an engineer staff assigned to the supported unit or through staff counterparts. In some cases, a supported unit may not have assigned engineer staff and the supporting unit will provide this support as well. Cases in which the supported unit does have an assigned engineer staff at EAB include the division, corps, and theater army headquarters. The engineer staff at these headquarters aid their commanders with the control of engineer forces by establishing control mechanisms and shaping the command and support relationships of the tailored force.

Control Mechanisms

3-55. Aided by staffs, commanders exercise control over all forces in their AO, including the airspace over it. Staffs contribute their greatest support in providing control and keeping commanders informed. Just as the operator establishes maneuver graphics, boundaries, axes of advance, and fire-support coordination lines to control fires and maneuver, the engineer employs standards, priorities, engineer work lines, and obstacle-free zones. Some of these control measures are put forth by the GCC and the JFC; others are established by the ASCC and the JFLCC.

3-56. The ENCOORD is responsible for coordinating the functional control (through the commander) of all engineer forces in support of the unit. The ENCOORD coordinates functional control by—

- Using the staff engineer cells and supporting engineer headquarters organizations to gather and refine RI impacting all engineer functions within the AO.
- Establishing and maintaining effective communication with supporting engineer staff cells, engineer units, and multifunctional CPs.
- Using the running estimate and the continuous link with supporting elements to compute resource and force requirements and recommend priorities and task organization.
- Developing specific missions and conveying them to subordinates through the orders and annexes.
- Using supporting unit CPs to assess and report to anticipate change and unforeseen requirements.

Plans and Orders

3-57. The staff prepares the plan or order by turning the selected COA into a clear, concise concept of operations and required supporting information. Plans and orders provide information subordinates need for execution. Mission orders avoid unnecessary constraints that inhibit subordinate initiative. The staff assists subordinate unit staffs with their planning and coordination. See appendix C for additional discussion of plans and orders.

3-58. The engineer staff planner provides input for the appropriate paragraphs in the base plan, annexes, and appendixes of the plan as found in FM 5-0 (CJCSM 3122.03C is used for joint planning). Engineer staff planners prepare an engineer annex and its associated appendixes and provide other input, depending on the mission and commander's intent.

Note. In CJCSM 3122.03C, the engineer annex is appendix 6 to annex D, Logistics.

3-59. Engineers review the force allocation to ensure sufficient capability to meet identified requirements. The engineer staff officer recommends task organization for engineer units considering C2 headquarters and command or support relationships. Additionally, planners provide input to the flow of the engineer forces as detailed on the time-phased force and deployment data (TPFDD).

3-60. Engineers review operations annexes and overlays and ensure the inclusion of obstacle effects or other graphics to assist in conveying the commander's intent for engineer operations on the overlay.

3-61. In the fire support annex, engineers work with the fire support coordinator and other members of the staff to integrate obstacles with fire. Of particular interest at EAB are SCATMINEs and related release authorities.

3-62. The engineer annex is the principal means through which the engineer defines engineer support to the maneuver commander's intent and coordinating instructions to subordinate commanders. It is not intended to function as the internal order for an engineer organization in which the engineer commander will articulate intent; concept of operations; and coordinating instructions to subordinate, supporting, and supported commanders. The preparation of an engineer annex seeks to clarify engineer support to the OPLAN or OPORD and includes the—

- ENCOORD's overall description of the concept for engineer operations.
- Priorities of work to shape the theater or AO (not in a tactical-level engineer annex).
- Operational project planning, preparation, and execution responsibilities (not in a tactical-level engineer annex).
- Engineer organization for combat.
- Essential mobility, countermobility, and survivability (M/CM/S) and other engineering tasks for subordinate units.

Note. Guidance to maneuver units on obstacle responsibilities should be listed in the body of the basic order under the *Tasks to Maneuver Units*, rather than in the engineer annex.

- Allocations of Class IV supplies and Class V supplies (munitions and demolition).

3-63. The ENCOORD may produce an overlay as an appendix to the engineer annex to highlight obstacle information, clearing operations, or breaching operations. A gap-crossing operation may require a separate annex as part of an order.

3-64. The ENCOORD performs as the staff integrator and advisor to the commander for environmental considerations. An environmental appendix to the engineer annex is a parallel document to Annex L in a joint OPLAN, OPORD, or concept plan (CONPLAN). See FM 3-34.5 for an example of this appendix. When specific command procedures dictate, other staff officers include some environmental considerations in logistics and medical annexes. Unit planning at the regimental or brigade level and below will normally include only those elements required by the higher headquarters orders or plans that are not already included in a unit standing operating procedure (SOP). If this appendix is not written, appropriate material may be placed in the coordinating instructions of the base order.

3-65. The ENCOORD performs as the staff integrator and advisor to the commander for GI&S. A GI&S appendix is a parallel document to annex M in a joint OPLAN, OPORD, or CONPLAN. See FM 3-34.230 for an example of this appendix.

Command and Support Relationships Common at All Echelons

3-66. Each of the three types of BCTs and the ACR are organized with organic engineer company-level units. The functional and multifunctional support brigades, including the engineer brigade and the MEB, do not have organic engineer units assigned but must be task-organized with these forces. The BCT engineer company has very limited capability to integrate augmenting engineer elements. In many situations the augmentation of a BCT by a task-organized engineer battalion task force is needed to provide the necessary additional C2 to orchestrate engineer operations and support. Similarly, a task-organized engineer battalion may be required in situations requiring engineer operations supporting one of the various support-type brigades. Additional engineer units augmenting the BCT or a support brigade are task-organized to the supported unit in either a command or support relationship.

3-67. Planners at all echelons must carefully consider the appropriate relationship needed for each situation to balance responsive support to the augmented unit (BCT or other brigade) with flexibility to distribute the low-density and high-demand engineer forces as necessary across the AO. Command relationships are used when the most responsive employment of the augmenting engineer units is required. Attached engineer units are temporarily associated with the gaining unit. They return to their parent unit when the reason for the attachment ends. OPCON relationships are temporary as well and may be only for a given mission. In both attached and OPCON relationships, the augmenting engineer unit is tasked and provided priorities by the gaining unit. A significant consideration in the OPCON relationship is that sustainment support and other ADCON responsibilities remain with the parent engineer unit unless coordinated with the gaining unit for certain classes of supply. In both cases, the gaining unit retains responsibility to furnish construction and barrier materials required to support their missions.

3-68. Commanders establish support relationships when subordination of one unit to another is inappropriate, such as when there are limited engineer capabilities that must support multiple BCTs. Support relationships are used when the greatest flexibility to distribute engineer forces across an AO is required. Support relationships are graduated from an exclusive supported and supporting relationship between two units—as in direct support (DS)—to a broad level of support extended to all units under the control of the higher headquarters—as in general support (GS). Support relationships do not normally alter ADCON. In a DS relationship, an engineer unit receives missions from the supported unit. A DS relationship is typically used when it is anticipated that a change to the engineer task-organization may require frequent shifting of an engineer unit to multiple locations. The logistics system can best support this in a DS role where the parent unit remains responsible for logistics and other types of support to the unit. In a GS relationship, an engineer unit receives missions and all support from its parent engineer unit. In a GS relationship, the engineer unit supports the maneuver element as a whole, and is appropriate when central control and flexibility in employing limited engineer forces is required. A GS relationship is typically used when a supported unit's higher headquarters either identifies a mission requirement within the subordinate echelon AO or accepts responsibility for a requirement identified by the subordinate. In either case, the requirement must be coordinated with the impacted unit responsible for the AO and any missions must be executed through close coordination with that unit.

Command and Support Relationships at Echelons Above Brigade

3-69. The ASCC is the primary vehicle for Army support to Army, joint, interagency and multinational forces operating across the CCDR's AOR. When the GCC acts as the JFC during major combat operations, the ASCC may provide the JFLCC and headquarters. In that case, it exercises OPCON over land forces deployed to a JOA. The ASCC headquarters continues to perform AOR-wide ASCC functions to include joint RSOI, joint logistics over the shore, and joint sustainment area coordinator.

3-70. *ADCON* is the direction or exercise of authority over subordinate or other organizations with respect to administration and support, including organization of Service forces, control of resources and equipment, personnel management, unit logistics, individual and unit training, readiness, mobilization, demobilization, discipline, and other matters not included in the operational missions of the subordinate or other organizations (JP 1). ADCON is closely associated with command relationships. However, joint doctrine does not classify it as a command relationship. ADCON of ARFOR is exercised through the chain of command's administrative branch. For units operating at the tactical level (division, brigade, and below), it normally follows the operational chain of command. When ARFOR are attached to a combatant command, the administrative chain of command switches from the parent Army command, ASCC, or direct reporting unit to the receiving headquarters, through the gaining ASCC. The gaining ASCC and parent command specify ADCON responsibilities retained by the parent command. Unless modified by higher headquarters, release from attachment returns ADCON responsibilities to the parent headquarters.

3-71. Army command and support relationships allow for flexibly allocating Army capabilities among various echelons. FM 3-0 lists responsibilities inherent in the Army's command and support relationships. Command and support relationships are the basis for building task organizations. Command relationships define superior and subordinate relationships between unit commanders. Command relationships identify the degree of control of the gaining or supported commander. The type of command relationship often relates to the expected longevity of the relationship between the headquarters involved. Table 3-2 lists the Army's command relationships.

Table 3-2. Army command relationships

If relationship is:	Then inherent responsibilities:							
	Have command relationship with—	May be task-organized by—[1]	Are ADCON by—	Are assigned position or AO by—	Provide liaison to—	Establish and or maintain communications with—	Have priorities established by—	Can impose on gaining unit further command or support relationship by—
Organic	All organic forces organized with the headquarters	Organic headquarters	Army delegated	Organic headquarters	Not applicable	Not applicable	Organic headquarters	Attached; OPCON; TACON; GS; GSR; R; DS
Assigned	Combatant command	Gaining headquarters	Army delegated	OPCON chain of command	As required by OPCON	As required by OPCON	ASCC or Service-assigned headquarters	As required by OPCON headquarters
Attached	Gaining unit	Gaining unit	Army delegated	Gaining unit	As required by gaining unit	Unit to which attached	Gaining unit	Attached; OPCON; TACON; GS; GSR; R; DS
OPCON	Gaining unit	Parent unit and gaining unit; gaining unit may pass OPCON to lower headquarters[1]	Parent unit	Gaining unit	As required by gaining unit	As required by gaining unit and parent unit	Gaining unit	OPCON; TACON; GS; GSR; R; DS
TACON	Gaining unit	Parent unit	Parent unit	Gaining unit	As required by gaining unit	As required by gaining unit and parent unit	Gaining unit	GS; GSR; R; DS

[1] In NATO, the gaining unit may not task-organize a multinational force. (See TACON.)

Legend:
ADCON administrative control
AO area of operations
ASCC Army Service component command
DS direct support
GS general support
GSR general support reinforcing

NATO North Atlantic Treaty Organization
OPCON operational control
R reinforcing
TACON tactical control

3-72. Table 3-3 lists support relationships. Commanders establish support relationships when subordination of one unit to another is inappropriate. They assign a support relationship when—

- The support is more effective when the supporting unit is controlled by a commander with the requisite technical and tactical expertise.
- The echelon of the supporting unit is the same as or higher than that of the supported unit. For example, the supporting unit may be a brigade, and the supported unit may be a battalion. It would be inappropriate for the brigade to be subordinated to the battalion, hence the use of an Army support relationship.
- The supporting unit supports several units simultaneously. The requirement to set support priorities to allocate resources to supported units exists. Assigning support relationships is one aspect of mission command.

Table 3-3. Army support relationships

If relation-ship is:	**Then inherent responsibilities:**							
	Have command relation-ship with—:	May be task-organized by—	Receive sustain-ment from—	Are assigned position or area of operations by—	Provide liaison to—	Establish and or maintain communi-cations with—	Have priorities established by—	Can impose on gaining unit further command or support relation-ship by—
Direct support[1]	Parent unit	Parent unit	Parent unit	Supported unit	Supported unit	Parent unit; supported unit	Supported unit	See note[1]
Reinforc-ing	Parent unit	Parent unit	Parent unit	Reinforced unit	Reinforced unit	Parent unit; reinforced unit	Reinforced unit; then parent unit	Not applicable
General support–reinforc-ing	Parent unit	Parent unit	Parent unit	Parent unit	Reinforced unit and as required by parent unit	Reinforced unit and as required by parent unit	Parent unit; then reinforced unit	Not applicable
General support	Parent unit	Parent unit	Parent unit	Parent unit	As required by parent unit	As required by parent unit	Parent unit	Not applicable

[1] Commanders of units in direct support may further assign support relationships between their subordinate units and elements of the supported unit after coordination with the supported commander.

3-73. Experience has generally shown that command relationships work well in offensive operations, but that support relationships allow for more efficient use of high-demand, low-density engineer capabilities during defensive and stability operations. However, each situation is unique and requires careful analysis in determining the appropriate relationship of engineers to the supported force. See below for more information about command and support relationships.

Balancing Responsiveness with Flexibility by Adjusting the Task Organization

During the offensive phase of OIF I, the command relationships of OPCON or attached were effective due to the fast pace of the operation and the responsiveness needed by BCT commanders. During the stability phase of OIF, these command relationships were gradually replaced by support relationships as the demand for critical low-density engineers increased and the corps needed the flexibility to quickly shift assets to where they were needed. This transition was difficult since BCT commanders were reluctant to give up the command relationship with these assets.

GS and GS-reinforcing relationships provided the engineer headquarters operating at corps and division echelons with flexibility to retask limited engineer assets as conditions changed in the AO. Some observed examples of support relationships:

- The corps engineer brigade task-organized an engineer battalion in a GS relationship to a division for a planned operation that included moving a BCT into an area that had not been occupied by coalition forces for some time.
- An engineer brigade attached to a division task-organized an engineer battalion in a GS relationship to a BCT to support both combat and general engineering requirements throughout the BCT AO.
- The corps engineer brigade task-organized facilities detachments and utilities detachments in GS relationships to divisions to support base camp requirements.
- The corps engineer brigade task-organized a platoon from a multirole bridge company in a GS–R relationship to an engineer battalion providing construction support to a division.

Adjusting the task organization or moving engineer assets between divisions remained difficult, regardless of the command or support relationship. Even with the GS relationship, a typical action by the corps engineer brigade to move an engineer battalion or company between divisions could take as long as two months to effect from concept to execution. However, the task organization using support relationships made these actions more efficient than the command relationships used in earlier rotations.

3-74. Several other relationships established by higher headquarters exist with units that are not in command or support relationships (see FM 3-0). These relationships are limited or specialized to a greater degree than the command and support relationships. These limited relationships are not used when tailoring or task-organizing ARFOR. Use of these specialized relationships helps clarify certain aspects of OPCON or ADCON.

Joint Considerations and Relationships

3-75. Army command relationships are similar but not identical to joint command authorities and relationships. Differences stem from the way ARFOR task-organize and the need for a system of support relationships. GCCs have broad authority and control over subordinate commands and forces. Particularly pertinent to engineer operations are—

- The directive authority for logistics that GCCs have and their authority to delegate directive authority for common support capabilities, which includes engineering support.
- The authority to employ mines, which originates with the President. See JP 3-15 for more information.

3-76. A subordinate JFC normally exercises OPCON over assigned or attached forces and is responsible for the employment of their capabilities to accomplish the assigned mission or objective. Additionally, the JFC ensures that cross-Service support is provided and that all engineering forces operate as an effective, mutually supporting team. The JFC assigns engineering tasks to subordinate commanders. Most often, joint forces are organized with a combination of Service and functional component commands (see FM 3-34 and JP 3-34).

3-77. Some operations, such as disaster relief or foreign humanitarian assistance (FHA), are engineer intensive. In such cases, the JFC may opt to establish a subordinate JTF to control extensive engineer operations and missions. Such a JTF may be formed around an existing TEC, engineer brigade, MEB, or naval construction regiment. The JFC designates the military engineer capabilities that will be made available for tasking and the appropriate command relationships. Engineer forces could be placed under OPCON, tactical control, or in a supporting role, depending on the degree of control that the JFC desires to delegate of the subordinate JTF. The engineer assets attached to the subordinate JTF will normally be made up of a mix of engineer assets drawn from the entire force's engineer resources. If the subordinate JTF is to provide a common support capability, it will require a specific delegation of directive authority from the GCC for the common support capability that is to be provided.

Chapter 4

Theater Army Echelon Engineer Operations

Initially, the Central Command (CENTCOM) Commander in Chief and staff determined that Operation Desert Shield was to be sustained in-theater by the premise of "minimum essential" support from troop units and maximum support from HN and contracting sources. The 20th Engineer Brigade's (Corps) (Airborne) commander initially served as the theater engineer, in addition to commanding engineer support to the forward fight. Fortunately, the Iraqi advance halted at the Saudi border, otherwise the XVIII Airborne Corps engineer commander would have been focused on the close fight vice the mission he assumed to provide theater troop beddown and logistic base-construction support.

The commander in chief made decisions not to deploy theater-engineer construction units, initially, because of their large strategic lift requirements and the prevailing attitude within the CENTCOM and Third U.S. Army leadership (who believed that support facilities, and by inference engineers were not critical to Army operations). During the initial stages of Operation Desert Shield, it became quickly apparent that HNS and contracting would not be able to handle the massive amount of construction needed to logistically sustain and move forces in-theater. The 20th Brigade, USACE's Middle East Area Project Office (MEAPO), and the Third U.S. Army's engineer staffs were not adequately staffed to control increasing theater-engineer requirements. The 416th Engineer Command (ENCOM) was mobilized and deployed to serve as the theater engineer.

Lieutenant General (Retired) Robert B. Flowers

Each theater army is designed to exercise C2 over land power in support of a GCC. The theater army headquarters structure is designed to provide its commander with maximum flexibility to meet the requirements to serve as both a Title 10 provider and as an operational commander. Even when configured with OPCON responsibilities, the theater army retains administrative and support functions that it must perform throughout the region. This chapter focuses on engineer operations at the theater army echelon and in support of both requirements. It describes foundational characteristics and considerations for providing engineer capabilities and conducting engineer operations at the theater army echelon. It discusses engineer integration within the operation designed by the theater army headquarters. It examines specific considerations for force tailoring of engineer units and capabilities at the theater army echelon. It examines considerations for each operational theme and discusses the elements of full spectrum operations from the theater army perspective. Finally, the chapter describes specific engineer considerations for the various operational configurations of the theater army headquarters.

INTEGRATION AT THEATER ECHELON

4-1.   The theater army engineer provides a focus on the relationship of the physical environment and infrastructure to the developing operational design. Other RI gained from the engineer analysis of the OE assists the commander in framing (and reframing) the problem, formulating the design, and refining the design. Operational engineer concepts are synchronized with and expressed through the framework of the elements of operational design (see FM 3-0).

THEATER PERSPECTIVE

4-2.   The echelons of command perceive differing requirements and constraints associated with command at each level of war. Between the levels of war, the horizons for planning, preparation, and execution are vastly different. Operational-level commanders typically orchestrate the activities of military and other U.S. government organizations across large areas and multiple operational themes. Operational commanders seek to create the most favorable conditions possible for subordinate commanders by shaping future events. The theater army echelon maintains a broad perspective typically considering simultaneous operational themes across the spectrum of conflict and throughout the theater. As figure 4-1 shows, the theater army echelon engineer views a similarly broad perspective of challenges and opportunities considering operational themes from peacetime military engagement to major combat operations and the various administrative and support functions required throughout the theater.

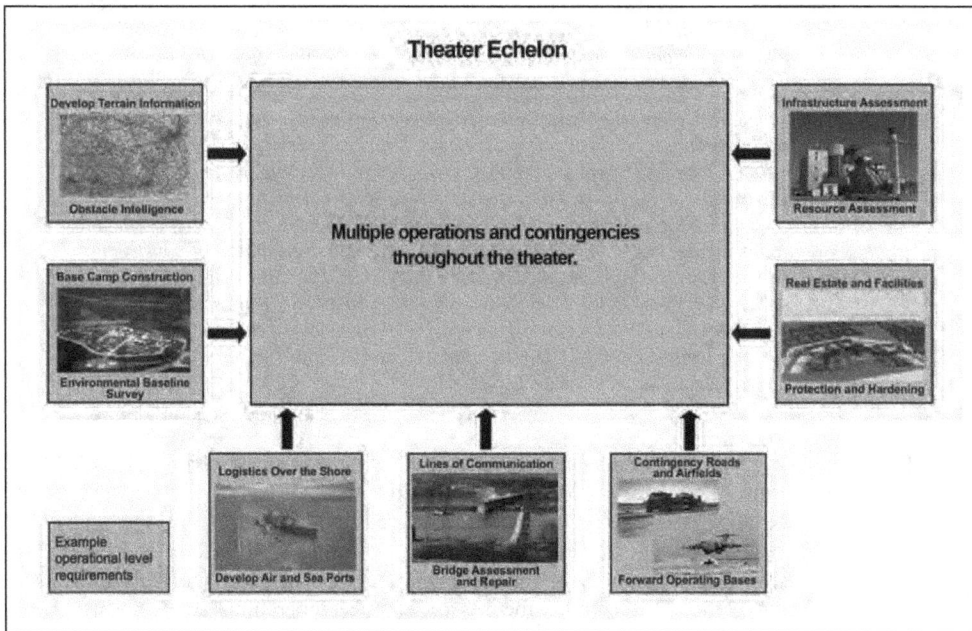

Figure 4-1. Theaterwide perspective of engineer requirements

4-3.   At the theater army echelon, the ENCOORD and other engineer staff assist in translating a broad operational design into a coherent, feasible concept for employing forces. The engineer examines the functional and multifunctional mobilization, deployment, employment, and sustainment requirements of the concept of operations. From the operational perspective, those requirements will typically include construction, real estate, and other general engineering support through both the sustainment and protection warfighting functions. The operational perspective also includes initially shaping the combat and general engineering capabilities most favorable for each subordinate echelon. Geospatial information and terrain analysis provide the foundation on which understanding the physical environment is based. Figure 4-2 shows how the warfighting functions and engineer functions are used to organize and integrate theater echelon engineer requirements.

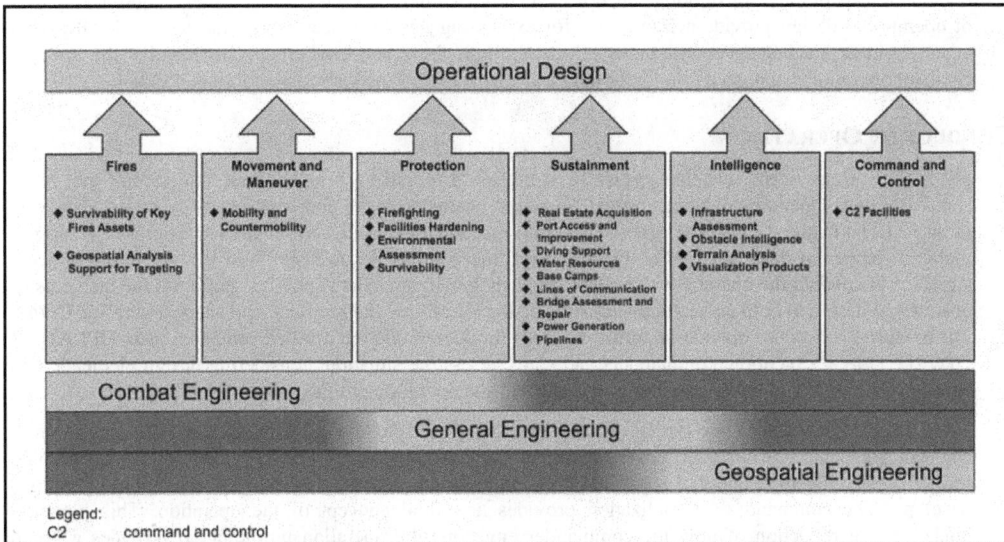

Figure 4-2. Theater echelon engineer requirements by function

4-4. As the operational design develops, the theater engineer collaborates with subordinate echelon engineers to identify and refine requirements for general and combat engineer support linked to both the movement and maneuver and protection warfighting functions. The theater must also ensure that adequate geospatial engineering support is provided for intelligence and C2 at each echelon. Communication enables collaboration, which continues throughout the operations process. To facilitate collaboration with engineer unit commanders and other unit engineer staff, each seeks to—

● Understand the higher commander's intent and planning guidance.

● Analyze the physical environment: have extensive knowledge of the terrain and geospatial products available, obstacle intelligence (OBSTINTEL), and threat capabilities.

● Know their engineer systems and capabilities to accomplish identified tasks and the time required. Identify risks where engineer capabilities are limited, or time is short, and identify methods to mitigate the risks, including leveraging reachback capabilities.

● Consider the depth of the AO and the impact of potentially simultaneous operational elements. Include the integration of environmental considerations.

● Plan for sustainment of engineer operations. Ensure that all logistical requirements, with special emphasis on engineer resources, are analyzed and accounted for to the end state of the operation, and facilitate future operations.

4-5. The theater ENCOORD's running estimate provides a working compilation of RI primarily focused on the physical environment while comprehensively accounting for engineer units, capabilities, and other resources. The running estimate is built from initial assessments framed by the operational variables of PMESII-PT (or mission variables—METT-TC). The operational-level running estimate evolves with the elements of operational design. The RI contained within the theater ENCOORD's running estimate logically connects each identified challenge or opportunity to an operational requirement. The running estimate can be organized by engineer function and warfighting function, as are the requirements shown in figure 4-2. The running estimate is continuously refined and updated as additional assessments are made, guidance and priorities are established, and feedback is gathered. Appendix B provides a tool for use in developing and maintaining the engineer running estimate.

4-6. Engineer operations act as one of many key enablers as the theater army commander drives the operational design to shape the conditions for tasks and objectives to achieve the military end state. To be effective as enablers, engineer staff must be integrated in the effort to assist the commander in framing (and reframing) the problem, formulating the design, and refining the design. Engineer functions assist in organizing capabilities; warfighting functions synchronize engineers with other enablers; and the elements of operational design provide a framework for expressing design concepts. The theater ENCOORD and other engineer staff integrate all these efforts through the operations process to identify the specific engineer operational approach (ways) for the theater or JOA and the refined operational concept.

CONDUCT OF OPERATIONS

4-7. The theater army echelon typically conducts a number of operations throughout the AOR simultaneously. Operational themes provide a way to characterize the dominant major operation underway in an AO. Throughout the AOR, the theater army headquarters could be required to conduct or support multiple themes in designated AOs. In each case, the commander and staff use the operations process activities to conduct the operations. Theater army echelon commanders and their staffs use the elements of operational design to help understand and describe the OE, frame the problem, and shape and refine COAs. The resulting concept of operations forms the basis for developing the detailed campaign plan, OPLAN, or OPORD. During execution, commanders and staffs assess the situation, considering design elements, and adjust both current and future operations and plans as the operation unfolds.

4-8. Engineer operations are typically resource-intensive (including the time factor). The theater army engineer perspective offers an extended planning horizon as an opportunity available at the operational level. To seize the opportunity, some initial decisionmaking is necessary even as the concept of operations develops. The commander's visualization provides an initial concept of the operation. This planning guidance is a reflection of how the commander envisions the operation unfolding. It provides a broad description of when, where, and how the commander intends to employ combat power within the higher commander's intent. Planning guidance also contains priorities for each warfighting function.

4-9. The theater army engineer seeks to exploit an extended operational planning horizon by prioritizing the need for the commander's decisions and shaping selected aspects of the operation as early as possible. For example, the provision of contingency basing and facilities for aviation capabilities can require extensive design and construction resources. Even if abundant design and construction capabilities are available, which would be a rare circumstance, an extensive amount of time may still be required to complete the effort. In this case, the operational engineer seeks to confirm the commander's priority for the project and obtain any necessary decisions on location and design for the project. With these initial decisions, the engineer effort can move to preparation and execution even as operational planning continues.

4-10. For the theater army engineer staff, the cyclic activities of the operations process are continuous and simultaneous (see figure 4-3). These activities will overlap and recur as circumstances demand. Assessment enables planning, which further enables assessment. Engineering preparations must in many cases occur as operational planning is conducted. Execution of selected engineer operations will nearly always precede operational execution, and operational assessments will generate additional engineer requirements. While the engineer staff will be cycling among selected activities demanded by engineer requirements, they must remain synchronized with their staff counterparts in the broader operations process.

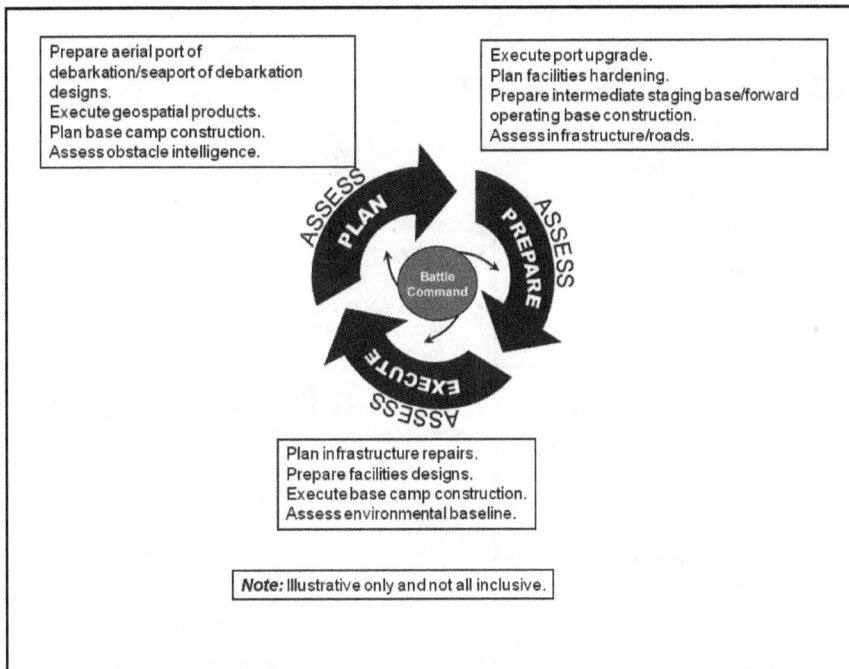

Figure 4-3. Simultaneous, overlapping activities

Planning Considerations

4-11. The CCDR plans joint operations based on analysis of national strategic objectives and development of theater strategic objectives supported by measurable strategic and operational desired effects. At the operational level, a subordinate JFC develops supporting plans, which can include objectives supported by measurable operational-level effects. Joint interdependence requires that the theater army headquarters understand doctrine addressing joint planning techniques (see chapter 3). For the theater echelon engineer, operational planning merges the engineer plan of the joint force, specific engineer missions assigned, and available engineer forces to support the operational design of the theater army commander.

4-12. Informed by their analysis of the OE, operational-level engineer planners assist in defining an AO, estimating forces required, and evaluating requirements for the operation. They use the planning processes—including joint processes—and tools described and referenced in chapter 3. Engineer operations also involve the use of some functionally unique analytic tools to solve construction, design, facilities, and other engineer-specific problems also discussed in chapter 3. They use the commander's intent to develop and refine COAs that contribute to setting the conditions in the AO that support the end state. They maintain a broad focus and seek to exploit the extended planning horizon. As units are identified to participate in the operation, they collaborate as fully as possible to gain depth for their view of the OE and to add to their planning and problem-solving capability. This collaboration also extends the subordinate engineer's planning, preparation, and execution horizon.

4-13. MDMP serves as the primary tool for Army operational planning. Operational engineer planners participate along with their staff counterparts in the process to translate the commander's visualization into a specific COA for preparation and execution. The theater army echelon engineers collaborate closely throughout the MDMP with their counterparts in the GCC joint engineer staff to develop a shared understanding of the mission. Table 3-1, page 3-12, provides some of the engineer planning considerations as they pertain to each step of the MDMP. As the plan develops, engineer planners remain synchronized with their theater army staff counterparts through warfighting functions as shown in table 4-1.

Table 4-1. Planning integrated across warfighting functions

Warfighting Function	Engineer Planning
Movement and Maneuver: • Deploy • Move • Maneuver • Conduct direct fires • Occupy an area • Conduct mobility and countermobility operations • Conduct battlefield obscuration	• Analyze infrastructure to support operational deployment and movement • Evaluate mobility and countermobility required to preserve operational freedom of maneuver, including clearance, crossing, and marking considerations • Develop engineer force and capabilities estimates • Consider infrastructure improvements, reconstruction, and other nonlethal applications for stability or civil support operations
Intelligence: • Support to force generation • Support to situational understanding • Conduct intelligence, surveillance, and reconnaissance • Provide intelligence support to targeting and information operations capabilities	• Identify requirements for geospatial information. Coordinate to provide the necessary terrain analysis, products, and other support • Estimate threat engineer capabilities • Gather and coordinate for obstacle intelligence • Disseminate specific explosive hazard, hazardous material, or other recognition and warning information • Coordinate for engineer assessments and surveys for technical information requirements
Fires: • Decide surface targets • Detect and locate surface targets • Provide fire support • Integrate command and control warfare	• Plan for survivability of key fires assets • Participate in the targeting process • Coordinate for command guidance on employment of scatterable mines and other munitions
Sustainment: • Provision of logistics • Provision of personnel services • Provision of health service support internment/resettlement operations	• Develop base development and support estimates • Estimate real estate and other facilities engineering support • Identify lines of communication and other key routes, and determine support requirements for establishing and maintaining distribution system • Estimate area damage control and other construction support • Determine specialized engineer requirements, such as power, water, and firefighting • Prepare construction and barrier material estimates • Prepare munitions estimates • Determine authorities, funding types, and levels of support

Table 4-1. Planning integrated across warfighting functions (continued)

Warfighting Function	Engineer Planning
Command and Control: • Execute the operations process • Conduct command post operations • Integrate the information superiority contributors • Conduct information engagement • Conduct civil affairs operations • Integrate airspace command and control • Execute command programs	• Coordinate for geospatial information, products, and analysis to enhance visualization of the OE, achieve situational understanding, and enable decisionmaking • Establish and participate on boards, working groups, and cells • Recommend command and support relationships • Recommend control measures: priorities, standards, and reports • Establish and maintain liaison
Protection: • Execute air and missile defense • Conduct personnel recovery • Conduct information protection • Conduct fratricide avoidance • Conduct operational area security • Conduct antiterrorism operations • Conduct survivability operations • Conduct force health protection • Conduct chemical, biological, radiological, and nuclear operations • Conduct safety operations • Conduct operations security • Execute explosive ordnance disposal operations	• Evaluate base camp and other survivability requirements • Consider facilities hardening • Plan for area damage control • Investigate environmental impacts • Conduct explosive hazard threat assessment and support

4-14. As operational planning proceeds through MDMP, the engineer relies heavily on analytic techniques to guide functional problem solving. These techniques demand technical information that may be available from existing assessments or may require additional assessments or surveys. Support available through reachback or through collaborative planning may be used to focus on technical details.

4-15. Control measures are established under the authority of a commander. However, staff officers and subordinate leaders can also establish them with the commander's authorization. Aided by their engineer staff, theater army commanders exercise control over all engineer forces in their AO. Staffs contribute their greatest support in providing control and keeping the commander informed. The following are some of the measures employed by the theater army echelon engineer staff to provide control and keep the commander informed:

- Construction priorities, directives, and standards.
- Policies and procedures.
- Reporting requirements.

4-16. It is essential to establish priorities to determine the distribution of engineering capabilities and resources and ensure unity of effort toward achieving the theater commander's intent. The theater contingency engineering management organization uses the contingency construction list developed during the planning process as a baseline. Initially, resources may only be assigned to the highest priority tasks that accomplish projects on the list. The theater commander issues directives establishing a broad priority system to serve as a guide for a detailed system using the generally accepted four priority groups—vital, critical, essential, and necessary—assigning specific categories of work to each group. For example, ADC of air base runways and critical communication facilities may be designated as vital; improvement to LOCs may be designated as critical. Subordinate echelon organizations develop an integrated priority list of general engineering work based on the priority groups and the changing tactical situation.

4-17. Theater army echelon engineer staff coordinates with their counterparts at the GCC to address construction standards in the AOR or a designated AO. See FM 3-34.400 for more discussion on construction standards.

4-18. The result of the MDMP is a plan or order which provides subordinates the information they need for execution. Engineer planners provide input to appropriate paragraphs, annexes, and appendixes for either the joint or Army format as described in chapter 3. The operational engineer staff continues to collaborate and assist subordinate unit staffs with their planning and coordination.

Preparation Considerations

4-19. Preparation consists of activities performed by the unit before execution to improve its ability to conduct the operation. Preparation requires staff, unit, and Soldier actions. Mission success depends on preparation as much as planning. A focus of operational engineer preparation activities is support to RSOI and establishment of the sustainment base. Construction activities, real estate management, and facilities engineering are predominant during preparation. Operational engineer forces conduct a variety of construction and other technical preparation activities focused on the specific mission. Construction and technical preparation activities include—

- Completing and reviewing designs. In a design-build process, the design will typically only be completed at a 10- to 30-percent resolution prior to execution.
- Conducting any necessary preconstruction studies or surveys.
- Identifying additional technical support required.
- Completing any detailed planning activities not yet completed from the project management process, such as estimates, bills of materials, and schedules.
- Preparing construction site as required, such as staging equipment, stockpiling materials, and completing temporary construction.

4-20. Operational engineer preparations include addressing requirements for facilities (to include the standards to be applied). The requirements should reflect the general engineering support necessary for the expected duration and intensity of operations, be limited to the forces employed (to include multinational, HN, and contractors), and time-phased. Adequate funding (see appendix D) must be available to undertake early engineer reconnaissance and acquisition of facilities to meet requirements, whether by construction or leasing. Facilities are grouped into six broad categories that emphasize the use of existing assets over new construction. To the maximum extent possible, facilities or real estate requirements should be met from these categories in the following priority order:

- U.S.-owned, -occupied, or -leased facilities (including captured facilities).
- U.S.-owned facility substitutes pre-positioned in-theater.
- HN and multinational support where an agreement exists for the HN or other nations to provide specific types and quantities of facilities at specified times in designated locations.
- Facilities available from commercial sources.
- U.S.-owned facility substitutes stored in the United States.
- Construction of facilities that are considered shortfall after an assessment of the availability of existing assets.

4-21. At the operational level, preparation activities may include the establishment of working groups, cells, or boards as described in chapter 3 to solve problems and coordinate actions. The conduct of theater army echelon construction operations may be managed by a theater contingency engineering management (TCEM) or a regional contingency engineering management (RCEM) cell. The composition and the procedures of the TCEM and the RCEM cells are governed by the respective GCCs. These cells are augmented by the staffs they support. The TCEM and the RCEM cells apply the commander's intent, merge engineer-support requirements, and orchestrate resources by—

- Establishing priorities and policy for theater construction and barrier materials.
- Establishing theater distribution protocols that are consistent with construction priorities.

- Monitoring and recommending the allocation and use of construction assets against priority operational requirements and recommending taskings for engineer assets.
- Developing construction standards and priorities.
- Providing input to the JCMEB.

Execution Considerations

4-22. During execution, commander's visualization helps commanders determine if, when, and what to decide. Commanders and their staffs continuously assess the progress of operations toward the envisioned end state and modify orders as required to accomplish the mission. Execution involves monitoring the situation, assessing the operation, and adjusting the order as needed. Throughout execution, commanders continuously assess the operation's progress based on information from the COP, running estimates, and assessments from subordinate commanders. When the situation varies from the assumptions the order was based on, commanders direct adjustments to exploit opportunities and counters threats. The staff, both the engineer unit commander's staff and the combined arms commander's engineer staff, assists the commander in execution through the integrating processes and continuing activities during execution (see FM 3-0). In addition, commanders, assisted by staff, perform the following activities specific to execution:

- Focus assets on the decisive operation.
- Adjust CCIR based on the situation.
- Adjust control measures.
- Manage movement and positioning of supporting units.
- Adjust unit missions and tasks as necessary.
- Modify the concept of operations as required.
- Position or relocate committed, supporting, and reserve units.

4-23. A focus of operational engineer execution activities is support to sustainment distribution and establishment of ISBs and FOBs. Construction activities, refinement and identification of new requirements, and ADC predominate during execution. As with preparation, engineer forces will conduct additional construction or other technically related activities during execution of the specific mission. Construction and technically related execution activities include—

- Implementation and maintenance of a construction safety program.
- Implementation and enforcement of quality controls.
- Periodic design and construction reviews.
- Preparation of as-built drawings.
- Response to construction contingencies.

4-24. As the theater sustainment base is established, focus shifts to requirements supporting distribution. Theater distribution includes aerial delivery and air drop, supply, maintenance, field services, contracting, contract management, procurement, and transportation. Operational engineer support for the developing distribution functions will include construction, bridging, and facilities engineering.

4-25. Considerations for the establishment of ISBs and FOBs include the size of the force projected to operate from the base camp(s), the duration the base camp will be required, and the level of construction standards to be applied. Other important parameters include geographical location, weather, available construction materials, resources, utilities, political concerns for permanency, localized environmental hazards and health threats, and impact on the local populace. Base development is discussed in detail in appendix E.

4-26. General engineering forces are prepared to conduct and support ADC. ADC comprises measures taken before, during, or after hostile action or natural or man-made disasters to reduce the probability of damage and minimize its effects (see JP 3-10). Commanders conduct ADC when the damage and scope of the attack is limited and they can recover with local assets and resources. Optimally, commanders aim to recover immediately. This recovery involves resuming operations, maintaining or restoring order, evacuating casualties, isolating danger areas, and mitigating personnel and materiel losses. Some attacks may rise to the level of incidents of operational significance and require additional resources for mitigation, recovery, and investigation.

Assessment Considerations

4-27. Assessment precedes and guides every activity in the operations process and concludes each operation or phase of an operation. Staffs analyze the situation in terms of mission variables to understand the mission and prepare their staff running estimates. They continuously assess the effects of new information on the conduct of the operation; they update their staff running estimates and determine if adjustment decisions are required.

4-28. Engineer capabilities may be applied to add technical detail to the commander's assessment. Engineer assessment and survey teams gather technically focused information on the physical environment, infrastructure, or other physical aspects of the AO. RI gathered adds to the depth of the commander's understanding and can provide a technical basis for measures of performance (MOPs) or measures of effectiveness (MOEs).

4-29. A focus of operational engineer assessment activities is monitoring RSOI requirements and the adequacy of the sustainment base. Operational engineer forces also conduct a variety of construction and other technical assessment activities focused on technical aspects of the support provided. Construction activities, real estate management, and facilities engineering are evaluated for adequacy to the requirements and conformance to quality standards. Construction and technical preparation activities include—

- Conducting any necessary postconstruction acceptance inspections.
- Identifying master planning activities not yet completed from the project management process.

FORCE TAILORING

4-30. Operational planning prepares the way for tactical activity on the most favorable terms through, among other considerations, adequate resourcing of units and other capabilities. Commanders are challenged to generate a force that is tailored for current and anticipated missions, flexible to changing circumstances, and fits the constraints of time and lift capabilities. Identified and anticipated requirements coupled with an analysis of the mission variables drive the initial tailoring of the force. The theater army considers an expansive shape for the required force, including a general outline of the tactical-level forces required and contemplation of effective operational configurations. Because the demands of any given operation vary, there is no set engineer force structure. A building-block approach that is based on need is used to tailor the force. Refer to appendix F for examples of tailored theater engineer forces based on various situations.

4-31. The tailored engineer force supporting the theater army echelon will in most cases result from a collaborative effort among the theater army engineer planners, their supported GCC engineer staff, elements at DA and DOD, supporting Army and joint force providers (including United States Army Forces Command [FORSCOM], TEC, and USACE), and the input from identified subordinate echelon units. The challenge is to generate the engineer force tailored to identified and anticipated requirements, lift, and other constraints. In many cases, leveraging reachback and other engineer capabilities mitigates the impact of these constraints (see figure 4-4). USACE and other contract capabilities may not be immediately available in the AO, requiring available military units to focus on the commander's highest priorities.

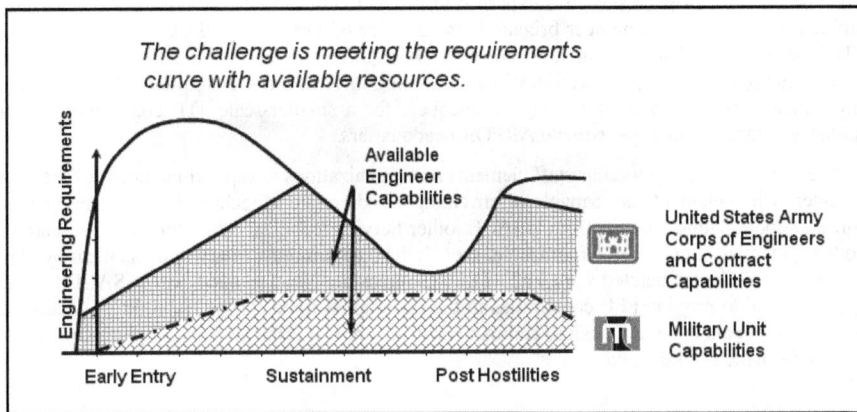

Figure 4-4. Engineer force generation challenge

THEATER ENGINEER COMMAND

4-32. Each TEC is routinely involved in various peacetime military engagement operations with associated theater army headquarters. For other major operations, the theater army ENCOORD collaborates with the TEC commander and staff as the operational design proceeds. A significant determination included in the force generation effort is timing and level for deployment of TEC capabilities. For major combat operations, the theater army echelon will typically require early or phased deployment of the full TEC headquarters. Stability or civil support operations will vary but may require deployment of the supporting TEC or its DCP.

4-33. The TEC is the only organization designed for operational command of engineer capabilities at EAC level and often will provide C2 for the JFC if an operational engineer headquarters is required. The TEC is focused on operational C2 of engineer operations across all three of the engineer functions and typically serves as the senior theater or land component engineer headquarters. When directed, the TEC provides C2 for engineers from other Service, multinational, and contract construction engineers according to joint relationships established by the JFC. The theater army operationally configured as a JFLCC will most certainly benefit from the early or phased deployment of the full TEC headquarters. In a JTF configuration, TEC deployment may still be advantageous, depending on the JTF mission's complexity and span of control. As discussed later in this section and in chapter 5, an engineer brigade may provide adequate engineer OPCON given a narrower span of control.

4-34. The TEC develops plans, procedures, and programs for engineer support for the theater army, including requirements determination, operational mobility and countermobility, general engineering, power generation, ADC, military construction, geospatial engineering, engineering design, construction materiel, and real property maintenance activities. The TEC commander receives policy guidance from the theater army based on the guidance of the GCC's joint force engineer. The TEC headquarters element provides C2 for operational-level engineer operations in the AO and reinforces engineer support to subordinate echelon forces. The TEC may support joint and multinational commands and other elements according to lead Service responsibilities as directed by the supported JFC. This headquarters maintains a collaborative planning relationship with the theater army and joint force staff engineers to help establish engineer policy for the theater. It also maintains coordination links with other Service and multinational command engineering staffs.

4-35. While the TEC is the organization primarily designed to provide an operational engineer headquarters for theater army and GCC echelons, in some cases a tailored engineer brigade may provide theater-level engineer support. The engineer brigade is one of several functional brigades available to support theater-level operations. They may be task-organized under theater-level functional commands, an engineer brigade organized under the C2 of the TEC, or directly subordinate to the theater army. When required, the theater army may also task-organize functional brigades to corps or divisions (see chapters 5 and 6). The engineer brigade provides expertise to the TEC but with a reduced capability. A significant determinant in tailoring the engineer brigade is the anticipated breadth of OPCON and support functions. The TEC is capable of supporting a broad array of requirements as is typical when the theater army functions in an operational configuration while continuing its ASCC responsibilities. The brigade provides a more concentrated capability that may be adequate for a smaller-scale JTF configuration with some functional assistance from a subordinate ARFOR headquarters.

4-36. The TEC can deploy modular staff elements and organizations to support the needs of the operational commander. These elements are capable of providing a wide range of technical engineering expertise and support and coordinating support from USACE, other Service technical laboratories and research centers, and other potential sources of expertise in the civilian community. They are enabled by the global reachback capabilities associated with FFE. TEC resources are synchronized with USACE for peacetime engagements and to provide FFE capabilities to the operational force. These capabilities include technical assistance, project planning and design, contract construction, real estate acquisition, infrastructure support, and support to nation-building capacities.

FIELD FORCE ENGINEERING

4-37. Each theater army headquarters receives support through USACE FFE, to include commercial contract construction acquisition and management, project and program management, real estate and environmental services, technical services, and access to the full suite of USACE (and other agency) capabilities through reachback. The theater army ENCOORD collaborates with an assigned USACE LNO for direct access to USACE resources to support engagement strategies and operations. The supporting USACE LNO will also typically assist the theater army in coordinating with the DOD-designated CCA. The designated CCA may have assets directly integrated into the military C2 structure and linked to a TEC or senior engineer headquarters or already be operating under contract in-theater. For major operations, the theater ENCOORD will typically consider timing and level for deployment of additional FFE capabilities, including appropriately tailored FESTs for support of the theater army and subordinate echelon headquarters.

4-38. Each FEST provides mission-tailored technical and contract engineering support, integrating its organic capabilities with those of other Services and other sources of engineering-related reachback support. Whether providing construction contract and design support in the AO or outside of the contingency area, the FEST can obtain necessary data, research, and specialized expertise not present in-theater through tele-engineering and other reachback capabilities. The two types of FESTs provide support to primarily general engineering efforts through forward-deployed engineer elements that can communicate with TeleEngineering Kits and reachback to technical experts within USACE. EFDs from the TECs provide a wide variety of services to forward-deployed forces in a public works capacity. These efforts can assist in the reception and staging of troops. Infrastructure assessment and base development teams are nondeployable capabilities available through reachback support.

4-39. Tailored FFE capabilities may also be employed to provide USACE expertise in support of operational-level engineer planning. Each FFE element can leverage reachback to technical subject matter experts in districts, divisions, labs and centers of expertise, other Services, and private industry. Teams can rapidly deploy to meet requirements for engineering assessments and analyses to support the conduct of engineer operations.

ENGINEER AND MULTIFUNCTIONAL FORCES

4-40. The units that make up the architecture of the theater army echelon engineer force are diverse with technical skill orientation ranging from highly specialized to multifunctional and sourcing that includes Army, joint, and multinational force providers. Operational engineer planners are challenged to comprehensively identify both current and future requirements across the range of organizational skill sets. Typically, operational-level priorities and substantially defined subordinate requirements are clear and the associated tasks and troop formations evident. For operational-level planners, requirements for supporting the less substantially defined tactical needs of subordinate echelons become increasingly ambiguous. To ensure adequate resourcing of units to meet these needs, planners must consider those troop formations and tasks that are evident but also provide for flexibility to mitigate uncertainty.

4-41. As previously discussed, planners use the engineer functions with their primary relationships to warfighting functions to organize and ensure an integrated view of operational requirements. At the theater army echelon, a significant focus is placed on general engineering capabilities that must be tailored based on operational requirements linked to the movement and maneuver, sustainment, and protection warfighting functions. These include construction requirements and a variety of specialized engineering requirements. Construction requirements will typically exceed Army unit capabilities and must be analyzed considering joint, multinational, contract, and other capabilities. Specialized requirements may require additional or more technical information to effectively associate with tasks and troops. FFE or reachback may be employed to guide the technical assessment needed. Theater army echelon engineer planners may, through their own analysis of the situation, determine the tailored force required by operational-level priorities and substantial subordinate requirements. They will need subordinate echelon input though, to more precisely tailor the force required to meet the tactical-level engineer requirements.

4-42. Theater echelon engineer planners typically develop a broad but less defined understanding of requirements at each lower echelon. Geospatial engineering support, though organic at each echelon down to BCT, may generate requirements for augmentation at either the operational or a selected subordinate echelon. General engineering support requirements linked to the movement and maneuver, sustainment, and protection warfighting functions at each subordinate echelon may be evident and either accepted as an operational force responsibility or considered in tailoring the subordinate echelon. Similarly, general engineering support as augmentation to combat engineering capabilities at lower echelons may be considered but will be less clearly defined. Finally, combat engineering requirements for each BCT and major tactical element is considered. Each BCT will include an organic engineer company but with only minimal M/CM/S support capabilities. Augmentation must typically be provided in the form of additional combat and general engineering capabilities and appropriate engineer and multifunctional headquarters elements. For the operational-level planner, the type and level of augmenting capabilities will likely be ambiguous. To ensure a flexible force adequate for comprehensive operational requirements, planners must employ more than their own broad understanding of those requirements.

4-43. When available for collaborative planning, subordinate echelon headquarters provide invaluable input not only for their assigned mission requirements but also for some operational-level requirements that may have been overlooked by the higher echelon. Subordinate echelon engineer units and the engineer staff supporting corps, division, and other headquarters develop an understanding through a more concentrated analysis of the situation. The resulting view adds depth to the understanding of engineer forces required for their support.

4-44. The tailored engineer force supporting the theater army echelon will typically include joint and multinational engineer formations. Planners mesh Service capabilities with joint and multinational formations, interagency, and NGOs. Operational engineer planners consider the joint engineer force capabilities and collaborate with joint force providers to effectively align joint capabilities with requirements. Consideration will typically include tactical limitations for joint engineer forces. While Navy and Air Force engineer forces include a variety of technical skill sets, they are often limited in ground combat capabilities. For example, certain Air Force engineer units possess highly skilled electrical, plumbing, and other utilities and construction capabilities; however, these units are limited in their capability to move to and secure a worksite. This type of unit would be appropriate as a joint resource for requirements within a base but not for requirements throughout a less secure operational area.

OTHER CAPABILITIES

4-45. With other Service augmentation, the theater army can provide JTF headquarters for contingencies. Other situations may generate requirements for individual augmentation within the theater army or a subordinate echelon headquarters. Similarly, the situation may require tailoring of individual augmentees for a provisional headquarters or for provisional teams (such as PRTs). The GCC supports the theater army with joint individual augmentees as available through its standing joint force headquarters. As requirements exceed the GCC capabilities, they are passed to joint force providers. The Army provides individual augmentees through its worldwide individual augmentee system.

4-46. Commanders may use an operational needs statement to document an urgent need for a material solution to correct a deficiency or to improve a capability that impacts on mission accomplishment. The operational needs statement provides an opportunity for the field commander, outside of the acquisition and combat development and training development communities, to initiate the requirements determination process. Response to the operational needs statement will vary, depending on the criticality of the need for the proposed item. Response can range from a Headquarters DA-directed requirement and fielding of a material system to the forwarding of the action to TRADOC for review and routine action. The theater army engineer staff may become involved in review and processing of engineer-related statements as part of the theater army echelon's ADCON responsibilities. Examples of engineer-related operational needs may include bridging or construction equipment, EH clearance improvements, and other nonstandard capabilities (see AR 71-9 for information on processing operational needs statements).

4-47. It will likely be important for theater army echelon engineers to understand contingency construction authorities and associated funding. These authorities provide the basis for legal spending to meet construction requirements and activities in support of contingency operations. Appendix D provides an introduction to contingency authorities and funding. However, the information in the appendix is subject to change due to changes in legislation, policy, or regulation. The theater army echelon engineer staff should consult with legal and financial management personnel for the latest definitive guidance.

OPERATIONAL THEMES

4-48. The theater army echelon maintains a broad perspective, typically considering simultaneous operational themes across the spectrum of conflict and throughout the theater. An *operational theme* is defined as the character of the dominant major operation being conducted at any time within a land force commander's AO. (FM 3-0) Table 4-2, page 4-15, groups various military operations with common characteristics under operational themes. Different themes usually demand different approaches and force packages, although some activities are common to all. Operational themes should not be confused with tactical tasks or activities. Operational themes are too general to be assigned as missions. Rather, they describe the major operation's general characteristics, not the details of its execution.

Table 4-2. Examples of joint operations conducted within operational themes

Peacetime Military Engagement	Limited Intervention	Peace Operations	Irregular Warfare
• Multinational training events and exercises • Security assistance • Joint combined exchange training • Recovery operations • Arms control • Counterdrug operations	• Noncombatant evacuation operations • Strike • Raid • Show of force • Foreign humanitarian assistance • Consequence management • Sanction enforcement	• Peacekeeping • Peacebuilding • Peacemaking • Peace enforcement • Conflict prevention	• Foreign internal defense • Support to insurgency • Counterinsurgency • Combating terrorism • Unconventional warfare
Note: Major combat operations are both an operational theme and its own descriptor; hence, it is not shown.			

4-49. Theater army echelon engineer operations are conducted considering multiple ongoing operational themes and smaller operations occurring throughout the theater. The theater army engineer staff routinely coordinates construction activities that assist the GCC in shaping the security environment in a particular region while maintaining presence within the AOR. The engineer staff may also participate in the conduct of exercise programs within a particular AOR as a tool to maintain presence and to foster strong military-to-military cooperation. USACE and other intergovernmental agencies are strategically engaged worldwide in activities that promote national-security objectives by improving the HN's infrastructure. Examples are products of the ERC Program, the HCA Program, and the Support-for-Others Program. Each theater army USACE LNO assists in coordinating these activities with the ENCOORD.

4-50. The theater army engineer staff coordinates engineer support required for limited intervention operations. Support may include tailored engineer modular forces and the application of a variety of joint and other engineer capabilities. The theater army USACE LNO may assist in integrating USACE and intergovernmental agency activities that support the operational objectives. Engineer operations are critical enablers in both foreign humanitarian assistance, which is conducted to relieve or reduce the results of natural or man-made disasters or other endemic conditions, such as human pain, disease, hunger, or privation (see JP 3-33), or consequence management actions, which are taken to manage and mitigate problems resulting from disasters and catastrophes, including natural, man-made, or terrorist incidents (see JP 3-28). The engineer response may include—

- Erecting temporary shelters and clinics.
- Removing debris.
- Performing temporary construction to reinforce weakened superstructures.
- Reestablishing transportation right of ways.
- Constructing diversion or protective structures.
- Constructing levees to contain rising floodwaters.
- Creating flood-prediction models for the mapping of disaster effects.
- Fighting fires.

4-51. Peace operations, irregular warfare, and major combat operations will typically involve the introduction of larger military forces into the operational area. These operational themes imply a degree of theater echelon engineer support for access, base development, establishing the sustainment base, and operational movement requirements. While each theater or JOA is unique, from a broad perspective each will follow a pattern from some level of immaturity at the beginning of operations through development to established standards and maintenance of those standards during the conduct of operations and finally the closure or turnover of bases and other facilities as operations conclude. Lesser-developed theaters or operational areas will tend to generate more operational engineer effort earlier in the operations process. A general comparison is provided in table 4-3, page 4-16, of considerations based on the level of development.

Table 4-3. Requirements comparison based on level of development

Lesser Developed Theater	Highly Developed Theater
Greater effort to establish seaports of debarkation and aerial ports of debarkation	Seaports of debarkation and aerial ports of debarkation may be available but require improvement
Geospatial data may require generation	Geospatial data may be available
Real estate acquisition is less likely	Real estate may be more available for acquisition
Environmental conditions may be unknown	Environmental baseline may be established
Austere base camps and forward operating bases may be required	Installations may be available for temporary use
Road network likely limited	Road network available
Natural obstacles predominate	Man-made obstacles predominate
Primitive or basic infrastructure	Complex or extensive infrastructure

4-52. While the operational theme describes the character of the dominant major operation being conducted, Army forces conduct full spectrum operations within this larger framework. All major operations conducted overseas combine offensive, defensive, and stability elements executed simultaneously at multiple echelons. Army forces provide a mix of land combat power that can be tailored for any combination of offensive, defensive, and stability or civil support operations as part of an interdependent joint force. At higher echelons, engineer operations are intrinsically full spectrum. They consist of more technically focused tasks that simultaneously support offensive, defensive, and stability or civil support operations. The technical aspects of engineer tasks at higher echelons become increasingly essential to their effective application. For example, from an operational-level perspective, the application of engineering efforts to repair and upgrade a road and its component bridges tends to retain a consistent set of technical tasks. Operational elements have less distinct impact than the technical aspects of the engineering tasks and, in fact, most operational-level engineering will simultaneously support all the operational elements. The example upgraded road supports the movement of forces into attack positions, the movement of counterattack forces repositioning in a mobile defense, and the movement of forces supporting civil security. Theater army echelon engineer operations apply technical capabilities to create favorable conditions for any combination of operational elements.

4-53. While the influence of distinct operational elements may be lessened for some technically focused engineering tasks, the overall engineer effort must remain integrated within the combined arms framework. The ENCOORD participates in operations process activities to synchronize both the orchestration and sustainment of primarily subordinate echelon engineer actions and the application of more technically focused engineer capabilities. Some generalities can be observed considering the operational elements and higher-echelon engineer operations.

4-54. For major combat operations, a significant portion of the tailored engineer force will tend to have command relationships to maneuver commanders. The tailored engineer force will be pushed, using command relationships in the task organization, to tactical echelons for close support of combat operations. This will be true for some general engineering capabilities and for most combat engineering capabilities. In major combat operations, the operational echelon engineer planners are less likely to accept responsibility, at least initially, for requirements linked to the movement and maneuver, sustainment, and protection warfighting functions at subordinate echelons. These requirements are not well defined at higher echelons and are more dynamic in combat operations. Tailored forces are pushed to subordinate echelons to address these requirements and add flexibility for those maneuver commanders to react to unforeseen challenges and opportunities.

4-55. For defensive operations, operational engineer planners will not typically be able to generate adequate construction capabilities to support all the subordinate requirements for both movement and maneuver (countermobility) and protection (survivability). Operational-level requirements will compete for these same construction capabilities. The operational planner must recommend priorities for these capabilities and then work collaboratively with subordinate elements to assist them in mitigating shortfalls.

4-56. When planning for stability operations, engineers consider the broadest range of potential requirements. The operational engineer planner considers all the theater echelon requirements linked to the movement and maneuver, sustainment, and protection warfighting functions, while also considering nonlethal applications supporting the objective end state. Subordinate echelons also require a broad range of general engineering support or may be conducting combat operations requiring combat engineering with appropriate augmenting general engineering capabilities. The tailored engineer force is distributed among echelons for both operational-level applications and close support of subordinate operations. Stability operations are most likely to occur in close coordination with multinational and interagency elements and among the local population. Construction capabilities will likely also be required to support infrastructure and reconstruction needs. The construction requirements will likely exceed Army unit capabilities. Operational, subordinate echelon, engineer leaders and staff will be required to coordinate efforts from a range of other capabilities to meet the extensive construction requirements.

4-57. Planning for civil support operations is significantly different from offensive, defensive, or stability operations because of the unique nature of the threat, although the basic tasks may be similar to those of stability operations. The threat will likely be a natural or man-made disaster, accident, or incident with unpredictable consequences. Additionally, planners must be aware of the number of statutes and regulations that restrict the Army's interaction with other governmental agencies and civilians during civil support operations. The local and state response normally leads the effort with a federal response providing support as required. Interagency response during civil support operations is governed by the NRF, which delegates responsibility to various federal agencies for emergency support functions. Each lead agency is responsible for planning within its assigned emergency support functions.

4-58. Army commanders will assume a support role to one or more designated agencies. Engineers can expect to be involved in planning for support of relief operations with geospatial products and analysis of potential areas to establish life-support areas. Engineers may be called on to provide manpower support or general engineering support from units with unique capabilities, such as water purification, temporary shelter, power generation, and firefighting. Engineer commanders and staff will work with the proponent planners to identify requirements and plan engineer applications. USACE and other engineering capabilities of the generating force will have a prominent role in civil support operations.

OPERATIONAL CONFIGURATIONS

4-59. Each theater army is organized, equipped, and trained to command and control land power in support of a GCC. By design, each GCC—USEUCOM, United States Pacific Command (USPACOM), USCENTCOM, United States Southern Command (USSOUTHCOM), United States Northern Command (USNORTHCOM), and United States Africa Command (USAFRICOM)—has an assigned theater army headquarters. The Secretary of Defense previously directed the Army to generate an additional theater army—Eighth United States Army for a subunified commander—United States Forces Korea. The normal command relationship between the GCC and the theater army is combatant command. Functional CCDRs—Strategic Command, Special Operations Command, Transportation Command, and Joint Forces Command—have their own unique ASCCs. These ASCCs are not theater armies.

4-60. A theater army performs two complementary functions for the GCC. First, it is the ASCC and ARFOR headquarters for all Army forces within the theater. In this capacity, the theater army commander—as the ASCC commander—is responsible for ADCON of all Army forces within the supported GCC's AOR. Second, the theater army is also organized and equipped to exercise OPCON of joint and multinational forces within a joint campaign while continuing to perform its theater responsibilities, with joint and multinational staff augmentation, as appropriate. This chapter has primarily focused on engineer support of the theater army's operational role. A significant theater echelon engineer effort is also required in support of the first role, that of support provider and ASCC. The theater army headquarters continues to perform AOR-wide functions in addition to its operational responsibilities. These functions include RSOI, logistics over-the-shore operations, and security coordination. The theater ENCOORD integrates and coordinates the theater echelon engineer staff and tailored engineer forces to best support the theater army in both of its roles and all of its operational configurations.

SUPPORT TO DEPLOYED ARMY, JOINT, AND MULTINATIONAL FORCES

4-61. The theater army headquarters is the primary vehicle for Army support to Army, joint, interagency, and multinational forces operating across the CCDR AOR. Joint forces rely on Army forces for support and services as designated in—

- Title 10, U.S. Code.
- Other applicable U.S. laws.
- DOD implementation directives and instructions.
- Inter-Service agreements.
- Multinational agreements.
- Other applicable authorities and federal regulations.

4-62. Support provided to joint forces and other support directed by CCDRs are broadly defined as Army support to other Services (ASOS). Similar directives govern the provision by the theater army to deployed joint, interagency, and multinational forces for common-user logistics (CUL). ASOS, CUL, and the support provided to deployed Army forces are continuous tasks performed by the theater army regardless of whether it is also controlling land forces in a major operation. The theater army—

- Tailors assigned land forces for joint operations.
- Supports theater security cooperation plans with Army forces and appropriate C2.
- Provides theater-level augmentation to Army forces in JOAs, including Army forces capabilities, liaison teams, and public affairs teams.
- Develops the mission-essential task list for conventional Army forces either assigned to the AOR or programmed to deploy to the AOR as part of an approved OPLAN.
- Provides training support, materials, and regional expertise to aligned Army forces.
- Provides Army support to the joint force as a whole, other Services, other U.S. government agencies, and multinational forces as directed.

- Establishes and secures theater bases and conducts RSOI through the TSC and gaining maneuver units.
- Orchestrates the deployment sequence and introduction of Army forces into the theater.

4-63. The theater army commander uses the main CP to control the support required, as directed by the GCC. The theater army provides its support responsibilities primarily through its supporting commands and brigades and by tailoring C2 capabilities organic and attached to it. For engineering support, the theater army ENCOORD coordinates activities of the assigned engineer staff and may use assistance from the TEC or its tailored C2 elements when available. The ENCOORD employs an assigned or supporting USACE FFE element to access additional capabilities through reachback. In-theater the supporting FFE element can assist in coordinating support from the CCA regardless of whether that agent is represented by USACE or NAVFAC.

4-64. Theater army echelon engineers will coordinate with the TSC to provide general engineering support to operational sustainment throughout the theater, including requirements for support to the joint force as a whole, the other Services, other U.S. government agencies, and multinational forces as directed. The TSC is the senior Army sustainment headquarters in an AOR. (While its focus is on sustainment, it does not normally provide the HSS component of sustainment, which is done by the MEDCOM.) The TSC provides the modular Army with a single operational echelon responsible for C2 of sustainment operations in support of Army, joint, interagency, and multinational forces. The TSC is capable of planning and executing all sustainment operations for the theater army or JFC. It provides C2 in support of operations during simultaneous deployment, employment, sustainment, redeployment, and reconstitution. The TSC also coordinates through the ENCOORD for geospatial engineering support. The ENCOORD may rely on the TEC to provide appropriate liaison elements to the TSC while the theater engineer staff coordinates with their sustainment counterparts on the staff.

4-65. Similarly, the theater army ENCOORD may rely on the TEC to provide liaison and coordination capabilities with other theater echelon supporting commands and brigades. An example is the theater-focused CA command (CACOM) aligned with theater army. The CACOM develops the CA-related portion of plans, policies, and programs for both the GCC and the theater army commander. The CACOM may deploy a theater-level civil-military operations center (CMOC) to coordinate, analyze, and enable policies, programs, and stability operations capabilities in support of the theater army. The ENCOORD will typically rely on the TEC for direct coordination and liaison with the CACOM and theater level CMOC.

ARMY SERVICE COMPONENT COMMAND

4-66. The theater army as ASCC exercises ADCON over Army forces in the AOR. ADCON is the direction or exercise of authority over subordinate or other organizations in respect to administration and support, including organization of Service forces, control of resources and equipment, personnel management, unit logistics, individual and unit training, readiness, mobilization, demobilization, discipline, and other matters not included in the operational missions of the subordinate or other organizations. The main CP is the organization primarily responsible for Army activities throughout the supported GCC's AOR. It focuses on—

- Developing and issuing Army AOR-wide policies and providing policy guidance.
- Reviewing and evaluating the performance of Army programs across the AOR.
- Allocating and distributing Army resources throughout the AOR.
- Conducting AOR-wide mid- and long-range planning, programming, and budgeting.

4-67. The ASCC ENCOORD identifies and addresses theaterwide requirements for construction and engineering support. The ENCOORD typically employs the various working groups and boards that are established and LNOs assigned from USACE and other elements. As requirements are identified, priorities are recommended, funding identified, and directives or contracts issued.

4-68. The ASCC ENCOORD will also provide a critical linkage for the provision of Title 10 support and requirements to deployed engineer forces. The ENCOORD provides information and coordinates activities impacting the training, equipping, supplying, and maintaining the AOR-specific engineer force.

JOINT FORCE LAND COMPONENT COMMAND

4-69. When the GCC acts as the JFC during major combat operations, the theater army headquarters may provide the JFLCC headquarters. In that case, it exercises OPCON over land forces deployed to a JOA. This may include controlling multiple divisions, corps-sized formations, and forces from other Services. Normally, during major combat operations the theater army's OCP provides a base for the JFLCC headquarters and responds directly to the GCC. The theater army headquarters continues to perform AOR-wide ASCC functions to include joint RSOI, joint logistics over the shore, and joint sustainment area coordinator.

4-70. The JFLCC ENCOORD typically relies on the TEC or its tailored C2 elements for the operational C2 of JFLCC engineer support. The JFLCC ENCOORD will also employ an assigned or supporting USACE FFE element to access additional technical and contract construction capabilities.

JOINT TASK FORCE

4-71. Although not organized primarily to act as a JTF headquarters, the theater army headquarters can use its OCP as a base from which to form a JTF headquarters for crisis response or limited contingency operations, with augmentation of the standing joint force headquarters (SJFHQ) and other joint Service manning. Within each GCC, these capabilities are emphasized or deemphasized through strategic tailoring of the Army forces assigned to that particular theater army headquarters.

4-72. Forming a JTF headquarters from the theater army's OCP has the advantage of using a regionally focused headquarters with a senior rank structure. It has disadvantages in that it curtails the capability of the theater army to perform as a JFLCC for another operation. The theater army is not designed to simultaneously serve as a JTF, a JFLCC, and the ASCC. When deployed as a JTF headquarters, the theater army headquarters retains its ADCON responsibilities; therefore, the theater army commander uses the OCP to provide the JTF headquarters, while the main CP continues to perform its theaterwide functions.

4-73. Because the theater army headquarters continues to perform AOR-wide functions in addition to its operational responsibilities, the theater army formed JTF may require a separate ENCOORD. The theater army ENCOORD may transition to become the JTF ENCOORD with a designated ASCC engineer staff officer assuming responsibilities as the new split ENCOORD. Similarly, the theater army formed JTF may identify requirements for separate engineer headquarters units supporting the JTF and the ASCC functions. The JTF ENCOORD may rely on a TEC element or an engineer brigade for the operational C2 of JTF engineer support while the ASCC may require an engineer battalion or brigade to provide C2 for engineer operations supporting the ASCC functions. The JTF ENCOORD will also employ an assigned or supporting USACE FFE element to access additional technical and contract construction capabilities.

4-74. The role of the JTF engineer is mission and situation dependent and will vary in response to the JTF commanders' intent. This critical decision is made early in the planning process by the JTF commander and dictates the location of the JTF engineer within the JTF staff. Mission analysis will determine whether engineer tasks will largely support operational movement, maneuver, and fires, or will predominantly support force sustainment (logistics). If mission analysis indicates that support to maneuver and fires comprises the principal engineer activities, then the JTF engineer will normally be an element directly under the J-3 and the joint operations center. If logistics support will be the majority of engineer missions, the J-4 will have staff responsibility for engineering. If engineering is essential to the success of the JTF mission, as frequently occurs in FHA and civil support operations, or if the JTF commander wants direct visibility of engineering issues, the JTF engineer may become a separate, primary staff function and report directly to the commander. This role sets the direction and composition of engineering planning teams. It is vital for naval civil engineering forces who are assigned to a JTF to seek out and contact the JTF engineer and ensure that they coordinate their planning effort with the JTF engineer's planning and guidance.

This page intentionally left blank.

Chapter 5

Corps Echelon Engineer Operations

In the early morning hours of 24 August 1992, Hurricane Andrew slammed into the southern tip of Florida. The eye of the hurricane passed directly over Homestead Air Force Base and the surrounding communities of Homestead and Florida City with an estimated wind speed of over 160 mph....

Late on 27 August 1992, the XVIII Airborne Corps was alerted and directed to send a logistical task force to aid in the relief operations. The 20th Engineer Brigade was directed to begin deployment of forces and to have an airborne engineer battalion on the ground within 24 hours....

During the time frame to deploy all military engineers, those units on the ground were busy with a varied amount of work. After the area's main roads were opened, debris operations became a lower priority mission. The clearing of areas for the establishment of disaster assistance centers (DACs), life-support centers (LSCs), mobile kitchen trailer (MKT) feeding sites, and the removal of associated trash and refuse from those areas, became priority tasks. Furthermore, the clearing of debris from schools grew in importance when local authorities decided to reopen them on 14 September 1992....

From "Hurricane Andrew: The 20th Engineer Brigade Perspective" by Major Robert M. Ralston and Lieutenant Colonel Douglas L. Horn, 20th Engineer Brigade, 1 October 1992.

The corps provides a headquarters that specializes in operations as a land component command headquarters, JTF for contingencies, or as an intermediate tactical headquarters within very large groupings of land forces. This chapter focuses on engineer operations at the corps echelon. It describes foundational characteristics and considerations for engineer operations supporting the corps. It discusses refinement of the operational design and integration within the operations process conducted by the corps headquarters. It examines specific considerations for force tailoring of engineer units and capabilities for the corps. It also examines implications of the assigned major operation and considerations for the operational elements from the corps perspective. Finally, the chapter describes specific engineer considerations for each operational configuration of the corps headquarters.

INTEGRATION AT CORPS ECHELON

5-1.   The corps echelon acts at both the tactical and operational levels of war. Typically employed for a specific major operation or contingency, the corps links the operational design from theater to its conduct at tactical echelons. It plans and conducts the major operations and battles. It creates and maintains the conditions for the success of current battles and sets up the conditions for the success of future battles. Corps operational planning concentrates on building on and filling in the design of campaigns and major operations. Corps tactical operations are generated from the implications within the operational design and made substantial by the corps commander's intent and conduct of the corps operations process. In conducting operations, the corps will synchronize and integrate warfighting functions from both the operational- and tactical-level perspective.

CORPS PERSPECTIVE

5-2. With minimum joint augmentation, the corps can initiate operations as a JTF or JFLCC for small-scale contingencies. The corps can also serve as a deployable base for a multinational headquarters directing protracted operations. The corps's flexibility allows the Army to meet the needs of JFCs for an intermediate land command while maintaining a set of headquarters for contingencies. It provides a capability that views challenges and opportunities associated with the operational approach and concentrates on the substance and shape of required tactical actions. The corps perspective is shaped by a specified contingency but retains flexibility to span operational approach (ways) as described by theater to tactical actions (means) inferred and defined by the corps and subordinate echelons. As figure 5-1 shows, the corps echelon engineer perspective similarly builds on a foundation of operational requirements while detailing tactical-level requirements for the selected contingency.

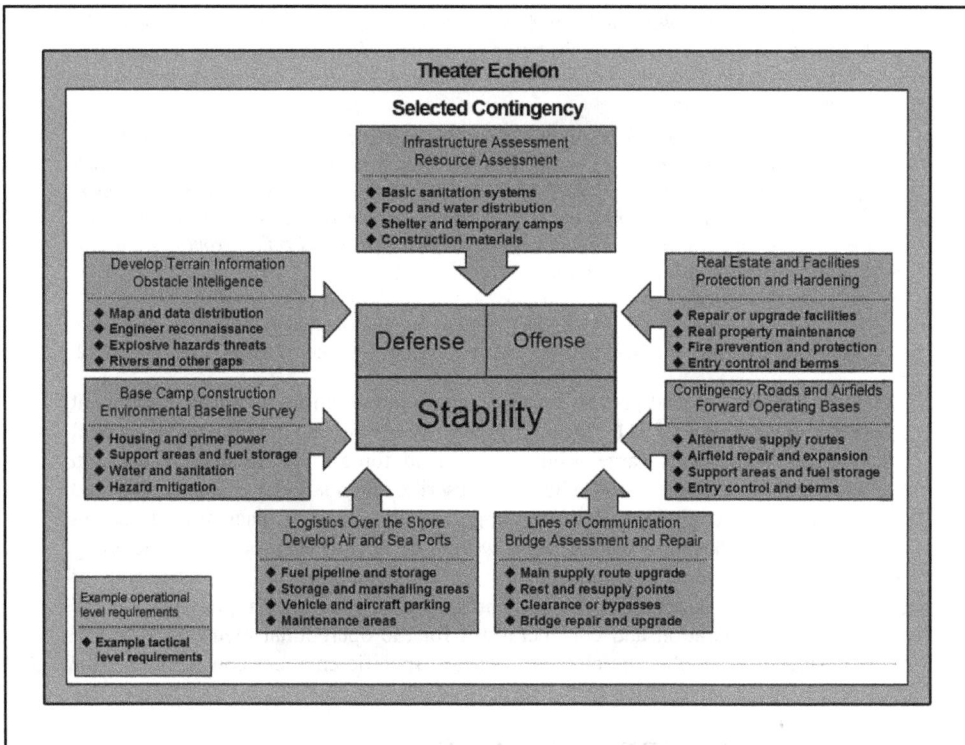

Figure 5-1. Contingency perspective of engineer requirements

5-3. At the corps echelon, the ENCOORD and other engineer staff assist in understanding and translating the operational design into a corps concept of operations. Corps engineer staff analyze the foundation provided by the theater and begin to concentrate on remaining problems. From the operational perspective, the corps engineer offers validation for the analysis supporting the theater engineer design. The corps engineer analysis may add detail or offer new information for theater consideration. Ultimately, as theater engineers refine and address requirements at their echelon, the corps echelon engineers gain understanding of the operational requirements that must be included in the conduct of corps operations. From the tactical perspective, corps echelon engineers concentrate on substantial development of engineering requirements and capabilities necessary to the corps concept of operation. The corps echelon engineer's analysis is broad enough to perceive general and geospatial engineering support considered in the operational design but more comprehensive in considering and shaping combat, general, and geospatial engineering support concentrating on the corps concept of operations.

5-4. Figure 5-2 shows how the corps echelon engineer integrates the operational engineer approach (below the dotted line in the illustration) and tactical engineer actions (above the dotted line in the illustration) through warfighting functions to support the corps concept of operations.

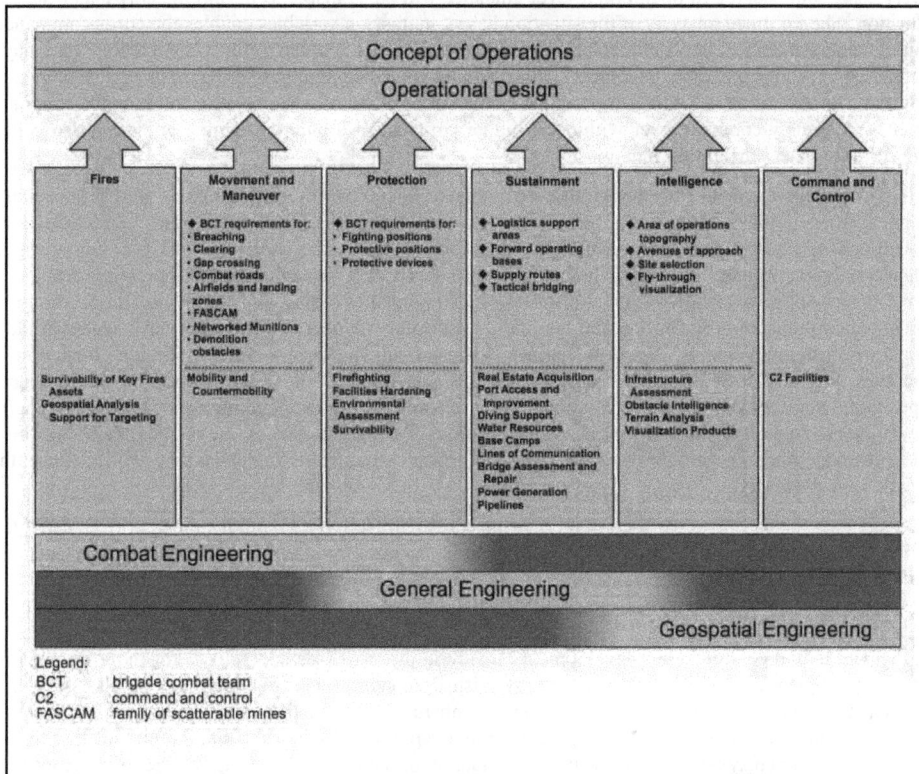

Figure 5-2. Corps echelon engineer requirements by function

5-5. Corps engineer staff collaborate with theater army engineer staff, supporting engineer headquarters, and subordinate echelon engineer staff to refine operational engineering concepts and add substance to the engineer actions required. The corps engineer staff's capacity to concentrate on detailing the capabilities required to support a specific major operation or contingency adds significantly to the depth of the theater engineer concept. Similarly, when an engineer unit headquarters is identified in support of the corps echelon, that engineer commander and staff bring additional capacity for developing engineer support concepts. Finally, when subordinate echelons are identified and available for collaborative planning, the corps echelon can gain even greater depth through those subordinate engineer support concepts.

5-6. The corps ENCOORD's running estimate provides a working compilation of RI primarily focused on the physical environment of the designated AO with a comprehensive accounting for engineer units, capabilities, and other resources associated with the assigned major operation or contingency. The running estimate is built on input from the theater army engineer's initial assessments and then further developed considering mission variables. The corps-level running estimate evolves with the development of the corps concept of operations. The RI contained within the corps ENCOORD's running estimate logically connects identified challenges and opportunities to either an operational requirement supported by the theater army or to a requirement for corps consideration. The running estimate can be organized by engineer function and warfighting function, as are the requirements shown in figure 5-2. The running estimate is continuously refined and updated as additional assessments are made, guidance and priorities are established, and feedback is gathered. Appendix B provides a tool for use in developing and maintaining the engineer running estimate.

5-7.   The theater army headquarters tailors the corps headquarters to meet mission requirements. Corps engineer and other staff planners enter the operations process for a major operation or contingency with at least the foundations of an operational design. Even in the situation in which the corps acts as JTF headquarters, the GCC or other higher headquarters will have begun developing the operational design. In every case, some degree of operational-level guidance will be available to inform the corps analysis of the situation. The informed analysis of the situation based on mission variables enables the corps commander's initial understanding. The commander's understanding forms the basis for visualization that may be expressed in corps planning guidance. This planning guidance is a reflection of how the commander envisions the operation unfolding. It provides a broad description of when, where, and how the commander intends to employ combat power within the higher commander's intent. Planning guidance also contains priorities for each warfighting function.

5-8.   The corps engineer may begin shaping engineer operations by understanding and influencing the commander's initial priorities. At the corps echelon, this effort requires an early understanding of operational engineer support responsibilities as defined by the theater echelon and GCC. Corps engineer planners should validate aspects of higher-echelon support. For example, the theater army echelon will typically accept responsibility for the provision of contingency basing and facilities. During design and construction preparation for basing and facilities, the theater engineer staff may not have access to the full depth of these requirements. As corps engineer planners validate theater engineer designs for basing and facilities, they adjust or refine the execution of the construction effort. This validation of the theater's operational engineer support is an important but peripheral effort to the planning concentration for engineer operations in support of the corps concept of operations. Both are guided by the commander's priorities in the planning guidance and provide the engineer planner improved understanding to influence those priorities as necessary.

5-9.   For any major operation or contingency, the corps will likely face a unique theater or JOA. While the discussion and comparison of levels of development in chapter 4 is applicable, from a corps perspective the GCC and theater army will typically expend some effort in mitigating the impact of those differences on the corps operation. In many cases the corps will inherit an accessible theater with a developed or developing sustainment base and real estate already acquired or in acquisition. Typically the corps will participate in and continue base development already in progress (see appendix E for more discussion on base development). Standards will likely be established, though some refinement may be necessary. Corps echelon engineers consider maintenance of those standards during the conduct of operations and finally the closure or turnover of bases and other facilities as operations conclude. In unique circumstances, corps echelon engineers may be presented with the broader assortment of engineering requirements generated by an undeveloped operational area.

5-10.   Engineer operations act as one of many key enablers as the corps commander drives both operational design and tactical concept of operations to shape conditions and achieve objectives. To be effective as enablers, engineer staff must be integrated in the effort to assist the commander in refining the operational design provided and formulating the concept of operations. As discussed previously in chapter 3, the engineer staff will be organized to meet the mission. Corps engineer staff may have representatives distributed across the staff or may organize as a special staff. The engineer staff must also integrate within planning horizons: plans, future operations, and current operations. The ENCOORD and engineer staff will have unique challenges coordinating and synchronizing engineer functions based on the organization selected. Engineer functions assist the staff in organizing capabilities; warfighting functions synchronize staff engineers with other enablers; and the elements of operational design provide a framework for refining design concepts. The corps ENCOORD and other engineer staff integrate all these efforts through the operations process to refine operational engineer support from theater and to develop the corps concept of engineer operations.

CONDUCT OF OPERATIONS

5-11.   In many situations the corps echelon will take on a design with some level of detail from the theater army or GCC. The corps echelon shares a broad operational-level view with higher echelons but is afforded a more singular focus by the established operational theme. The corps echelon engineer staff must understand the elements of operational design to participate in its refinement. Corps echelon commanders and their staffs also use more objectives-focused problem solving to develop the detailed corps concept of operations. The resulting concept of operations forms the basis for developing the OPLAN or OPORD. During execution, corps commanders and staffs assess the situation, from both the operational and tactical perspective, to adjust current and future operations and plans as the operation unfolds.

5-12. Engineer operations require coordination throughout the corps echelon operations process. The corps echelon engineering effort will require consideration of engineer requirements identified from both an operational- and tactical-level perspective and linked through the warfighting functions to the operational design and the corps concept of operations. For the corps echelon engineer staff, the activities of the operations process are increasingly simultaneous, as was the case for the theater echelon (see figure 4-3, page 4-5). For the corps, however, these activities will have a singular focus on the assigned major operation. Assessments, including some technical assessments, will be required to enable planning, and engineering preparations must in many cases occur as operational planning is conducted. Execution of selected engineer operations will nearly always precede operational execution, and operational assessments will generate additional engineer requirements. While the engineer staff will be cycling among selected activities demanded by engineer requirements, they must remain synchronized with their staff counterparts in the broader operations process.

Planning Considerations

5-13. The corps trains as joint headquarters for contingency operations. At the operational level, a subordinate JFC develops supporting plans, which can include objectives supported by measurable operation-level effects. Joint interdependence requires that the corps headquarters understand joint doctrine addressing these planning techniques. See chapter 3 of this manual and JP 3-34 when required to participate in joint planning.

5-14. Corps echelon engineer planners assist in defining an AO, estimating forces required, and evaluating the requirements for the operation. They also assist in determining specific objectives and detailing the COA selected for achieving those objectives. They use the planning processes—including joint processes—when required, and tools described and referenced in chapter 3. They use the commander's intent to develop and refine COAs that contribute to setting the conditions and achieving objectives in the AO. They maintain a peripheral view of the operational-level engineer support required while concentrating on supporting the corps concept of operations. As units are identified to participate in the operation, they collaborate as fully as possible to gain depth for their view of the OE and to add to their planning and problem-solving capability. This collaboration also extends the subordinate engineer's planning, preparation, and execution horizon.

5-15. MDMP serves as the primary tool for deliberate planning. Corps engineer planners participate along with their staff counterparts in the process to translate the commander's visualization into a specific COA for preparation and execution. The corps echelon engineers collaborate closely throughout the MDMP with their counterparts in the theater army and GCC engineer staff to develop a shared understanding of the mission. Table 3-1, page 3-12, provides some of the engineer planning considerations as they pertain to each step of the MDMP. Route clearance and bridging are two examples of essential mobility tasks that are both typical requirements and fairly important at the operational level. As the plan develops, engineer planners remain synchronized through warfighting functions as shown in table 4-1, page 4-6.

5-16. As operational planning proceeds through MDMP, the engineer relies heavily on analytic techniques to guide functional problem solving. These techniques demand technical information that may be available from existing assessments or may require additional assessments or surveys. Support available through reachback or through collaborative planning may be used to focus on technical details.

5-17. Control measures are established under the authority of a commander. However, staff officers and subordinate leaders can also establish them with the commander's authorization. Aided by their engineer staff, the corps commander exercises control over engineer forces in the corps AO. Staffs contribute their greatest support in providing control and keeping the commander informed through some of the measures below:

- Construction priorities and project lists.
- Engineer task organization and command and support relationships.
- Engineer work lines and other graphic control measures.

- Obstacle control measures (authorities retained or released).
- Reporting requirements.
- Engineer staff procedures and battle drills.
- Engineer-specific boards and working groups (acquisition review, JFUB, basing, EH, and geospatial).
- Engineer-specific programs and policies (new equipment fielding and training, EH policies, and construction standards).

5-18. The result of the MDMP is a plan or order that provides subordinates the information they need for execution. Engineer planners provide input to appropriate paragraphs, annexes, and appendixes for either the joint or Army format as described in chapter 3. The corps engineer staff continues to collaborate and assist subordinate unit staffs with their planning and coordination.

Preparation Considerations

5-19. The corps echelon gives significant focus to integration of engineer support within combined arms forces. Implementing the engineer task organization and linking up engineers with their gaining or supported units is an important and challenging preparation activity. The ENCOORD in the headquarters directing the task organization initiates the coordination effort by ensuring that the necessary linkup instructions are contained in the gaining or supported unit's order. In many cases, corps echelon and subordinate engineer units conduct preparation activities integrated within the combined arms task organizations required by the operation. Combined arms rehearsals are especially critical to the success of a breaching, clearing, or gap-crossing operation. Engineer integration within the reconnaissance efforts at corps and subordinate echelons are another important yet challenging preparation activity.

5-20. Preparation considerations include in-depth terrain analysis of the OE, using reachback support from the NGA, Topographic Engineering Center, and ERDC as required. Preparation considerations also include development of survivability standards and resourcing construction and barrier materials to support corps operations. Engineer task organization is further refined to support combat operations, specifically any breach or gap-crossing operations. Analysis of how to shape the AO through obstacles, mainly by destroying enemy LOCs and through family of scatterable mines (FASCAM) emplacement, may also be included in preparation considerations.

5-21. The corps echelon engineer must apply peripheral attention during preparation activities to review and refine operational-level engineer support. The corps may rely on theater army support for reception and staging in-theater and the establishment of the sustainment base, or these may be included with other corps preparation responsibilities. A more concentrated focus is applied to preparation activities supporting onward movement and integration of the corps. Construction activities, real estate management, and facilities engineering are predominant during preparation. Operational engineer forces conduct a variety of construction and other technical preparation activities focused on the specific mission. Construction and technical preparation activities include—

- Completing and reviewing designs. In a design-build process the design will typically only be completed at a 10- to 30-percent resolution prior to execution.
- Conducting any necessary preconstruction studies or surveys.
- Identifying additional technical support required.
- Completing any detailed planning activities not yet completed from the project management process, such as estimates, bill of materials, or schedules.
- Preparing the construction site as required, such as staging equipment, stockpiling materials, or completing temporary construction.

5-22. Operational engineer preparations include addressing requirements for facilities (to include the standards to be applied). The requirements should reflect the general engineering support necessary for the expected duration and intensity of operations; be limited to the forces employed (to include multinational, HN, and contractors); and be time-phased. Adequate funding (see appendix D) must be available to undertake early engineer reconnaissance and acquisition of facilities to meet requirements, whether by construction or leasing. Facilities are grouped into six broad categories that emphasize the use of existing assets over new construction. To the maximum extent possible, facilities or real estate requirements should be met from these categories in priority order as described in chapter 4.

5-23. Corps-level preparation activities may also include the establishment of or participation in working groups, cells, or boards (as described in chapter 3) to solve problems and coordinate actions. The conduct of theater army echelon engineer operations may be managed by a TCEM or a RCEM cell requiring corps participation. The composition and the procedures of the TCEM and the RCEM cells are governed by the respective GCCs. These cells are augmented from the staffs they support, including the corps when appropriate. The TCEM and the RCEM cells apply the commander's intent, merge engineer-support requirements, and orchestrate resources as described in chapter 4.

Execution Considerations

5-24. A focus of corps echelon operational engineer execution activities is support to sustainment distribution and establishment of ISBs and FOBs. Construction activities, refinement and identification of new requirements, and ADC predominate during execution. As with preparation, engineer forces will conduct additional construction or other technically related activities during execution of the specific mission. Construction and technically related execution activities include—

- Implementation and maintenance of a construction safety program.
- Implementation and enforcement of quality controls.
- Periodic design and construction reviews.
- Preparation of as-built drawings.
- Response to construction contingencies.

5-25. As the theater sustainment base is established, focus shifts to requirements supporting distribution. Theater distribution includes aerial delivery and air drop, supply, maintenance, field services, contracting, contract management, procurement, and transportation. Operational engineer support for the developing distribution functions will include construction, bridging, and facilities engineering.

5-26. Considerations for the establishment of ISBs and FOBs include the size of the force projected to operate from the base camp(s), the duration the base camp will be required, and the level of construction standards to be applied. Other important parameters include geographical location, weather, available construction materials, resources, utilities, political concerns for permanency, localized environmental hazards and health threats, and impact on the local populace. Base development is discussed in detail in appendix E.

5-27. During execution, corps engineers consider more than support to sustainment operations and base construction, although these are major focuses of operational-level engineering. The corps engineer staff must assess division and BCT engineer operations to determine if additional resources or task organization changes are required. Corps engineer staff also monitor and assess enemy operations in order to recommend effective countermeasures and enhance situational understanding. Geospatial engineering provides the foundational layer for the corps COP. Engineer staff also provide input to corps boards and working groups to maintain integration of engineer functions throughout corps operations. During execution, corps engineers may leverage FFE to provide necessary technical expertise to emerging problems.

Assessment Considerations

5-28. The corps echelon assessment will include some tactical detail down to subordinate BCT levels. These assessments inform the theater echelon operational assessments. The corps staff analyzes the situation in terms of mission variables to understand changes in conditions and objectives and maintain their staff running estimates. They continuously assess the effects of new information on the conduct of the operation; they update their staff running estimates and determine if adjustment decisions are required.

5-29. Engineer capabilities may be applied to add technical detail to the commander's assessment. Engineer assessment and survey teams gather technically focused information on the physical environment, infrastructure, or other physical aspects of the AO. RI gathered adds to the depth of the commander's understanding and can provide a technical basis for MOPs or MOEs.

5-30. A focus of operational engineer assessment activities is monitoring RSOI requirements and the adequacy of the sustainment base. Operational engineer forces also conduct a variety of construction and other technical assessment activities focused on technical aspects of the support provided. Construction activities, real estate management, and facilities engineering are evaluated for adequacy to the requirements and conformance to quality standards. Construction and technical preparation activities include—

- Conducting any necessary postconstruction acceptance inspections.
- Identifying master planning activities not yet completed from the project management process.

FORCE TAILORING

5-31. Operational planning prepares the way for tactical activity on the most favorable terms through, among other considerations, adequate resourcing of units and other capabilities. Commanders are challenged to generate a force that is tailored for current and anticipated missions, flexible to changing circumstances, and fits the constraints of time and lift capabilities. Identified and anticipated requirements, coupled with analysis of mission variables at operational echelons, drive the initial tailoring of the corps force. Typically the initial tailoring is shaped for the anticipated operational configuration for the corps, the assigned AO, and the concept for corps operations. The corps headquarters may have significant input for refining the tailored force and providing detailed considerations down to the tactical level. Because the demands of any given operation vary, there is no set engineer force structure. A building-block approach that is based on need is used to tailor the force. See appendix F for examples of tailored corps engineer forces based on various situations.

5-32. The tailored engineer force supporting the corps echelon will in most cases result from a collaborative effort among corps and theater army engineer planners, their supported GCC engineer staff, elements at DA and DOD, supporting Army and joint force providers (including the TEC and USACE), and the input from identified subordinate echelon units. The challenge is to generate the engineer force tailored to identified and anticipated requirements, time, lift, and other constraints. In many cases, leveraging reachback and other engineer capabilities mitigates the impact of these constraints (see figure 4-4, page 4-11).

COMMAND AND CONTROL OF ENGINEER FORCES

5-33. A significant determination included in the force generation effort is timing and level for deployment of engineer headquarters. The corps does not have echelon-specific units other than the organic corps headquarters. Each corps does have habitual associations established with engineer brigade headquarters, but each of the three echelons of engineer headquarters units is capable of serving, within its inherent span of control limitations, directly under the corps headquarters in any of its operational configurations. The engineer brigade headquarters incorporates training focused on support to corps echelon operations. The brigade is capable of providing effective C2 of engineer operations for most contingencies in which the corps headquarters is required and is the most likely headquarters to be tailored for a corps echelon engineer headquarters. For major combat operations, the corps echelon will typically require early or phased deployment of at least one engineer brigade headquarters because the engineer brigade is best suited for integrating engineer capabilities across the entire force. Additional engineer brigades and MEBs may be required in support of the corps and its subordinate divisions (discussed in chapter 6). Stability or civil support operations will vary, but most operations or contingencies requiring the deployment of the corps headquarters in one of its configurations will also require an engineer brigade headquarters element.

5-34. The TEC is designed for operational command of engineer capabilities at EAC level and often will provide C2 of engineer operations for the JFC if an operational engineer headquarters is required. The TEC typically serves as the senior theater or land component engineer headquarters. The corps headquarters operationally configured as a JFLCC may benefit from an early or phased deployment of a TEC headquarters, but more typically will rely on the engineer brigade to provide C2 of engineer operations. In a JTF configuration, TEC deployment may still be advantageous depending on the JTF mission's complexity, but an engineer brigade will typically provide adequate capability given the narrower span of control.

5-35. The engineer brigade is capable of developing plans, procedures, and programs for engineer support for the corps, including requirements determination, operational mobility and countermobility, general engineering, power generation, ADC, military construction, geospatial engineering, engineering design, construction materiel, and real property maintenance activities. The brigade's force-tailored engineer units are responsible for infrastructure planning, development, construction, and maintenance. The brigade commander receives policy guidance from the corps based on the guidance of the theater army and GCC engineer staff. If the corps is configured as an intermediate tactical headquarters, a TEC is likely also providing guidance in its role supporting the theater. The brigade headquarters provides staff supervision over corps engineer operations in the AO and reinforces engineer support to subordinate corps forces. The brigade also may support joint and multinational commands and other elements according to lead Service responsibilities as directed by the supported JFC. It provides policy and technical guidance to subordinate engineer units in the AO and maintains a collaborative planning relationship with the corps, theater army, joint force staff engineers, and the TEC when appropriate.

5-36. The engineer brigade is capable of rapid deployment in modular elements to support the needs of the operational commander. These elements are capable of providing a wide range of technical engineering expertise and support and coordinating support from USACE, other Service technical laboratories and research centers, and other potential sources of expertise in the civilian community. The engineer brigade can provide C2 for the low-density, high-demand engineer assets supporting the corps, to include military working dogs, EFDs, bridge units, and others. The brigade is enabled by the global reachback capabilities associated with FFE. These capabilities include technical assistance, project planning and design, contract construction, real estate acquisition, infrastructure support, and support to nation-building capacities.

FIELD FORCE ENGINEERING

5-37. A corps headquarters will also receive support through USACE FFE for an appropriately tailored FEST. The corps ENCOORD collaborates with theater army ENCOORD, the theater USACE LNO, and the TEC to determine the appropriate level of support. USACE FFE provides the corps a means to access specialized engineer capabilities and contract construction support.

5-38. USACE support provides for technical and contract engineering support, integrating its organic capabilities with those of other Services and other sources of engineering-related reachback support. USACE may have assets directly integrated into the military C2 structure and linked to a TEC or senior engineer headquarters or already be operating under contract in-theater. Whether providing construction contract and design support in the AO or outside of the contingency area, USACE can obtain necessary data, research, and specialized expertise not present in-theater through tele-engineering and other reachback capabilities.

5-39. USACE expertise may support corps-level engineer planning and operations and can leverage reachback to technical subject matter experts in districts, divisions, labs and centers of expertise, other Services, and private industry in its role as part of the generating force. Teams can rapidly deploy to meet requirements for engineering assessments and analyses in support of the full array of engineer operations. The two types of FESTs provide support to primarily general engineering efforts through forward-deployed engineer elements that can communicate with TeleEngineering Kits and reachback to technical experts within USACE. EFDs from the TECs provide a wide variety of services to forward-deployed forces in a public works capacity. Infrastructure assessment and base development teams are nondeployable capabilities available through reachback support.

ENGINEER AND MULTIFUNCTIONAL FORCES

5-40. The units that make up the architecture of the corps echelon engineer force are diverse, with technical skill orientation ranging from highly specialized to multifunctional and sourcing that includes Army, joint, and multinational force providers. Corps engineer planners are challenged to comprehensively identify both current and future requirements across the range of organizational skill sets. Typically, operational-level priorities and substantially defined subordinate requirements are clear, and the associated tasks and troop formations evident. For operational-level planners, requirements for supporting subordinate echelons become increasingly ambiguous. To ensure adequate resourcing of units, planners must consider those troop formations and tasks that are evident but also provide for flexibility to mitigate the uncertainty.

5-41. As previously discussed, planners use the engineer functions with their primary relationships to warfighting functions to organize and ensure an integrated view of operational requirements. Corps echelon engineer planners must consider those general engineering capabilities tailored by the theater or other higher-echelon planners based on operational requirements linked to the movement and maneuver, sustainment, and protection warfighting functions. These include construction requirements and a variety of specialized engineering requirements. Construction requirements will typically exceed Army unit capabilities and must be analyzed considering joint, multinational, contract, and other capabilities. Specialized requirements may require additional or more technical information to effectively associate with tasks and troops. FFE or reachback may be employed to guide the technical assessment needed. A more significant focus for corps echelon engineer planners will typically be adding substance to the analysis of requirements linked to the movement and maneuver, sustainment, and protection warfighting functions for the corps and its subordinate forces. Consideration includes airborne or air-assault-capable elements when required to support corps or subordinate echelon forced-entry operations.

5-42. Corps engineer planners refine the tailored force required to support operational-level priorities and develop a more substantial understanding of the tailored force required to support lower echelons. Geospatial engineering support, though organic at each echelon down to BCT, may generate requirements for augmentation at corps or subordinate echelons. General engineering support for requirements linked to the movement and maneuver, sustainment, and protection warfighting functions at each subordinate echelon may be accepted as a corps responsibility or considered in tailoring the subordinate echelon. General engineering support as augmentation to combat engineering capabilities at lower echelons is also considered. Finally, combat engineering requirements for each BCT and major tactical element are considered. Each BCT will include an organic engineer company but with only minimal M/CM/S support capabilities. Augmentation must typically be provided in the form of additional combat and general engineering capabilities and appropriate engineer and multifunctional headquarters elements. The type and level of augmenting capabilities will likely receive a more concentrated analysis at corps echelon than applied in the comprehensive theater review.

5-43. When available for collaborative planning, subordinate echelon headquarters provide invaluable input not only for their assigned mission requirements but also for some operational-level requirements that may have been overlooked by the higher echelon. Subordinate echelon engineer and multifunctional units and the engineer staff supporting division and other headquarters develop an understanding through a more concentrated analysis of the situation. The resulting view adds depth to the understanding of engineer forces required for their support.

5-44. The tailored engineer force supporting the corps echelon will typically include joint and multinational engineer formations. Planners mesh Service capabilities with joint and multinational formations, interagency, and NGOs. Corps engineer planners give significant consideration to the joint engineer capabilities. Whenever feasible, they align joint forces with optimum capabilities. For example, Navy engineer units routinely train to support Marine forces. The optimal alignment for general engineering in support of subordinate Marine forces will be Navy engineer units. Army engineers retain capability to support Marine forces but will be a secondary option to available Navy units. Corps engineer planners collaborate with the theater army and joint force providers to effectively align joint capabilities with requirements. Significant consideration is also given to the tactical limitations for joint engineer forces, such as a joint engineer unit's capability for self-mobility in a contested AO.

OTHER CAPABILITIES

5-45. With minimum joint augmentation, the corps headquarters can initiate operations as a JTF or land component command for contingencies. For sustained operations in this role, a corps is augmented according to an appropriate joint manning document (JMD). Other situations may generate requirements for individual augmentation within the tailored corps headquarters or a subordinate echelon headquarters. Similarly, the situation may require tailoring of individual augmentees for a provisional headquarters or for provisional teams. The GCC supports subordinate joint force requirements for joint individual augmentees as available through its standing joint force headquarters. As requirements exceed the GCC capabilities, they are passed to joint force providers.

5-46. An engineer is typically assigned on the staff of PRTs. The engineer may be an assigned individual augmentee or provided by USACE through FFE. The engineer trains and advises HN engineers working on provincial development projects. The engineer assists the PRT Provincial Reconstruction Development Committee with project assessments, designing scope-of-work statements for contracts with local companies, site supervision, and project management. The engineer advises the PRT team leader on reconstruction projects and development activities in the province.

5-47. As discussed in chapter 4, commanders may use an operational needs statement to document an urgent need for a materiel solution to correct a deficiency or to improve a capability that impacts on mission accomplishment. The corps echelon engineer staff may become involved in review and processing of engineer-related statements in support of the theater army echelon's process or to meet its own ADCON responsibilities. Examples of engineer-related operational needs may include bridging or construction equipment, EH clearance improvements, and other nonstandard capabilities (see AR 71-9 for information on processing operational needs statements).

5-48. Corps echelon engineers must also understand contingency construction authorities and associated funding. These authorities provide the basis for legal spending to meet construction requirements and activities in support of contingency operations. Appendix D provides an introduction to contingency authorities and funding. However, the information in the appendix is subject to change due to changes in legislation, policy, or regulation. Corps and theater army echelon engineer staff collaborate and consult with legal and financial management personnel for the latest definitive guidance.

OPERATIONAL THEMES AND ELEMENTS

5-49. The corps echelon maintains an operational-level perspective but will typically focus on an assigned major operation or contingency. The character of most major operations is likely to evolve and vary with time. Major operations comprise many smaller operations conducted simultaneously, but the corps should be involved in a single operational theme within a designated AO at any one time. Different themes usually demand different approaches and force packages, and the corps will have a foundation from which to refine both.

5-50. Corps echelon forces are tailored with a mix of land combat power effective for any combination of offensive, defensive, and stability or civil support operations as part of an interdependent joint force. Since the corps spans the operational- to tactical-level perspectives, corps echelon engineer operations will include operational engineering efforts that simultaneously support offensive, defensive, stability or civil support operations, and tactical engineer operations that are significantly influenced by the distinct operational element they support. For example, the corps engineer perspective may include the application of engineering efforts to repair and upgrade a road influenced significantly by the technical aspects of the engineering tasks. Simultaneously, from a tactical perspective, the corps may control major combat operations of its subordinates. In this example, the corps may be supporting gap-crossing requirements for a subordinate element conducting an attack. The characteristics distinct in offensive operations shape and constrain the engineering tasks supporting the gap crossing. Assault-crossing means are selected, C2 unique for the assault crossing is employed, and other tactical requirements constrain technical standards. The example, upgraded road, supports movement of forces conducting any military operation, while the gap crossing is tactically focused on projecting combat power across the obstacle. Even though operational applications are more technically influenced, corps echelon engineer operations at both the operational and tactical levels must remain integrated within the combined arms framework.

5-51. The corps echelon orchestrates and sustains tactical actions employed to achieve operational objectives. Engineer combat power applications are key enablers in achieving objectives for any combination of operational elements. The corps echelon engineer staff is integral to the process of orchestrating and sustaining enabling tactical engineer actions, but the focus for operational engineer applications is significantly influenced by technical aspects of the tasks. The corps ENCOORD may rely significantly on a supporting engineer headquarters unit and FFE element for the conduct and control of these applications. Chapter 4 included a discussion of generalities observed considering the operational elements and engineer operations. From a tactical perspective, operational element considerations become more distinct.

5-52. Offensive operations defeat enemy forces that control important areas or contest the HN government's authority. Army forces perform the following primary offensive tasks (FM 3-90 discusses them in detail). A movement to contact develops the situation and establishes or regains contact. It also creates favorable conditions for subsequent tactical actions. Movements to contact include search-and-attack and cordon-and-search operations. An attack destroys or defeats enemy forces, seizes and secures terrain, or both. Attacks require maneuver supported by direct and indirect fires. Success depends on skillfully massing the effects of combat power. Exploitation rapidly follows a successful attack and disorganizes the enemy in depth. Exploitations seek to expand an attack to the point where enemy forces have no alternatives but to surrender or flee. A pursuit is designed to catch or cut off a hostile force attempting to escape with the aim of destroying it. Pursuits often follow successful exploitations. However, they can develop at any point when enemy forces are beginning to disintegrate or disengage.

5-53. During offensive operations, engineer units will tend to have command relationships to maneuver commanders. OPCON is the most common command relationship for engineers during offensive operations because it provides the gaining commander flexibility of a command relationship without the burden of ADCON responsibilities. Although the forms of offensive maneuver have different intentions, the planning phase must always begin with predicting the adversary's intent through a thorough understanding of the threat, threat engineer capabilities, and how the terrain will affect operations. Geospatial products and information become the foundation and common reference for planning. Of all the forms of maneuver, knowledge of the threat's disposition is especially critical and required for an infiltration or penetration due to the requirements for stealth and surprise. Engineer planning tends to focus on mobility support, including a robust reconnaissance effort. A greater degree of planning is required for a penetration from the breach to the ultimate control of the decisive objective.

5-54. An enemy offensive may compel forces to conduct major defensive operations that may require defeating or preventing attacks across international borders, defeating conventional attacks, or halting an insurgent movement's mobilization. The following primary tasks are associated with the defense. Defending commanders combine these tasks to fit the situation. (FM 3-90 discusses them in detail.) In a mobile defense, the defender withholds a large portion of available forces for use as a striking force in a counterattack. As enemy forces extend themselves in the defended area and lose momentum and organization, the defender surprises and overwhelms them with a powerful counterattack. In an area defense, the defender concentrates on denying enemy forces access to designated terrain for a specific time, limiting their freedom of maneuver, and channeling them into killing areas. Retrograde involves organized movement away from the enemy. This includes delays, withdrawals, and retirements. Retrograde operations gain time, preserve forces, place the enemy in unfavorable positions, or avoid combat under undesirable conditions. All three primary defensive tasks use mobile and static elements. In mobile defenses, static positions help control the depth and breadth of the enemy penetration and retain ground from which to launch counterattacks. In area defenses, commanders closely integrate mobile patrols, security forces, sensors, and reserves to cover gaps among defensive positions. In retrograde operations, some units conduct area or mobile defenses along with security operations to protect other units executing carefully controlled maneuver or movement rearward. Static elements fix, disrupt, turn, or block the attackers and gain time for other forces to pull back. Mobile elements maneuver constantly to confuse the enemy and prevent enemy exploitation.

5-55. Planning for defensive operations is inextricably linked to offensive operations and, for planning purposes, must consider the transition from offensive operations and the follow-on offensive operations. During defensive operations, engineers use terrain products to describe the best position for units within the defense. Engineers then work with intelligence staff to describe the threat functions to predict where the threat is likely to attack friendly forces. Engineers work in conjunction with intelligence personnel to determine which sensor capabilities to leverage and best predict and prevent the threat from maneuvering freely into the defended area. Construction planning includes security and survivability considerations. The consideration of counterattack planning or support for the mobile strike force is the same as the typical mobility planning for offensive operations. The ENCOORD works with the other staff members to ensure that the counterattack force can mass its effects on the enemy for decisive operations. The type of defensive operation will define the amount and focus of engineer effort required. Support relationships for engineer units to maneuver commanders would be preferred to maximize the application of limited assets. An area defense will typically require more effort due to the increased survivability requirements. A mobile defense will require less effort (although mobility requirements may increase) because it has greater flexibility and takes advantage of the terrain in depth. During defensive operations, engineer units will tend to have support relationships to the maneuver commander except for those combat engineer forces task-organized to the reserve or the mobile strike force.

5-56. Just as planning for defensive operations is linked to offensive operations, planners must consider the transition from combat operations to follow-on stability operations. Stability operations are designed to establish a safe and secure environment and facilitate reconciliation among local or regional adversaries. Stability operations can also establish political, legal, social, and economic institutions and support the transition to legitimate local governance. The combination of tasks conducted during stability operations depends on the situation. Army forces perform five primary stability tasks. Civil security involves protecting the populace from external and internal threats. Ideally, Army forces defeat external threats posed by enemy forces that can attack population centers. Simultaneously, they assist HN police and security elements as the HN maintains internal security against criminals and small, hostile groups. In some situations, there is no adequate HN capability for civil security and Army forces provide most of it. Civil security is required for the other stability tasks to be effective. Civil control regulates selected behavior and activities of individuals and groups. This control reduces risk to individuals or groups and promotes security. Civil control channels the populace's activities to allow provision of security and essential services while coexisting with a military force conducting operations. Army forces establish or restore the most basic services and protect them until a civil authority or the HN can provide them. Normally, Army forces support civilian and HN agencies. When the HN cannot perform its role, Army forces may provide the basics directly. Essential services may include the following:

- Providing emergency medical care and rescue.
- Preventing epidemic disease.
- Providing food and water.
- Providing emergency shelter.
- Providing basic sanitation (sewage and garbage disposal).

5-57. Stability operations establish conditions that enable actions by civilian and HN agencies to succeed. By establishing security and control, stability operations provide a foundation for transitioning authority to civilian agencies and eventually to the HN. Once this transition is complete, commanders focus on transferring control to a legitimate civil authority according to the desired end state. Support to governance may include the following:

- Supporting transitional administrations.
- Supporting development of local governance.
- Supporting anticorruption initiatives.
- Supporting elections.

5-58. In stability operations, the engineer assesses the OE focusing on different aspects of the terrain and friendly and threat capabilities. Terrain products continue to have a great deal of importance, but political and cultural considerations may be more important than strictly a combat terrain analysis. Terrain analysts will work with the intelligence staff to develop usable products for the commander to reflect this information if it is available. Support relationships for engineer units to maneuver commanders are employed to maximize the application of limited assets. When analyzing the troops available, the ENCOORD should consider if there are HN, third-party NGOs, or other multinational forces involved with engineering capabilities. Interaction with these other parties requires engineers to address interoperability, common standards, and mutual agreements. Engineers should also plan for engineer units operating among civilians or in conjunction with NGOs and other international organizations. Engineer elements may be tasked with managing capacity-building programs (both military and civilian) during stability operations. The EAB engineer staff assesses technical capacity and includes consideration for these requirements in the conduct of stability operations.

5-59. PRTs may be employed as part of a longer-term effort to transition the functions of security, governance, and economics to provincial governments. The PRT is a potential combat multiplier for EAB engineer efforts supporting stability operations. The PRT provides expertise to programs designed to strengthen infrastructure and the perception of local governments. The PRT focuses on developing institutional capacity for governance, security, and reconstruction. An assigned engineer on the staff of the PRT assists in developing the PRT economic development work plan, including its assistance projects. The PRT emphasizes the construction of infrastructure, including schools, clinics, community centers, and government buildings. The PRT also focuses on developing human capacity through training and advisory programs.

5-60. Though USNORTHCOM maintains a standing JTF for operations in the United States, any corps headquarters may be required to provide civil support. Civil support operations address the consequences of natural or man-made disasters, accidents, and incidents within the United States and its territories. Army civil support operations include three primary tasks. Policies issued by the federal government govern the essential services Army forces provide in response to disaster. Essential services include the following:

- Providing rescue.
- Providing emergency medical care.
- Preventing epidemic disease.
- Providing food and water.
- Providing emergency shelter.
- Providing basic sanitation (sewage and garbage disposal).
- Providing minimum essential access to affected areas.

5-61. Army forces work directly with state and federal officials to help restore and return control of services to civil authorities as rapidly as possible. As a result of disaster or attack, state and local governments' capacities may be reduced or overextended. Army forces provide C2, protection, and sustainment to government agencies at all levels until they can function normally. When authorized and directed, ARFOR provide support to local, state, and federal law enforcement officers. In extreme cases, when directed by the President, regular ARFOR maintain law and order. The Army is frequently called on to provide other support to civil authorities apart from disaster response and law enforcement. Most of this support is identified well in advance and planned with civil authorities. Much of the support is routine; it consists of providing support to communities surrounding Army units' home stations. Examples of other types of support provided to civil authorities include the following:

- Supporting state funerals.
- Participating in major public sporting events.
- Providing military equipment and Soldiers to community events.

5-62. Planning for civil support operations is significantly different from offensive, defensive, or stability operations because of the unique nature of the threat, although the basic missions may be very similar to those of stability operations. Civil support operations are similar to stability operations in that they both interact with the populace and civil authorities and the engineer tasks are similar but within a domestic versus foreign environment. The focus for engineer capabilities on essential services is similar in both stability and civil support operations. In most stability operations, materials or capabilities are typically scarce after a natural disaster or conflict. However, in civil support operations, they are plentiful in almost all situations, so the Army will typically be called on to help states facilitate the orderly movement of manpower and material from the civilian sector. Engineer planners consider statutes and regulations that restrict the Army's interaction with other government agencies and civilians during civil support operations. The local and state response normally leads the effort with a federal response providing support as required.

5-63. Army commanders will assume a support role to one or more designated agencies. The deploying headquarters will likely be configured as a JTF and interact directly with the designated lead agencies. Disaster operations are normally conducted in four phases: planning, response, recovery, and restoration. The role of the military is most intense in the planning and response phases, decreasing steadily as the operation moves into the recovery and restoration stages.

5-64. Engineers can expect to be involved in planning for support of relief operations with geospatial products and analysis of potential areas to establish life-support areas. Engineers may be called on to provide manpower support or general engineering support from units with unique capabilities such as water purification, temporary shelter, power generation, and firefighting. Engineer commanders and staff will work with the proponent planners to identify requirements and plan engineer applications. USACE and other engineering capabilities of the generating force typically have a prominent role in civil support operations. The ENCOORD may leverage coordination with USACE elements involved in the civil support to add depth to the understanding of the OE and to access reachback support.

5-65. Restoration is the return of normality to the area. The corps would disengage before complete restoration. As civil authorities assume full control of remaining emergency operations and normal services, the corps transfers those responsibilities to replacement agencies and begins redeployment from the area. During restoration, the ENCOORD assists the corps commander in considering items such as—

- Disengagement criteria.
- Redeployment plans while recovery continues in the affected area.

OPERATIONAL CONFIGURATIONS

5-66. The primary mission of a corps headquarters is to serve as a base on which a GCC can build a JTF headquarters. The secondary mission of the corps is to serve as a JFLC headquarters. Both of these missions involve the provision of operational-level C2 and the integration and synchronization of joint, interagency, and multinational actions within a JOA. Serving as an intermediate-level tactical headquarters during the conduct of major combat operations is a tertiary mission for a corps headquarters.

5-67. The modular corps headquarters design promotes joint and multinational operational planning efficiency. It ensures that the corps headquarters has essential C2 capabilities while remaining rapidly deployable to any GCC's AOR to provide C2 for Army, joint, and multinational forces engaged in operations. The basic design includes the following characteristics:

- The headquarters is organized around one main CP and one tactical CP.
- The commander has a mobile command group.
- The corps special troops battalion (STB) provides life support and network support to the headquarters. The corps normally tasks its subordinate units to provide security assets for each command node based on mission variables. Alternatively, security could be provided by multinational, HN, or contracted assets. Regardless of its source, the corps headquarters security elements come under the control of the corps STB commander.

5-68. In every operational configuration, the theater army headquarters retains its responsibilities as ASCC. Therefore the corps will have an ASCC that includes regional expertise and is tailored for the needs of the AOR. This provides the corps with a degree of higher-echelon support in any of its operational configurations and regardless of whether the corps is also functioning as the ARFOR headquarters. While some support or other ADCON responsibilities will be placed upon the corps headquarters, it will function with a more singular focus on the contingency or major operation than the theater army headquarters.

JOINT TASK FORCE

5-69. A corps headquarters provides a base structure on which a JTF headquarters can be built for a smaller-scale contingency without additional initial Army augmentation. Normally, this occurs when the preponderance of forces involved are land units. It does require joint augmentation when assigned this mission. That joint manning may be provided by the GCC's standing joint force headquarters (core element) (SJFHQ[CE]) or by other joint manning, such as a joint manpower exchange program. The theater army normally provides a corps-based JTF headquarters with elements from the theater sustainment command, theater signal command, and other theater-level functional organizations. While acting as a JTF headquarters, the corps headquarters should not also be the ARFOR headquarters. This is because the wide difference in roles and responsibilities between a JTF and an ARFOR headquarters means that two separate staffs are required in all but the most benign circumstances. The corps headquarters will use joint doctrine and procedures when it is acting as a JTF headquarters.

5-70. With minimum joint manning (about 20 other Service officers), the headquarters is capable of initiating operations as a JTF. This includes initiating joint campaign planning, deploying the corps early-entry CP and advance elements to establish initial C2 capabilities in the JOA, initiating shaping operations, and coordinating with HN and multinational partners within the JOA. Figure 5-3 shows a corps configured as a JTF headquarters. The conduct of sustained joint operations may require additional joint personnel. Note the multirole expeditionary sustainment command (ESC) CP with assets for providing support across the JOA. The ESC CP may support both Army and joint forces. In this example, the MEB has been tailored to allow its commander to perform the duties of the joint security area coordinator. However, the corps deputy commanding general is routinely assigned those responsibilities as outlined in JP 3-10.

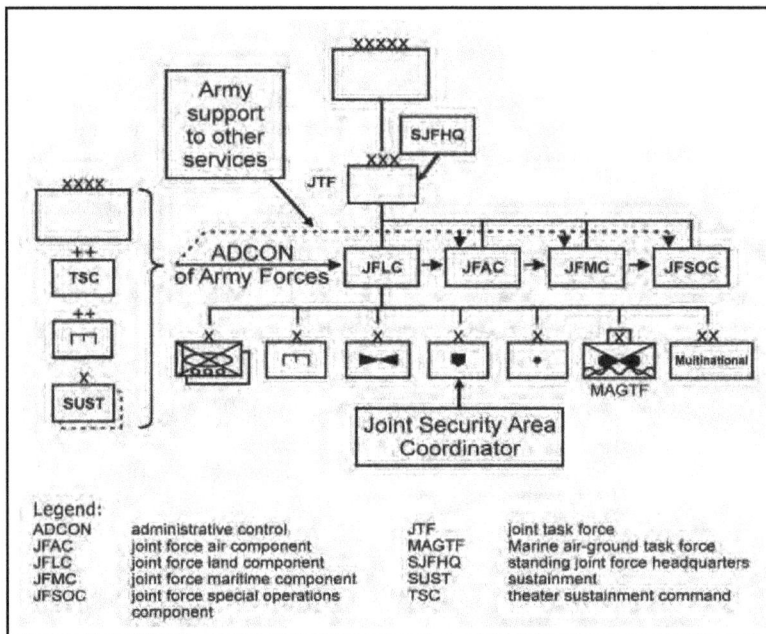

Figure 5-3. Corps headquarters as a joint task force headquarters in a crisis response or limited contingency operation

5-71. Unlike the theater army-formed JTF, the corps configured as a JTF will not require a separate ENCOORD. The corps ENCOORD transitions to become the JTF ENCOORD and will not have additional responsibilities associated with the ARFOR. Similarly, the corps-formed JTF should only require engineer headquarters units to support the JTF—a TEC element or an engineer brigade for the operational C2 of JTF engineer support. The theater army continues its ASCC functions and may require an engineer battalion or brigade to provide C2 for engineer operations supporting those functions. The JTF ENCOORD will also employ an assigned or supporting USACE FFE element to access additional technical and contract construction capabilities.

JOINT FORCE LAND COMPONENT COMMAND

5-72. The corps headquarters is also designed to provide the core headquarters on which a JFLCC or combined force land component headquarters can be built (see figure 5-4). This headquarters can exercise OPCON over land forces in a campaign or major operation. This may include controlling multiple Army, USMC, and multinational division- and brigade-size formations. The composition of the headquarters should roughly reflect the composition of the joint and multinational land forces involved. While acting as a JFLCC headquarters, the corps headquarters will also perform the duties of an ARFOR headquarters. Like the theater army's OCP, the corps will use Army doctrine and procedures but refer to joint doctrine for a list of duties when it is tasked to perform as a JFLCC headquarters.

5-73. In its ARFOR role, the corps headquarters commands all Army forces assigned or attached to the JTF except those Army forces assigned to or attached to the JFLCC USMC or multinational formations. As an Army forces headquarters, the corps headquarters coordinates ADCON support for Army forces within its JOA and provides ASOS and other government agencies, and multinational forces as required by the JFC. An Army forces commander may not have OPCON of all Army forces provided to the JFC; however, the Army forces commander remains responsible for their ADCON.

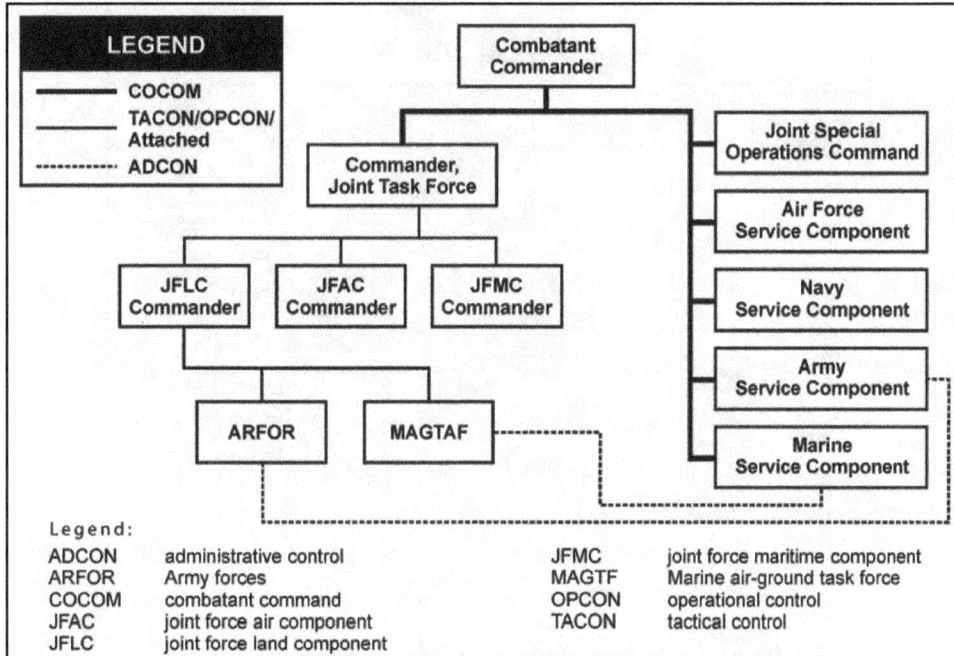

Figure 5-4. Corps headquarters as a joint force land component headquarters

INTERMEDIATE TACTICAL HEADQUARTERS

5-74. Large land forces require an intermediate echelon between the divisions that control BCTs and the theater army serving as the land component command. Other factors requiring an intermediate headquarters may include—

- The mission's complexity.
- Multinational participation.
- Span of control.

5-75. In major combat operations, the corps may be tasked to be an intermediate land tactical headquarters under the command of a JFLCC (see figure 5-5, page 5-18). Complexity, span of command, or multinational considerations may require the use of a second tactical controlling echelon above the brigades. When required, the Army tailors the theater army with a corps headquarters to serve as this intermediate tactical level. As the major combat operation transitions to a protracted stability operation, the corps headquarters may become the joint force headquarters or multinational land component headquarters. When the corps is acting as an intermediate level tactical headquarters, it will employ Army doctrine and procedures. When used as an intermediate tactical headquarters, the corps may also be designated as the Army force headquarters, or ARFOR, with responsibility for ADCON of Army forces.

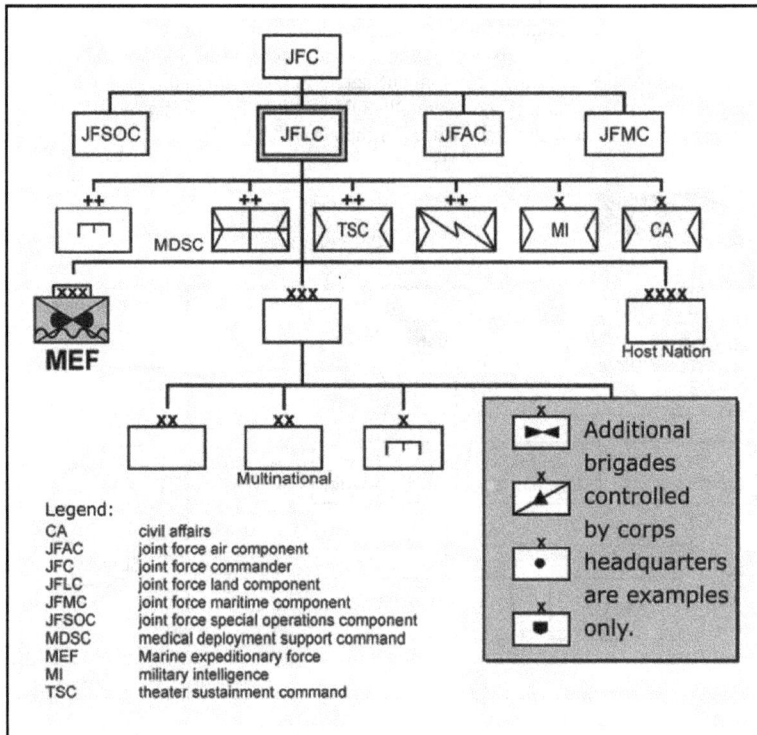

Figure 5-5. Corps headquarters as an intermediate tactical headquarters

5-76. When performing this mission, the headquarters role involves requesting and tailoring of its available division headquarters and modular brigades for land operations in support of the JFC. It assigns a command or support relationship between its available BCTs, supporting brigades to available division headquarters, or the corps commander may choose to retain direct control of selected brigade-size elements. Conduct of battles and engagements is a tactical function exercised through the BCT and supporting brigade headquarters and monitored by division headquarters. The corps headquarters focuses on shaping the future battlefield and setting the conditions that allow the success of subordinate tactical units. This capability relieves the JFLCC or the GCC of the requirement for planning and synchronizing multiple land operations conducted by very large formations (two or more divisions).

Chapter 6

Division Echelon Engineer Operations

...[Y]ou may fly over a land forever; you may bomb it, atomize it, pulverize it and wipe it clean of life—but if you desire to defend it, protect it, and keep it for civilization, you must do this on the ground, the way the Roman legions did, by putting your young men into the mud.

T.R. Fehrenbach, *This Kind of War*

Divisions are the Army's primary tactical warfighting headquarters. Their principal task is directing subordinate brigade operations. The division headquarters structure is designed to exercise C2 over any mix of brigades. This chapter focuses on engineer operations at the division echelon. It describes foundational characteristics and considerations for engineer operations supporting the division. It discusses engineer integration within the operations process conducted by the division headquarters. It examines specific considerations for force tailoring of engineer units and capabilities at the division echelon. It also examines considerations unique to each element of full spectrum operations from the division perspective. Finally, the chapter describes specific engineer considerations for each operational configuration of the division headquarters.

INTEGRATION AT DIVISION ECHELON

6-1.   The division is optimized for tactical control of brigades during land operations. Typically employed within a broader operational design, the division focuses a tailored mix of forces on the tasks and objectives contributing to achieving end state conditions. The division commander arranges forces for engagements and employs combat power in battles. In major combat operations, a division will typically operate along a line of operations or in an AO. Some situations will require the division to shift perspective from primarily tactical to the operational level as well. In smaller-scale contingencies, a division may be configured as JTF or JFLCC and be required to influence the operational design. Similarly, in protracted stability or in civil support operations the division will likely fulfill an operational-level role of shaping conditions for the success of current and future military operations. Division tactical operations are generated from the implications within the operational design and made substantial by the division commander's intent and conduct of the division operations process. In conducting operations, the division synchronizes and integrates warfighting functions primarily from the tactical-level perspective.

DIVISION PERSPECTIVE

6-2.   Operational commanders seek to create the most favorable conditions possible for the employment of divisions. The division meets the needs of joint force commanders for tactical command capable of translating design into concept and decisions into action. It synchronizes forces and warfighting functions in time, space, and purpose—to accomplish missions. The division perspective is substantially shaped by the operational approach (ways) described by theater and is focused on the tactical actions (means) inferred from that approach. As figure 6-1, page 6-2, shows, the division echelon engineer perspective similarly includes a solid operational foundation from which to focus on the detailed tactical-level requirements for a selected operation.

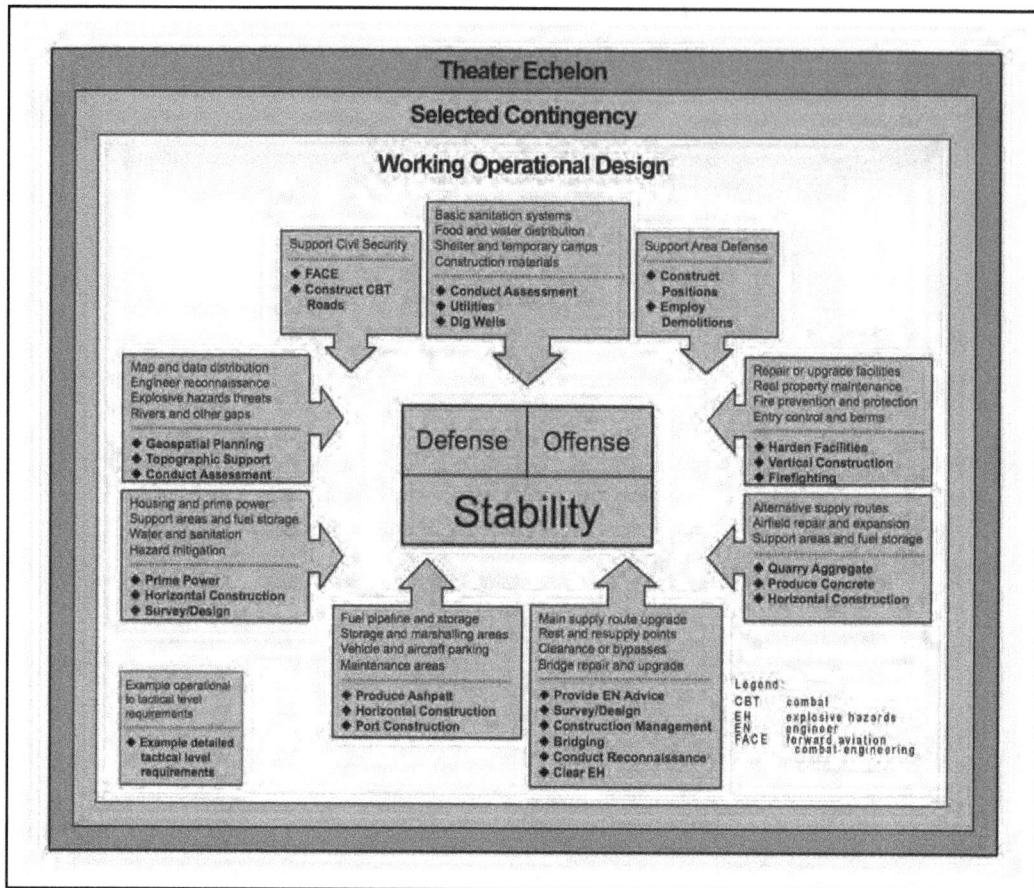

Figure 6-1. Detailed engineer requirements shaped by operational design

6-3. At the division echelon, the ENCOORD and other engineer staff assist in understanding and translating the operational design into a division concept of operations. The division engineer staff analyzes the operation and begins to concentrate on COAs for arranging forces in relation to each other and employing combat power to accomplish the mission. Just as corps echelon engineers validate analysis supporting the operational engineer design, the divisional engineer analysis adds detail or offers new information for operational consideration. Ultimately, as operational-level engineers refine and address requirements at their echelon, the division echelon engineers gain understanding of the operational requirements that must be included in the conduct of division operations. Division echelon engineers concentrate on substantial development of engineering requirements and capabilities necessary to the division concept of operation. The divisional engineer analysis is operationally broad enough to include general and geospatial engineering support not included in the operational design. The analysis is more comprehensive and detailed in considering and shaping combat, general, and geospatial engineering requirements for arranging and employing divisional forces. Figure 6-2 shows how the division echelon engineer integrates tactical engineer actions (shown above as the topmost set of tasks, resting on the foundation from theater and corps echelons in the illustration) through warfighting functions to support the division concept of operations.

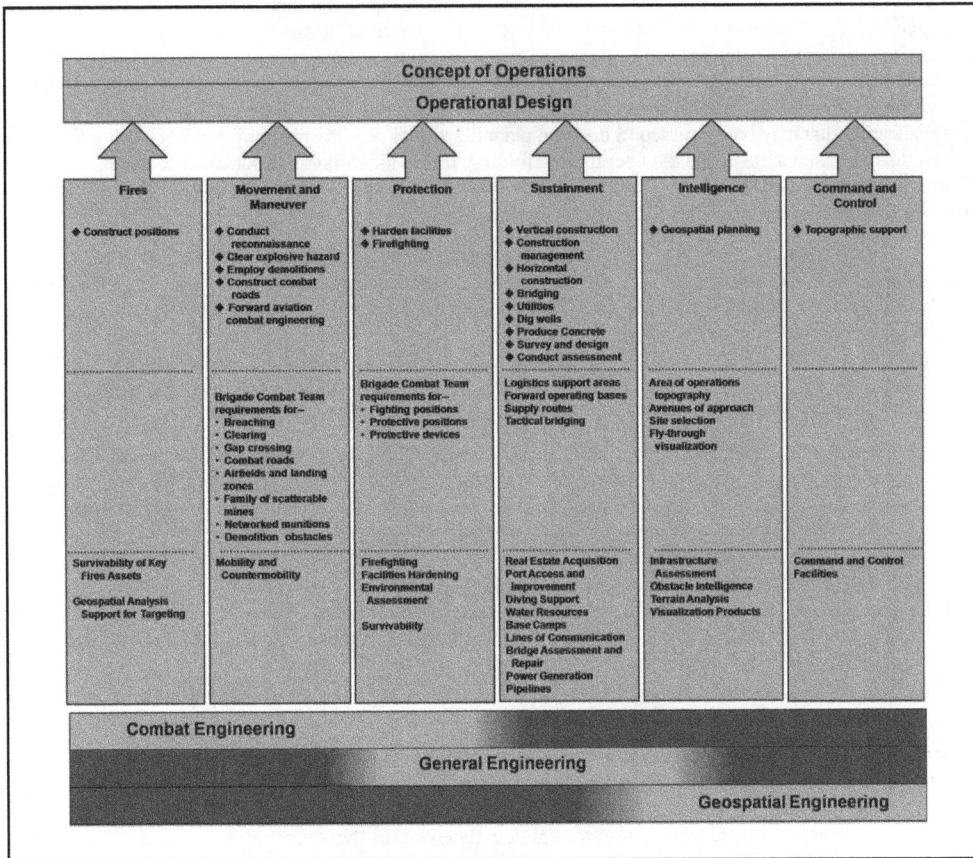

Figure 6-2. Division echelon engineer requirements by function

6-4. As the concept of operations develops, the division engineer staff collaborates with the corps or theater army engineer staff, supporting engineer and multifunctional headquarters, and subordinate echelon engineer staff to refine engineering support from higher echelons and clearly define division echelon engineer actions required. The division engineer staff's concentration on the detailed capabilities and actions required to support division operations adds significant depth to the operational engineer concept. Similarly, engineer and multifunctional unit headquarters identified as divisional forces bring additional capacity for developing engineer support concepts. When subordinate BCTs are identified and available for collaborative planning, divisional engineers gain greater depth through the BCT engineer staff.

6-5. The division ENCOORD's running estimate provides a working compilation of RI primarily focused on the physical environment within the division AO with a comprehensive accounting for engineer units, capabilities, and other resources tailored for the operation. The running estimate is built on input from the corps or theater army engineer's initial assessments and then further developed considering mission variables. The division-level running estimate evolves with the development of the division concept of operations. The RI contained within the division ENCOORD's running estimate logically connects identified challenges and opportunities to either support included in the operational design or to requirements for division-level action. The running estimate can be organized by engineer function and warfighting function, as are the requirements shown in figure 6-2. The running estimate is continuously refined and updated as additional assessments are made, guidance and priorities are refined, and actions are fulfilled. Appendix B provides a tool for use in developing and maintaining the engineer running estimate.

6-6. The theater army tailors the division headquarters to meet mission requirements. Though some degree of refinement of operational-level guidance will be required based on the divisional analysis of the situation, the division engineer and other staff planners enter the operations process with an established operational design. The division-level analysis of the situation based on mission variables enables the division commander's initial understanding. The commander's understanding forms the basis for visualization that may be expressed in division planning guidance. This planning guidance is a reflection of how the commander envisions the operation unfolding. It provides a broad description of when, where, and how the commander intends to employ combat power within the higher commander's intent. Planning guidance also contains priorities for each warfighting function.

6-7. The division engineer may begin shaping engineer operations by understanding and influencing the commander's initial priorities. This effort requires an understanding of operational engineer support responsibilities as defined by the theater echelon and GCC. As division engineer planners validate higher-echelon support, that support is adjusted or refined accordingly. Validation of operational engineer support is an important but peripheral effort to the planning concentration for engineer operations in support of the division concept of operations. Both are guided by the commander's priorities in the planning guidance and provide the engineer planner improved understanding to influence those priorities as necessary.

6-8. For any major operation or contingency, the division will likely face a unique theater or JOA. While the discussion and comparison of levels of development in chapter 4 is applicable, from a division perspective the GCC and theater army will typically expend some effort in mitigating the impact of those differences on the division operation. In many cases, the division will inherit an accessible theater with a developed or developing sustainment base and real estate already acquired or in acquisition. Typically, the division will participate in and continue base development already in progress (see appendix E for more discussion on base development). Standards will likely be established, though some refinement may be necessary. Division echelon engineers consider maintenance of those standards during the conduct of operations and finally the closure or turnover of bases and other facilities as operations conclude. In unique circumstances, division echelon engineers may be presented with the broader assortment of engineering requirements generated by an undeveloped operational area.

6-9. Engineer operations act as one of many key enablers as the division commander employs combat power to achieve objectives. To be effective as enablers, engineer staff must be integrated in the effort to assist the commander in formulating the concept of operations. Engineer functions assist in organizing capabilities that are integrated through warfighting functions in the synchronized application of combat power. The division ENCOORD and other engineer staff integrate their efforts through the operations process to refine operational engineer support and to develop the division concept of engineer operations.

CONDUCT OF OPERATIONS

6-10. In most situations, the division echelon will take on an established operational design from the corps, theater army, or GCC. Division echelon commanders and their staffs must recognize the elements of operational design to help understand that design and translate a supporting concept of operation. The division echelon staff must also recognize the elements of operational design to participate in its refinement (see FM 3-0). Division echelon commanders and their staffs use more objective and task-focused problem solving to develop the detailed division concept of operations. The resulting concept of operations forms the basis for developing the OPLAN or OPORD. During execution, division commanders and staffs assess the situation and adjust current and future actions as the operation unfolds.

6-11. For division-level engineer staff, the cyclic activities of the operations process may be sequential or simultaneous. Though not completely separate or unconnected, activities at division level tend to be more distinct than for higher echelons. They are narrowly focused on tasks and objectives supporting operations within an established operational theme. Division commanders use the operations process to help them decide when and where to make decisions, control operations, and provide command presence. Throughout the operations process, the division staff synchronizes forces and warfighting functions to accomplish missions. The division-level engineer staff synchronizes the application of engineer functions through the warfighting function framework by integrating into the operations process.

Planning Considerations

6-12. In smaller-scale contingencies, a division may be configured as JTF or JFLCC and be required to influence the operational design. At the operational level, a subordinate JFC develops supporting plans, which can include objectives supported by measurable operation-level effects. Joint interdependence requires that division headquarters understand joint doctrine addressing these planning techniques. See chapter 3 of this manual and JP 3-34 when required to participate in joint planning.

6-13. The division echelon engineering effort will require consideration of engineer requirements linked through the warfighting functions to the division concept of operations. Division echelon engineer planners assist in determining specific objectives and detailing the tasks required to achieve those objectives. They use the planning processes, including joint processes when required, and tools described and referenced in chapter 3. They use the commander's intent to develop and refine COAs that contribute to achieving objectives in the AO. They concentrate on supporting the division concept of operations and collaborate to gain depth for their view of the OE and to add to their planning and problem-solving capability. Collaboration extends both to corps or theater army echelon and to the tailored subordinate engineer units and staff.

6-14. The MDMP serves as the primary tool for deliberate planning. Division engineer planners participate along with their staff counterparts in the process to translate the commander's visualization into a specific COA for preparation and execution. Table 3-1, page 3-12, provides some of the engineer planning considerations as they pertain to each step of the MDMP. As the plan develops, engineer planners remain synchronized through warfighting functions as shown in table 4-1, page 4-6.

6-15. Engineer operations will also involve the use of some functionally unique analytic tools to solve construction, design, facilities, and other engineer-specific problems as discussed in chapter 3. As planning proceeds through the MDMP, the engineer relies heavily on the analytic techniques that support design and project management to guide functional problem solving. These techniques demand technical information that may be available from existing assessments or may require additional assessments or surveys. Support available through reachback or through collaborative planning may be used to focus on technical details.

6-16. Aided by engineer staff, the division commander exercises control over engineer forces in the division AO. Staffs contribute their greatest support in providing control and keeping the commander informed. The following are some of the measures employed by the division echelon engineer staff to provide control and keep the commander informed:

● Engineer unit missions and tasks.
● Engineer task organization and command and support relationships.
● Obstacle integration and control measures.

6-17. The role of the division staff involves identifying missions, allocating resources, and synchronizing and controlling engineer actions. In a defense, the engineer running estimate incorporates the obstacle planning process. The division echelon perspective provides a pivotal linkage from obstacle integration coordinated by lower echelons to obstacle control established at higher echelons (see FM 90-7 for specific obstacle synchronization techniques and control measures at tactical planning levels). Divisions, brigades, and task forces plan obstacle zones, belts, and groups, respectively. While in some cases corps may designate obstacle zones, normally obstacle zone planning is initiated by division. Obstacle control measures enable tactical obstacle placement while synchronizing the obstacle effort with future operational plans. The obstacle control measures not only focus obstacle effort on a specified area but can also guide the desired obstacle effect (disrupt, turn, fix, and block). See FM 90-7 for additional discussion of obstacle integration.

6-18. The result of the MDMP is a plan or order that provides subordinates the information they need for execution. Engineer planners provide input to appropriate paragraphs, annexes, and appendixes for either the joint or Army format as described in chapter 3. The division engineer staff continues to collaborate and assist subordinate unit staffs with their planning and coordination.

Preparation Considerations

6-19. Division preparation consists of activities performed by units before execution to improve the division's ability to conduct the operation. Preparation requires staff, unit, and Soldier actions. Mission success depends as much on preparation as planning. Rehearsals help staffs, units, and individuals to better understand their specific role in upcoming operations, practice complicated tasks before execution, and ensure that equipment and weapons function properly. Key preparation activities include—

- Revision and refinement of the plan.
- Rehearsals.
- Task organizing.
- Surveillance and reconnaissance.
- Training.
- Troop movements.
- Preoperation checks and inspections.
- Sustainment preparations.
- Integration of new Soldiers and units.
- Subordinate confirmation backbriefs.

6-20. In many cases, engineer units conduct these preparation activities integrated within the combined arms task organizations required by the operation. Combined arms rehearsals are critical to the success of a breaching, clearing, or gap-crossing operation. Similarly, engineer reconnaissance teams can be employed as integrated elements in a combined arms reconnaissance formation. In every case, engineer reconnaissance efforts must be integrated within the intelligence, surveillance, and reconnaissance (ISR) plan. At the division echelon, some specific engineer preparation considerations may include—

- Integrated engineer participation in all combined arms planning, backbriefs, and rehearsals before the operation. Construction of mock-up complex obstacle systems and other terrain features that may be encountered, allowing integrated, combined arms, breaching rehearsals.
- Provided analysis and terrain products for geospatial engineering support of routes that assist planners in the IPB process. Engineer planners may focus on these products to help identify obstacle and bypass locations or other RI in the physical environment.
- Completed direct obstacle zones and reserve demolition obstacles. Deconflicted subordinate obstacle and other engineer actions to ensure mutual support and access for division forces.
- Staged engineer units in forward positions with other combined arms units to enable execution at the desired tempo.
- Engineer participation with route reconnaissance forces ensuring that follow-on engineer forces are task-organized to meet the mobility requirements needed to keep the maneuver force moving.
- Pre-positioned bridge stocks and obstacle-breaching material to enable effective employment.
- Prepared and loaded materials and munitions to enable effective employment during the operation.
- Constructed forward logistics bases and MSRs, when feasible, to enable uninterrupted sustainment during the operation.

6-21. The division engineer may be required to apply some attention during preparation activities to review and refine operational-level engineer support. From the operational perspective, construction activities, real estate management, and facilities engineering are predominant during preparation. Operational engineer preparations include addressing requirements for facilities and may include the establishment of working groups, cells, or boards as described in chapter 3 to solve problems and coordinate actions. See the discussion of operational-level preparation in chapters 4 and 5.

Execution Considerations

6-22. During execution, commander's visualization helps commanders determine if, when, and what to decide. Commanders and their staffs continuously assess the progress of operations toward the envisioned end state and modify orders as required to accomplish the mission. Situational understanding forms the basis of commander's visualization.

6-23. Execution involves monitoring the situation, assessing the operation, and adjusting the order as needed. Throughout execution, commanders continuously assess the operation's progress based on information from the COP, running estimates, and assessments from subordinate commanders. When the situation varies from the assumptions the order was based on, commanders direct adjustments to exploit opportunities and counter threats. The staff, both the engineer unit commander's staff and the combined arms commander's engineer staff, assists the commander in execution through the integrating processes and continuing activities during execution (see FM 3-0). In addition, commanders, assisted by the staff, perform the following activities specific to execution:

- Focus assets on the decisive operation.
- Adjust CCIR based on the situation.
- Adjust control measures.
- Manage movement and positioning of supporting units.
- Adjust unit missions and task as necessary.
- Modify the concept of operations as required.
- Position or relocate committed, supporting, and reserve units.

6-24. As with preparation, engineer forces will conduct additional construction or other technically related activities during execution of the specific mission. These activities include—

- Implementation and maintenance of a construction safety program.
- Implementation and enforcement of quality controls.
- Periodic design and construction reviews.
- Preparation of as-built drawings.
- Response to construction contingencies.
- Geospatial database replication and synchronization.

6-25. The division engineer may be required to apply some attention, including during preparation activities, to the further refinement of operational-level engineer support. From the operational perspective, construction supporting operational sustainment, considerations for the establishment of ISBs and FOBs, and ADC predominate during execution. See the discussion of operational-level execution in chapters 4 and 5.

Assessment Considerations

6-26. The division echelon assessment will include tactical detail down to subordinate BCT and battalion levels. These assessments inform higher-echelon operational assessments. The division staff analyzes the situation in terms of mission variables to understand changes in objectives and tasks and maintain their staff running estimates. They continuously assess the effects of new information on the conduct of the operation; they update their staff running estimates and determine if adjustment decisions are required.

6-27. Engineer capabilities may be applied to add technical detail to the commander's assessment. Engineer assessment and survey teams gather technically focused information on the physical environment, infrastructure, or other physical aspects of the AO. RI gathered adds to the depth of the commander's understanding and can provide a technical basis for MOPs or MOEs. Engineer forces also conduct a variety of construction and other technical assessment activities focused on technical aspects of the support provided. General engineering activities are typically evaluated for adequacy to the requirements and conformance to quality standards.

FORCE TAILORING

6-28. Operational planning results in a division echelon force that is tailored for current and anticipated missions, flexible to changing circumstances, and fits the constraints of time and lift capabilities. Identified and anticipated requirements, coupled with analysis of the mission variables by higher echelons, influence the initial tailoring of the division force. Refinements at the division level are narrowly focused on analysis bounded by the assigned mission and AO. Because the demands of any given operation vary, there is no set engineer force structure. A building-block approach that is based on need is used to tailor the force. Refer to appendix F for examples of tailored division engineer forces based on various situations.

6-29. Higher echelons achieve combined arms capabilities by tailoring and task-organizing different types of brigades and battalions under corps or division headquarters. Divisions can typically control up to six BCTs in major combat operations. They can control more BCTs in protracted stability operations. A division force package may include any mix of heavy, infantry, and Stryker BCTs. In addition to BCTs, each division controls a tailored array of modular support brigades and functional brigades. In some operations, divisions may control multiple support brigades of the same type. However, for major combat operations, divisions should have at least one of each type of support brigade OPCON or attached (except for sustainment brigades, which provide general or direct support to a division or corps). They may also control functional groups, battalions, or separate companies; however, these are normally task-organized to a brigade.

6-30. The tailored engineer force supporting the division echelon will in most cases result from a collaborative effort among division, corps and theater army engineer planners; their supported GCC engineer staff; elements at DA and DOD; supporting Army and joint force providers (including the TEC and USACE); and the input from identified subordinate echelon units. The challenge is to generate the engineer force tailored to identified and anticipated requirements, time, lift, and other constraints. In many cases, leveraging reachback and other engineer capabilities mitigates the impact of these constraints (see figure 4-4, page 4-11).

COMMAND AND CONTROL OF ENGINEER FORCES

6-31. A significant determination included in the force generation effort is timing and level for deployment of engineer headquarters. Divisions are not fixed formations. They do not have organic engineer units and do not establish habitual associations with echelon-specific engineer headquarters units. Typically, the division will be tailored with at least one MEB, which provides C2 of engineer operations in cases where engineer support is integral to the mission of the MEB. The MEB's mission will likely be associated with owning or controlling terrain. Additionally, the engineer brigade can be tailored, if necessary, as a division echelon engineer headquarters. In most cases, the addition of an engineer brigade headquarters would be in addition to an allocated MEB and as a result of analysis of mission variables indicating the division would require the increased C2 capability for engineer functional missions. The primary consideration for placing a functional engineer brigade at division level is whether the division has the capability to integrate and synchronize engineer capabilities across the entire division. A prime example is in stability operations, in which the MEB within a division is given an AO to control, limiting its ability to also control engineer operations. The engineer brigade headquarters incorporates training focused on support to division echelon operations. For major combat operations, the division echelon will typically require at least one MEB and the early or phased deployment of an engineer brigade headquarters. Additional engineer brigades and MEBs may be required in support of the division for stability or civil support operations. Most operations or contingencies requiring the deployment of the division headquarters in one of its configurations will also require appropriate engineer headquarters in support of subordinate BCTs (see FM 3-34.22 for discussion of engineer operations in support of the BCT and its subordinate elements). Table 6-1 provides a comparison of C2 capabilities, span, and allocation for the MEB and the engineer brigade (see appendix A for additional unit reference information).

Table 6-1. Comparison of MEB and engineer brigade C2

	MEB	Engineer Brigade
Capabilities	Provides command and control for multifunctional operations, including maneuver support, support area, consequence management, and stability operations. Provides a tactical command post as an early-entry command post if required. Integrates and synchronizes engineer capability within its own area of operation (if assigned control of an area of operation).	Provides command and control for engineer operations, including combat, general, and geospatial engineering missions. Provides supervision for contract construction. Provides two scalable, deployable command posts as required. Serves, with augmentation, as a joint engineer headquarters and may be the senior engineer headquarters deployed in a joint operations area if full theater engineer command deployment is not required. Integrates and synchronizes engineer capability across the entire supported force (does not control an area of operation without significant augmentation).
Span of C2	Conducts multifunctional missions with a mix of modular units from detachments to battalions. Requires a subordinate engineer battalion headquarters for two or more subordinate engineer modules. Typically will not be task-organized with more than two subordinate engineer battalion headquarters.	Conducts engineer missions with two to five task-organized engineer battalions and other force pool units.
Allocation	One maneuver enhancement brigade per division conducting major combat or contingency operations. As required, in support of higher-echelon, joint, and multinational forces.	One engineer brigade headquarters per 2-5 engineer battalions. Mission-tailored to support each corps conducting major combat or contingency operations. May also be tailored in support of divisions when the functional nature of engineer missions calls for brigade-level command and control capability.

6-32. Allocated engineer brigade and MEB commanders will provide significant advice to the division commander and C2 for assigned engineer forces. The division ENCOORD must establish and maintain a collaborative relationship with the engineer brigade and MEB commanders and their headquarters to ensure a coordinated engineer effort. Though the engineer brigade headquarters does not possess an integral capability to augment division engineer staff sections, they will typically provide a significant contribution for the ENCOORD's conduct of engineer operations. They will also, depending on task organization and other mission variables, provide C2 for much of the tailored division engineer force conducting operations.

6-33. The MEB, one of the multifunctional brigades, is designed as a headquarters to provide C2 for primarily those units providing engineer, EOD (company), MP, AMD, CBRN, and signal capabilities. The number of MEBs placed under the control of a division headquarters depends on analysis of the mission variables. The MEB is designed to receive and control forces to provide protection and mobility to prevent or mitigate the effects of hostile action against divisional forces. Their mission is to preserve freedom of maneuver for operational and tactical commanders by controlling terrain and facilities, and by preventing or mitigating hostile actions against the protected force. An MEB is a combined arms organization rather than a functional brigade that is task-organized based on mission requirements. It has a combined arms staff and C2 capabilities that suit it for a variety of missions. They typically control combinations of several different types of battalions and separate companies, such as CBRN, CA, engineer, EOD (company), MP and, in selected situations, AMD and a TCF. The MEB has the ability to control an AO. However, once assigned an AO, its ability to synchronize engineer effort across the force is greatly reduced.

6-34. One or more engineer brigades is required in the division whenever the number of engineer units or the functional nature of engineer missions calls for a functional engineer brigade-level C2 capability. The brigade's span of control exceeds the engineer functional C2 capability of the multifunctional MEB. Examples of when the engineer brigade would be required are division operations involving large construction requirements (airfield, port, or base camp development), significant reconstruction efforts in urban terrain supporting stability operations, a division AO that exceeds the capability of the MEB's span of control capability, or operations requiring HN engineer training to build technical capacity. Once deployed, engineer brigades integrate and synchronize engineer capability across the division AO and become the focal point for apportioning and allocating mission-tailored engineer forces within the AO. The engineer brigade is capable of supporting the division configured as a JTF or component command and providing C2 to all Service engineers and contracted engineering within an operational area. The engineer brigade has the capability to simultaneously provide two deployable CPs with engineer functional staff expertise to provide C2 as required. It provides engineer-specific technical planning, design, and quality assurance and quality control during 24-hour operations.

FIELD FORCE ENGINEERING

6-35. In many situations a division headquarters may receive support through USACE FFE for an appropriately tailored FEST. The division ENCOORD collaborates with the corps and theater army ENCOORD, the theater USACE LNO, and the TEC to determine the appropriate level of support.

6-36. USACE support provides for technical and contract engineering support, integrating its organic capabilities with those of other Services and other sources of engineering-related reachback support. USACE may have assets directly integrated into the military C2 structure and linked to a TEC or senior engineer headquarters or already be operating under contract in-theater. Whether providing construction contract and design support in the AO or outside of the contingency area, USACE can obtain necessary data, research, and specialized expertise not present in-theater through tele-engineering and other reachback capabilities.

6-37. USACE expertise may support division-level engineer planning and operations and can leverage reachback to technical subject matter experts in districts, divisions, labs and centers of expertise, other Services, and private industry in its role as part of the generating force. Teams can rapidly deploy to meet requirements for engineering assessments and analyses in support of the full array of engineer operations. The two types of FESTs provide support to primarily general engineering efforts through forward-deployed engineer elements that can communicate with TeleEngineering Kits and reachback to technical experts within USACE. EFDs from the TECs provide a wide variety of services to forward-deployed forces in a public works capacity. Infrastructure assessment and base development teams are nondeployable capabilities available through reachback support.

ENGINEER AND MULTIFUNCTIONAL FORCES

6-38. The units that make up the architecture higher-echelon engineer force are diverse with technical skill orientation ranging from highly specialized to multifunctional and sourcing that includes Army, joint, and multinational force providers. Corps and higher-echelon engineer planners typically consider in detail general engineering forces and capabilities based on operational requirements linked to the movement and maneuver, sustainment, and protection warfighting functions. These include construction requirements and a variety of specialized engineering requirements. Division engineer planners are challenged to comprehensively identify combat, general and geospatial engineering requirements linked to the movement and maneuver, sustainment, and protection warfighting functions for the division and its subordinate forces.

6-39. Division engineer planners may refine the tailored force required to support operational-level priorities but focus on developing a more substantial understanding of the tailored force required to support lower echelons. Geospatial engineering support, though organic at division echelon and each BCT, may generate requirements for augmentation. Corps or higher echelons may provide some general engineering support for requirements linked to the movement and maneuver, sustainment, and protection warfighting functions within the division AO, but this may need augmentation for division-identified priorities. General engineering support as augmentation to combat engineering capabilities at lower echelons must also be considered. Finally, combat engineering requirements for each BCT and major tactical element must be considered. Each BCT will include an organic engineer company, but with only minimal M/CM/S support capabilities. Augmentation must typically be provided in the form of additional combat and general engineering capabilities and appropriate engineer and multifunctional headquarters elements. The type and level of augmenting capabilities will likely receive a more concentrated analysis at division echelon than applied in the higher-echelon review.

6-40. When available for collaborative planning, subordinate echelon headquarters provide invaluable input not only for their assigned mission requirements but also for some operational-level requirements that may have been overlooked by the higher echelon. Subordinate echelon engineer and multifunctional units and the engineer staff supporting BCTs and other headquarters develop an understanding through a more concentrated analysis of the situation. The resulting view adds depth to the understanding of engineer forces required for their support.

6-41. The tailored engineer force supporting the division echelon may include joint and multinational engineer formations. Planners mesh Service capabilities with joint and multinational formations and interagency and NGOs. Division engineer planners give significant consideration to the joint engineer capabilities. Whenever feasible, they align joint forces with optimum capabilities. For example, Navy engineer units routinely train to support Marine forces with general engineering capabilities. The optimal alignment for general engineering in support of subordinate Marine forces will typically be Navy engineer units. Army engineers retain capability to support Marine forces but will be a secondary option to available Navy units. Division engineer planners collaborate with the corps, theater army, and joint force providers to effectively align joint capabilities with requirements. Significant consideration is also given to the tactical limitations for joint engineer forces.

OTHER CAPABILITIES

6-42. With appropriate joint augmentation, a division can be the JTF or land component command headquarters for small contingencies. For sustained operations in this role, a division is augmented according to an appropriate JMD. Other situations may generate requirements for individual augmentation within the tailored division headquarters. Similarly, the situation may require tailoring of individual augmentees for a provisional headquarters or for provisional teams. The GCC supports subordinate joint force requirements for joint individual augmentees as available through its standing joint force headquarters. As requirements exceed the GCC capabilities, they are passed to joint force providers.

6-43. As discussed in chapter 4, commanders may use an operational needs statement to document an urgent need for a material solution to correct a deficiency or to improve a capability that impacts on mission accomplishment. The division echelon engineer staff will likely be involved in the initial identification and documentation of such needs and the review and processing of statements through the established ASCC procedures. Examples of engineer-related operational needs may include bridging or construction equipment, EH clearance improvements, and other nonstandard capabilities (see AR 71-9 for information on processing operational needs statements).

6-44. Division echelon engineers must also understand contingency construction authorities and associated funding. These authorities provide the basis for legal spending to meet construction requirements and activities in support of contingency operations. Appendix D provides an introduction to contingency authorities and funding. However, the information in the appendix is subject to change due to changes in legislation, policy, or regulation. EAB engineer staff collaborates and consults with legal and financial management personnel for the latest definitive guidance.

OPERATIONAL ELEMENTS

6-45. Divisions are optimized for tactical control of brigades during full spectrum operations. The division's principal task is directing its subordinate brigades that are tailored for any combination of offensive, defensive, and stability or civil support operations. It is typically at the division echelon where these operational elements are combined and conducted simultaneously. During major combat operations, a division may be attacking in one area, defending in another, and focusing on stability tasks in a third. Simultaneous combinations are also present in operational themes dominated by stability or (in some cases) civil support. While the division echelon retains a perspective on operational engineering efforts, the primary focus is on providing tactical control of the engineer operations supporting its brigades.

6-46. The division echelon engineer considers the implications of distinct operational elements on the arrangement of forces and employment of combat power. Engineer support provided to a BCT is focused on maneuver at the tactical level. The engineer organizations organic to the BCT are optimized to perform combat engineering (primarily mobility with limited capabilities in countermobility and survivability) tasks along with geospatial engineering support provided by the organic terrain teams. Additional engineering support (combat and general engineering) comes from modular engineer organizations task-organized to the BCTs or providing support from EAB organizations. General engineering at this echelon focuses primarily on reinforcing the combat engineering capabilities and supporting the sustainment of BCT operations. Engineer operations conducted below the division echelon are significantly influenced by the tactical focus of the operational element they support. These distinct engineer operations supporting offensive, defensive, and stability or civil support operational elements are combined and conducted simultaneously at the division level.

6-47. The division echelon engineer's consideration includes the arrangement of multifunctional forces and employment of their combat power. MEB operations contribute significant combat power, both lethal and nonlethal in nature, to all the components of full spectrum operations (see FM 3-90.31 for additional discussion on MEB operations). Based on an analysis of the mission variables, the MEB will be task-organized with additional modular capabilities to meet mission requirements. The MEB conducts only very limited offensive and defensive operations as a brigade but typically supports other organizations in performing them. Force-tailored MEB capabilities can provide critical nonlethal capabilities to conduct or support stability or civil support operations.

OFFENSIVE OPERATIONS

6-48. In major combat operations, a division will typically operate along a line of operations or in an AO. In combat operations, the offense is the decisive element of full spectrum operations. The offensive operation is the division's primary means of gaining and maintaining the initiative. Offensive operations aim at defeating, destroying, or neutralizing the enemy. A commander may conduct offensive operations to deprive the enemy of resources, seize decisive terrain, develop intelligence, hold an enemy in position, or facilitate other friendly operations. Maneuver commanders sustain the initiative by committing their forces aggressively against enemy weaknesses; attacks are force- or terrain-oriented and facilitate the defeat of the enemy or the continuation of the attack. Surprise, concentration, audacity, and tempo characterize successful offensive operations, as explained below:

- Factors that contribute to surprise include the tempo and intensity in executing the attack plan and employing unexpected factors, such as selecting a less-than-optimal COA, varying operational tactics and methods, conducting deception operations, and ensuring operations security. An enhanced COP and terrain visualization enable engineer commanders to achieve surprise because they better understand enemy defensive preparation. Engineers achieve surprise through obstacle reduction and the use of situational obstacles. They enable surprise by rapidly overcoming obstacles, thus increasing the force tempo.
- Concentration requires careful prior coordination within the combined arms team and with other Services and partners as required. Engineers consider concentration in planning by integrating geospatial products and templating threat obstacles and hazards. This effort is further enhanced with the employment of engineer reconnaissance that can provide the necessary OBSTINTEL and other technical information essential for detailed planning. This allows the maneuver force and the engineers that support them to concentrate reduction assets and overcome obstacles or other hazards as part of the maneuver unit breaching plan.
- Engineers operating in a decentralized role and who comprehend the commander's intent can enable the commander to see the OE and anticipate future operations. With enhanced situational understanding, commanders can be more audacious.
- Engineer speed and flexibility are crucial to the attack. Rapid mobility operations by engineers ensure the maneuver force tempo. The ability to quickly reduce, mark, and guide the supported maneuver unit through an obstacle is the engineer's hallmark.

6-49. Engineer operations in support of offensive operations focus on enabling movement and maneuver. A significant consideration for the division echelon is ensuring that subordinate BCTs conducting offensive operations are provided adequate additional combat engineering capabilities to enable the maneuver commander's freedom of action. Required combat engineering augmentation is typically task-organized in command relationships to provide the gaining commander with maximum flexibility to employ the assets.

6-50. Engineer support at division echelon for offensive operations also considers the selected forms of offensive maneuver—the envelopment, turning movement, penetration, infiltration, and frontal attack. Executing the forms of maneuver translates into four types of offensive operations at the tactical level: the movement to contact, attack, exploitation, and the pursuit. See FM 3-90 for an in-depth discussion of these forms and types of offensive maneuver. Table 6-2 provides a summary of engineer considerations for each type of offensive operation. See FM 3-34.22 for a more detailed discussion.

Table 6-2. Engineer considerations in offensive operations

Type of Operation or Form of Maneuver	Engineer Consideration
Movement to contact	Priority for combat engineer support is typically to mobility, though it may rapidly shift to countermobility in anticipation of an enemy attack. The task organization of engineers must balance task-organizing mobility capabilities with the lead element to optimize response time and tempo without increasing the risk to the mobility of the main body or limiting the ability to mass breaching assets against complex obstacles.
Attacks	The employment of engineer reconnaissance as part of the intelligence, surveillance, and reconnaissance effort helps generate obstacle intelligence that provides the necessary detailed picture of the enemy situation. If breaching operations are anticipated, the breach organization is established based on detailed reverse planning. Engineer priority of effort is toward mobility with priority of support to the main effort. Countermobility effort, primarily through the employment of situational obstacles, is initially directed at supporting the isolation and fixing of enemy forces, and to protecting the flanks. Upon seizure of the objective, and depending on the follow-on mission, engineers are prepared to conduct countermobility and survivability operations in support of a defense, while mobility operations center on clearing obstacles or improving lanes to support friendly movement.
Exploitation	Engineers support an exploitation by breaching obstacles to facilitate the maneuver of ground forces, keeping supply routes open, and emplacing situational obstacles to protect the flanks.
Pursuits	The direct-pressure and encircling forces require engineers to be forward in movement formations to quickly breach any obstacles that cannot be bypassed to ensure unimpeded movement. Engineers also conduct countermobility and survivability tasks in support of the encircling force.

6-51. Though the forms of offensive maneuver and the types of offensive operations have different intentions, the planning phase must always begin with predicting the adversary's intent through a thorough understanding of the threat, threat engineer capabilities, and how the terrain will affect operations. Geospatial products and information become the foundation and common reference for planning. Engineer planning tends to focus on mobility support and will likely include a robust reconnaissance effort. Since engineer units will tend to have command relationships to maneuver commanders conducting offensive operations, parallel planning between division and subordinate echelons is vital in allowing engineer units to position critical assets and to establish linkup and task-organize into their supported units. A significantly greater degree of planning centralized at the division echelon is required when operations will require division-level control of maneuvering brigade-level forces such as a breaching operation or a gap crossing.

DEFENSIVE OPERATIONS

6-52. Defensive operations are a prelude to the offense. Defense plans should not be designed simply to resist enemy attack. Rather, they should aim at reverting to the offense and decisively defeating the enemy. Defensive operations defeat an enemy attack, buy time, economize forces, or develop conditions favorable for offensive operations. Engineer focus is on attacking the enemy's ability to influence operating areas (countermobility through combined arms obstacle integration and survivability of the defending force) and on assuring mobility for friendly repositioning or counterattacking forces.

6-53. The defending force arrives first on the battlefield and, with the help of engineers, shapes the battlefield to its advantage. Based on the higher commander's intent, maneuver commanders—along with their fire support officer and engineer—site tactical obstacles to enhance the effects of direct and indirect fires on the enemy. Engineers provide technical expertise and advice to the commander on tactical obstacle emplacement. Fortifications allow fires from positions that best disrupt and destroy the attacker. Because of defending force survivability, the defender can postpone the commitment of major forces until the attack develops and then strike the extended enemy over selected, prepared terrain.

6-54. Preparation, security, disruption, massed effects, and flexibility characterize successful defensive operations (see FM 3-90). Defensive operations have a distinct preparation phase that is vital to setting the conditions for combat and giving the defender the edge against an attacker. The mission of the ENCOORD and engineer commanders is to plan and execute engineer efforts that enhance the defending unit's ability to combine fires, obstacles, and maneuver to destroy an attacking enemy. Success of engineers in preparation for defensive operations depends largely on the ability of the division echelon engineer to conduct integrated planning with the division staff and parallel planning with supporting and subordinate engineer units. The division echelon engineer uses parallel planning to disseminate information and intent needed to foster early planning and the preparation efforts required at subordinate levels. The division scheme of engineer operations, task organization, obstacle control, survivability guidance, and allocation of resources (barrier materials, munitions, and construction equipment) enables and focuses subordinate unit engineer efforts. With the information provided, subordinate units can anticipate limitations of allocated capabilities and prioritize efforts and resources to mitigate the limitations.

6-55. A significant consideration for the division echelon is ensuring that subordinate BCTs conducting defensive operations are provided adequate additional combat and general engineering capabilities to meet requirements. The division echelon must balance the availability of combat engineering and horizontal construction-oriented general engineering capabilities against extensive requirements in support of the protection and movement and maneuver warfighting functions. Typically, these assets are task-organized in support relationships to optimize their availability. An exception is that some general engineering units may be task-organized in a command relationship to a combat engineering or an engineer headquarters unit to facilitate their integration into the combined arms operation.

6-56. Defending forces await the enemy's attack and counter it. Waiting for the attack is not a passive activity. Commanders conduct aggressive ISR and security operations to find enemy forces and deny them information. Successful defenses are aggressive. Commanders use all available means to disrupt enemy forces. They disrupt attackers and isolate them from mutual support to defeat them in detail. Defenders seek to increase their freedom of maneuver while denying it to attackers. Commanders use combined arms and joint capabilities to attack enemy vulnerabilities and seize the initiative.

6-57. The three types of defensive operations are mobile defense, area defense, and retrograde operations (see FM 3-34.22 for a more detailed discussion). These three types have significantly different concepts and must be dealt with differently during planning and execution, as explained below:

- **Mobile defense.** Engineer support to a mobile defense focuses on using obstacles to attack enemy maneuver and providing mobility to the striking force and reserve. The majority of the countermobility and survivability assets support the fixing force, while the majority of the mobility assets support the striking force. Obstacle control coordinated at division echelon is directed at the enemy's most likely COA rather than the terrain and may be restrictive to assure the mobility of the striking force. Situational obstacles are advantageous in the mobile defense by allowing the commander to exploit enemy vulnerabilities, exploit success, separate follow-on forces, and provide flank protection.

- **Area defense.** In an area defense, the focus of the engineer effort is on providing the maneuver commander with the ability to hold terrain while enabling maneuver units to concentrate fires from static positions. Engineers help to identify key and decisive terrain that supports the commander's concept of the operation with a focus on where the commander wants to kill the enemy. During obstacle planning, obstacle control measures are designed to give maximum flexibility to subordinate units, while focusing the tactical obstacle effort on terrain retention. The ENCOORD must advise the maneuver commander of the resource requirements of each subordinate unit based on its assigned essential M/CM/S and other engineering tasks. The division echelon must balance these engineer resource requirements.

- **Retrograde operations.** Mobility and countermobility operations are normally the focus of engineer support to retrograde operations. The actual priority of effort depends on whether or not the unit is in contact with the enemy. The underlying purpose of engineer support to retrograde operations is twofold. First, the mobility of the force must be maintained, regardless of the type of retrograde operation being conducted. Mobility operations focus on maintaining the ability of the force in contact to disengage while preserving the main body freedom of maneuver. Second, the force must be protected because it is particularly vulnerable to enemy actions during retrograde operations. Consequently, retrograde operations are normally conducted under limited visibility conditions. Engineers support units left in contact and extend the time available to the commander by reducing enemy mobility through obstacles, fires, and terrain optimization.

STABILITY OPERATIONS

6-58. Stability operations are part of full spectrum operations. They are intended to promote and protect U.S. interests by influencing the military, political, and information variables of the OE through a combination of peacetime developmental, cooperative activities, and coercive actions in response to crisis. The focus for most stability operations is on sustaining the outcome achieved from combat operations to prevent the threat or the conditions for a threat to return and realize strategic results. Army forces perform the following five primary stability tasks:

- **Civil security.** Protecting the populace from external and internal threats.

- **Civil control.** Regulating the behavior and activity of individuals and groups. Control limits the population's activity to allow for the provision of security and essential services. A curfew is an example of civil control.

- **Essential services.** Restoring emergency lifesaving medical care, veterinary service, prevention of epidemic disease, food and water, emergency shelter from the elements, and basic sanitation (sewage and garbage disposal). This is an area that typically receives significant engineer focus.

- **Support to governance.** Providing societal control functions that include regulation of public activity, rule of law, taxation, maintenance of security, control and essential services, and normalizing means of succession of power.

- **Support to economic and infrastructure development.** Providing direct and indirect military assistance to local, regional, and national entities to provide an indigenous capacity and capability for continued economic and infrastructure development.

6-59. Stability operations tend to be of a longer duration compared to the other full spectrum operations. While combat engineer route clearance and other close support capabilities may be critical tasks applied through the movement and maneuver warfighting function, a larger portion of the engineer requirements within BCT and MEB AOs will likely be met with significant general engineering and other specialized engineer capabilities. MEBs controlling an AO in stability operations will likely have the same mission as BCTs but within more permissive conditions. In these cases, MEBs will become focused on their own AO, creating the need to consider a functional engineer brigade to provide synchronization for engineer operations across the division. The general engineering level of effort may be relatively high at the onset or during transition from combat operations. This level will gradually decrease as the operation matures, but stability operations typically require a much higher level of technical engineer expertise than during combat operations. The division echelon must coordinate the simultaneous execution of these engineer efforts throughout the depth of the AO and among the subordinate brigades. When the required engineer augmentation is unavailable, the ENCOORD must rely on contracted engineering support, reachback, or collaborative planning with other engineer elements for the necessary technical support to provide the required engineer capabilities. As the operation matures, the general engineering effort may transfer to civilian contractors such as those that operate under LOGCAP. Engineer missions tend to focus on the long-term sustainment of the force. Likely missions include the following:

- Construction of base camps and force beddown facilities.
- Survivability and other protection support.
- Robust support area facilities.
- Infrastructure support.
- Reliable power generation and distribution facilities.
- LOC construction, maintenance, and repair.

6-60. Stability operations involve both coercive and constructive military actions. They are designed to establish a safe and secure environment and facilitate reconciliation among local or regional adversaries. In addition to the support provided to the military force, a significant engineer effort is focused on infrastructure repair and restoration to reconstruct or establish services that support the population. Given the nature of stability operations, the risks associated with environmental hazards may have a greater importance and impact in stability operations than in offensive or defensive operations. Analysis of mission variables focuses on different aspects of the terrain and friendly and threat capabilities. Terrain products continue to have a great deal of importance, but political and cultural considerations become more important than in a strictly combat terrain analysis. Terrain analysts will work with the intelligence staff to develop usable products for the commander to reflect this information if it is available. When analyzing the troops available, the ENCOORD has an increased interest in HN, third-party NGOs, contract or other multinational forces involved with engineering capabilities. Increased interaction with these other parties requires engineers to address interoperability, common standards, and mutual agreements. Engineer planners must also consider that military engineer units employed will be operating among civilians or in conjunction with NGOs and other international organizations.

6-61. The ENCOORD and supporting engineer unit commander will likely have a requirement to integrate the activities of general and more specialized engineer capabilities assessments, engineering services, and emergency repairs) within the AO. Typically these assets are task-organized in support relationships to optimize their availability. In a major reconstruction effort, additional engineer brigades could be task-organized to the division. These units are equipped and manned to fulfill design, construction management, and C2 requirements needed to accomplish these missions, which likely will include the following:

- Base camp construction and power generation.
- Emergency restoration of critical public services and facilities.
- Infrastructure reconnaissance, technical assistance, and damage assessment.
- Emergency demolition.
- Debris or route clearing operations.
- Construction and repair of expedient (temporary) roads and trails.
- FACE, to include the repair of paved, asphalt, and concrete runways and airfields.
- Installation of assets that prevent foreign object damage to rotary-wing aircraft.
- Construction of temporary bridging.
- Conducting ADC missions that support the mobility of the civil support force.
- Ensuring access to the region through the construction and upgrade of ports, airfields, and facilities.

6-62. Stability operations typically fall into ten broad types that are neither discrete nor mutually exclusive. For example, a force engaged in a peace operation may also find itself conducting arms control or a show of force to set the conditions for achieving an end state. Engineer operations remain synchronized throughout the various types of stability operations through the warfighting functions. For more detailed information, see FM 3-0 and FM 3-07. The ten types of stability operations are—

- Peace operations.
  - Peacekeeping.
  - Peacebuilding.
  - Peacemaking.

- ■ Peace enforcement.
- ■ Conflict prevention.
- ● Foreign internal defense.
- ● Security assistance.
- ● Humanitarian and civic assistance.
- ● Support to insurgencies.
- ● Support to counterdrug operations.
- ● Combating terrorism.
  - ■ Antiterrorism.
  - ■ Counterterrorism.
- ● Noncombatant evacuation operations.
- ● Arms control.
- ● Show of force.

6-63. The clearance of mines by engineers during stability operations is based on necessity to support military operations. Humanitarian mine action organizations provide the preponderance of mine clearance in support of local populations, and such action is ultimately an HN responsibility. United States Army participation in humanitarian mine action focuses on training HN personnel, including demining training, the establishment of national mine action centers, and mine risk education. U.S. military personnel may assist and train others in demining techniques and procedures, but they are prohibited by federal statute from detecting, lifting, or destroying land mines unless done for the concurrent purpose of supporting a U.S. military operation. Humanitarian mine action training missions are normally conducted by special operations forces and assisted by EOD. CA personnel help establish national mine action centers, and psychological operations personnel provide mine risk education.

6-64. HCA provides support to the local populace with military operations and exercises by predominantly U.S. forces. ARFOR (including engineer headquarters) may be tasked to provide the C2 support necessary to plan and execute the ground portion of any humanitarian assistance operation. Such assistance must fulfill unit training requirements that incidentally create a humanitarian benefit to the local populace. The assistance that engineers may provide under HCA is limited to—

- ● The construction of rudimentary surface transportation systems.
- ● Well drilling and the construction of basic sanitation facilities.
- ● Rudimentary construction and repair of public facilities and utilities. Engineer assistance may also include constructing feeding centers and disposing of human and hazardous wastes.
- ● The detection and clearance of land mines, including activities relating to furnishing education, training, and technical assistance with respect to the detection and clearance of land mines.

CIVIL SUPPORT OPERATIONS

6-65. The overall purpose of civil support operations is to meet the immediate needs of the citizens of the United States in time of emergency until civil authorities can accomplish these tasks without assistance. Civil support operations are similar to stability operations, but differ because they are conducted within the United States and its territories and are executed under U.S. law. For example, ARNG forces under state control have law enforcement authorities when operating within the United States that are not granted to Regular Army units. In addition to legal differences, operations conducted within the United States are conducted in support of other government agencies to assist state and local authorities. These agencies are trained, resourced, and equipped far more extensively than counterpart agencies involved in many stability operations overseas. Army civil support operations include three primary tasks:

- ● **Provide support in response to disaster or terrorist attacks.** During disaster or terrorist attacks, Army forces provide essential services to an affected area. Essential services include rescue, emergency medical care, veterinary service, preventing epidemic disease, providing food and water, providing emergency shelter, providing basic sanitation (sewage and garbage disposal), and providing minimum essential access to affected areas. Army forces work directly with state and federal officials to restore and return control of essential services to civil authorities as rapidly as possible. As a result of disaster or attack, the capacity of government may be reduced or overextended. Army forces provide C2, protection, and sustainment to government agencies at all levels until they can function normally.

- **Provide support to civil law enforcement.** When authorized and directed, Army forces provide support to local, state, and federal law enforcement officials. Support is normally provided when an emergency overwhelms the capabilities of civil authorities. Typical contingencies include support to antiterrorism, counterdrug, civil disturbances, border security, and disaster response. In extreme cases, when directed by the President, Regular Army forces maintain law and order under martial law.

- **Provide other support as required.** This task primarily denotes planned, routine, and periodic support not related to a disaster, such as military support for parades, funeral details, and community relations.

6-66. The Army supports civil authority during civil support operations in a unity of effort. Most disasters are handled at the state level and below. The Army, whether ARNG or a federal Army unit, may be involved at the local through state levels under immediate response authority or ordered by their respective chains of command. Federal resources are committed when requested by the state in need. A civilian federal agency may be placed in charge of a disaster response if the state government is overwhelmed or the incident triggering the disaster is an incident of national significance.

6-67. The division headquarters will likely be configured as a JTF and interact directly with the designated lead agencies. Army commanders will assume a support role to one or more designated agencies. Disaster operations are normally conducted in four phases: planning, response, recovery, and restoration. The role of the military is most intense in the planning and response phases, decreasing steadily as the operation moves into the recovery and restoration stages.

6-68. General engineering support for the restoration of essential services is the primary focus in most civil support operations; however, all three engineer functions may be applied simultaneously to some degree. The generating force elements of the Engineer Regiment such as USACE will play a critical and significant role in civil support operations. USACE authority to respond to civil emergencies is provided in public law. USACE is authorized to undertake activities that create a comprehensive flood response infrastructure. Flood response infrastructure is divided into six categories: disaster preparation, emergency response, rehabilitation, water assistance, advance measures, and hazard mitigation. The appropriation provides funding for most USACE preparedness activities in support of the NRF. The Robert T. Stafford Disaster Relief and Emergency Assistance Act enables FEMA to direct federal agencies to use available personnel, supplies, facilities, and other resources to provide assistance in the event of a major disaster or emergency declaration within the NRF. Under the NRF, DOD has responsibility for emergency support function #3, Public Works and Engineering. DOD has designated USACE as its operating agent for emergency support function #3. In addition, USACE supports lead federal agencies for other emergency support functions upon the request of the lead agency and direction of FEMA.

6-69. Engineers can expect to be involved in planning for support of relief operations with geospatial products and analysis of potential areas to establish life-support areas. Engineers may be called on to provide manpower support or general engineering support from units with unique capabilities such as water purification, temporary shelter, power generation, and firefighting. Engineer commanders and staff will work with the proponent planners to identify requirements and plan engineer applications. The ENCOORD may leverage coordination with USACE elements involved in the civil support to add depth to the understanding of the OE and to access reachback support.

6-70. Division echelon engineer planners consider statutes and regulations that restrict the Army's interaction with other government agencies and civilians during civil support operations. The local and state response normally leads the effort with a federal response providing support as required.

6-71. The division would disengage before complete restoration (the return of normality to the area). As civil authorities assume full control of remaining emergency operations and normal services, the division transfers those responsibilities to replacement agencies and begins redeployment from the area. During restoration, the ENCOORD assists the division commander in considering items such as—

- Disengagement criteria.
- Redeployment plans while recovery continues in the affected area.

OPERATIONAL CONFIGURATIONS

6-72. The primary mission of the division headquarters is to serve as a tactical warfighting headquarters directing subordinate brigade operations. The secondary mission is to serve as a JTF or land component command headquarters for small contingencies. The division does not need additional Army augmentation but does require joint augmentation to act as a JTF or JFLCC headquarters. Performing the functions of an ARFOR command is a tertiary mission for a division headquarters but will not typically be required when configured as a JTF and requires significant additional Army augmentation when configured as JFLCC.

6-73. The division headquarters itself is a self-contained organization consisting of the division command group, a main CP, a tactical CP, a mobile command group, and a supporting division STB with the signal and sustainment necessary for the division headquarters to function. The division is not a fixed formation. It is a completely modular entity designed to exercise C2 over several brigades.

6-74. In every operational configuration, the division—like the corps—will have an ASCC, the theater army headquarters that includes regional expertise and is tailored for the needs of the AOR. This provides the division with a degree of higher-echelon support in any of its operational configurations and regardless of whether the division is also functioning as the ARFOR headquarters. While some support or other ADCON responsibilities will be placed on the division headquarters, it will function with a more singular focus on the assigned contingency or major operation.

TACTICAL WARFIGHTING HEADQUARTERS

6-75. As a tactical warfighting headquarters, the division—

- Employs land forces as part of a joint, interagency, multinational force.
- Executes offensive, defensive, and stability operations in an assigned AO.
- Conducts decisive, shaping, and sustaining operations through mission command.
- Assigns missions with required resources to subordinate brigades.
- Integrates and synchronizes operations of brigades to achieve operationally significant results in the entire AO.
- Adjusts operations to account for changing mission variables.

6-76. The division will most likely be configured as a tactical warfighting headquarters in major combat operations. In this configuration, the division may be task-organized in a command relationship to a corps configured as intermediate tactical headquarters or configured as the JFLCC. In major combat operations, a division will typically operate along a line of operations or in an AO. A division can control up to six BCTs with appropriate supporting brigades during the conduct of major combat operations. These BCTs may include any mix of heavy, infantry, or Stryker BCTs. The division requires at least one of each of the five types of support brigades—combat aviation, fires, MEB, battlefield surveillance, and sustainment—to have a complete combined arms team during the conduct of major combat operations. The sustainment brigade normally remains attached to the theater sustainment command, but is given the mission of supporting the division. The division may have OPCON of a sustainment brigade during the conduct of large-scale exploitation and pursuit operations.

6-77. The division may continue to act as tactical warfighting headquarters in a transition from major combat operations or may operate in that configuration for other larger-scale operations. During protracted operations focused primarily on stability, the number of BCTs and supporting brigades controlled by a division headquarters is adjusted to meet mission variables and may exceed the numbers listed for major combat operations. The division may not be supported by all five types of support brigades during these later protracted types of operations, since their capabilities may not be required or appropriate to ongoing operations.

6-78. The engineer perspective in a tactical warfighting configuration focuses on the needs of the BCTs without losing sight of operational requirements. BCTs conducting full spectrum operations will generate requirements for combat and general engineering capabilities to support the movement and maneuver and protection warfighting functions. General engineering capabilities will be required in support of sustainment of the division while geospatial and engineering reconnaissance capabilities may be required for C2 and intelligence requirements. The division should be force-tailored with at least one MEB that can provide multifunctional C2 for a portion of the engineer effort. An engineer brigade may or may not be task-organized in support of the division, depending on the mission variables (including the scope of technical engineering requirements as well as the size of the engineering effort required). Similarly, engineer battalion headquarters units may be available for division-level support or as augmentation to brigade(s) depending on mission variables. The division ENCOORD ensures that the division engineer staff conducts operations integrated within the division CP structure and collaborates in the conduct of engineer operations with supporting engineer headquarters and subordinate unit engineer staff.

JOINT TASK FORCE OR JOINT FORCE LAND COMPONENT COMMAND

6-79. The division may be configured as a JTF or JFLCC smaller-scale operations. A JTF configuration is likely for either consequence management or FHA. In either configuration, the division will require augmentation, and a division headquarters designated as a JTF headquarters should not also be designated as a JFLCC headquarters without significant augmentation. The division staff must transition to a joint staff structure when so designated. However, only appropriate joint boards, centers, and cells should be established—not all possible doctrinal ones. Joint and multinational representation on the staff should be provided in those areas where Army personnel do not have the appropriate expertise. This will allow joint and multinational components to participate in staff processes.

6-80. The JFC establishing authority is responsible for providing joint personnel and other resources to the division when the division headquarters is designated as the JFC headquarters. However, the division commander, as the JFC commander, must determine what additional augmentation is needed and coordinate support through the establishing authority. The division commander has the option of retaining the functional organization of his headquarters or converting it into a standard J-staff configuration. The analysis of the situation in terms of mission variables will determine which option the commander chooses. The JFC commander tailors the staff augmentation based on analysis of the situation in terms of mission variables. The following areas usually require augmentation:

- Joint and special staff sections.
- Communications support, to ensure joint communications connectivity.

6-81. The engineer perspective in a JFC configuration likely focuses more on general engineering requirements for restoration of essential services and infrastructure development without losing sight of the support required for the movement and maneuver, protection, and sustainment warfighting functions. A tailored mix of subordinate Army brigades and joint and multinational elements will make up the division force. Similarly, a mix of Army modular engineer elements—along with joint, multinational, interagency, contract, and other engineer capabilities—may be available for employment. General engineering capabilities may be retained under the division echelon control to facilitate applications of JFC priority. The division should be force-tailored with an appropriate mix of functional and multifunctional headquarters to provide C2 for the engineer effort. An engineer brigade—or in some cases a portion of the TEC—may be tailored in support of the division, depending on mission variables. The division ENCOORD ensures that the JFC engineer staff conducts operations integrated within the JFC CP structure and collaborates in the conduct of engineer operations with supporting engineer headquarters and subordinate unit engineer staff.

ARMY FORCES COMMAND

6-82. In its ARFOR role, the division headquarters commands all Army forces assigned or attached to the JTF except those Army forces assigned to or attached to the JFLCC, USMC, or multinational formations. As an Army forces headquarters, the division headquarters coordinates ADCON support for Army forces within its JOA and provides ASOS, support to other government agencies, and support to multinational forces as required by the JFC. An Army forces commander may not have OPCON of all the Army forces provided to the JFC; however, the Army forces commander remains responsible for their ADCON. When a significant level of engineer effort is required by the division Army forces role, appropriate additional engineer units may be tailored with the division or other engineer capabilities made available.

6-83. Usually, the size, scope, and nature of the operation—for which a division headquarters is appropriate for designation as the JTF headquarter—is such that the division headquarters cannot also be the Army forces headquarters without significant Army augmentation. Doctrinally, another division or brigade-size headquarters will be designated as the ARFOR headquarters. Therefore, the division headquarters, serving as the JTF headquarters, normally does not have ADCON responsibilities toward subordinate Army units located within the JTF JOA.

This page intentionally left blank.

Chapter 7

Sustainment Support for the Engineer Unit

"Faced with such demands, engineer supply personnel had to operate under difficulties involving more than just their own understrength forces. Many supply ships were necessarily diverted from original destinations while en route and discharged throughout the Theater where little or no engineer depot personnel or facilities were available. Yet, these ships were packed and loaded in the United States for receipt at a central depot in Theater. But no central engineer depot could be maintained in this theater where fast, widespread movements scattered operational areas a across vast distances. Such conflicting factors contributed to the development of further difficulties. Large excesses of some engineer supplies accumulated at certain points while critical shortages of the same item existed at others".

Engineers of the Southwest Pacific 1941-1945

Army transformation into an expeditionary force includes significant changes in the structure and systems providing logistics and other sustainment support. One key feature is a logistics system that relies on asset visibility and flexibility instead of mass. Within the transformed framework, distributed support and sustainment are keys to maintaining freedom of action with the smallest feasible deployed logistical footprint. Support planning and execution must be closely integrated into tactical and operational battle rhythms. Successful engineer operations include effective incorporation of sustainment support. Sustainment for engineer elements includes the functions of supply, field services, transportation, maintenance, EOD, HSS, human resources (HR) support, financial management support, legal support, religious support, and band support. For units augmenting the BCT engineers and all other units operating at EAB, integration into an area and or theater support structure will be required. This chapter focuses on sustainment support for engineer capabilities and highlights the sustainment considerations that will affect engineer operations (see FM 4-0 for additional discussion of sustainment support).

ORGANIZATIONS AND FUNCTIONS

STRATEGIC-LEVEL SUPPORT

7-1. Within the transformed framework, distribution has transitioned to a single distribution manager, who provides unity of control. The manager directs the flow throughout the entire network—using asset visibility, capacity, and control information available from the COP—while supported by a networkwide view of distribution operations. A single distribution manager will be used at each level of war within a distribution management center (DMC) and will interact as appropriate to provide sustainment support.

7-2. The strategic-level manager is concerned with centrally controlling the distribution network in support of the Secretary of Defense, the Joint Chiefs of Staff and, when appropriate, Service components. The operational-level manager, working at the theater army or JFLCC level, controls the flow of personnel, equipment, and materiel entering, leaving, or being distributed within the GCC's JOA. The tactical-level distribution managers, working in the modular force support battalion, manage according to the designated tactical commander's priorities.

7-3. DLA is DOD's primary strategic-level logistics provider and is responsible for providing a variety of logistics support to the military Services. DLA has the capability of providing a forward presence in the operational area via the Defense Logistics Agency contingency support teams (DCSTs). DLA normally provides a DCST to each major joint operation that serves as the focal point for coordinating DLA activities within a specific AOR, theater of operation, or JOA. The DCSTs may either locate with the JFC J-4 or the TSC DMC and Army field service brigade (AFSB) when the Army is the lead Service for significant CUL support. The in-theater DCST integrates strategic- to operational-level materiel management support of DLA common commodities such as subsistence, clothing and other general supplies, Class IV construction and barrier materials, package and bulk petroleum, and medical materiel.

7-4. DLA also provides in-theater Defense Reutilization and Marketing Service (DRMS). In coordination with the joint force commander J-4, DLA establishes theater-specific procedures for the reuse, demilitarization, or disposal of facilities, equipment, and supplies, to include hazardous materiel and waste. Initially, salvage and excess materiel destined for the DRMS is collected in the theater sustainment area or the BCT areas as the situation permits. As the theater matures, DLA evacuates this material to collection points for inspection, classification, and disposal by DLA-directed activities. The TSC or sustainment brigade DMC coordinates DRMS operations for the Army forces to ensure that usable materiel is not disposed of or evacuated from the theater.

7-5. United States Army Materiel Command (USAMC) support to deployed Army forces is executed through AFSBs and contracting support brigades. These two separate colonel (O-6) level commands are theater-committed headquarters which, upon deployment, are normally placed OPCON to the TSC. The AFSB is responsible for planning and controlling all Army acquisition, logistics, and technology (ALT) functions, less theater support contracting and LOGCAP support, in the operational area. The AFSB is a small, highly modular MTOE headquarters that leverages reach capabilities to provide ALT technical and call-forward support from the national sustainment base. In addition to the small MTOE command and staff element, each AFSB has a tailored table of distribution and allowances (TDA) structure and can call forward significant USAMC and ALT support capabilities necessary to meet specific mission requirements. Specific AFSB functions include, but are not limited to—

- Providing C2 and management of the logistics assistance program (LAP).
- Coordinating system contract support to new or partially fielded systems.
- Providing Army science and technology functions and all materiel fielding organizations providing new equipment training.
- Coordinating Army pre-positioned stock support to include off-loading and property accountability.
- Providing C2 of sustainment maintenance organizations deployed to the theater.
- Maintaining accountability of all Army contractor personnel who deploy with the force.

7-6. AFSBs provide ALT support through two primary subordinate units: the logistics support element (LSE) and the brigade logistics support team (BLST). LSEs are small, tailorable, deployable, battalion-level TDA organizations of about 20 personnel, mostly Life Cycle Management Command logistics assistance representatives. BLSTs are similar to LSEs, but are smaller organizations that provide DS LAP support to a specific BCT or CAB. The LSE commander is primarily responsible for coordinating and controlling GS technical LAP support to the corps or division headquarters and Army units such as the MEB that do not have a DS BLST. Additional information on the AFSB can be found in FMI 4-93.41.

OPERATIONAL-LEVEL SUPPORT

7-7. The JFC directs operations through Service component commanders or establishes functional commands. Such functional commands include a joint forces land component to provide centralized direction and control of all land operations (See JP 1, JP 3-31 and JP 4-07). For sustainment support, the JFC assigns a lead Service to provide CUL wherever possible, to avoid redundancy and achieve greater efficiency.

7-8. The TSC is the senior Army sustainment headquarters in a theater of operations and the single Army sustainment headquarters for the theater army or JFC. The TSC consolidates most of the functions previously performed by corps support commands and TSCs into a single operational echelon and is responsible for C2 of sustainment operations conducted in support of Army, joint, interagency, and multinational forces. The TSC is regionally focused, and globally employable. Its modular design provides the TSC commander with the flexibility to adapt his C2 as requirements develop—with ESC providing an additional measure of responsiveness, agility, and flexibility for employment or deterrence.

7-9. The TSC rapidly establishes C2 of operational-level sustainment in a specified AO by employing one or more ESC. Each ESC provides a rapidly deployable, regionally focused, forward-based C2 capability that mirrors the organizational structure of the TSC. By design, the ESC executes sustainment operations that are limited in scale and scope; employs reach capabilities to provide full spectrum support across the spectrum of conflict; and conducts sustainment operations according to TSC plans, policies, programs, and mission guidance. In some situations, the ASCC may choose to use a TEC or MEDCOM as the senior headquarters for support if dictated by the mission circumstances.

TACTICAL-LEVEL SUPPORT

7-10. Engineers operating above the BCT level will work closely with and receive sustainment support from the sustainment brigade. Sustainment brigades are one of the five types of support brigades and are subordinate commands of the TSC. They consolidate selected functions previously performed by corps and division support commands and area support groups into a single operational echelon. They provide C2 of the full range of logistics operations conducted at the operational (theater level) or higher tactical (corps and division) levels. They perform theater opening, distribution, and sustainment functions. Each of these functions is interrelated, and throughout the course of an operation a sustainment brigade will likely perform one or more of these functions simultaneously.

7-11. The sustainment brigade is a flexible, modular organization. Organic to the sustainment brigade are the brigade headquarters and an STB. All other assets are task-organized to the sustainment brigade to enable it to accomplish its role and mission (see FMI 4-93.2 for more information on the organic and modular units within the sustainment brigade). Sustainment brigades are assigned to a TSC but may be task-organized based on mission variables. The sustainment brigade may be assigned at either the operational level (tasked to provide operational sustainment, tasked to conduct theater opening operations, or tasked to provide theater distribution) or the tactical level (tasked to provide tactical logistics support to the division).

7-12. The sustainment brigade provides support within an AO. Each sustainment brigade is a multifunctional logistics organization providing support for multiple brigade-size units. It is tailored and task-organized and uses modular subunits (battalions, companies, platoons) to perform specific functions. At the tactical level, multifunctional sustainment brigades normally operate within the division AO. The sustainment brigade is primarily concerned with the continuous management and flow of stocks and allocation of reinforcing maintenance support in the AO to provide operational reach to maneuver commanders. When task-organized to provide sustainment support within an AO, the sustainment brigade capabilities include—

- Coordinating supply of arms, munitions, and equipment.
- Synchronizing supply and distribution of fuel and water.
- Maintaining equipment and stocks that support the supply system.
- Coordinating support of forces, including HR, field services, HSS, religious support, financial management, and legal services.
- Managing materiel, controlling movement, and managing distribution.
- Providing lead Service CUL to other Services, multinational partners, and civilian agencies on order.
- Establishing, managing, and maintaining facilities (including storage areas) and maintenance areas.
- Planning, coordinating, managing, and supervising the positioning and security of activities.

ENGINEER LEADER AND STAFF RESPONSIBILITIES FOR SUSTAINMENT

7-13. Engineer staff and commanders are essential to the sustainment of engineer organizations and capabilities operating at every echelon. Sustainment for engineer units and capabilities organic, assigned, or attached directly to a supported unit is the responsibility of the leaders and staff of the unit they support, but the higher-echelon ENCOORD will retain an interest in status of their support. The ENCOORD must also work closely with the supported unit logistics staff to assist in planning, preparing, executing, and assessing operations that will likely require extensive engineer materials and resources. When engineer or multifunctional modular headquarters units are provided, the organic logistics staff within that headquarters provides sustainment planning for the engineer force under its C2. Engineer battalions provide logistics support to subordinate units through organic forward support companies (FSCs).

7-14. At the engineer unit level, the basic sustainment responsibilities are to monitor, report, and request requirements through the correct channels and to ensure that sustainment requirements are met when sustainment is brought forward to the engineer unit. The engineer company executive officer and first sergeant are normally in charge of these functions within the engineer companies, and they receive guidance and oversight from the commander. They are also responsible for supporting any augmentation they may receive. Accurate and timely submission of personnel and logistics reports, and other necessary information and requests, is essential.

ENGINEER COORDINATOR

7-15. The ENCOORD at each echelon is responsible for engineer logistics estimates and plans and monitors engineer-related sustainment support for engineer capabilities operating at that echelon. When an engineer unit or capability is task-organized in support of the unit, the ENCOORD recommends the most effective command or support relationship, including considering the impact of inherent sustainment responsibilities. The ENCOORD—

- Writes the engineer annex and associated appendixes to the OPLAN or OPORD to support the commander's intent. Included in these is a recommended distribution for any engineer-related, command-regulated classes of supply and special equipment.
- Assists in planning the location(s) of the engineer forward supply point for the delivery of engineer-configured loads of Class IV and Class V materials. This site(s) is coordinated with the unit responsible for the terrain and the appropriate Logistics staff officer (S-4) or assistant chief of staff, logistics (G-4).
- Assists in planning the location(s) of the engineer equipment parks for pre-positioning of critical equipment sets, such as tactical bridging. This site(s) is coordinated with the unit responsible for the terrain and the appropriate S-4 or G-4.
- Works closely with the sustainment staff to identify available haul assets (including HN) and recommends priorities to the sustainment planners.
- Identifies extraordinary medical evacuation (MEDEVAC) requirements or coverage issues for engineer units and coordinates with sustainment planners to ensure that the supporting unit can accomplish these special workloads.
- Identifies critical engineer equipment and engineer mission logistics shortages.
- Provides the appropriate S-4 or G-4 with an initial estimate of required Class IV and Class V supplies for countermobility/survivability efforts.
- Provides the appropriate S-4 or G-4 with an initial estimate of required Class IV supplies in support of construction. Monitors and advises, as required, implications of statutory, regulatory, and command policies for the procurement of construction materials. The critical issue for the ENCOORD is the timely delivery at required specifications whatever the source for construction materials.
- Tracks the flow of mission-critical Class IV and Class V supplies into support areas and forward to the supporting engineer units. Coordinates to provide engineer assistance as required to accept delivery of construction materials.

- Coordinates MSR clearing operations and tracks their status at the main CP.
- Coordinates for EH support and integration as necessary.

ENGINEER UNIT COMMANDER

7-16. The unit commander ensures that sustainment operations maintain the mission capabilities of the unit and its ability to provide combat power. The unit commander provides critical insight during the supported unit planning process. The unit commander—

- Coordinates for sustainment support requirements external to the engineer unit.
- Anticipates problems, works to avoid delays in planning and transition, and tracks sustainment status.
- Communicates with subordinate leaders to identify the need for push packages, ensures their arrival, and tracks their expenditure.
- Determines the location of the unit resupply points and monitors the operation.
- Ensures that the unit is executing sustainment operations according to supported unit SOP and OPORD.
- Monitors equipment locations and maintenance status.
- Updates the engineer-specific Class IV and Class V supply requirements based on reconnaissance of mission sites. The engineer brigade or battalion, in some circumstances, may need to manage and maintain a level of Class IV stockage to ensure flexible and timely general engineering support to the force.
- Tracks engineer equipment use, maintenance deadlines, and fuel consumption.
- Receives, consolidates, and forwards all logistical, administrative, personnel, and casualty reports to the parent or supported unit.
- Directs and supervises the medical support within the unit, coordinating for additional support as required.
- Supervises and monitors the evacuation of casualties, detainees, and damaged equipment.
- Orients personnel replacements and assigns personnel to subordinate units.
- Conducts sustainment rehearsals at the unit level.
- Maintains and provides supplies for unit field sanitation activities.
- Integrates EH support as necessary.

PRINCIPLES OF LOGISTICS

7-17. During the operations process cycle, the ENCOORD and the engineer unit commander(s) must plan, prepare, execute, and continuously assess sustainment support for engineer capabilities. Concurrent with other operational planning, the unit develops a sustainment plan during the mission analysis and refines it in the war-gaming portion of the MDMP. Sustainment rehearsals are normally conducted at brigade, battalion, and company levels to ensure a smooth, continuous flow of materiel and services.

7-18. Engineers ensure that they identify all sustainment requirements in advance—taking into consideration support relationships of subordinate units. This information must be passed into sustainment channels and tracked through delivery. It involves identifying, accumulating, and maintaining the minimum assets, capabilities, and information necessary to meet support requirements. On the other hand, the force that accumulates enough material and personnel reserves to address every possible contingency usually cedes the initiative to the enemy. The sustainment system must keep pace with rapid decision cycles and mission execution to react quickly to crises or opportunities. It must continually respond to a changing situation and the shifting of engineer units in the AO. Interim contingency sustainment support must be planned until the task organization is modified or changed. When possible, the plan should include aerial resupply.

7-19. Personnel losses and unit capabilities must also be anticipated to plan for continuous operations and future missions. Forward engineer units depend on the sustainment system of their parent unit or of the unit they are supporting and may require significant support to accomplish their engineer tasks. The brigade (and battalion) engineer must anticipate likely task organization changes that will affect the flow of sustainment to engineer organizations. Additional missions will be created by the sustainment support plan (for example, clearing a landing zone [LZ] for aerial resupply). These missions and tasks must be anticipated and planned for during the mission analysis.

7-20. Versatile sustainment systems enhance the engineer unit's responsiveness and adapt to changing requirements without interrupting the flow of support. In this respect, responsiveness is closely tied with improvisation. Theater sustainment planners structure the logistics force to be versatile enough to complement engineer plans and operations, yet be robust enough to ensure that engineer services are not interrupted. The structure must be responsive enough to allow the engineer commander to seize and maintain the initiative.

7-21. Engineers plan to meet the changing requirements of the operation on short notice. The engineer sustainment system should be versatile enough to keep pace with rapid decision cycles and mission execution and also react rapidly to crises or opportunities. Engineer planners are sensitive to engineer task organization changes. Engineer units can normally respond to a change in task organization much more quickly than theater sustainment packages can. Because of this, contingency engineer sustainment plans are normally developed.

7-22. Engineers consider joint, multinational, contract civilian, and interagency assets when planning support for engineer operations. They—

- Use all available resources to the fullest, especially HN assets.
- Prioritize critical engineer activities based on the concept of operations.
- Anticipate engineer requirements based on war-gaming and rock drills incorporating experience and historical knowledge.
- Do not think linearly or sequentially; organize and resource for simultaneous and noncontiguous operations.
- Participate in and evaluate the engineer significance of each phase of the operation during the entire command estimate process, to include mission analysis and COA development, analysis and war-gaming, recommendation, and execution.

7-23. The ENCOORD and the engineer unit commander forecast future requirements and accumulate assets needed to accommodate likely contingencies. Engineer operations frequently require—

- High fuel consumption rates (higher than most equipment found in a light brigade).
- Engineer-specific Class IX repair parts, which often necessitates extraordinary coordination to obtain.
- Large amounts of Class IV and Class V supplies.
- Demolitions for offensive and defensive operations.
- A large commitment of maintenance and transportation support.
- Financial management support to procurement and contracting of locally available commercial services and materials.
- High consumption rates of geospatial printing and plotting supplies which are not found in supply systems.

7-24. Engineer commanders and staffs establish priorities and allocate classes of supply and services to simplify sustainment operations. Engineers use preconfigured loads of specialized classes of supply to simplify transport.

7-25. Due to the inherently changing world environment, engineer missions will change. Engineers require flexibility and coordination with higher staffs to provide sustainment and logistical support. As ENCOORDs work future branch or sequel plans, they ensure that sustainment and logistical support are planned and resourced.

7-26. Extraordinary methods may be necessary to ensure success during operations. Sustainment planners attempt to push support to engineer units forward to ensure smooth combat operations. Sometimes this is not feasible or supportable. In such cases, engineers improvise by making, inventing, devising, or fabricating what is needed. One example is the creation of a demolition cratering charge using common fertilizer and diesel fuel.

7-27. The engineer, in conjunction with the logistician, completes the sustainment estimate and initiates resource identification based on the supported commander's requirements and priorities. An operation should not begin until minimum essential levels of support are on hand. For engineers, attainability is at the very core of decisions that are made. Trade-offs may be necessary to attain a given goal or level and quality of product. Since engineer materials must meet specific technical requirements, engineers work closely with the logistics staff to help them understand these requirements and obtain acceptable and suitable alternatives when trade-off decisions are required.

7-28. Sustainability ensures the longevity of logistics support to engineers throughout the AO for the duration of the operation. Sustainability focuses on the engineer commander's attention for long-term objectives and capabilities of the engineer forces. Long-term support is a challenge for the engineer staff, which must not only attain the minimum essential materiel levels to initiate operations but must also sustain those operations through the end state. The ENCOORD must ensure that logistical requirements are known and are flowing based on available transportation assets.

7-29. Engineers are either committed to the current operation or preparing for the next one. The tempo of operations requires a constant vigilance by the logistician and engineer commander to ensure a constant flow of support. Supplies are pushed (unit distribution method) forward whenever logistically feasible. Maneuver units rely on lulls in the tempo of an operation to conduct sustainment operations, while engineers may not. Engineers usually do not have this opportunity, since many of their missions occur during a lull in operations and this may deny them the opportunity to use the supply point method. This increases the need for engineers to plan for continuous, routine, and emergency logistics support.

7-30. General engineering involves constructing, repairing, operating, and maintaining infrastructure and facilities to enhance provision of sustainment and services (see FM 3-34.400). Contracting support obtains and provides supplies, services, and construction labor and materiel—often providing a responsive option or enhancement to support the force (see FMI 4-93.41). General engineers will often be required to provide subject matter expertise for the supervision of contracted materials and services.

7-31. The logistics principle of survivability is related to, but not exactly the same as, the discussion of survivability operations. It is based on being able to protect support functions from destruction or degradation. Engineers contribute to ensuring that sustainment means are survivable by constructing sustainment bases and clearing LOCs. They may also construct ammunition holding areas and provide revetments and other hardening for petroleum products.

7-32. Operational and tactical plans integrate all sustainment support to create a synergy with the concept of operation. Engineer planners participate in and evaluate the sustainment significance of each phase of the operation during the entire command estimate process. They create a clear and concise concept of support that integrates the commander's intent and concept of operation. This includes analyzing the mission; developing, analyzing, war-gaming, and recommending a COA; and executing the plan.

SUSTAINMENT PLANNING

7-33. The efforts of engineer leaders and staff to plan and coordinate engineer sustainment are essential to the full integration of engineer operations. The ENCOORD, the engineer unit commander, the supported unit S-4 or G-4, and the sustainment support unit work closely to synchronize sustainment for engineer capabilities.

7-34. When the supported unit receives a warning order (directly or implied) as part of the MDMP, the ENCOORD initiates the engineer portion of the logistics estimate process. The ENCOORD focuses the logistics estimate on the requirements for the upcoming mission and the sustainment of all subordinate engineer units that are organic and task-organized in support of the unit. Classes I, III, IV, and V supplies and personnel losses are the essential elements in the estimate process. Close integration with the sustainment support unit can simplify and accelerate this process through the use of the automated systems logistics status report to ensure that the sustainment support unit is able to maintain an up-to-date picture of the engineer unit sustainment requirements. During continuous operations, the estimate process supporting execution decisions may need to be abbreviated because of time constraints.

7-35. After conducting the estimate process to determine the requirements for unit and mission sustainment, the ENCOORD, with the respective S-4 or G-4, compares the requirements with the reported status of subordinate units to determine the specific amount of supplies needed to support the operation. These requirements are then coordinated with the sustainment support unit or forward support element to ensure that the needed supplies are identified and resourced higher-echelon stocks.

7-36. The ENCOORD then translates the estimate into specific plans that are used to determine the supportability of supported unit COAs. After a COA is selected, the specific sustainment input to the supported unit base OPORD and paragraph four of the engineer annex is developed and incorporated.

7-37. In each of the different types of BCTs, the ENCOORD, working with the appropriate sustainment planner and executor, tracks essential sustainment tasks involving all engineer units supporting the brigade. Accurate and timely status reporting assists the ENCOORD in providing the overall engineer status to the brigade commander and allows the ENCOORD to intercede in critical sustainment problems when necessary. The ENCOORD also ensures that supplies needed by augmenting EAB engineer units to execute missions for the brigade are integrated into the brigade sustainment plans. For the ENCOORD to execute these missions properly, accurate and timely reporting and close coordination among the ENCOORD, sustainment planners and providers, task force engineers (or in some cases the engineer unit commander in the Stryker BCT), and supporting EAB engineers are essential. Supporting EAB engineer units must affect linkup with the existing engineer sustainment to ensure their synchronization of effort.

SUSTAINMENT SUPPORT FUNCTIONS

7-38. Sustainment support can be broadly categorized and discussed within subordinate functions. The functions assist planners and leaders in coordinating for sustainment support. The functions include tasks associated with maintenance, ammunition support, supply and field services, transportation, HSS, transportation, HR support, and financial management.

MAINTENANCE

7-39. The ENCOORD ensures that the full range of field-level maintenance is identified for each supporting engineer unit. This is particularly important in identifying the maintenance evacuation chain from operator or crew through organizational maintenance support to the field maintenance (DS) company.

7-40. Unit commanders ensure that vehicle crews and equipment operators perform preventive maintenance checks and services. To provide quick turnaround of maintenance problems, each engineer unit should coordinate for a field maintenance team (FMT) from their supporting maintenance company. These FMTs have contact maintenance trucks and mechanics trained to repair the unit's equipment.

SUPPLY AND FIELD SERVICES

7-41. Providing the force with general supplies and services is the mission of the attached or assigned elements of the sustainment brigade and functional battalions. Supply and service elements generally provide the subsistence, general supplies, bulk fuel, heavy materiel, repair parts, laundry and shower services, mortuary affairs, and water. Personal demand items (Class VI) and medical supplies are not typically provided by units under the C2 of the sustainment brigade, but must be considered during the planning process.

7-42. Class IV consists of construction materials, including all fortification and barrier materials. These are items for which allowances are not prescribed. Units deploy with a limited amount of Class IV barrier materiel, primarily for protection of unit perimeters and key positions. This materiel is considered the unit's basic load and usually is carried on tactical vehicles. Replenishment is ordered by company supply sergeants.

7-43. Much larger quantities of Class IV materials are nearly always required by any significant application of engineer effort. Large quantities of Class IV materials may require significant transportation efforts. Statutory, regulatory, and command policies may dictate the source, requiring the maximum use of local procurement, for example. Engineer units, while not designed to manage Class IV material stocks, will typically expend extraordinary means to ensure that the supplies required to enable the engineer effort is made available. A significant effort on the part of supported unit commanders and staff is required to adequately address the challenge of providing the large quantities of construction and other Class IV materials required.

7-44. The management of these Class IV supplies is most efficient when there is a shared interest among the maneuver, sustainment, and engineer logisticians. The ENCOORD must coordinate closely with the logistics staff to assist in management of required construction materials. The ENCOORD assists the logistics staff in adequately forecasting the requirements and ensuring that a quality control process is in place for receipt of the materials.

7-45. Class V consists of all types of ammunition, including chemical, radiological, and special weapons; bombs; explosives; mines; networked munitions; fuses; detonators; pyrotechnics; missiles; rockets; propellants; and other associated items. Class V supplies are based on a required supply rate (RSR) and controlled supply rate (CSR). RSR is the amount of ammunition, usually expressed in rounds per weapon per day, estimated to be required to sustain operations, without restriction, for a specific period. CSR is the rate of ammunition consumption that can be supported (considering availability, facilities, and transportation) for a given period. The CSR may well be less than the RSR. If the RSR exceeds the CSR, the commander determines who receives the ammunition. The ENCOORD coordinates supporting engineer unit ammunition requirements, including demolitions, munitions, and mines, with the S-4 or G-4.

7-46. Ammunition support activities like the theater storage area (TSA), ASPs, and ammunition transfer and holding points (ATHPs) provide the capability to receive, store, issue, inspect, and perform field level munitions maintenance support. The sustainment brigade gains such capability when it is assigned one or more ammunition ordnance companies. The TSA encompasses the storage facilities located at the operational level. This is where the bulk of the theater reserve ammunition stocks are located. The primary mission of the TSA is to receive munitions from the national level, conduct the bulk of operational-level reconfiguration, and distribute munitions to forward ASP locations and BCT ATHPs. The TSA will build those configured loads that cannot be shipped into theater due to explosive compatibility conflicts for international shipment. Engineer units may provide general engineering support to the ammunition support activities.

TRANSPORTATION

7-47. Transportation assets of the sustainment brigade and functional transportation battalions provide distribution from the sustainment brigades forward and retrograde of damaged or surplus items. The mobility branch of the TSC support officer (SPO), operations, provides staff supervision of all transportation and coordinates directly with the movement control battalion (MCB). The MCB and its movement control teams (MCTs) coordinate all movement in the JOA or AO to include in, out, and through all divisional areas. Sustainment brigades with lift assets physically located adjacent to divisional units may or may not provide transportation support to move materiel when requests from tactical units are processed by the TSC DMC.

7-48. MCTs process movement requests and arrange transport for moving personnel, equipment, and sustainment supplies. They process convoy clearance requests and special hauling permits. MCTs coordinate for the optimal mode (air, rail, inland waterway, or highway) for unprogrammed moves, and commit the mode operators from the sustainment brigade, LOGCAP, multinational elements, and the HN. They also assist in carrying out the movement program. (For more information see FM 4-01.30.)

HEALTH SERVICE SUPPORT

7-49. Medical care in the Army health system includes immediate lifesaving measures, emergency medical treatment, advanced trauma management, disease prevention, combat and operational stress control, casualty collection, and evacuation from supported unit to supporting medical treatment facility (MTF). These elements include the trauma specialist assisted by first aid (self-aid and buddy aid) and advanced first aid (combat lifesaver) and the MTF (battalion aid station). When an MTF is not present in a unit, this support is provided on an area support basis by the supporting medical unit. See FM 4-02 for an overarching discussion of HSS.

7-50. MEDEVAC elements use the most expedient means available for evacuation of sick, injured, or wounded Soldiers. The use of air ambulance is METT-TC-dependent since they may not always be available. The combat aviation brigade GS aviation battalion will determine where to position the forward support MEDEVAC teams and the number of aircraft in support will be based on mission requirements. The aviation element and surgeon coordinate the use and positioning of the forward support MEDEVAC team. They integrate air ambulance support, to include coordinating of Army airspace C2 requirements, establishing clear lines of authority to launch a MEDEVAC, and identifying of pickup zones and LZs.

HUMAN RESOURCES SUPPORT

7-51. The unit human resources staff officer (S-1) is the principal coordinating staff responsible for the planning, integration, coordination, and delivery of HR support. The S-1 is responsible for the execution of the HR core competencies and capabilities listed below, and the S-1 serves as the point of contact for command interest programs, such as voting assistance, Army Emergency Relief, equal opportunity, and retention. External HR support is coordinated through the SPO, HR Operations Branch, of the sustainment brigade supporting the unit. The S-1 relies on the availability of both secure and nonsecure data and voice systems and its location in the AO must allow for full connectivity with SIPRNET and nonsecure Internet protocol router network (NIPRNET). Brigade-level S-1 sections provide staff control of subordinate S-1 sections.

7-52. HR support encompasses ten core competencies. These core competencies are—

- Personnel readiness management.
- Personnel accountability and strength reporting.
- Personnel information management.
- Reception, replacement, redeployment, rest and recuperation, and return to duty.
- Casualty operations.
- Essential personnel services.
- HR planning and operations.
- Postal operations.
- Morale, welfare, and recreation.
- Band operations (when applicable).

FINANCIAL MANAGEMENT SUPPORT

7-53. Financial management support enhances the commander's ability to manage and apply available resources at the right time and place in a fiscally responsible manner. It is composed of two mutually supporting core functions: finance operations and resource management operations. Financial management capabilities are organic to the TSC.

INTERNMENT/RESETTLEMENT OPERATIONS

7-54. Internment/resettlement (I/R) operations are operations that take or keep selected individuals in custody or control as a result of military operations to control their movement, restrict their activity, provide safety, or gain intelligence. These operations comprise the measures necessary to guard, protect, and account for people that are captured, detained, confined, or evacuated from their homes by the U.S. armed forces. I/R operations require detailed advanced planning to provide a safe and secure environment. U.S. policy and international law mandate that all individuals captured, interned, evacuated, or held by U.S. armed forces be treated humanely. This policy applies from the moment they are under the control of U.S. armed forces until they are released, repatriated, or resettled. See FM 3-39.40 for more in-depth information regarding I/R operations.

7-55. I/R operations are perhaps the most sustainment-intensive of all missions. The Army is DOD's executive agent for all detainee operations. Additionally, the Army is DOD's executive agent for long-term confinement of U.S. military prisoners. Within the Army and through the GCC, MP units are tasked with coordinating shelter, protection, accountability, and sustainment for detainees. This effort may include significant engineering support. Engineer participation in managing internee activities includes providing construction support for building or renovating facilities and employing internee labor in engineer tasks where appropriate. See FM 3-34.400 for further discussion of engineer participation in I/R operations. There are several classes of detainees, each with specific sustainment requirements. FM 3-39.40 has an entire appendix that covers I/R facility design and logistical considerations.

OTHER SUSTAINMENT SUPPORT

7-56. In addition to the support provided by U.S. military organizations, sustainment support may incorporate support provided by contractors and HN support into plans and operations. These sources of support offer greater economy and may reduce demands on strategic lift. However, their use must be balanced with the greater burden of protection that they also bring.

CONTRACTED SUPPORT

7-57. Contracting is a key source of support for deployed forces conducting full spectrum operations. Because of the importance and unique challenges of contracted support, engineer commanders and staff need to fully understand their role in planning for and managing contracted support. Key to understanding contracting and contractor management is being familiar with the doctrine laid out in FMI 4-93.41 and FM 3-100.21. These FMs describe three broad types of contracted support:

- **Theater support.** Theater support contractors support deployed operational forces under prearranged contracts, or contracts awarded from the mission area, by contracting officers under the OPCON of the contracting support brigade or joint contracting command (if established). Theater support contractors provide goods, services, and minor construction—usually from the local commercial sources—to meet the immediate needs of operational commanders. Theater support contracts are typically associated with contingency contracting.

- **External support.** External support contractors provide a variety of sustainment support to deployed forces. External support contracts may be prearranged contracts or contracts awarded during the contingency itself to support the mission and may include a mix of U.S. citizens, third-country nationals, and local national subcontractor employees. The largest and most commonly used external support contract is LOGCAP. This Army program is commonly used to provide life support, transportation support, and many other support functions to deployed Army forces and other elements of the joint force as well.

- **Systems support.** Systems support contracts are prearranged contracts by the ALT program executive officer (PEO) and program management offices. Supported systems include, but are not limited to, newly fielded weapon systems, aircraft, C2 infrastructure (such as the Army Battle Command Systems), and communications equipment. System support contractors, made up mostly of U.S. citizens, often provide support in garrison and may deploy with the force to both training and real-world operations. They may provide either temporary support during the initial fielding of a system, called interim contracted support, or long-term support for selected materiel systems, often referred to as contractor logistic support.

7-58. For engineer units, the major challenge is ensuring that the engineer-related requirements are properly identified in the ESP and that all requirements that cannot be met via military or HN support means are identified. It is imperative that the staff engineer work closely with the TSC or ESC SPO, the Army forces G-4, and the supporting contracting support brigade to ensure that engineer requirements are properly integrated and captured in the contracting support plan and/or specifically addressed in the ESP. It is also important to understand that most engineer units (less FEST–A teams) do not have any dedicated contingency contracting teams and that this support will be provided on a GS basis from the supporting contracting support brigade (or joint contracting command if established).

7-59. It is also imperative that the engineer commanders and staff fully understand the key differences between contracted and organic military support. These differences include—

● Contractor personnel authorized to accompany the force are neither combatants nor noncombatants; they are civilians "authorized" to accompany the force in the field.

● Contractors are not in the chain of command. They are managed through their contracts and the contract management system, which should always include a unit contracting officer's representative.

● Contractors perform only tasks specified in contracts. "Other duties as assigned" does not apply.

GENERATING FORCE SUSTAINMENT OF FORCES AND OPERATIONS

7-60. The increasingly interconnected global environment allows the generating force to apply its sustainment capabilities directly within the theater of operations. These capabilities include contingency and sustainment contracting; the maintenance and repair of equipment; acquisition, logistic and technology functions; and HSS and force health protection. The generating force supports deployed operational Army units employing a combination of forward presence, call-forward support, and technical reach. The Army field support brigade coordinates generating force sustainment support of operations in the theater of operations.

7-61. The Army Support Command, through its deployable AFSBs, is the primary generating force integrator of ALT support. The AFSB, normally in DS to the TSC, is responsible to integrate, coordinate and, when appropriate, command Army ALT support organizations in support of deployed Army forces. Using reach and call-forward methodologies, the AFSB leverages national sustainment-level generating force capabilities. Specific AFSB generating force-related capabilities include, but are not limited to—

● Calling forward TDA or contracted forward repair activities.

● Coordinating technical advice from various ALT organizations.

● Coordinating PEO and project management system fielding and modification efforts.

● Integrating and assisting in the management of systems support contracts.

7-62. The MEDCOM provides enterprise-level HSS to the joint force that provides continuity of care from the theater of operations through the generating force. MEDCOM integrates the capabilities of its subordinate operational Army units with generating force assets like military treatment facilities: research, development, and acquisition capabilities. MEDCOM's generating force capabilities not only augment those of operational Army units but also provide significant assistance in coping with unanticipated health threats.

HOST NATION SUPPORT

7-63. The TSC will coordinate for HN support (negotiated by the DOS) as required in support of its mission. HN support and local procurement may provide a full range of logistics, operational, and tactical support. HN support agreements fulfilling the command requirements for support need to be prenegotiated. Such support arrangements must be integrated into the distribution plan and coordinated with other Services and multinational partners to prevent competition for resources and ensure that high-priority requirements are met.

7-64. HN support may include functional or area support and use of HN facilities, government agencies, civilians, or military units. Preestablished arrangements for HN support can reduce the requirement for early deployment of U.S. assets and can offset requirements for early strategic lift by reducing requirements for moving resources to the theater.

MULTINATIONAL SUPPORT

7-65. Multinational support may consist of CUL support provided from one multinational partner to another. One or more of the following organizational and management options facilitates multinational support:

- National support elements provide national support.
- Individual acquisition and cross-servicing agreements provide limited support.
- A lead nation provides specific support to other contributing-nation military forces.
- A role-specialist nation provides a specific common supply item or service.
- A multinational integrated logistics unit provides limited common supply and service support.
- A multinational joint logistics center manages CUL support.

7-66. In all cases, the multinational force commander directs specific multinational CUL support within the applicable laws and regulations of the HN. When operating within a formal alliance, the TSC commander and staff execute CUL support according to applicable standardization agreements or quadripartite standardization agreements. FM 4-0, JP 4-07, and JP 4-08 discuss multinational logistics support.

This page intentionally left blank.

Appendix A

Engineer Organization: Units, Staffs, and Selected Cells, Workgroups, and Boards

This appendix provides a quick reference for the organization and capabilities of engineer headquarters units and the MEB. It also describes engineer staff and geospatial engineering organizations at each echelon from division to theater army. It also highlights many of the key cells, workgroups, and boards with which the engineer staff may interact.

ENGINEER HEADQUARTERS UNITS AND THE MANEUVER ENHANCEMENT BRIGADE

A-1. The modular construct of the Army engineer operational force is a complementary and interdependent relationship among four major categories of units (and includes USACE-provided technical engineering and contract support as already discussed). The four categories include organic engineers (and staff elements) and three categories in an engineer force pool (all operational force engineer units not organic to a BCT, organic to the ACR, or in a headquarters staff). The assets in the force pool exist to augment organic BCT engineers and provide echelons above the BCT with necessary engineer capabilities. The force pool is organized into engineer headquarters units, baseline units, and specialized engineer units. See appendix B of FM 3-34 for a complete quick reference guide for modular engineer operational force.

A-2. Table A-1 provides a quick reference index for the C2 units described in this appendix.

Table A-1. Headquarters units

Unit	Figure Number	Page Number
Theater Engineer Command	A-1	A-2
Engineer Brigade	A-2	A-3
Engineer Battalion	A-3	A-4
Maneuver Enhancement Brigade	A-4	A-5

THEATER ENGINEER COMMAND
05800G000

++

96-7-142-245

40-6-68-114

CMD
2-0-4-6

DCS
2-0-1-3

DCP
26-0-34-61

MISSION

To provide a senior engineer headquarters for command and control of engineer operations in a theater of operations.

CAPABILITIES

Provides command and control for theater engineer operations including combat, general, and geospatial engineering missions. The theater engineer command is organized in three modules. This design allows the theater engineer command to be deployed in its entirety or in mission tailored modules. The modules are--

(1) **Early Entry Module.** Responsible for preoperations engineer planning and early deployment requirements as outlined in the strategic theater Universal Joint Task List. The deputy commander controls and deploys with elements from the intelligence, plans and operations, engineer, facility engineer, information, and material sections.

(2) **Functional Module.** As the engineer mission expands beyond the capability of the early entry module, the Commander deploys with enough personnel to conduct the expanded engineer operations.

(3) **Command and Control Module.** As the Army service component command increases mission functionality and requirements the command and control module will deploy with the remaining theater engineer command personnel from the intelligence, information management, public affairs, inspector general, staff judge advocate, materiel section, comptroller, internal review, and the company headquarters.

DEPENDENCIES

Transportation Command, for supplemental transportation. Signal Company (Command Operations) (Theater), for supplemental signal support. Legal support organization, for supervision of the administration of military justice and other legal matters in the command. Theater Aviation Brigade, for aviation support.

SUPPORTS

Mission tailored to conduct theater Army or other operational echelon engineer operations.

RULE OF ALLOCATION

One theater engineer command per major combat operations. Mission tailored theater engineer command modules as required for contingency operations.

Legend:
CMD   command
DCP   deployable command post
DCS   Deputy Chief of Staff

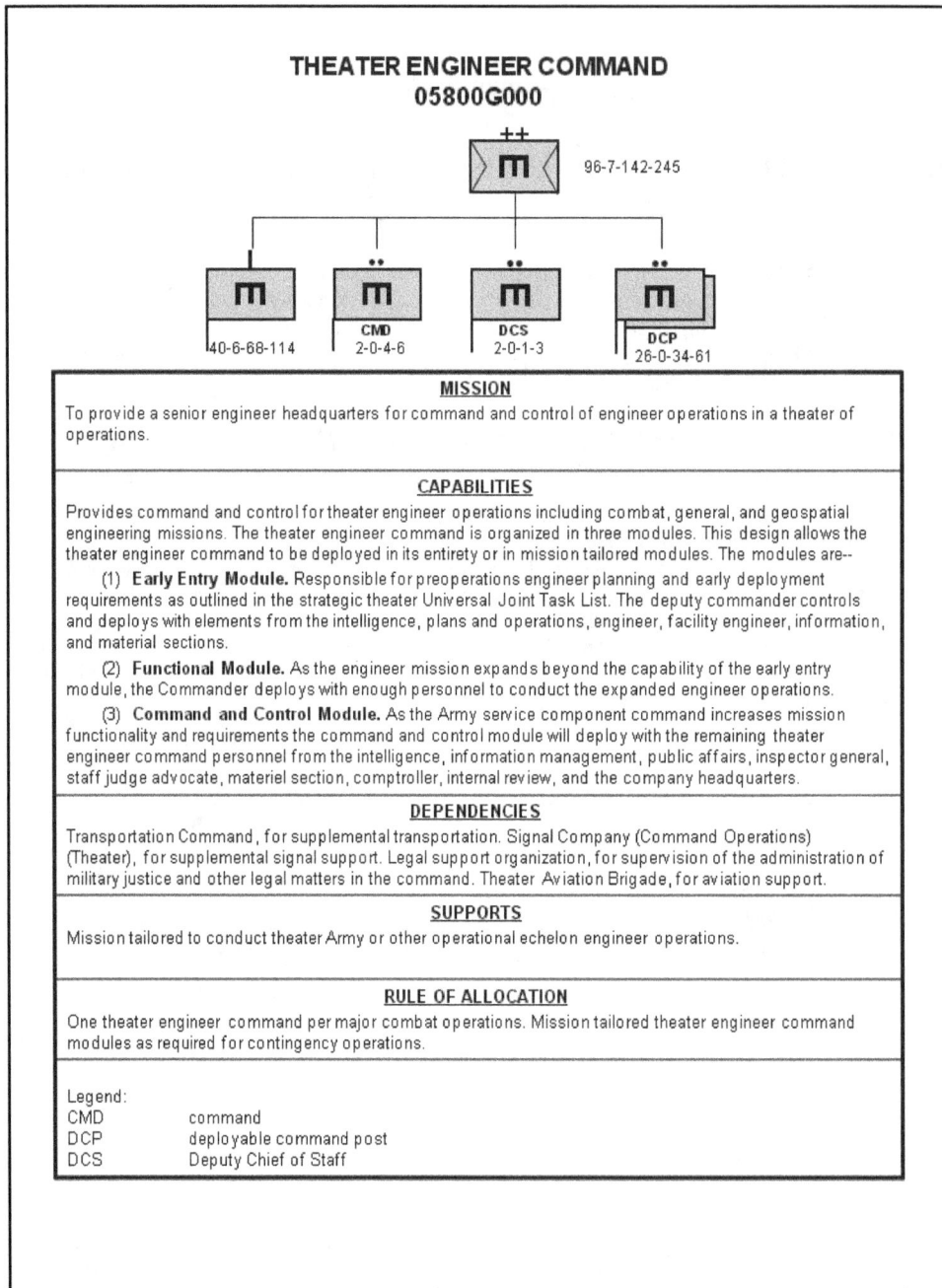

Figure A-1. Theater engineer command

ENGINEER BRIGADE
05402G000

X
m 33-4-87-124

m	m CMD	m Integration	m Technical	m Sustain	
2-0-9-11	4-0-6-10	12-0-31-43	5-1-19-25	8-3-21-32	2-0-1-3

m Intelligence
2-0-5-7

m Plans
3-0-2-5

m DCP
6-0-18-24

m Liaison Officer
1-0-1-2

m
3-0-5-8

m Procurement
2-0-1-3

m Survey and Design
0-1-13-14

MISSION
To provide an engineer headquarters for command and control of engineer operations throughout the area of operations.

CAPABILITIES
- Conducts engineer missions with 2 to 5 task-organized engineer battalions and other force pool units.
- Provides command and control for engineer operations including combat, general, and geospatial engineering missions.
- Provides supervision for contract construction.
- Provides two scalable, deployable command posts as required.
- Integrates and synchronizes engineer capabilities across the supported force.

DEPENDENCIES
- Appropriate elements of corps or division for religious, legal, health service support, finance, personnel and administrative, and logistical services.
- This unit requires table of organization and equipment 63357G000, Forward Support Company Engineer Battalion, to perform field support maintenance on engineer construction and other organic equipment, except communications security and medical equipment.

SUPPORTS
- The brigade headquarters provides command and control for engineer operations supporting a division or corps.
- The brigade provides an intermediate headquarters for command and control of assigned engineer operations when task-organized to a theater engineer command.
- The brigade headquarters provides command and control for joint or multinational engineer operations with augmentation.

RULE OF ALLOCATION
One engineer brigade headquarters per 2 to 5 engineer battalions. Mission tailored to support each corps conducting major combat or contingency operations. May also be tailored in support of divisions when the functional nature of engineer missions calls for brigade level command and control capability.

Legend:
CMD   command
DCP   deployable command post

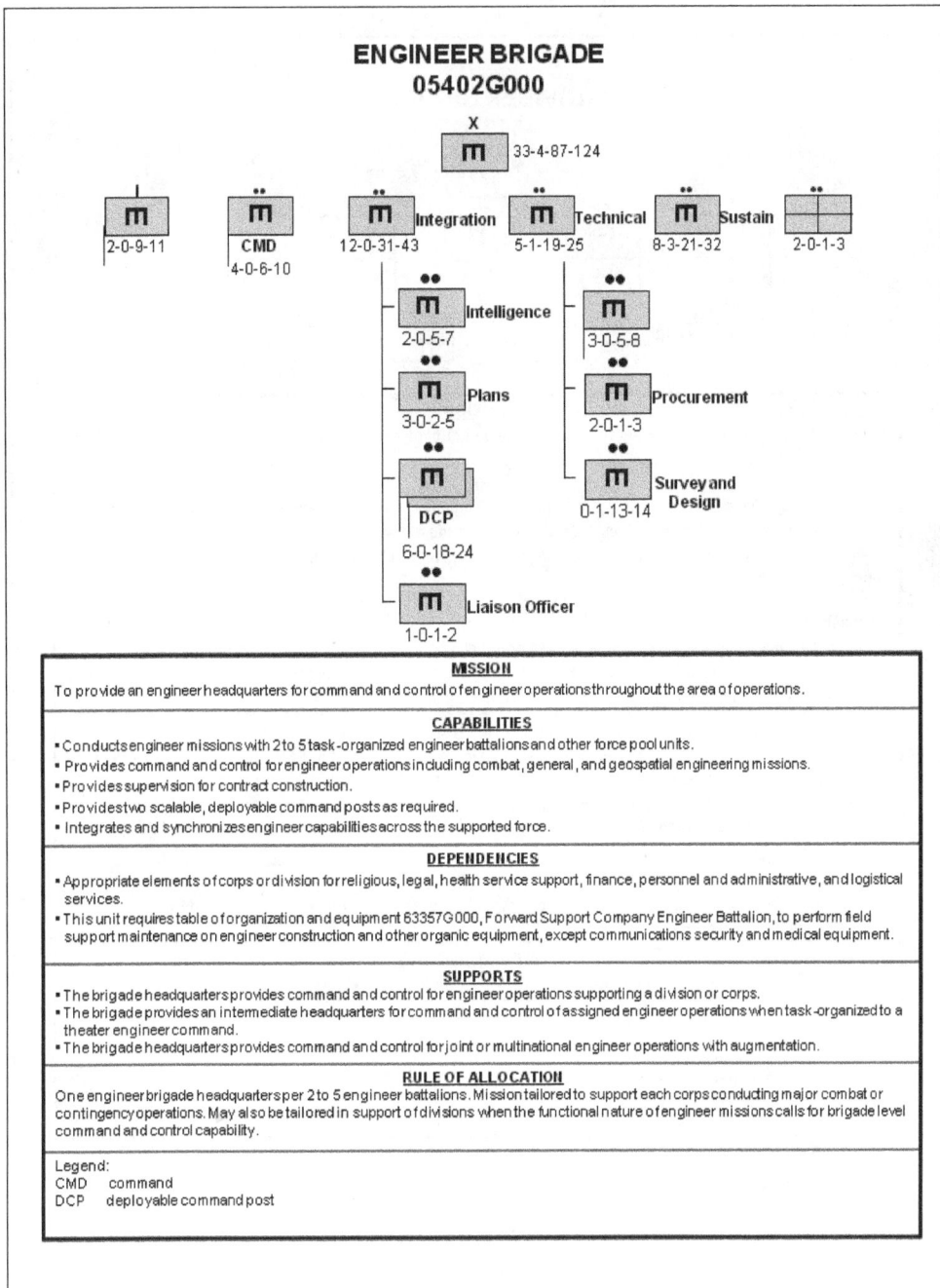

Figure A-2. Engineer brigade

ENGINEER BATTALION
05435G000

▥	18-2-63-83
CSS	5-2-83-90

▥	▥	▥	▥	PS
2-0-10-12	CMD 2-0-4-6	DCP1 3-0-8-11	DCP2 3-0-8-11	2-0-10-12

▥ Intelligence	▥ Plans		
2-0-6-8	2-0-3-5	1-0-7-8	1-2-7-10

MISSION

To provide an engineer headquarters for command and control of engineer operations in the area of operations.

CAPABILITIES

- Conducts engineer missions with 2 to 5 task-organized engineer companies and other force pool units.
- Provides command and control of units task-organized to the battalion.
- With task-organized engineer units, the battalion is capable of conducting engineer operations including combat and general engineering missions.
- With task-organized combined arms units, the unit is capable of conducting of combat missions, when required.
- With task-organized units, the unit is capable of conducting area damage control, when required.
- Provides unit administration, religious, and logistic support to task-organized units.
- Provides two scalable, deployable command posts as required.

DEPENDENCIES

- Appropriate elements of corps or division for religious, legal, health service support, finance, personnel and administrative, and logistical services.
- Table of organization and equipment 63357G000, Forward Support Company Engineer Battalion, for field feeding support, fuel and supplemental transportation of Class IV and V supplies, as well as support for limited field maintenance.

SUPPORTS

- The battalion headquarters provides command and control for engineer operations supporting brigade, division, or corps operations.

RULE OF ALLOCATION

One engineer battalion headquarters per 2 to 5 engineer companies.

Legend:
CMD   command
CSS   combat service support
DCP   deployable command post
PS   personnel services

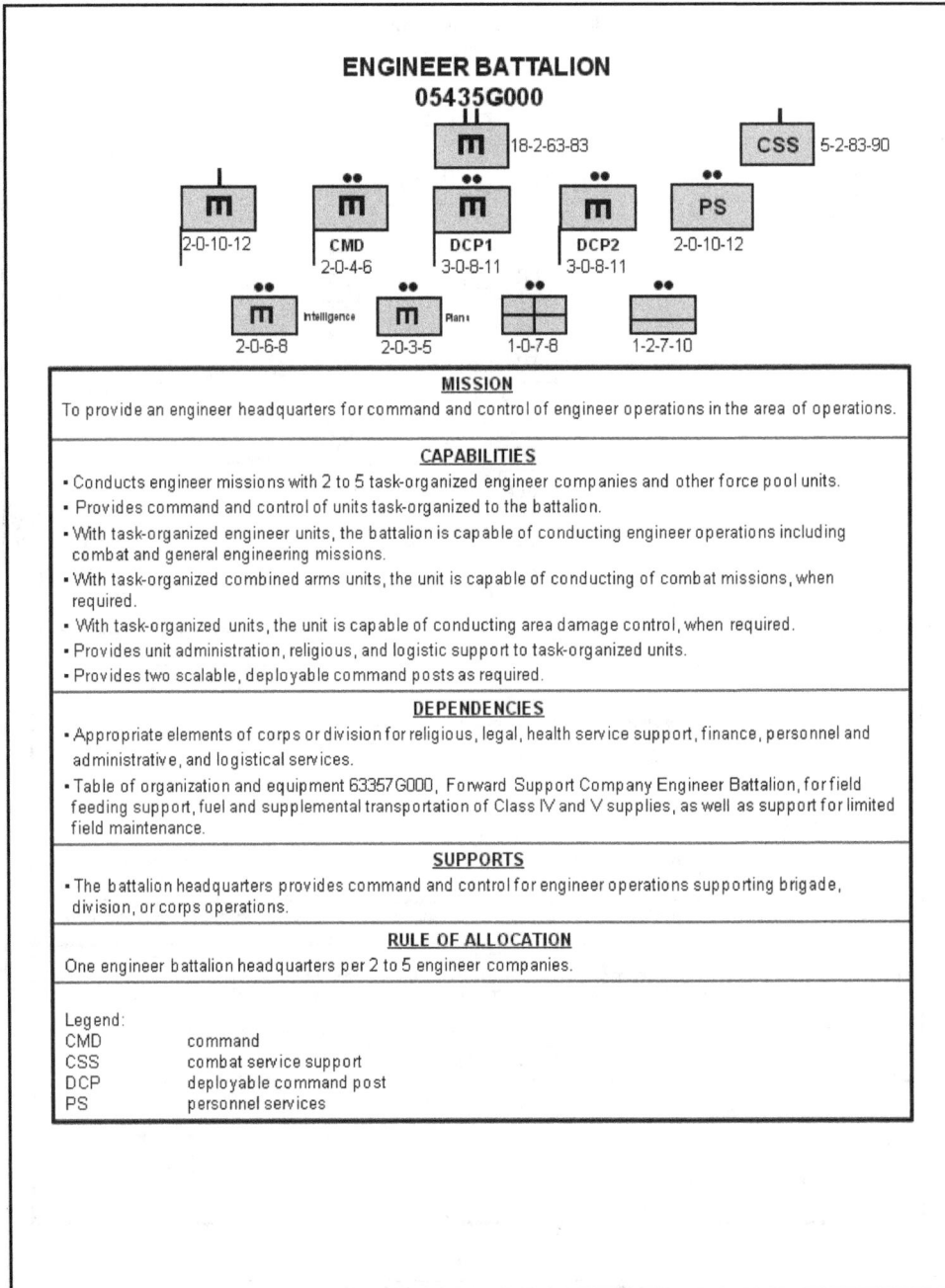

Figure A-3. Engineer battalion

MANEUVER ENHANCEMENT BRIGADE

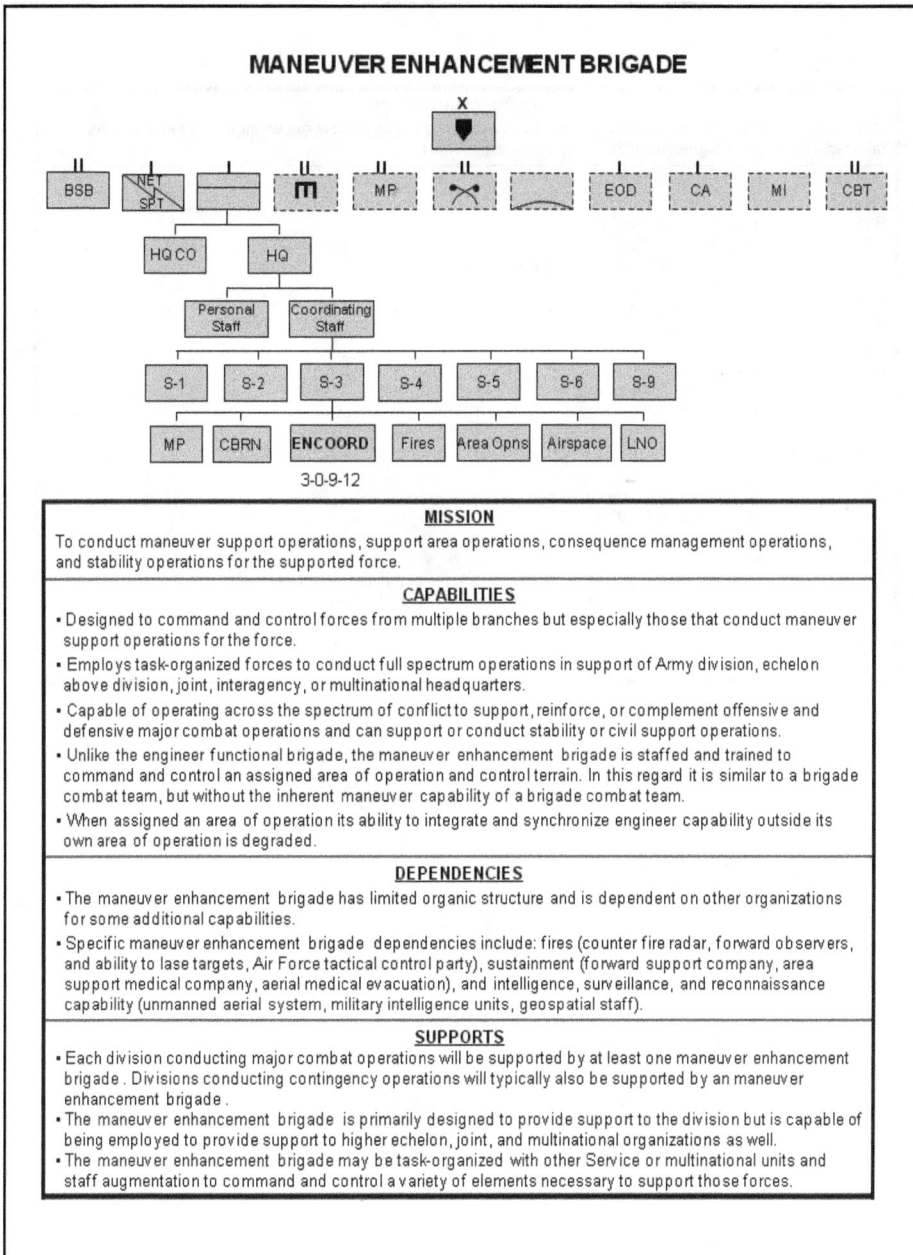

3-0-9-12

MISSION

To conduct maneuver support operations, support area operations, consequence management operations, and stability operations for the supported force.

CAPABILITIES

- Designed to command and control forces from multiple branches but especially those that conduct maneuver support operations for the force.
- Employs task-organized forces to conduct full spectrum operations in support of Army division, echelon above division, joint, interagency, or multinational headquarters.
- Capable of operating across the spectrum of conflict to support, reinforce, or complement offensive and defensive major combat operations and can support or conduct stability or civil support operations.
- Unlike the engineer functional brigade, the maneuver enhancement brigade is staffed and trained to command and control an assigned area of operation and control terrain. In this regard it is similar to a brigade combat team, but without the inherent maneuver capability of a brigade combat team.
- When assigned an area of operation its ability to integrate and synchronize engineer capability outside its own area of operation is degraded.

DEPENDENCIES

- The maneuver enhancement brigade has limited organic structure and is dependent on other organizations for some additional capabilities.
- Specific maneuver enhancement brigade dependencies include: fires (counter fire radar, forward observers, and ability to lase targets, Air Force tactical control party), sustainment (forward support company, area support medical company, aerial medical evacuation), and intelligence, surveillance, and reconnaissance capability (unmanned aerial system, military intelligence units, geospatial staff).

SUPPORTS

- Each division conducting major combat operations will be supported by at least one maneuver enhancement brigade. Divisions conducting contingency operations will typically also be supported by an maneuver enhancement brigade.
- The maneuver enhancement brigade is primarily designed to provide support to the division but is capable of being employed to provide support to higher echelon, joint, and multinational organizations as well.
- The maneuver enhancement brigade may be task-organized with other Service or multinational units and staff augmentation to command and control a variety of elements necessary to support those forces.

Figure A-4. MEB

RULE OF ALLOCATION
One maneuver enhancement brigade per division conducting major combat or contingency operations. As required in support of higher echelon, joint, and multinational forces.

Legend:
BSB   brigade support battalion
CA   civil affairs
CBRN   chemical, biological, radiological, and nuclear
CBT   combat
EOD   explosive ordnance disposal
ENCOORD   engineer coordinator
LNO   liaison officer
HQ   headquarters
HQ CO   headquarters company
MI   military intelligence
MP   military police
NET   network
opns   operations
S-1   human resources staff officer
S-2   intelligence staff officer
S-3   operations staff officer
S-4   logistics staff officer
S-5   civilian affairs/public affairs staff officer at the battalion/brigade level
S-6   communications and information management staff officer
S-9   facilities management staff officer
SPT   support

Figure A-4. MEB (continued)

ECHELONS ABOVE BRIGADE ENGINEER STAFF AND GEOSPATIAL ENGINEERING SUPPORT

A-3. The organic structure of the staff at each EAB will vary slightly from unit to unit. This is especially true at theater army echelon. The basic structure of authorizations is described in this appendix, but readers must investigate variations based on the specific division, corps, or theater army headquarters in which they are interested.

A-4. As discussed in chapter 3, staff authorizations provide a starting point for organizing an operational engineer staff. Mission variables are considered in determining the operational configuration for the headquarters, and the mission also determines which activities the operationally configured headquarters must accomplish. These activities determine how commanders organize, tailor, or adapt their staff to accomplish the mission. Ultimately, the distribution of engineer staff among CPs and cells may differ significantly from the basic structures shown. Similarly, the engineer staff may be more consolidated into a functional cell than shown when that organization better fits mission variables. In every case, an ENCOORD must coordinate the efforts of the entire engineer staff, and the staff will use working groups as necessary to further integrate efforts across functions.

DIVISION ENGINEER STAFF

A-5. The organic engineer staff authorizations within the division headquarters are shown in figure A-5.

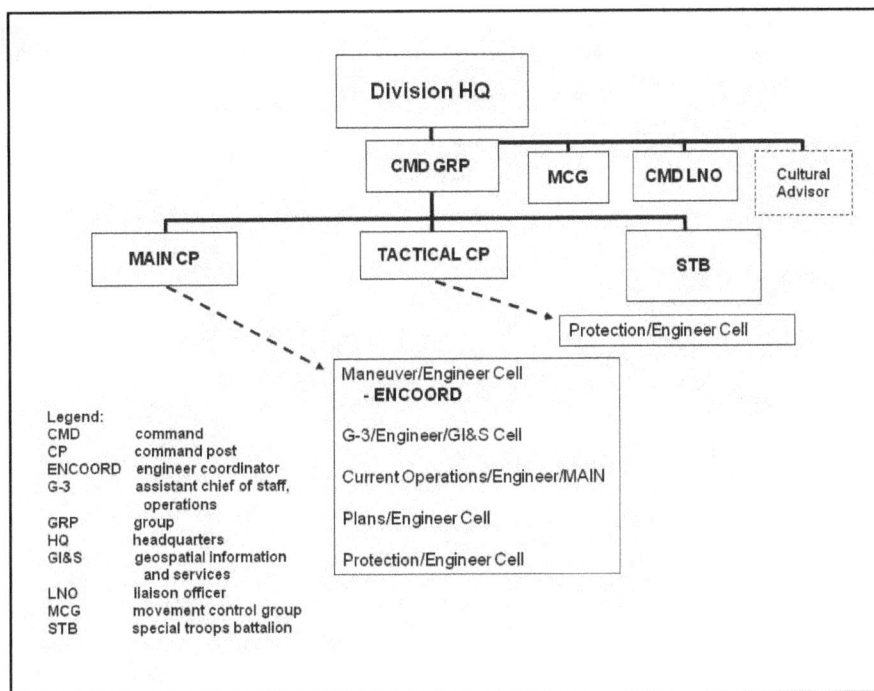

Figure A-5. Organic engineer staff in the division headquarters

A-6. The division engineer or ENCOORD is an engineer lieutenant colonel who is assisted by a senior engineer noncommissioned officer (NCO) and a chief warrant officer utilities operations maintenance technician. In addition to the ENCOORD, the division headquarters is assigned engineer staff cells in both the main CP and tactical CP. An engineer major, captain, and NCO provide an engineer operations cell in both the main CP and tactical CP. An additional engineer major and NCO are assigned to the protection cell in the main CP, and an engineer major serves as engineer plans officer in the main CP.

A-7. The organic GI&S cell assigned to the division main CP is led by a chief warrant officer geospatial information technician and a senior geospatial engineer sergeant. In addition, the cell has two geospatial engineer NCOs and five geospatial engineer Soldiers. The geospatial engineer cell has the capability to—

- Generate and analyze terrain data.
- Prepare decision graphics.
- Produce image maps.
- Provide three-dimensional terrain perspective views.
- Manage the theater geospatial database.
- Update maps.
- Produce tactical decision aids.
- Produce IPB overlays.
- Operate on a 24-hour basis.

A-8. Equipment assigned to the geospatial engineer section includes—

- One each digital topographic support system (DTSS): AN/TYQ-67 (light).
- One each truck cargo: 4x4 light to medium tactical truck (LMTV) with towed generator.
- One each truck utility: 1-1/4 ton 4x4 with equipment high-mobility multipurpose wheeled vehicle (HMMWV).

Corps Engineer Staff

A-9. The organic engineer staff authorizations within the corps headquarters are shown in figure A-6, page A-8.

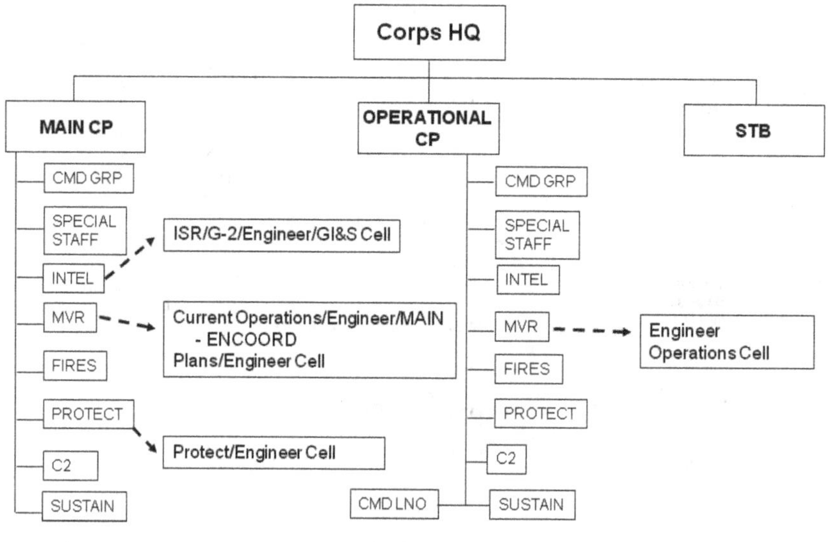

Legend:

C2	command and control
CMD	command
CP	command post
ENCOORD	engineer coordinator
G-2	assistant chief of staff, intelligence
GI&S	geospatial information and services
GRP	group
HQ	headquarters
INTEL	intelligence
ISR	intelligence, surveillance, and reconnaissance
LNO	liaison officer
MVR	maneuver
STB	special troops battalion

Figure A-6. Organic engineer staff in the corps headquarters

A-10. The corps engineer or ENCOORD is an engineer colonel who is assisted by an engineer sergeant major. In addition to the ENCOORD, the corps headquarters is assigned engineer staff cells in both the main CP and operational CP. An engineer major and captain provide an engineer operations cell in the main CP. The engineer operations cell in the operational CP consists of an engineer lieutenant colonel, two majors, an engineer NCO, and two combat engineer Soldiers. An additional engineer major serves as engineer plans officer in the main CP.

A-11. The organic GI&S cell assigned to the corps main CP has the same structure, manning, and equipment as the division geospatial cell (see paragraphs A-7 and A-8).

THEATER ARMY ENGINEER STAFF

A-12. The organic engineer staff authorizations within the theater army headquarters are shown in figure A-7.

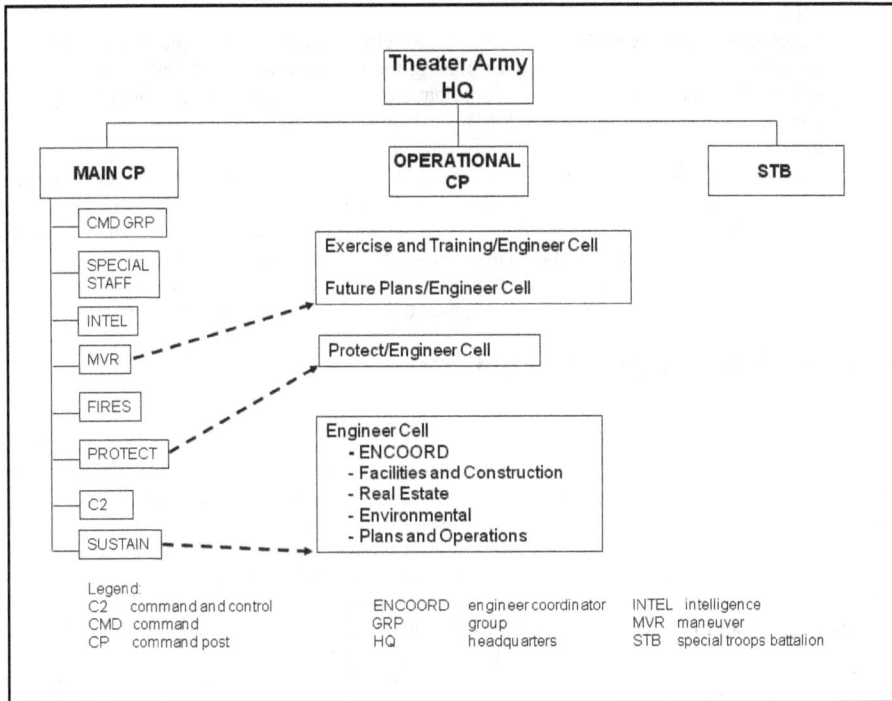

Figure A-7. Organic engineer staff in the Army headquarters

A-13. The theater army engineer, ENCOORD, is an engineer colonel who is assisted by an engineer sergeant major. In addition to the ENCOORD, the theater army headquarters is assigned engineer staff cells within the protection, maneuver, and sustainment sections of the main CP. Within the sustainment section, a total of seven engineer lieutenant colonels lead subordinate engineer staff cells with majors, captains, NCOs, and combat engineer Soldiers to assist. An additional engineer lieutenant colonel and two majors serve within the maneuver section and an engineer major serves in the protection section.

A-14. The theater army headquarters relies on a topographic engineer company or geospatial planning cell task-organized to provide geospatial engineering support. See FM 3-34 for a description of these organizations.

JOINT FORCE ENGINEER STAFF AND GEOSPATIAL SUPPORT

A-15. Each JFC has a unique engineer staff structure. The specific JMD describes the engineer staff organization and should reflect representation from each Service. Staff engineers should work closely with civilian and multinational partner organizations to develop wartime organization augmentation manning.

The JMD should be built based on analysis of the mission and the engineer staff capabilities required to support the operation.

A-16. The JFC will organize their staffs to carry out their respective assigned duties and responsibilities. Based on mission-specific requirements, the engineer staff may be placed within the J-3, J-4, or organized as a separate staff to the JFC. The JFC may choose to organize geospatial engineers or GI&S officers within the J-2, J-3, J-4, or doctrine and training directorate of a joint staff (J-7), depending on the specific organizational structure of the unit. Considerations for each option include the following:

- **Operations directorate staff.** When the focus of engineer effort predominantly supports the operational movement and maneuver, fires, and protection warfighting functions, the JFC should consider placing the engineer staff as a cell within the J-3. This option will provide the fastest exchange of information during crisis action planning and optimize the use of supporting capabilities.
- **Logistics directorate staff.** When the engineer effort predominantly supports sustainment of the joint force, the JFC should consider placing the engineer staff as a cell within the J-4. This option facilitates planning and coordination among engineers and logisticians for the construction and repair of LOCs, MSRs, airfields, other logistic facilities, and infrastructure in general.
- **Separate engineer staff.** When the engineer effort is a significant focus or a key element of the joint operation, or where the engineer effort is equally divided between combat and general engineering functions, the JFC should consider establishing a separate engineer staff element that reports directly to the JFC. This option provides the greatest flexibility in orchestrating diverse engineer operations, and it provides the greatest visibility of engineer capabilities, requirements, and responsibilities throughout the staff. This is the preferred option.

CELLS, WORKGROUPS, AND BOARDS

COMMAND POST CELLS

A-17. In the context of CPs, a cell is a grouping of personnel and equipment by warfighting function or purpose to facilitate C2. There are two types of CP cells: functional and integrating (see figure A-8). Functional cells group personnel and equipment by warfighting function. Integrating cells group personnel and equipment to integrate functional cell activities. Integrating cells normally focus on different time horizons. For example, the plans cell focuses on the long-range time horizon, while the current operations cell focuses on the short-range time horizons. FM 3-0 discusses time horizons. This is not to say that the functional cells do not integrate. The sustainment cell integrates numerous logistic areas and services; the fires cell integrates the contributions of all warfighting functions to targeting through the targeting working group. This integration, however, generally focuses on maximizing the effects of a single warfighting function. Integrating cells focus the efforts of functional cells on planning, preparing for, or executing the overall operation within a time horizon.

A-18. Functional cells and integrating cells are not single staff sections. In a sense, they are combined arms staff components. For example, in a corps main CP, G-2 section personnel often form elements of the intelligence, fires, current operations, and plans cells. They form elements of the intelligence, fires, current operations, and future operations cells in the tactical CP.

A-19. Not all cells depicted in figure A-8 are in every CP. A battalion or brigade tactical CP, for example, is usually not divided into cells: the entire tactical CP is the current operations cell. It comprises representatives from various staff sections. A corps operational CP, in contrast, has all the cells listed in paragraph B-15, except for plans.

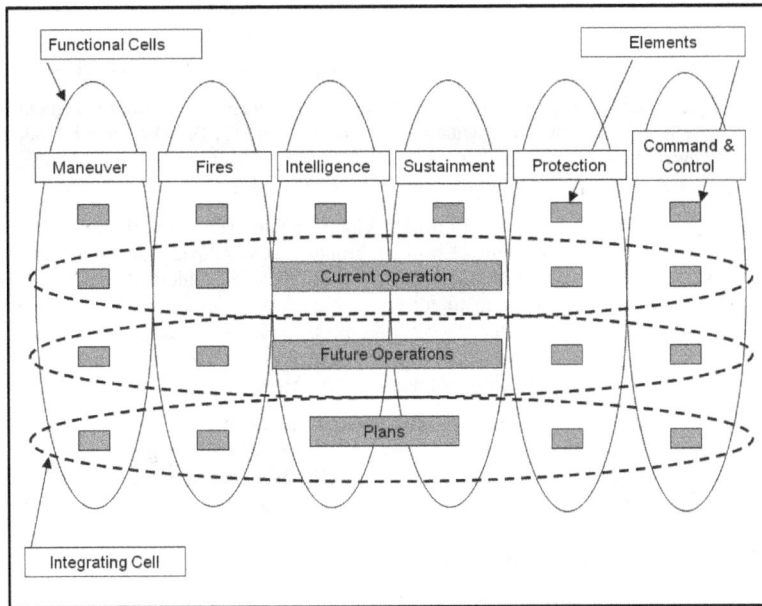

Figure A-8. Command post organization

MEETINGS, WORKING GROUPS, AND BOARDS

A-20. Periodically or as required, ad hoc groupings form to solve problems and coordinate actions. These groups include representatives from within or outside a CP. Their composition depends on the issue. These groups are called meetings, working groups, and boards. Each is a control mechanism for regulating a specific action, process, or function.

A-21. Meetings (sometimes called huddles) are informal gatherings used to present and exchange information. Cell chiefs and staff section representatives hold meetings as needed to synchronize their activities.

A-22. Working groups are temporary groupings of predetermined staff representatives who meet to coordinate and provide recommendations for a particular purpose or function. Some working groups may be thought of as ad hoc cells. Others are the forum used to synchronize the contributions of multiple cells to a process. For example, the targeting working group brings together representatives of all staff elements concerned with targeting. It synchronizes the contributions of all staff elements to the work of the fires cell. It also synchronizes fires with current or future operations. Working groups may be held at a central location, by teleconference, by video teleconference, or by a combination of all of these. They are formed as needed or when the commander directs. Typical working groups and the lead cell or staff section at division and corps headquarters include—

- Operations synchronization (current operations cell).
- Plans (plans cell).
- Targeting (fires cell).
- Information operations (G-7 section).
- ISR (current operations cell).
- GEOINT (GEOINT cell).
- Intelligence synchronization (intelligence cell).
- Protection (protection cell).
- Logistics synchronization (sustainment cell).

- Movements (sustainment cell).
- Civil-military operations (assistant chief of staff, civil affairs operations [G-9] section).
- Information management (assistant chief of staff, information management [G-6] section).

A-23. For example, a corps CP may form working groups to address enemy improvised explosive device (IED) tactics or refugee return and resettlement of displaced civilians. Battalion and brigade headquarters normally have fewer working groups than higher echelons, and working groups are often less formal. Groups may gather daily, weekly, or monthly, depending on the subject, situation, and echelon.

A-24. Working groups form a major part of a CP's battle rhythm. The chief of staff or executive officer oversees the battle rhythm and scheduling of working groups. Each group should be logically sequenced so that one group's outputs are available as another's inputs when needed. Chiefs of staff or executive officers balance the time required to plan, prepare for, and hold working groups with other staff duties and responsibilities. They also examine attendance requirements critically. Some staff sections and cells may not have enough personnel to attend all working groups. Chiefs of staff and cell leaders constantly look for ways to combine working groups and eliminate unproductive ones.

A-25. Boards are temporary groupings of selected staff representatives who are delegated decision authority for a particular purpose or function. They are similar to working groups. When the process or activity being synchronized requires command approval, a board is the appropriate forum. The unit's SOP establishes each board's purpose, frequency, required inputs, expected outputs, attendees, and agenda.

ENGINEER BOARDS, CENTERS, AND CELLS

A-26. A JFC may establish engineer boards or cells to manage engineer-intensive activities and to ensure an effective use of resources to meet mission requirements. Engineer boards establish policies, procedures, priorities, and oversight to coordinate efficient use of engineer resources. Engineer boards serve as the forum to address issues outside of daily operations and to ensure coordination at the leadership level and across staff directorates. The joint force engineer and staff will carry out responsibilities of the engineer-specific boards until the boards are formed. An important distinction between a board and a working group is that a board is usually a decisionmaking body. Working groups conduct staff coordination at the action officer level and prepare materials for decisions to be made at a board. Cells within the JTF are a group of personnel with specific skills who are listed together on the headquarters JMD to accomplish key functions. It is important for the Services and components to be represented on the engineer boards to facilitate vertical and horizontal integration that will allow the joint force engineer to capitalize on the advantages of joint capabilities. Collaborative tools allow components to participate in boards without having to physically be present at the joint force headquarters. The joint force engineer is responsible for the boards described below.

A-27. The CCDR or subordinate JFC may establish a JCMEB to assist in managing civil-military construction and engineer projects and resources. The JCMEB is a temporary board, chaired by the CCDR or his designated representative, such as the combatant command J-4, combatant command engineer, subordinate joint force engineer, or CA officer. The joint force engineer will provide the secretariat and manage the administrative details of the board. Key members on the board include the J-3 future plans officer, J-4, engineer, CA officer, staff judge advocate, and force structure, resources, and assessment of a joint staff (J-8). Other personnel from the staff, components, DOD agencies or activities in support of the combatant command may also participate. According to CCDR guidelines, the JCMEB establishes policies, procedures, priorities, and overall direction for general military construction and engineering requirements in-theater. Figure A-9 depicts some typical inputs and outputs for the board, primary membership, and outside stakeholders. The board gauges mission impact from engineering activities and recommends actions as needed. A primary task of the board is to deconflict requirements between the military and civilian aspects of construction during a joint operation. The board should also facilitate synchronization of the joint force engineer effort with similar efforts being undertaken at the strategic level. The JCMEB will coordinate its activities with the combatant command's engineering and CA staff. The JCMEB will elevate construction and engineering requirements it cannot satisfy from within joint force resources to the next appropriate level for support. The JCMEB may arbitrate issues referred to it by the JFUB. The JCMEB, in conjunction with the JFUB, also provides guidance on development of the ESP to an OPLAN or OPORD and, if appropriate, assumes responsibility for preparation of the ESP.

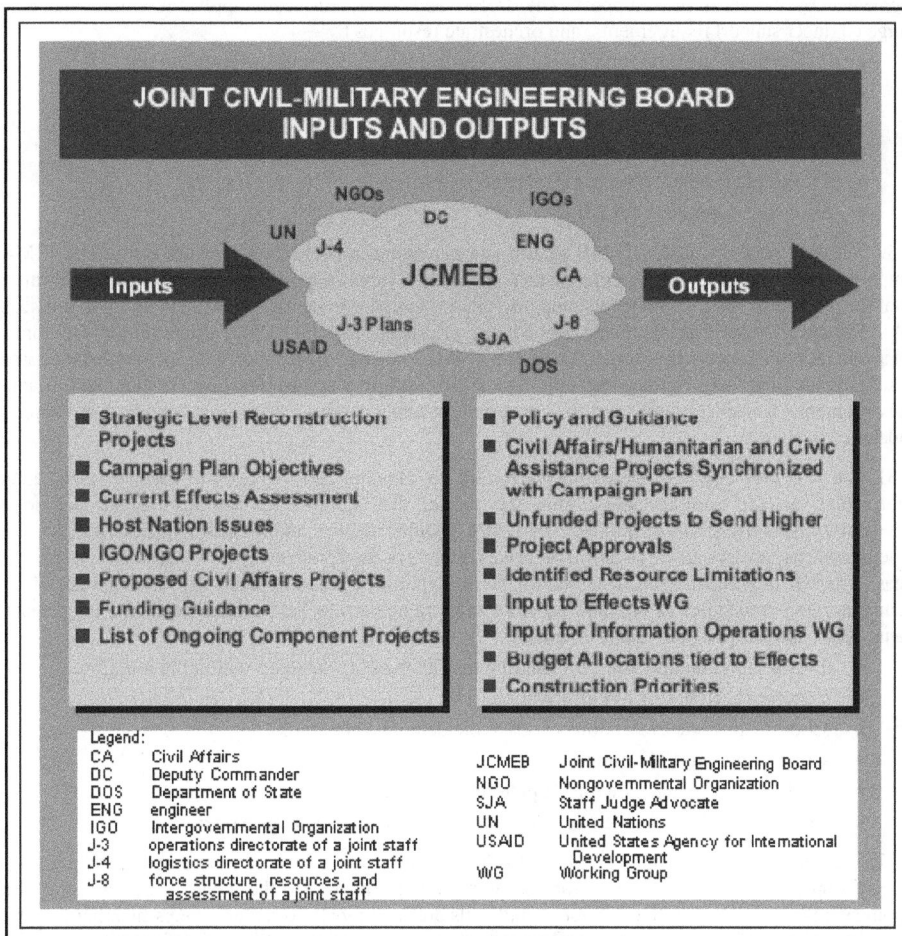

JOINT CIVIL-MILITARY ENGINEERING BOARD INPUTS AND OUTPUTS

NGOs   IGOs

UN   DC   ENG

J-4   **JCMEB**   CA

Inputs   →   ←   **Outputs**

J-3 Plans   J-8

USAID   SJA

DOS

- Strategic Level Reconstruction Projects
- Campaign Plan Objectives
- Current Effects Assessment
- Host Nation Issues
- IGO/NGO Projects
- Proposed Civil Affairs Projects
- Funding Guidance
- List of Ongoing Component Projects

- Policy and Guidance
- Civil Affairs/Humanitarian and Civic Assistance Projects Synchronized with Campaign Plan
- Unfunded Projects to Send Higher
- Project Approvals
- Identified Resource Limitations
- Input to Effects WG
- Input for Information Operations WG
- Budget Allocations tied to Effects
- Construction Priorities

Legend:
CA	Civil Affairs	JCMEB	Joint Civil-Military Engineering Board
DC	Deputy Commander	NGO	Nongovernmental Organization
DOS	Department of State	SJA	Staff Judge Advocate
ENG	engineer	UN	United Nations
IGO	Intergovernmental Organization	USAID	United States Agency for International
J-3	operations directorate of a joint staff		Development
J-4	logistics directorate of a joint staff	WG	Working Group
J-8	force structure, resources, and assessment of a joint staff		

Figure A-9. Joint civil-military engineering board inputs and outputs

A-28. The JFC may establish a JFUB to assist in managing Service component use of real estate and existing facilities. The JFUB is a temporary board chaired by the combatant command or subordinate joint force engineer, with members from the joint force staff, components, and any other required special activities (such as legal, contracting, and CA). If the JFC decides that all engineer-related decisions will be made at the JCMEB, then the JFUB functions as a working group to forward recommendations for decision to the JCMEB. The JFUB evaluates and reconciles component requests for real estate, use of existing facilities, inter-Service support, and construction to ensure compliance with priorities established by the JFC. It serves as the primary coordination body within the JTF for approving construction projects within the wire to support troop beddown and mission requirements. For long-standing JTFs, the JFUB may issue master planning guidance and develop the JTF military construction program to support enduring base operations. The joint force engineer handles most of the JFUB's work with assistance from other selected board members. Unresolved issues may be forwarded to the JCMEB.

A-29. Contingency engineering management organizations are an option to augment the joint force staff, providing additional service engineering expertise to support both contingency and crisis action planning and provide construction management in contingency and major combat operations. The conduct of theater army echelon construction operations may be managed by a TCEM or an RCEM cell. The composition and the procedures of the TCEM and the RCEM cells are governed by the respective GCCs. These cells are augmented by the staffs they support. The TCEM and the RCEM cells apply the commander's intent, merge engineer support requirements, and orchestrate resources by—

- Establishing priorities and policy for theater construction and barrier materials.
- Establishing theater distribution protocols that are consistent with construction priorities.
- Monitoring and recommending the allocation and use of construction assets against priority operational requirements and recommending taskings for engineer assets.
- Developing construction standards and priorities.
- Providing input to the JCMEB.

A-30. The JFC may establish a JEMB to assist in managing environmental requirements. The JEMB is a temporary board, chaired by the combatant command or subordinate joint force engineer, with members from the joint force staff, components, and any other required special activities (such as legal, medical, and CA). The board establishes policies, procedures, priorities, and the overall direction for environmental management requirements in a JOA. The JEMB will coordinate its activities with the combatant command or subordinate joint force engineering staff. The JEMB also provides guidance on development of annex L, "Environmental Considerations," and, if appropriate, assumes responsibility for preparation and appropriate updates of this annex.

A-31. The JFC may establish the explosive hazard coordination cell (EHCC) to predict, track, distribute information on, and mitigate EH within the theater that affect force application, focused logistics, survivability, and awareness of the OE. The EHCC should establish and maintain an EH database, conduct pattern analysis, investigate mine and IED strikes, and track unexploded explosive ordnance (UXO) hazard areas. The cell provides technical advice on the mitigation of EH, including the development of tactics, techniques, and procedures (TTP), and provides training updates to field units. The EHCC coordinates EH teams. Key capabilities of the EHCC include—

- Establishing, maintaining, and sharing the EH tracking database within the joint force.
- Ensuring accuracy of EH information.
- Coordinating site evaluations or strike incident investigations.
- Conducting unit EH training.
- Assisting ISR planners with EH pattern analysis and ISR synchronization.
- Providing updated TTP and guidance for route and area clearance operations.

A-32. Engineer participation in a number of other boards, centers, and cells is essential to joint mission accomplishment. Compared to the formal, nonstanding nature of the boards, centers are standing organizations typically operating 24 hours, and cells are functionally oriented groups meeting on a regular basis. Engineer staff participation and support to these organizations will be significant, but the resultant exchange of RI is vital in maintaining situational awareness and facilitating the horizontal staff integration of the joint force engineer. Joint force engineer participation in the following boards, centers, and cells includes—

- **Joint planning group.** Engineers are represented on the joint planning group to enhance the formulation of joint force plans. The engineer planner ensures that joint force plans are supportable from an engineer perspective. Support by the rest of the joint force engineer cell with products facilitates engineer input and impact into the planning cycle. The engineer planner should leverage the rest of the engineer staff to provide products throughout the planning process. The key for the engineer is to ensure representation and establish handoff procedures for products developed within all three planning horizons within the joint force: future plans, future operations, and current operations.
- **Joint intelligence support element.** Representation on the joint intelligence support element provides engineers with MI related to infrastructure, hydrography, and other geospatial engineering and GEOINT topics.
- **Joint operations center.** The joint operations center plans, monitors, and guides the execution of the JFC's decisions. The joint force engineer maintains a presence in or close contact with this center. This is the engineer's link to current operations and the engineer watch officer is responsible for keeping the rest of the engineer staff situationally aware.

- **Joint targeting coordination board.** On the joint targeting coordination board, the joint force engineer contributes to the planning and integration of munition fields into the barrier plan and participates in target coordination to ensure critical infrastructure preservation. Of particular engineer concern are remotely delivered mines scattered beyond the intended location and the related reporting, marking, and clearing of those mines. The joint force engineer should ensure that implications on stability operations are considered during the targeting process for decisive operations. Engineer expertise can enable the JFC to achieve desired effects with minimal long-term infrastructure damage and protection of significant cultural and natural resources in the operational area.

- **Information operations cell.** In the information operations cell, the joint force engineer coordinates with other staff elements on the preservation of critical adversary facilities and infrastructure. During stability operations, engineer reconstruction efforts focused on the HN can help support the commander's strategic communications plan.

- **Civil-military operations center.** The CMOC provides the joint force engineer a meeting place to coordinate nonmilitary activities with other agencies, departments, organizations, and the HN. If formed, the CMOC is the focal point where engineers coordinate any support to NGOs. Outputs from the CMOC (such as lists of intergovernmental and NGO projects) are useful input into the JCMEB and help facilitate unity of effort.

- **Joint logistics operations center.** Engineers are represented at the joint logistics operations center to respond to information received from supporting command, Service components, and external sources for presentation to the CCDR.

- **Force protection working group.** The force protection working group will often generate engineer requirements as they develop or modify JTF force protection policy and guidance. Examples include hardening of key facilities and modifications to entry control points.

- **Special purpose boards, centers, working groups, and cells.** Through necessity, new boards, centers, and cells may be formed and require engineer participation. For example, an IED working group may be required as a central clearinghouse for developing solutions to an IED problem within the JOA. The engineer should also have representation at the force protection and effects assessment working groups and boards, if established. Engineer construction efforts, whether inside or outside the wire, are closely tied to the issues addressed at these two working groups and boards.

This page intentionally left blank.

Appendix B
Engineer Running Estimate

The running estimate is a staff section's continuous assessment of current and future operations to determine if the current operation is proceeding according to the commander's intent and if future operations are supportable (FM 3-0). The engineer staff develops a running estimate to embody its evaluation of the situation and then refines and maintains it based on new information gathered while monitoring the operation. The running estimate incorporates all the staff tools used by the engineer in planning, preparing, and executing an operation and represents a tangible form for the engineer staff member's continuous assessment. The ENCOORD uses the running estimate to coordinate the unique perspectives of the various engineer staff elements supporting the headquarters. This appendix is intended as a tool for organizing the various aspects of the running estimate in the conduct of engineer operations. Running estimates follow the generic format in FM 5-0, and are also discussed further in FM 3-0 and FM 6-0.

NAVIGATING MAJOR ACTIVITIES DURING OPERATIONS

B-1. Applications of engineer support efforts at EAB must remain integrated within the combined arms framework. Integration enables a synchronized application of combat power, maximizing the effect of the engineering effort. Integration is a foundation of engineer operations—integration within the supported unit staff, throughout the operations process, and across the force. In general, the engineer staff at EAB or of a joint force assists their commander by furnishing engineer advice and recommendations to the commander and other staff members; preparing those portions of plans, estimates, and orders that pertain to engineering; participating on boards and working groups as necessary; and coordinating and supervising engineer units and other activities within the engineer staff's span of control. The running estimate roadmap shown in figure B-1, page B-2, is a tool to assist the engineer staff in navigating the various processes and activities involved in conducting operations while considering the application of engineer combat power.

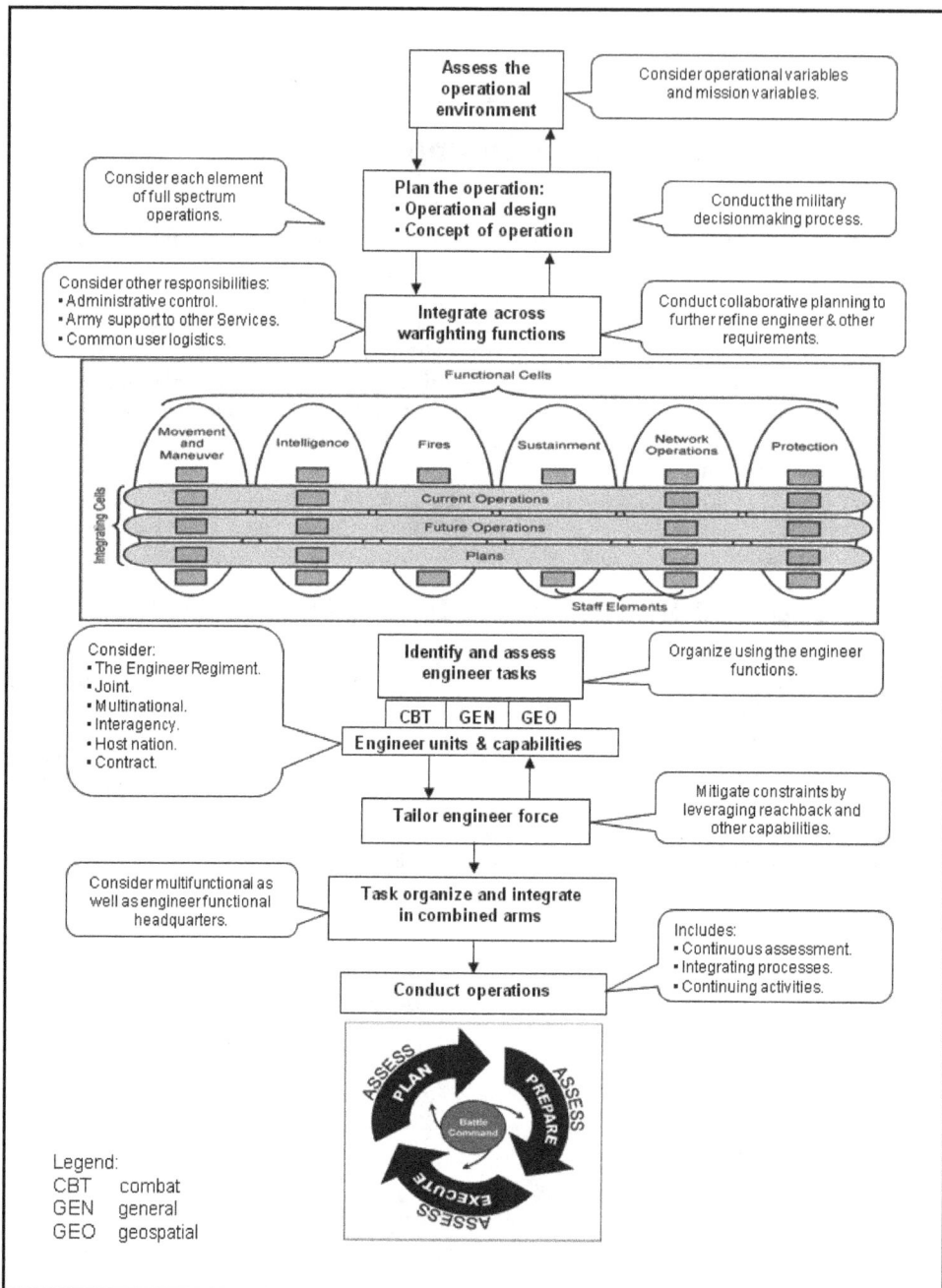

Figure B-1. Roadmap for the engineer running estimate

ASSESSING THE OPERATIONAL ENVIRONMENT

B-2. Army doctrine describes an OE in terms of eight operational variables, PMESII-PT. Table B-1 provides some engineer considerations within each of these variables. The examples are not meant to restate the more complete treatment of the operational variables provided in FM 3-0, nor are they meant to be an all-inclusive treatment of the engineer aspects within each of the operational variables.

Table B-1. Assessment using operational variables

Operational Variables	Engineer Considerations
Political	• Political circumstances permitting or denying access to key ports of entry or critical sustainment facilities. • Alternative access routes. • The effect of laws, agreements, or positions of partners that might prevent the shipment of construction, hazardous, or other materials across borders. • Political considerations that might affect real estate acquisition or engineer planning and operations.
Military	• An adversary's capability to employ explosive hazards or other obstacles and the capability to challenge traditional survivability standards. • Existing military installations and other infrastructure. • Understanding of engineer capabilities in a joint, interagency, and multinational context.
Economic	• Production or availability of key materials and construction resources. • Potential for new or improved production facilities that might be added.
Social	• Specific cultural or religious buildings or installations. • Impact of language barriers or unique local dialects on the availability of labor and engineer resources. • Potential to provide for culturally related building requirements might be a consideration.
Information	• Physical deficiencies in the supporting architecture (including electrical power) or nodes. • Provision for humanitarian projects or services.
Infrastructure	• Deficiencies in the basic infrastructure (see FM 3-34.170 for a discussion of assessment of infrastructure using the sewer, water, electrical power, academics, trash, medical, safety, and other considerations framework). • Access to existing infrastructure; building, deconstructing, or transferring infrastructure needed for base camps. • Opportunities for improvements to existing infrastructure and specific new projects.
Physical Environment	• Defining factors are urban settings (supersurface, surface, and subsurface features), other types of complex terrain, weather, topography, hydrology, and environmental conditions. • Natural and man-made obstacles. • Existing routes, installations, and resources.
Time	• Challenges associated with completing required construction projects in the time allotted. • Potential to accelerate priority projects.

B-3. When commanders receive a mission, they require a mission analysis focused on their specific situation. The Army uses mission variables, METT–TC, as a framework for this mission analysis (see table B-2). Assessment using the mission variables is substantially refined during the mission analysis portion of MDMP, but the framework remains useful throughout the conduct of operations. It serves as the major subject categories into which RI is grouped.

Table B-2. Assessment using mission variables

Mission Variables	Engineer Considerations
Mission	• Understand the friendly mission, commander's intent, and concept of the operation (two levels up), and understand how engineer capabilities contribute to the mission. • Analyze and monitor the status of engineer missions—planned, prepared, executed (see mission analysis portion of the military decisionmaking process for planning considerations).
Enemy	• Enemy disposition (organization, strength, location). • Obstacle intelligence (results of intelligence, surveillance, and reconnaissance, engineer reconnaissance, mine strikes). • Enemy engineer capabilities. • Enemy vulnerabilities. • Probable enemy COAs.
Terrain and Weather	• Updated terrain information to reflect the effects of combat and nature. • Environmental considerations.

Troops and Support Available	• Current task organization.
	• Engineer combat power.
	  ▪ Unit readiness (normally two levels down):
	    - Personnel strength (critical specialties).
	    - Maintenance status.
	    - Supply status.
	  ▪ Mobility/countermobility/survivability and other engineer capabilities.
	• Resources and support available from:
	  ▪ Joint, multinational, and interagency forces.
	  ▪ Department of Defense or Department of State civilians.
	  ▪ Contractors.

Time Available	• Information related to how much time is available to plan, prepare, and execute operations. • Critical milestones that have been or will need to be identified.

Civil Considerations	• Influences and immediate impacts on engineer operations in the area of operation areas, structures, capabilities, organizations, people, events:
	  ▪ Areas (district boundaries, economic centers, religious or tribal enclaves).
	  ▪ Structures (bridges, dams, power plants, cultural sites).
	  ▪ Capabilities (status of essential services, host nation resources and services that can support military operations).
	  ▪ Organizations (nonmilitary groups or institutions that can influence the population).
	  ▪ People (attitudes and activities of civil leaders and populations), to include the criminal dimension and its effect on engineer operations.
	  ▪ Events (holidays, elections, natural or man-made disasters).

INTELLIGENCE PREPARATION OF THE BATTLEFIELD

B-4. Engineer staff participate in various integrating processes and continuing activities to add engineer perspectives and remain synchronized with the conduct of operations. IPB is an integrating process that is critical to the success of planning. It is also a systematic and continuous process of analyzing and visualizing the OE in a specific geographic area for a specific mission or in anticipation of a specific mission. Analysis includes terrain, weather, and civil considerations. The IPB centers on templating the enemy; anticipating its capabilities; and predicting its intentions based on threat doctrinal norms, patterns of operation, and the order of battle. Defining the OE identifies the characteristics of the environment that influence friendly and threat operations. The engineer must understand the intelligence officer's threat template and situational template (SITEMP) to analyze enemy engineer capabilities. Engineer reconnaissance (as discussed in chapter 2) may be required to support IPB, and the ENCOORD must be proactive in recognizing these requirements and coordinating the tasking of appropriate engineer elements.

B-5. The IPB consists of four steps:

- **Step 1. Define the operational environment.** This includes identifying characteristics that influence friendly and threat operations. It helps determine the area of interest and identifies gaps in intelligence. It is also the basis for analyzing terrain, weather, civil considerations, and threat forces.
- **Step 2. Describe the operational environment's effects.** This involves evaluating the effects of all aspects of the OE with which both sides must contend and always includes an examination of terrain, weather, and civil considerations.
- **Step 3. Evaluate the threat.** This is a detailed study of enemy forces, their composition and organization, tactical doctrine, patterns of operation, weapons and equipment, and supporting systems. This step identifies threat capabilities based on threat missions and objectives.
- **Step 4. Determine threat courses of action.** This involves developing possible enemy COAs, based on the analysis performed during the previous steps.

RUNNING ESTIMATE IN SUPPORT OF PLANNING

B-6. Operational design provides the bridge between strategic end state and execution of tactical tasks. Higher-echelon engineer staff will participate in the assessments and planning that lead to the design of an operational approach. Table B-3, page B-6, provides engineer considerations for the elements of operational design.

Table B-3. Assessment using elements of operational design

Design Elements	Engineer Focus
End state	Ensure that the image of the physical environment is consistent with the operational environment.
Conditions	Ensure that the physical conditions are supportive of the end state.
Centers of gravity	Expose, exploit physical vulnerabilities.
Operational approach	Defeat and stability mechanisms supported.
Decisive points	Understand, leverage geographic points.
Lines of operations, effort	Support the physics of geography, logic.
Operational reach	Extend tether of distance and duration.
Tempo	Maintain initiative to enhance control.
Simultaneity and depth	Collaborate among echelons and units.
Phasing and transitions	Anticipate challenges and opportunities.
Culmination	Preserve resources.
Risk	Prioritize engineer resources.

B-7. Tactically focused echelons will typically gain substantial initial context for their assessments from a higher-echelon's operational design. Prior to receipt of a mission, the running estimate consists of a broad analysis of the OE and assessment of engineer capabilities. Upon receipt of the mission, the running estimate parallels the MDMP and becomes focused on RI to assist the commander's decisionmaking. Table B-4 provides engineer considerations through the MDMP.

Table B-4. Assessment in the military decisionmaking process

Steps of the Military Decisionmaking Process	Engineer Considerations
Receipt of the Mission	• Receive higher headquarters plans, orders, and construction directive(s). • Understand commander's intent and time constraints. • Request geospatial information about the area of operation; provide geospatial products to the staff for use during military decisionmaking process. • Establish and participate on engineer-related boards.
Mission Analysis	• Analyze available intelligence on existing obstacles. Evaluate terrain, weather, and threat capabilities to determine potential impact on mobility/countermobility/survivability. • Develop essential mobility/countermobility/survivability and other engineering tasks. • Identify available information on routes and key facilities. Evaluate lines of communication, aerial port of debarkation, and seaport of debarkation requirements. • Determine availability of construction and other engineering materials. • Review availability of engineer capabilities, to include Army, joint, multinational, host nation, and contract. • Determine beddown requirements for supported force. Review theater construction standards and base camp master planning documentation. Review unified facilities criteria as required.

Table B-4. Assessment in the military decisionmaking process (continued)

Steps of the military decisionmaking process	Engineer Considerations
Mission Analysis (Continued)	• Review existing geospatial data on potential sites, conduct site reconnaissance (if possible), and determine the threat (to include environmental and explosive hazards). • Obtain necessary geologic, hydrologic, and climatic data. • Determine the level of interagency cooperation required. • Determine funding sources as required. • Determine terrain and mobility restraints, obstacle intelligence, threat engineer capabilities, and critical infrastructure. Recommend combatant commander. • Integrate reconnaissance effort.
Course of Action Development	• Identify priority engineer requirements, including essential mobility/countermobility/survivability and other engineering tasks developed during mission analysis. • Integrate engineer operations into course of action development. • Recommend an appropriate level of survivability effort for each course of action based on the expected threat. • Produce construction designs that meet the commander's intent. (Use Theater Construction Management System when the project is of sufficient size and scope.) • Determine alternate construction location, methods, means, materials, and timelines to give the commander options. • Determine real property and real estate requirements.
Course of Action Analysis	• War-game and refine the engineer plan. • Use the critical path method to determine length of different courses of action and the ability to accelerate the project.
Course of Action Comparison	• Determine the most feas ble, acceptable, and suitable methods of completing the engineering effort. • Determine and compare the risks of each engineering course of action.
Course of Action Approval	• Gain approval of the essential tasks for mobility/countermobility/survivability, construction management plan, safety plan, security plan, logistics plan, and environmental plan as required.
Orders Production	• Produce construction directives as required. • Provide input to the appropriate plans and orders. • Ensure that all resources are properly allocated.
Rehearsal	• Coordinate arms rehearsals as appropriate. • Conduct construction prebriefings. • Conduct preinspections and construction meetings. • Synchronize construction plan with local and adjacent units.
Execution and Assessment	• Implement survivability construction standards, including requirements for security fencing, lighting, barriers, and guard posts. • Conduct quality assurance and midproject inspections. • Participate in engineer-related boards. • Maintain "As Built" and "Red Line" drawings. • Project turnover activities.

B-8.   The result of the MDMP is a concept of operations. The running estimate is refined through detailed consideration of engineer requirements in support of the concept of operations. Assessment considers each of the elements of full spectrum operations, see table B-5, page B-8.

Table B-5. Elements of full spectrum operations

Offense	
Tasks: • Movement to contact • Attack • Exploitation • Pursuit	*Considerations:* • Engineer planning begins with predicting the adversary's intent through a thorough understanding of the threat, threat engineer capabilities, and how the terrain will affect operations. • Engineer planning tends to focus on mobility support, including a robust reconnaissance effort. • Engineer planning also includes planning to ensure a smooth, resourced transition from offensive to defensive or stability operations. • Engineer units will tend to have command relationships to maneuver commanders.
Defense	
Tasks: • Mobile defense • Area defense • Retrograde	*Considerations:* • Engineer planning begins with use of terrain products to visualize how best to shape the terrain, to include describing the best positions from which to defend. • Engineer planning tends to focus on countermobility and survivability support, including a significant construction effort. • Construction planning includes security and survivability considerations. • Engineer units will tend to have support relationships to the maneuver commander except for those combat engineer forces task-organized to the reserve or the mobile strike force.
Stability	
Tasks: • Civil security • Civil control • Restore essential services • Support governance • Support to economic and infrastructure development	*Considerations:* • Engineer assessment of the operational environment includes a greater focus on political and cultural considerations. • Engineer planning will tend to focus on construction support, including engineer forces working among and in conjunction with civilians. • Engineer units will likely be distributed among echelons of command. Engineer units will tend to have support relationships to the maneuver commander; however, there are cases where responsiveness and proximity to higher engineer command and control will dictate a command relationship.
Civil Support	
Tasks: • Support to civil law enforcement • Provide support in response to disaster or terrorist attack • Provide other support as required	*Considerations:* • Engineer planners consider statutes and regulations that restrict the Army's interaction with other government agencies and civilians during civil support operations. • Engineer planning will tend to focus on construction support, including engineer forces working among and in support of civilian agencies. • Engineer units will likely be distributed among echelons of command. Engineer units will tend to have support relationships to the maneuver commander; however, there are cases where responsiveness and proximity to higher engineer command and control will dictate a command relationship.

CONTINUOUS REFINEMENT

B-9. As more detailed engineer requirements are refined in collaborative planning with subordinate echelons and headquarters, the engineer effort remains synchronized with the combined arms team by integrating across warfighting functions (see table B-6).

Table B-6. Engineer running estimate integrated across warfighting functions

Warfighting Function	Engineer Planning
Movement and Maneuver • Deploy • Move • Maneuver • Conduct direct fires • Occupy an area • Conduct mobility and countermobility operations • Conduct battlefield obscuration	• Analyze infrastructure to support operational deployment and movement. • Evaluate mobility and countermobility required to preserve operational freedom of maneuver, including clearance, crossing, and terrain reinforcement considerations. • Develop engineer force and capabilities estimates. • Consider infrastructure improvements, reconstruction, and other nonlethal applications for stability or civil support operations.
Intelligence • Provide support to force generation • Provide support to situational understanding • Conduct intelligence, surveillance, and reconnaissance • Provide intelligence support to targeting and information operations capabilities	• Coordinate for geospatial information and products to enhance visualization of the operational environment, achieve situational understanding, and enable decisionmaking. • Estimate threat engineer capabilities. • Gather and coordinate for obstacle intelligence. • Disseminate specific explosive hazards, hazardous material, or other recognition and warning information. • Coordinate for engineer assessments and surveys for technical information requirements.
Fires • Decide surface targets • Detect and locate surface targets • Provide fire support • Assess effectiveness • Integrate command and control warfare	• Participate in the targeting process. • Coordinate for command guidance on employment of scatterable mines and other munitions.
Sustainment • Provision of logistics • Provision of personnel services • Provision of health service support • Internment/resettlement operations	• Develop base development and support estimates. • Estimate real estate and other facilities engineering support. • Identify lines of communications and other key routes, and determine support requirements for establishing and maintaining distribution system. • Estimate area damage control and other construction support. • Determine specialized engineer requirements, such as power, water, and firefighting. • Prepare construction and barrier material estimates. • Prepare munitions estimates. • Determine authorities, funding types, and levels of support.

Table B-6. Engineer running estimate integrated across warfighting functions (continued)

Warfighting Function	Engineer Planning
Command and Control • Execute the operations process • Conduct CP operations • Integrate the information superiority contributors • Conduct information engagement • Conduct civil affairs operations. • Integrate airspace command and control • Execute command programs	• Coordinate for geospatial products to enhance visualization of the operational environment, achieve situational understanding, and enable decisionmaking. • Establish and participate on boards, working groups, and cells. • Recommend command and support relationships. • Recommend control measures: priorities, standards, and reports. • Establish and maintain liaison.
Protection • Air and missile defense • Personnel recovery • Information protection • Fratricide avoidance • Operational area security • Antiterrorism • Survivability • Force health protection • Chemical, biological, radiological, and nuclear operations • Safety • Operations security • Explosive ordnance disposal	• Evaluate base camp and other survivability requirements. • Evaluate survivability of key assets. • Consider facilities hardening. • Consider the use of networked munitions as part of base defense. • Plan for area damage control. • Investigate environmental impacts. • Conduct explosive hazard threat assessment and support.

B-10. As engineer requirements are identified and continually refined, the engineer functions offer organization into categories of related capabilities and activities (see table B-7). Assessment of engineer requirements in terms of the engineer functions assist in tailoring the engineer force.

Table B-7. Capabilities and activities organized by engineer functions

Combat Engineering	

Capabilities:
• Organic engineer elements
• Force pool
• Other
  ▪ Joint (Marines)
  ▪ Multinational
  ▪ Host nation
	Activities:
	• Conduct mobility operations.
	• Conduct countermobility operations.
	• Conduct survivability operations.

General Engineering	

Capabilities:
• Force pool
• United States Army Corps of Engineers field force engineering
• Other
  ▪ Joint (Navy, Air Force)
  ▪ Multinational
  ▪ Host nation
  ▪ Interagency
  ▪ Contract
	Activities:
	• Restore damaged areas.
	• Restore essential services.
	• Construct and maintain sustainment lines of communication.
	• Provide engineer construction support (including support to combat engineering activities).
	• Supply mobile electric power.
	• Provide facilities engineer support.

Geospatial Engineering	

Capabilities:
• Organic engineer elements
• Force pool
• United States Army Corps of Engineers field force engineering
• Other
  ▪ Joint (Navy, Air Force, National Geospatial-Intelligence Agency)
  ▪ Multinational
  ▪ Host nation
  ▪ Interagency
	Activities:
	Conduct geospatial engineering operations and functions.

COORDINATION AND CONTROL

TASK-ORGANIZE ENGINEER CAPABILITIES

B-11. A significant consideration for the integration of engineer capabilities is the task organization of engineer forces. Task organization includes allocating available engineer assets to subordinate commanders and establishing their command and support relationships. In some cases, engineer forces may be task-organized to subordinate nonengineer headquarters—for example, when a Sapper company is attached to a BCT or a clearance company placed OPCON to an MEB. In most cases, an engineer brigade or battalion headquarters will provide the longer-term C2 of tailored engineer forces and may be required at various echelons for C2 of engineer operations at each level. The analysis of the mission variables, within the construct of the running estimate, helps determine the engineer task organization. FM 3-0 (summarized in chapter 3 of this manual) describes command, support, and other relationships that may be established in the task organization. Table B-8 is intended to summarize considerations for the three engineer headquarters elements available from the force pool to provide C2 for engineer functional capabilities and missions.

Table B-8. Considerations for the task organization of engineer headquarters

Theater Engineer Command	
Capabilities:	Considerations:
• Provided command and control for task-organized Army engineer brigades and other engineer units and missions for the joint force, land component, or Army commander. • Deployed its main command post and two deployable command posts to provide flexibility and rotational capability. • Augmented command posts with field force engineering assets from United States Army Corps of Engineers to enhance technical capabilities and joint or multinational assets to extend span of control.	The theater engineer command is the only organization designed for operational command of engineer capabilities at echelons above corps level and often will provide command and control for the joint force commander if an operational engineer headquarters is required.
Engineer Brigade	
Capabilities:	Considerations:
• Capable of conducting engineer missions and controlling up to five mission-tailored engineer battalions, including capabilities from all three of the engineer functions. • Integrated and synchronized engineer capabilities across the supported force. • Deployed its main command and control or two deployable command posts to provide flexibility and rotational capability. • Served, with augmentation, as a joint engineer headquarters, and may be the senior engineer headquarters deployed in a joint operations area if full theater engineer command deployment is not required. • Augmented with field force engineering assets from United States Army Corps of Engineers to enhance technical capabilities.	• One or more engineer brigades are required in the division or corps whenever the number of engineer units or the functional nature of engineer missions calls for brigade-level command and control capability. • Most operations or contingencies requiring the deployment of the corps headquarters in one of its configurations will also require an engineer brigade headquarters element. • Unlike a brigade combat team or maneuver enhancement brigade, the functional engineer brigade is not designed to control terrain. It would require significant augmentation to accomplish such a mission.

Table B-8. Considerations for the task organization of engineer headquarters (continued)

Maneuver Enhancement Brigade	
Capabilities:	Considerations:
• Designed to command and control forces from multiple branches, but especially those that conduct maneuver support operations for the force. • Employed task-organized forces to conduct full spectrum operations in support of Army division, echelons above division, joint, interagency, or multinational headquarters. • Capable of operating across the spectrum of conflict to support, reinforce, or complement offensive and defensive major combat operations and can support or conduct stability or civil support operations. • Staffed and trained to command and control an assigned area of operation and control terrain, unlike the engineer functional brigade. In this regard, it is similar to, but without the inherent maneuver capability of a brigade combat team.	• Each division conducting major combat operations will be supported by at least one maneuver enhancement brigade. Divisions conducting contingency operations will typically also be supported by an maneuver enhancement brigade. • The maneuver enhancement brigade is primarily designed to provide support to the division but is capable of being employed to provide support to higher-echelon, joint, and multinational organizations as well. • When given control of an area of operation, the maneuver enhancement brigade's ability to integrate and synchronize engineer capabilities outside its area of operation is degraded.
Engineer Battalion	
Capabilities:	Considerations:
• Capable of conducting engineer missions controlling any mix of up to five mission-tailored engineer companies. • Capable of providing command and control for either combat or general engineering missions when they have been task-organized to perform those roles, except the prime power battalion, which performs a specific technical role.	• Whenever two or more engineer modules are task-organized in support of a brigade combat team, maneuver enhancement brigade, engineer brigade, or other unit, an engineer battalion headquarters may be required for the command and control and sustainment of those modules. • Typically found within the engineer brigade, the maneuver enhancement brigade, or in support of a brigade combat team. • For the conduct of construction or explosive hazard clearance missions, the battalion will receive survey and design or explosive hazard teams to facilitate those missions.

CONTROL MECHANISMS

B-12. Control mechanisms of significant interest to the engineer include, but are not limited to, the following:

- Establishing policies and construction standards.
- Assigning priorities (such as funding, construction, priority of effort, or priority of support).
- Delegating authority (to employ FASCAM or other munitions).
- Assigning of missions and tasks to subordinates.
- Establishing engineer portions of plans and orders, including their components and subordinate plans, such as the following:
  - Unit mission.
  - Task organization.
  - Concept of operations.
  - Project lists.
  - ISR and Service support plans.
- Establishing graphic control measures (including engineer work lines).
- Establishing intelligence synchronization matrix.
- Performing routine reports and returns.

RISK ASSESSMENT

B-13. Composite risk management (CRM) is an integrating process that occurs during all operations process activities. CRM is the process of identifying, assessing, and controlling hazards (risks) that arise from operational factors and balancing that risk with mission benefits (see FM 5-19). CRM involves the following five steps:

- **Step 1.** Identify hazards.
- **Step 2.** Assess hazards to determine risk.
- **Step 3.** Develop controls and make risk decisions.
- **Step 4.** Implement controls.
- **Step 5.** Supervise and evaluate.

B-14. Commanders integrate CRM into the MDMP. During mission analysis, the focus is on performing the first two steps which are assessment steps. Hazards are identified using METT-TC as a standard format. Hazards can be associated with enemy activity, accident potential, weather or environmental conditions, health, sanitation, behavior, and or material or equipment. Hazards are then assessed and risk is assigned in terms of probability and severity. Step 3 is accomplished during COA development, COA analysis, COA comparison, and COA approval. Controls are implemented (step 4) through mission orders, mission briefings, running estimates, and SOPs. Step 5 (supervise and evaluate) is conducted continuously throughout the operations process. See FM 5-19 for detailed information on CRM.

PREPARATION AND EXECUTION

B-15. Planning offers a premium opportunity for the integration of engineer operations, but only through participation throughout the operations process is the engineer effort truly an integrated application within the combined arms operation. The engineer staff uses the running estimate as a basis for participation in various activities during preparation and execution. Likewise, through participation in these activities, the running estimate is continually refined and updated. Maintaining the running estimate is one of the staff functions that directly contributes to controlling ongoing operations and planning future operations. The construct of the running estimate also provides a framework for organizing and arranging information displays within the CP or cell.

B-16. During preparation and execution, staffs analyze the situation within their fields of interest in terms of the mission variables to maintain their running estimates. Maintaining the running estimate helps the staff make recommendations (within their areas of expertise) to support the commander's decisionmaking. Staffs also use the running estimate in offering recommendations to other staff elements and subordinate commanders (for information and assistance only). Staff recommendations may be in writing, but are usually presented orally during preparation and execution. Presentations may be formal or informal and in the form of briefings, written estimates, or staff studies.

B-17. During preparation, running estimates continue to track resource status. Priority for assessment is on answering priority intelligence requirements, friendly force information requirements, priority civil information requirements, and especially CCIRs that fall within the engineer's area of expertise.

B-18. During execution, running estimates focus on identifying any variances, assessing their effect on achieving the end state, and recommending corrective actions to keep the operation within the commander's intent. Assessments also address the supportability of possible sequels and future operations.

This page intentionally left blank.

Appendix C

Plans and Orders

Plans and orders are key tools used by commanders, with staff assistance, in directing operations, including engineer operations. Engineer operations typically require direction expressed both within the plans and orders of the supported combined arms headquarters and in the plans and orders of controlling engineer unit headquarters. The engineer staff assists combined arms commanders with input to the mission orders that direct supporting engineer operations. Engineer staff planners collaborate with mission-tailored engineer headquarters commanders and staff to enable their use of plans and orders to direct engineer unit operations. Interaction with joint operations planning increases at higher echelons, and so EAB engineer planners will also frequently draw on and use the ESP. This appendix discusses engineer direction expressed in mission orders and in the ESP. It does not provide a format guide for either, but does broadly follow an order outline. See FM 5-0 for a detailed discussion of order formats. The format for the ESP is described in CJCSM 3122.03C.

PURPOSE OF PLANS AND ORDERS

C-1. Commanders issue plans and orders to subordinates to communicate their visualization of an operation. Plans and orders summarize the situation (current conditions) and describe the operation's end state (desired future conditions). Effective plans focus on the results commanders expect to achieve rather than how to achieve them. Plans and orders convey the unit's mission, commander's intent, and the concept of operations. These serve as the guiding constructs for coordinating the force during execution. A concept of operations sequences forces in time, space, and purpose to accomplish the mission and achieve the operation's end state. Plans and orders task-organize the force, allocate resources, and assign tasks to subordinate units. A concept of sustainment and a concept of C2 complete the base plan or order. Details regarding the situation and instructions necessary to synchronize the force are contained in annexes. FM 5-0 provides the format for Army plans and orders. The format for joint plans and orders is in JP 5-0 and CJCSM 3122.03C.

C-2. Plans and orders vary in scope, complexity, and planning horizon length. Different types of plans and orders include OPLAN; CONPLAN with or without TPFDD, OPORD, Service support order, or warning order; and FRAGO.

C-3. The Army's OPORD format must be usable at all echelons and in all situations. Strategic plans cover the overall conduct of a war or a crisis from a national perspective. Operational and campaign plans cover a series of related military operations aimed at accomplishing strategic and operational objectives within an AOR or a JOA. Tactical plans cover the employment of corps and lower level units in operations. Tactical plans and orders also vary greatly. A division OPORD covering the conduct of a 12-month operation and a rifle platoon OPORD for an ambush patrol, for example, are significantly different in scope, complexity, and length of planning horizon. While each type of plan or order serves a particular purpose, they all follow the basic five-paragraph format: situation, mission, execution, administration and logistics (Service support), and C2. Figure C-1, page C-2 through page C-7, is a sample engineer annex.

UNCLASSIFIED

ANNEX F (ENGINEER) TO Multinational Division–North (MND–N) OPORD 07-06 (IRON STRIKE)

1. SITUATION.

    a. Enemy Forces. Refer to Annex B (Intelligence).

    b. Friendly Forces. Refer to Annex A (Task Organization).

        (1) Multinational Corps–Iraq (MNC–I) military and contractor elements work on Coalition projects in AO Ironsides in support of Coalition Forces. For example, some civilian contractors provide base operations support, and other civilian contractors provide construction and repair support. NGO and other elements conduct work on humanitarian projects.

        (2) Iraqi army (IA) forces operate throughout AO Ironsides. Coordination is conducted through LNOs.

        (3) Iraqi police (IP) are operational in most of AO Ironsides.

    c. Environment.

        (1) Terrain. Refer to Annex B (Intelligence).

        (2) Weather. Refer to Annex B (Intelligence).

        (3) Civil Considerations. Refer to Annex Q (Civil Military Operations).

            (a) AO Ironsides is rural but contains several large communities linked with gravel or hardtop roads. Infrastructure is generally antiquated with conditions such as poor sewage treatment and sporadic power.

            (b) Structures consist of expanded two-story structures, mud huts, and temporary tent or frame structures.

            (c) Municipal services are sporadic. Garbage collection and health services are poor but improving.

    d. Attachments and Detachments. Refer to Annex A (Task Organization).

2. MISSION. MND–N and BCT engineer units provide mobility (M), countermobility (CM), survivability (S), and limited general construction in support of MND–N forces in AO Ironsides. BPT conduct M, CM, and S training for IA forces operating in AO Ironsides.

Figure C-1. Sample engineer annex

3. EXECUTION.

  a. Scheme of Engineer Operations. MND–N and BCT engineer units support MND–N forces with a focus on support to maneuver task forces conducting full spectrum operations.

    (1) Priority of effort remains on mobility operations. Mobility tasks focus on areas such as removal of IED threats, inspection of MSRs, bridges, facilities, and LZs to eliminate potential threats to MND–N forces. Conduct patrolling and combat operations as required to maintain mobility throughout AO Ironsides.

    (2) Secondary effort is providing engineer support and training to IA forces to enable them to assume a primary role in stability operations.

    (3) Tertiary effort is providing general engineering support to humanitarian efforts and infrastructure repair and maintenance.

    (4) Priority of support is to 2BCT, then 2Stryker Cavalry Regiment (2SCR).

  b. Conduct mobility tasks to provide maneuver TFs access to the entire AO. Access to every location in the AO is critical to finding and destroying anti-Iraqi forces (AIF).

    (1) IED-defeat operations are critical. Request EOD support to render safe or dispose of IEDs located in the AO.

      (a) Conduct clearing of areas such as roads, bridges, and overpasses, as needed.

      (b) Mark IEDs, mines, and unexploded explosive ordnance (UXO) for day and night recognition, report, and secure until removed.

      (c) Areas requiring extensive UXO clearing will be marked and reported to BCTs for contracted removal.

    (2) Survey MSRs regularly for danger areas and condition (ambush sites, IED sites, and slow travel areas) and report problem areas. Inspect bridges regularly for explosives and structural damage. Use contractors to remove items such as debris and abandoned automobiles near the MSRs. Destroy or block possible ambush sites. Survey alternate mobility routes.

    (3) Conduct assessments and clearing for potential and active LZs. Update listings of LZs per SOP.

Figure C-1. Sample engineer annex (continued)

c. Focus countermobility efforts on denying the enemy freedom of maneuver to and from IED emplacement sites, ambush sites, and overwatch sites.

(1) Priority of countermobility effort is to denying access and occupation of locations that support IEDs and ambushes.

(2) Support interdiction operations of insurgent forces moving to and from known IED and ambush sites.

d. Focus survivability efforts on facilities improvements.

(1) Priority of survivability support is to aviation refuel/rearm facilities, C2 nodes, ammunition and fuel transfer points, and troop facilities.

(2) Maximum effort must be made to harden fixed sites, route control points, entry control points, and guard posts (permanent and temporary). IA and IP facilities must also be considered for improvements. Employ barriers and control measures to minimize impact from and on local citizens.

(3) Continue to improve and upgrade current fixed sites, FOBs, and operating bases, including sites scheduled for transfer to IA. Upon transfer to IA, responsibility for improvements of facilities may transfer as well. BCTs will review plans for facility transfer.

e. General engineering tasks focus on the evaluation and repair of Iraqi infrastructure and upgrade of U.S. facilities.

(1) Identify potential projects and submit them to the Commander, MNC-I for contracting support. Project execution will be according to MNC–I procedures.

(2) All units are responsible for initiating local projects to improve Iraqi communities and overall living conditions. Prioritize projects as follows:

(a) Emergency repair of essential services (for example, power supply, water supply, medical, police, fire protection, waste disposal) damaged by AIF attacks or sectarian violence.

(b) Other projects supporting essential services.

(c) Projects supporting fuel pipelines and storage facilities.

(d) Projects supporting local hospitals, schools, and public administration facilities.

(3) Develop long-range plans for infrastructure improvements.

Figure C-1. Sample engineer annex (continued)

(4) Commander's Emergency Response Program (CERP) projects in AO Ironsides are currently under construction by NGOs and private contractors. The BCT ENCOORD has oversight responsibility. See Tab C (Current CERP Projects), appendix 1 (CERP), Annex Q (Civil Military Operations) for current project list.

(5) Consider environmental issues with special emphasis on camp closure and cleanup before redeployment; camp sanitary waste and medical waste; hazardous materials; destroyed or damaged military property; and oil, gas, batteries, tires, and other waste that could endanger Iraqi citizens and/or affect MNC-I operations.

f. Tasks to subordinate units.

(1) BCT engineer units will:

(a) Recommend EH support matrix to BCT Commander.

(b) Conduct routine patrolling of MSRs, LZs, bridges, overpasses, and possible IED sites.

(c) Provide countermobility and survivability upgrades for temporary and permanent checkpoints, guard facilities, and site protection.

(d) Develop post conflict plan for restitution/repair of damaged infrastructure.

(e) Coordinate temporary repair of facilities damaged by attacks such as those caused by random mortars, IEDs, and vehicle-borne improvised explosive devices.

(f) Identify existing and or possible environmental hazards to units and local population.

(g) Coordinate base camp maintenance, construction, and decommissioning.

(h) Develop plans for local infrastructure repair and improvements.

(i) Develop plans to repair and improve schools and health care facilities.

(j) Identify local resources and assets available to assist in reconstruction.

Figure C-1. Sample engineer annex (continued)

(2) BCT engineer tasks in support of Iraqi forces.

    (a) Assess and upgrade survivability status on IA and IP facilities for temporary and permanent checkpoints, guard facilities, and site protection.

    (b) BPT provide Explosive Hazard Awareness Training (EHAT) to IA down to company level, if appropriate.

    (c) BPT provide training element to IA engineer force in AO, if appropriate. Develop training package and coordinate with BCT ENCOORD for approval.

g. Coordinating Instructions.

    (1) Minimize destruction of civilian public and private property (land and facilities) consistent with mission. MNC-I Commander's approval is required to destroy or damage bridges, natural or man-made dams, dikes, or levees.

    (2) BCTs handle payment for destruction of civilian property. Provide estimate of repairs within four hours of damage or arrival on the scene. Destruction of property must correlate with combat necessity of the situation.

    (3) Contracting for facilities and real estate requires coordination through the MND–N contracting office. Identification and evaluation of required facilities and real estate remains an engineer responsibility at each BCT.

4. SERVICE SUPPORT. Refer to Annex I (Service Support).

5. COMMAND AND CONTROL. Refer to Base OPORD.

ACKNOWLEDGE:

                    MG

Appendixes:
1-Obstacle Overlay (Not Used)
2-Environmental Considerations (Not Used)
3-Terrain (Not Used)
4-Mobility/Countermobility/Survivability Execution Matrix/Timeline (Not Used)
5-EOD (Not Used)

Figure C-1. Sample engineer annex (continued)

Legend:
BPT   be prepared to
CERP   Commander's Emergency Response Program
CM   countermobility
IA   Iraqi army
ISF   Iraq security forces
IP   Iraqi police
LZ   landing zone
M   mobility
MG   Major General
MNC–I   Multinational Corps–Iraq
MND–N   Multinational Division–North
TBP   to be published
S   survivability
SCR   Stryker Cavalry Regiment
UXO   unexploded explosive ordnance

Figure C-1. Sample engineer annex (continued)

MISSION ORDERS

C-4. Mission orders use a technique for developing orders that emphasizes to subordinates the results to be attained, not how they are to achieve them; they provide maximum freedom of action in determining how to best accomplish assigned missions (FM 3-0). Commanders focus their orders on the purpose of the operation rather than the details of how to perform assigned tasks. Effective mission orders help subordinates to better understand the situation, their commander's mission and intent, and their own mission. The commander's intent and concept of operations set guidelines that ensure unity of effort while allowing subordinate commanders to exercise initiative.

C-5. A sample engineer brigade warning order (WARNO) follows (see figure C-2).

Copy ___ of ___ Copies
xx EN BDE
FOB xxxxx
062300FEB08

(U) xx EN BDE WARNO # 1 (GS engineering operations in division AO).

(U) References: DIVISION OPORD 08-04

(U) Time Zone Used throughout the OPORD: Alpha (local)

(U) Task Organization. No change.

1. (U) SITUATION. To be published (TBP).

2. (U) MISSION. TBP.

3. (U) EXECUTION.

    a. (U) Purpose. TBP.

    b. (U) Concept of Operations. TBP.

    c. (U) Tasks to subordinate units.

        1. (U) TF 54 EN (-) (combat).

            a. (U) BPT conduct route clearance operations in support of maneuver BCTs in AO Ironsides.

            b. (U) BPT conduct escort of the WIT and EOD teams in AO Ironsides.

            c. (U) BPT provide backup support to ISF units as required in AO Ironsides.

        2. (U) TF 94 EN (CONST).

            a. (U) BPT conduct steady state MSR repair and maintenance in AO Ironsides.

            b. (U) BPT conduct FOB expansion and improvement in AO Ironsides.

            c. (U) BPT conduct bridge repair operations as required in AO Ironsides.

            d. (U) BPT receive and accept attachment of a multirole bridge company no later than (NLT) 15 APR 08.

Figure C-2. Sample engineer brigade warning order

e. (U) BPT conduct bridging operations in AO Ironsides.

f. (U) BPT develop a plan for the improvement and expansion of the short takeoff and landing strip vicinity of QV 120576 in AO Ironsides.

g. (U) BPT provide backup support to ISF units as required in AO Ironsides.

3. (U) HHC, 162 EN CO (-) (combat), EOD Mobile Unit (MU) 8, Civil Affairs (CA) Team, Weapons Intelligence Team (WIT). TBP.

d. (U) Coordinating Instructions. TBP.

4. (U) SERVICE SUPPORT. TBP.

5. (U) COMMAND AND SIGNAL.

a. (U) Command. TBP.

b. (U) Signal. (Points of Contact). (U) Brigade S-3 Operations POC is CPT xxxxxx at DSN 370-xxxx, NIPR: <xxxx@army.mil>.

commander
COL

OFFICIAL:
major
S-3

Distribution:
HHC
TF 54 EN (-) (Combat)
TF 94 EN (CONST)
162 EN CO (-) (Combat)
EOD Mobile Unit (MU) 8
Civil Affairs (CA) Team
Weapons Intelligence Team (WIT)
Staff Primaries

Figure C-2. Sample engineer brigade warning order (continued)

ENGINEER SUPPORT PLAN

C-6. Joint interdependence requires higher headquarters to understand joint planning doctrine. Army force headquarters must be prepared to serve as the Army component of a joint force. Army division and corps headquarters may serve as the base for a JTF headquarters. Engineer staff and engineer organizations supporting these headquarters will participate in joint planning and must understand the ESP. The ESP (appendix 6, Annex D of a joint OPLAN) is produced by a joint engineer staff for input to a joint OPLAN as part of the planning process. It ensures that essential engineering capabilities are identified and will be provided at the required locations and times. It is the most critical appendix for engineering in a joint OPLAN.

C-7. GCSS–EN is a tool used to support quantitative aspects of engineer support planning and execution. It provides the general requirements for the ESP and provides a common automated system for the joint force engineer planners to determine the appropriate amount of engineer assets and capabilities to support the selected COA. GCSS–EN is the engineer component of the Global Combat Support System, a web-based application residing on the SIPRNET. GCSS–EN assists the engineer planners in determining the correct engineer capability for the proper location, timed correctly to support the concept of operations. GCSS-EN includes a TCMS module to assist with facilities planning and links into construction resource and materials planning. It also includes an environmental module. GCSS–EN is used to—

- Generate time-phased facility requirements based on the OPLAN.
- Analyze and assess engineering support by comparing facility requirements to in-theater facility assets and HN, contract, and troop engineering capability.
- Provide facility feasibility assessment, manpower, material, and nonunit cargo requirements for other processes.
- Provide infrastructure data to assist in mission analysis and COA development.
- Provide real-time monitoring capability needed to track plan execution.

C-8. A sample ESP follows (see figure C-3, page C-12 through page C-16).

HEADQUARTERS, JFC
APO XX XXXXX
28 February XXXX

APPENDIX 6 TO ANNEX D TO JFC OPLAN XXXX-XX ( )
ENGINEER SUPPORT PLAN ( )

( ) References: List references that provide guidance and the applicable SOP.

1. ( ) General.

    a. ( ) Purpose, Scope, and Limitations. State in general terms what will and will not be addressed. State the general character and magnitude of the engineer effort. Include gross estimate of expected environment and any constraints affecting the engineer operation.

    b. ( ) Engineer Intelligence.

        (1) ( ) Refer to Annex B for significant intelligence concerning climatology, terrain, hydrography, and natural and industrial resources in the operational area.

        (2) ( ) List sources of geospatial intelligence data, including dates of information.

    c. ( ) Concept of Engineer Support. Explain the general concept for satisfying engineer requirements. Identify the overall facility requirements and summarize the existing U.S., HN, multinational, contract, and other assets and construction capabilities to satisfy those requirements. Include requirements for accomplishing construction and other engineering in support of base camp development, air and seaport development, sustainment and other facilities, ground LOCs and MSRs, survivability and other protection support, restoration of essential services and other stability support, and acquisition of construction and engineering services. Identify the essential M/CM/S and other engineering tasks.

    d. ( ) Definitions. List definitions that are necessary to understand this plan but are not included in JP 1-02.

    e. ( ) International Agreements and Political Factors.

        (1) ( ) General. Summarize agreements, other arrangements, and political factors affecting the engineer operation.

        (2) ( ) Real Property. Discuss policies for real property acquisition and use.

Figure C-3. Sample engineer support plan

(3) ( ) HN Support. Discuss use of the following, including resources that are expected to be made available. Specify quantity where possible.

(a) ( ) Indigenous labor.

(b) ( ) Local availability of construction materiel, supplies, and equipment.

(c) ( ) Third-world country labor force.

(d) ( ) Local contractor.

(e) ( ) Local facilities.

(4) ( ) Limiting Factors. Identify rights, agreements, or other arrangements not now in existence that will be required to execute the plan.

f. ( ) Construction Standards. Indicate the construction standards to be used by all Service components in the operational area and explain proposed deviations from the established standards.

g. ( ) Planning Factors. Explain proposed deviations from the joint planning factors for military construction in contingency operations.

h. ( ) General Priority of Development. Provide any general guidance for prioritizing engineer efforts. Include areas such as relative geographic, functional, and base priorities, theater construction policy, and other general guidance.

i. ( ) Protective Construction Policy. Define the command policy for protective construction and repair of damage. Include:

(1) ( ) Statement of the enemy's capability to inflict damage. (A quantitative evaluation is not required.)

(2) ( ) Protection required for weapon systems, personnel, and materiel.

(3) ( ) Self-help versus engineer troop effort.

j. ( ) Contractor. Discuss the availability and possible use of U.S. or third-world country construction contractors.

k. ( ) Multinational Forces. Discuss the availability and possible use of multinational engineering forces.

l. ( ) Construction Policy. Provide the supported commander's guidance for construction of new facilities. In general, the supported commander should plan expeditious facility construction to meet shortfall requirements (for example, those facilities that cannot be sourced from existing assets). Contracting support should be used to augment military capabilities. Because construction is time-consuming and entails the risk of not being

Figure C-3. Sample engineer support plan (continued)

finished in time to meet mission requirements, supported commanders should seek alternative solutions to new construction. Expedient construction should also be considered, which includes several types of rapid construction techniques such as prefabricated buildings, inflatable buildings, and clamshell structures. These construction techniques entail minimal time, cost, and risk.

2. ( ) Responsibilities for Engineer Support Planning.

    a. ( ) Primary Responsibility. Identify each joint command echelon responsible for engineering support planning (for example, unified command, subunified command, or JTF) and identify each one's specific tasks.

    b. ( ) Supporting Responsibility. Identify each Service component command's engineer support planning responsibilities addressed in the OPLAN. Note that LOCs, bases, ports, depots, and airfields may be jointly used and will require assignment of responsibility to one component commander to ensure complete integrated planning, subsequent programming, and necessary coordination and construction.

3. ( ) Command Relationships. Indicate in this paragraph any recommendations to deviate from existing command relationships as they relate to the execution of support described in this appendix.

4. ( ) Time-Phased Requirements. Summarize construction and other engineer support requirements and identify U.S. forces available for accomplishing those requirements. Provide time-phased summaries and analysis of engineer forces to meet the requirements at least in terms of the five areas listed below.

    a. ( ) Facility Shortfalls. Indicate alternate means of accommodating major functions.

    b. ( ) Materiel Requirements. Indicate in the analysis significant out-of-theater requirements by general type and gross tonnage.

    c. ( ) Engineer Force Shortfalls. Analyze required versus available work hours at theater and regional levels. Identify shortfalls by area, duration, and specific skill types. Summarize shortfalls in terms of unsatisfied requirements and assess the impact on OPLAN execution.

    d. ( ) War Damage Repair. Identify locations where heavy attacks are anticipated and estimate percent of engineer workload for repairs. Assess the potential effect on materiel, equipment, personnel readiness, and adequacy of assigned engineer force to repair.

    e. ( ) Host Nation Assignments. Identify extent of reliance on host nation engineer assets and impact if host nation engineers are not available.

Figure C-3. Sample engineer support plan (continued)

5. ( ) Summary of Critical Factors Affecting the ESP. Summarize major problem areas addressed in GCCS-EN that may inhibit OPLAN implementation. Analyze possible solutions to these problems and evaluate the implications of each alternative in terms of its effect on the OPLAN.

Tabs
A—Construction Standards for Military Construction and Engineer Support of Joint Operations

Figure C-3. Sample engineer support plan (continued)

Tab A to Appendix 5 to Annex D to JFC OPLAN XXXX-XX () Standards of Construction ()

STANDARDS OF CONSTRUCTION		
TYPE OF CONSTRUCTION	INITIAL	TEMPORARY
Site preparation	Clearing and grading for facilities sites, including drainage, revetments for POL and ammunition storage and aircraft parking, aggregate for heavily used hardstands and soil stabilization.	Engineering site preparation, including pavement for vehicle traffic areas and aircraft parking, building foundations and concrete floor slabs.
Troop housing/dining/admin/mission structures	Organic tentage with wooden floors.	Relocatable structures such as: 1) Harvest Eagle and Harvest Falcon. 2) Hard backed (rigid walls and floors) 3) Force provider.
Electricity	Tactical generators, high-voltage and low-voltage distribution.	Nontactical and/or high-voltage distribution.
Water	Water points.	Limited distribution to hospitals, dining halls, and other large users.
Cold storage	Portable reefer with freezer units for medical, food service, and maintenance storage.	Refrigeration installed in temporary structures.
Sanitation	Organic equipment evaporative ponds, pit or burnout latrines, lagoons for hospitals, and sewage lift stations.	Waterborne to austere treatment facility. Priority: hospitals, dining halls, bathhouses, decontamination sites, and other high-volume water users.
Airfield pavement	Tactical surfacing including matting, aggregate, and soil stabilization.	Conventional pavement.[1]
Fuel storage	Bladders.	Bladders and steel tanks.

[1] The type of airfield surfacing to be used will be based on the expected number, types, and weight of aircraft involved in operations, as well as material availability.

Figure C-3. Sample engineer support plan (continued)

Appendix D

Contract Construction

Use of construction contracting and contingency funding can play an important role in support of EAB engineer operations. Civilian construction contractors and HN engineering support provide the JFC with a significant engineering capability that becomes a force multiplier when combined with joint force military engineering units. Construction agents provide the ability to harness and direct this means of support.

CONSTRUCTION CONTRACTING AND ENGINEERING SUPPORT

D-1. The DOD construction agents are USACE, NAVFAC, or other approved DOD activities (see DOD Directive 4270.5). These organizations and their contractors are a powerful force multiplier, allowing military engineers to concentrate on engineering missions in high-threat areas. USACE and NAVFAC also provide the JFC with a significant engineering capability to be leveraged in joint operations. They are DOD's principal organizations to plan, design, construct, and acquire (lease or buy) facilities and real estate. Inherent in their mission support capabilities is a planning and engineering capability for theater advanced base and infrastructure development. These organizations also maintain in-depth engineering expertise in their operating field organizations and laboratories.

D-2. The responsibilities of the DOD construction agents include designing, awarding and managing the construction contracts for projects associated with the peacetime military construction program. Overseas, USACE, NAVFAC, and the Air Force are assigned specific geographical areas under DOD Directive 4270.5 (see table D-1, page D-2). Related to these responsibilities is the leasing of real estate. The CCAs are fee-for-service organizations that require funding from the JFC or other user to execute taskings.

D-3. The CCDR may also use USACE and NAVFAC as contingency CCAs for design, award, and management of construction contracts in support of military operations. For geographical areas where there is no designated DOD construction agent, the CCDR usually designates a CCA for support during a contingency. USACE and NAVFAC also provide facilities planning, contract administration, and technical engineering support to JFCs (such as advanced base master planning, geospatial engineering, facilities hardening, environmental engineering, and cold-weather mobility assessments). The Air Force also maintains a limited capability in contract construction in contingencies and facilities and real estate acquisition in England, Turkey, Spain, and Israel.

Table D-1. Designated geographical areas of Department of Defense construction agents

Department of the Army	Department of the Navy	Department of the Air Force
Afghanistan	Atlantic Ocean area	British Isles
Canada, excluding Newfoundland	Australia and New Zealand	
Central America	Caribbean Sea area	
Europe, excluding Spain, Portugal, Italy, Greece, and the British Isles	Greece	
Northern Eurasia, which makes up Russia and the former Soviet republics	Iceland	
Greenland	Indian Ocean area	
Iraq	Italy	
Japan, including the Ryuku Island (Okinawa)	Newfoundland	
Korea	North Africa, including Somalia and Kenya but excluding Egypt	
Marshall Islands	Pacific Ocean area, including the Commonwealth of the Northern Marianas Islands, but excluding the Marshall Islands	
Mexico	Portugal, including the Azores	
Middle East, including the Saudi Arabian Peninsula	Republic of the Philippines	
South America	Southeast Asia, from Thailand to Vietnam	
Southern Asia, from Iran to Myanmar (Burma)	Spain	
Sub-Sahara Africa, excluding Kenya and Somalia		
Taiwan		
Turkey		

FIELD FORCE ENGINEERING REACHBACK PROCESS

D-4. FFE refers to linking well-trained and well-equipped military and civilian deployed forces with reachback teams for technical expertise. The objective of FFE is to effectively execute USACE roles such as engineering expertise, contract construction, real estate acquisition and disposal, and environmental engineering in the AO and to maximize the use of reachback to assist the CCDR. FFE reachback teams provide rapid, actionable engineering analyses across the full operational and natural disaster response spectrum in support of the armed forces and the nation. They provide support for technical engineering analyses, base camp planning, geographic information systems, intelligence support, training, and equipment.

D-5. Accessing reachback support is simple. Deployed personnel from all military Services or other U.S. government organizations can submit a request for information (RFI) via unclassified or classified Web sites, e-mail, video teleconference, or telephone to the USACE Reachback Center. Once a request is submitted, it is routed to trained response teams, centers of expertise, or labs for solutions. The personnel working the RFI will provide the response to the requestor to solve the problem and the data will be archived in a repository. Army, Navy, Air Force, Marine Corps, the DOS, and FEMA, among others, can benefit from USACE expertise (see figure D-1).

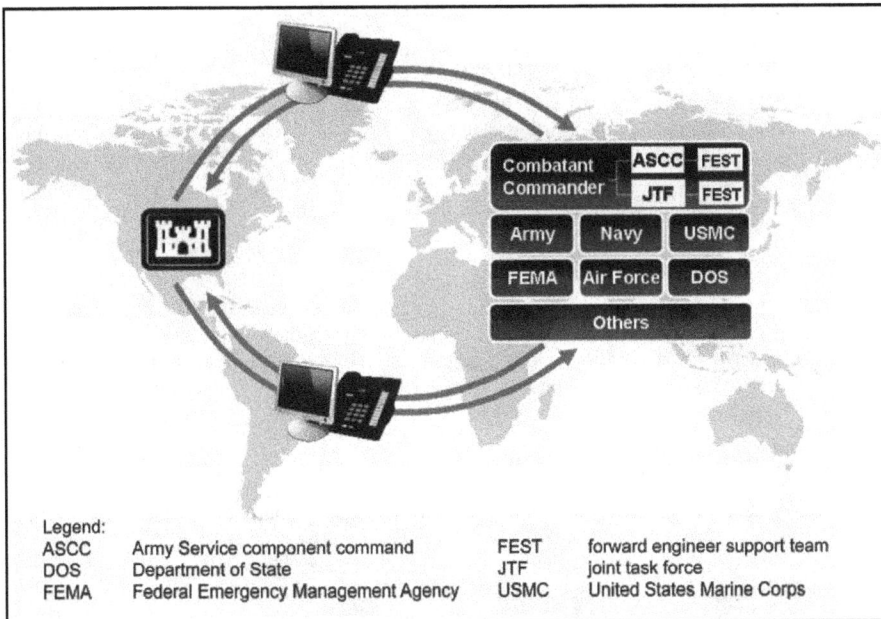

Legend:
ASCC   Army Service component command   FEST   forward engineer support team
DOS   Department of State   JTF   joint task force
FEMA   Federal Emergency Management Agency USMC   United States Marine Corps

Figure D-1. Reachback process

D-6. The engineer providing support is the preferred access point to USACE reachback capability. The engineer will determine if the required technical assistance is beyond available capabilities and can then develop an appropriate RFI for reachback support. Table D-2, page D-4, provides general contact information for reachback support.

Table D-2. Reachback contact information

	Web site	E-Mail	Mail	Telephone
Unclassified	https:// reachback.usace	UROC@usace.army.mil UROC–VTC@usace.army.mil	CEERD–GM, UROC–Mobile 109 Saint Joseph Street Mobile, AL 36602 CEER–GM, UROC–Vicksburg 3909 Halls Ferry Road Vicksburg, MS 39180-6199	Commercial 251-690-2039 Commercial 601-634-2735 Defense Switched Network 312-446-2735
Classified	https://reachback.usace.army.smil.mil	rfi@usace.army.smil.mil		Defense Switched Network 601-634-4231 (STUIII)
Korea	http://ei2rc.korea.army.mil.rmil.mil	usacerfi@korea.army.rmil.mil		Defense Switched Network 312-457-2039 (STUIII)

CONTINGENCY AUTHORITIES AND FUNDING

D-7. It is especially important that engineers understand contingency authorities and the associated funding. These are the tools that set the conditions for success during contingency operations and provide the basis for legal spending to take care of DOD personnel and activities in support of contingency operations—which comprise a large portion of the operations conducted by Army and joint forces. This appendix provides an introduction to contingency authorities and funding. However, the information in this appendix is subject to change due to changes in legislation, policy, or regulation. The reader should consult with legal and financial management personnel for the latest definitive guidance.

LEGAL PERSONNEL

D-8. Legal personnel can provide invaluable advice and guidance on authorities and sources of funding for civil engineering activities in a variety of situations. From the earliest stages of planning, execution, and redeployment, legal professionals play a vital role in preparing the JOA by identifying and assisting in the resolution of legal and political constraints and providing relevant and responsive readiness programs to the individual civil engineering members.

TYPES OF AUTHORIZATIONS AND SOURCES OF FUNDING

D-9. Services are authorized to use annual operation and maintenance (O&M) funds for construction projects costing less than $750,000 on U.S.-controlled or -owned real property ($1.5 million to correct a life-threatening condition or for new construction and $3 million for maintenance and repair when the repair-to-replacement ratio is less than 50 percent). This is a peacetime provision, applicable during contingencies and emergencies; however, "life-threatening" is generally considered a safety issue vice an emergency in the context of contingency operations. During combat or designated contingency operations, O&M may be used to fund construction projects exceeding these thresholds. The JFC must consult with the staff judge advocate before making a determination to use O&M in such a case.

D-10. Several broad authorities have been established under Title 10 U.S. Code that enable the JFC to carry out contingency construction, including procuring materials for construction by military forces and funding of civilian contracts in support of contingency operations. Figures D-2 and D-3, pages D-6 and D-7, depict decision trees for the contingency construction funding options below:

- Section 2803, Emergency Construction, authorizes each Service to use $45 million per year of nonobligated military construction funds for projects that cannot wait for the normal military construction submission procedures. Projects must comply with a 21-day congressional notice and wait period before proceeding. Generally, a previously congressionally approved project must be canceled to free the $45 million.

- Section 2804, Contingency Construction, authorizes the Secretary of Defense a specific military construction line item amount for contingency construction projects that cannot wait for the normal military construction program submission process. A project must comply with a 21-day congressional notice and wait period before proceeding. Generally, funding for this section has been limited to less than $10 million per year.

- Section 2805, Unspecified Minor Construction, authorizes each Service a specific military construction line item amount that varies annually for unspecified minor construction. Projects must be less than $1.5 million each (or $3.0 million for life-, safety-, or health-focused projects). Projects greater than $750,000 require a 21-day congressional notice and wait period before proceeding.

- Section 2808, Construction Authority, in the event of a declaration of war or national emergency, requires a Presidential declaration of war or national emergency and authorizes the Secretary of Defense to carry out any military construction project for the war or national emergency within the total amount of unobligated military construction funds available. Congress must be notified of each project, but there is no wait requirement before the project may begin.

- Section 2811, "Repair of Facilities," authorizes the Secretary of Defense to use funds available to carry out repair of facilities. Repair projects over $10 million must be submitted to congress for approval.

D-11. CCDRs do not need specific authority to request projects under Sections 2803 and 2804. To gain approval for a project under either authority, it is necessary to provide the appropriate Service Secretary or Secretary of Defense with a justification of need, estimated costs, and source of funding.

Identify Requirement

Appropriate to lease?

NO / YES

All maintenance and repair — YES → **Service approves (O&M)**

NO

Construction >$750K

YES / NO

Construction <1.5M — YES → **Determine if unspecified minor MILCON applies** — YES → **Unspecified minor MILCON model**

2805

2805

NO

Declaration of war or national emergency

NO

Deferral is not in the national interest — FALSE

YES

Vital to national security or vital to health, safety, or environment

YES / NO

YES

Can project wait until next MILCON submission

YES

TRUE

Can project wait until next MILCON submission

YES →

NO

Can project wait until next MILCON submission

NO

Unobligated SecDef contingency funding available

NO

Is total requirement <$45M/FY for the service

NO →

CCDR submits prioritized projects

YES

CBT CDR validates need

YES

YES

Adequate unobligated MILCON funds available — NO →

NO

SecDef approves and notifies Congress (no wait)

SecDef approves for execution after 21-day Congressional notification

YES

Service Secretary approves for execution After 21-day Congressional notification

Submit through the appropriate service in next MILCON program

2808

2804

2803

Legend:
CBT CDR — combat commander
CCDR — combatant commander
FY — fiscal year

MILCON — military construction
O & M — operation and maintenance
SecDef — Secretary of Defense

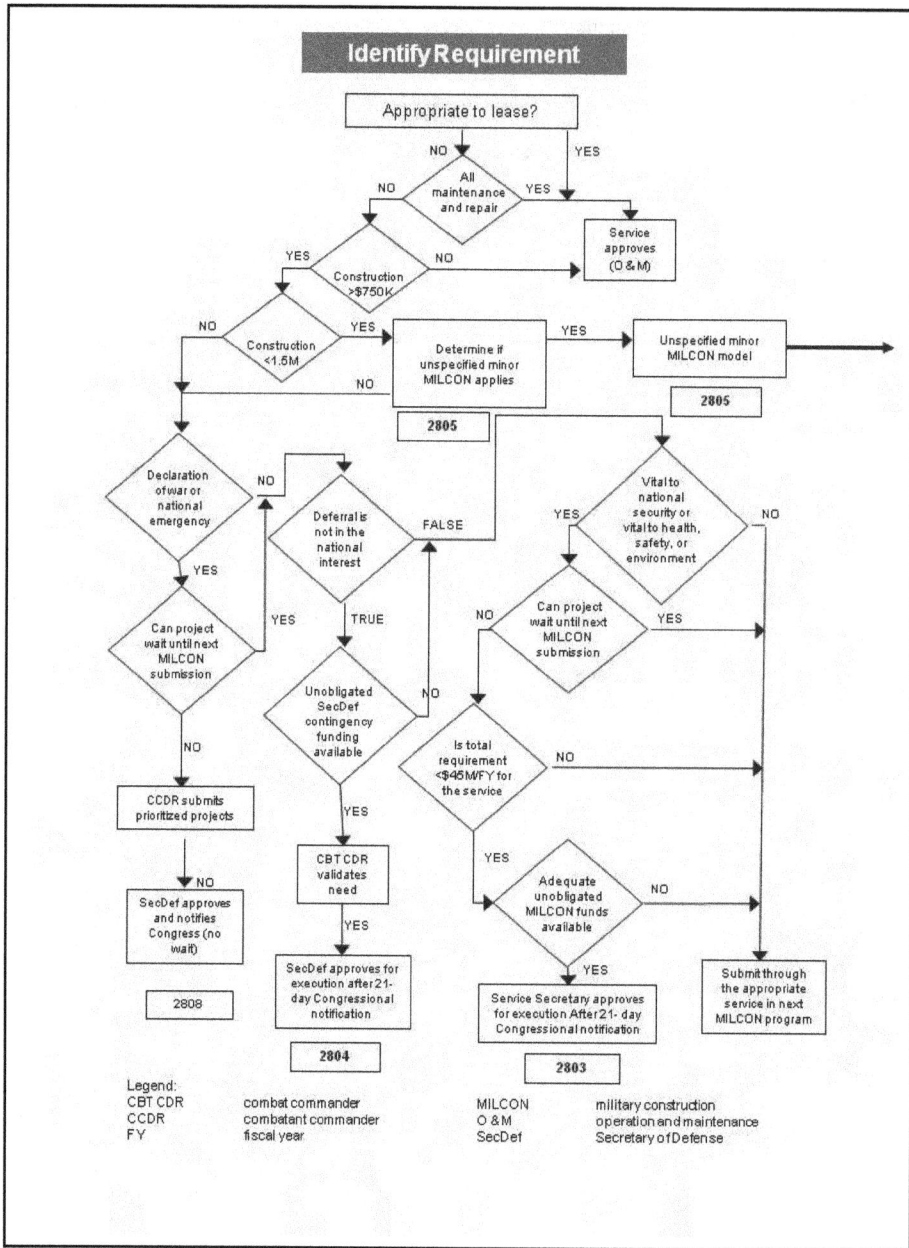

Figure D-2. Contingency construction funding model

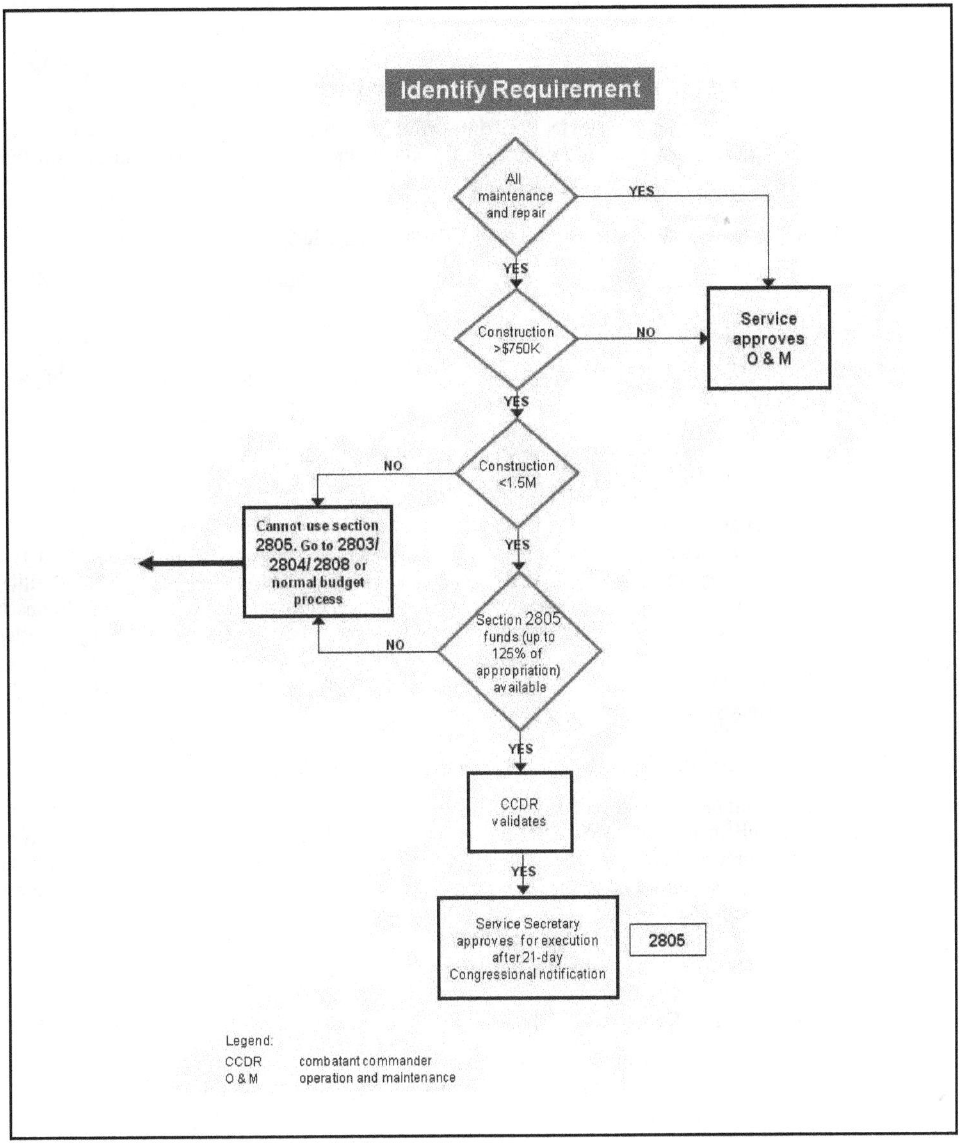

Figure D-3. Contingency construction funding model (unspecified minor, $750,000–$1.5 million)

OTHER AUTHORITIES AND SOURCES OF FUNDING

Burden Sharing (Title 10 United States Code 2350.J)

D-12. This portion of law authorized the Secretary of Defense, after consultation with the Secretary of State, to accept burden-sharing cash contributions from any country or regional organization designated for certain purposes (to include military construction projects) for DOD. Written approval from the Under Secretary of Defense (Comptroller) is required for the use of such contributions to carry out military construction projects. For additional information see DOD Financial Management Regulation (DOD 7000.14-R), volume 12, chapter 24.

Section 607A of the Foreign Assistance Act of 1961 (Public Law 87-195, as amended)

D-13. This act provides restoration of HN civil infrastructure. This provision of law allows any U.S. Government agency to provide goods and services to friendly countries and NGOs on an advance-of-funds or reimbursable basis.

Arms Export Control Act of 1976 (Public Law 90-629, as amended)

D-14. HN military facilities may be restored under the foreign military sales provisions of this authority.

Economy in Government Act (Title 31 United States Code 1535)

D-15. This act allows USG agencies to support each other provided that the supported agency has the funds and authority to do the work requested.

Humanitarian and Civic Assistance Projects Provided in Conjunction With Military Operations Projects (Title 10 United States Code 401)

D-16. In humanitarian and civic assistance facilities projects, the JFC and joint force engineers may work with HN government agencies to repair or improve infrastructure and public facilities. These authorized and funded projects are designed to provide assistance to the HN populace in conjunction with a military operation or exercise. They are usually planned well in advance and are not usually planned in response to disasters, though humanitarian and civic assistance activities have been executed following disasters. Specific engineer activities for which humanitarian and civic assistance funds can be used include construction of rudimentary surface transportation systems, well drilling, construction of basic sanitation facilities, and rudimentary construction and repair of facilities.

Foreign Humanitarian Assistance (Title 10 United States Code 2551)

D-17. In disaster operations, the United Nations and the DOS, Office of Foreign Disaster Assistance may generate funded requirements for DOD assistance. FHA programs focus on the use of DOD excess property, emergency transportation support, disaster relief, or other support, as necessary, to alleviate urgent needs caused by some type of disaster or catastrophe in an HN. While other elements of the joint force are focused on immediate humanitarian assistance, civil engineering planning may focus on projects that provide immediate shelter for dislocated civilians. The joint force engineers must work in a close relationship with the representatives of the HN and U.S. country team.

Drawdown of Department of Defense Articles and Services (Title 22, United States Code 2318)

D-18. Drawdown authority is a means to respond to unforeseen military emergencies or humanitarian relief situations. These recurring authorities have placed annual limitations on the value of articles and services that may be drawn down in any fiscal year.

Foreign Disaster Relief (Department of Defense Directive 5100.46)

D-19. Normally, DOD components may participate in foreign disaster relief operations only after a determination is made by the DOS. This directive allows the military commander at the scene of a disaster to undertake disaster relief operations without prior approval of the ambassador or chief of the mission when the emergency is so acute that immediate action is required to save life and property.

Appendix E

Base Camp Development

This appendix serves as a quick reference for leaders conducting base camp development by explaining the base camp development planning process and providing some of the basic planning factors for base camp construction. While construction standards are established by commanders, typically at the theater echelon, engineers at all echelons must understand and implement those standards. See FM 3-34.400 and JP 3-34 for more information.

OVERVIEW OF BASE CAMPS

E-1. Base camps are vital in supporting the deployment and operational reach of joint forces. In today's OEs, base camp planners will be challenged with varying degrees of theater entry and threat conditions, uncertainty in mission durations, and likely fluctuations in troop strength compounded with frequent repositioning of forces, in determining the magnitude, positioning, and posturing of base camps. Failure to grasp the complexity of base camp development and address the inherent difficulties early in the planning process will present tremendous challenges to the deployed force and those supporting it. Effective base camps hinge on proper planning, coordination, and oversight.

DEFINITIONS

E-2. A *base* is a locality from which operations are projected or supported. (JP 1-02) Army bases overseas typically fall into two general categories: base camps and permanent bases or installations. Base camps are discussed further in paragraph E-5 below. Permanent bases or installations are generally located in HNs in which the United States has a long-term lease agreement and a status-of-forces agreement.

E-3. *Base development* (less force beddown) is defined as the acquisition, development, expansion, improvement, and construction and/or replacement of the facilities and resources of an area or location to support forces employed in military operations or deployed in accordance with strategic plans. (JP 3-34)

E-4. A *base development planning cell* is a nondeployable working group that can quickly provide base development engineering and planning and facilities design for staging bases, base camps, FOBs, displaced persons camps, and any similar requirement (FM 3-34). The cell's resources and expertise are available to support FFE teams and operational forces through the USACE reachback center.

E-5. A *base camp* is an evolving military facility that supports the military operations of a deployed unit and provides the necessary support and services for sustained operations. (FM 3-37) Base camps consist of ISBs and FOBs. Base camps support the tenants and their equipment. While they are not permanent bases or installations, they develop many of the same functions and facilities the longer they exist and can eventually evolve to permanent bases.

E-6. An *intermediate staging base* is a tailorable, temporary location used for staging forces, sustainment, and or extraction into and out of an operational area. (JP 3-35)

E-7. A *forward operating base* is defined as an area used to support tactical operations without establishing full support facilities. (FM 3-0) An FOB extends and maintains the operational reach of Army forces, providing a secure location from which to conduct and sustain operations. Such bases may be used for an extended time. During protracted operations, they may be expanded and improved to establish a more permanent presence. Typically, an FOB is established adjacent to a regional distribution hub, such as a large airfield (civilian or military), rail terminal, or major highway junction.

CONSTRUCTION STANDARDS

E-8. The CCDR specifies the construction standards for facilities in-theater to minimize the engineer effort expended on any given facility, while assuring that the facilities are adequate for health, safety, and mission accomplishment. Typically, the CCDR will develop command-specific base camp construction standards using the guidelines provided in JP 3-34. Figure 3-4, page 3-16, shows the beddown and basing continuum and highlights the need for early planning efforts to help facilitate transition to more permanent facilities as the operation develops. While the timelines provide a standard framework, the situation may warrant deviations. Planners must recommend the most feasible solutions to each requirement based on construction guidelines and other planning factors.

E-9. Base camp planners must consider all construction standards and guidebooks established by CCDRs and ASCCs for the AOR such as CENTCOM's *Sandbook* and United States Army Europe's *Redbook*. These standards books typically provide the planners with the initial guidance necessary to determine the facilities desired by the command and the associated square footage allowances. CCDRs may also establish construction standards in OPLANs, OPORDs, FRAGOs, and directives that may take precedence over guidebooks. Standards may also provide priorities for construction within base camps. Planners must be very familiar with the appropriate standards to execute construction and maintenance activities in a decentralized manner.

E-10. As described in JP 3-34, there are two broad categories of construction that are based on the anticipated length of the operation of the base camp—contingency (up to 2 years) and enduring (2 to 10 years or more). Based on the category, there are five possible standards: organic, initial, temporary, semipermanent, and permanent. See table E-1.

Table E-1. Base camp standards

Base Camp Standards (Duration)	Characteristics
Organic (up to 6 months)	• Use unit equipment and capabilities. • Use minimal engineer support or construction effort.
Initial (up to 2 years)	• Use unit equipment augmented with additional assets. • Use limited military engineer or contractor support and some new construction effort.
Temporary (up to 5 years–bridges the gap between contingency and enduring phases)	• Use a high degree of engineer support. • Use new construction or repair of existing facilities. • Cross the gap into the enduring phase.
Semipermanent (2 to 10 years)	• Design effort exceeds military engineer unit capabilities. • Beyond the scope of construction for military engineers. • Design and build for moderate energy efficiency, maintenance, and life-cycle management.
Permanent (5 to 10 years or more)	• Require significant design effort. • Beyond the scope of construction for military engineer units completely. • Design and build for a high degree of energy efficiency, maintenance, and life-cycle management.

BASE CAMP DEVELOPMENT PLANNING

E-11. Effective base camp planning requires a multidisciplined approach with a host of participants from various organizations that can provide the necessary expertise such as civil engineering, design, environmental, safety, preventive medicine, antiterrorism, and real estate. The base camp development planning process shown in figure E-1 provides a framework for locating, designing, constructing, and eventually closing base camps. The process is not an absolute, is rarely performed in sequence, and is dependent on both the mission and operational variables that require planners to constantly assess, revise, and coordinate their efforts. The steps of the base camp development planning process are—

- Initiate preliminary planning.
- Select location.
- Plan land use.
- Develop facility requirements.
- Plan general site.
- Design guide, programming, and construction.
- Maintain and update plans.
- Clean up, effect closure, and archive.

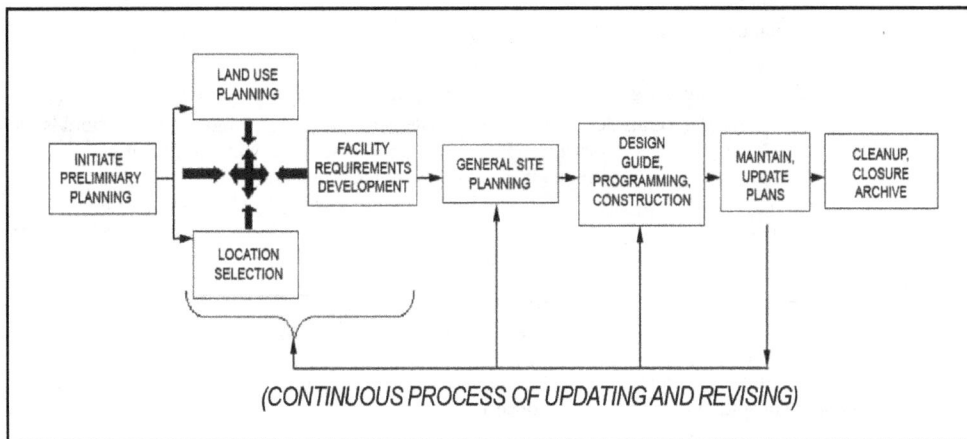

Figure E-1. Base camp development planning process

E-12. When conducting the base camp development planning process, base camp planners must constantly consider—

- Integration of survivability measures.
- Functional area requirements and their arrangement based on base camp size and commander's guidance.
- Availability and acceptability of existing facilities and the real estate support required to acquire them.
- Facility construction standards based on the appropriate governing documents.
- Means of facility construction based on the availability of labor and resources.
- Infrastructure requirements based on base camp size, location, and life span.
- Environmental considerations.

INITIATE PRELIMINARY PLANNING

E-13. This step centers on understanding the scope and magnitude of the mission and correlates to mission analysis of the MDMP. Base camp planners analyze the supported unit's OPORD to determine unit organization, strength (personnel and equipment), commander's intent, functional requirements, and the mission and operational variables affecting planning.

E-14. Critical facts and assumptions are developed and requests for information are submitted through appropriate channels to begin developing information that may not yet be available. Initially, the major variables that planners must contend with—

- Using existing facilities or constructing new ones.
- Using military assets and resources, HN labor and materials, or those from other sources.
- Construction standards and allowances.

E-15. A review of doctrine and governing policies and directives aids planners in determining constraints on facility design and construction standards, as does determining the availability of resources (labor and material). It is important to determine the facility types and standards as early in the process as possible to allow for the time required for the contracting of services and acquisition of materials. The major planning considerations include—

- Survivability.
- Facility construction (materials, troop labor, HN, or contracted).
- Infrastructure requirements, which include—
  - Sanitation (latrines and solid waste).
  - Hygiene (water supply, showers, and laundry).
  - Electrical (military generators, prime power, and contracted generators).
  - Environmental considerations (dust abatement, drainage, hazardous materials and petroleum, oil, and lubricants [POL] storage areas, toxic industrial materials hazards, disease vectors, and natural and/or cultural resource protection).

LOCATION SELECTION

E-16. The objective of this step is determining the optimal location for a base camp. It consists of developing, evaluating, and comparing a series of possible locations against criteria such as mission requirements, survivability measures, tactical suitability, resource availability, environmental considerations, and commander's guidance. An important part of this step is gathering and analyzing all available geospatial and intelligence products. This also includes obtaining specialized expertise through various reachback capabilities, such as tele-engineering.

E-17. The initial environmental baseline survey for a base camp should occur as early as possible (within 30 days of occupation at a minimum) and should occur in conjunction with an environmental health site assessment. The assessment is normally requested through the Center for Health Promotion and Preventive Medicine. The resulting information is critical not only for the health of U.S. Service members and civilians, but it also provides a baseline of information about the site to ensure that the United States does not incur liability for preexisting environmental conditions.

E-18. Selection may not be required when the location is predetermined based on HN directives, U.S. government land acquisitions, or when the OE or tactical requirements dictate a specific location, such as an existing airfield. Coordinating this step through proper channels with the DOS ensures important factors involving diplomatic procedures and international laws have been properly considered. When the situation allows, this step is greatly enhanced with "on-the-ground" surveys and assessments by the location selection team. Figure E-2 shows an example of the composition of a location selection team. The major location selection considerations include—

- Defensible terrain.
- Existing infrastructure (facilities, sewage, transportation networks, and power).
- Civil considerations (labor market and resources).
- Potential for base camp expansion.
- Environmental conditions (such as toxic industrial materials hazards; proximity to industrial facilities that may expose personnel to contaminants; health hazards; presence of historic, cultural, or religious sites; and potential of interference with the normal routine of local civilians).
- Probability of natural events.
- Soil conditions.

- Water sources.
- Suitability for communication systems.
- Proximity to medical facilities.

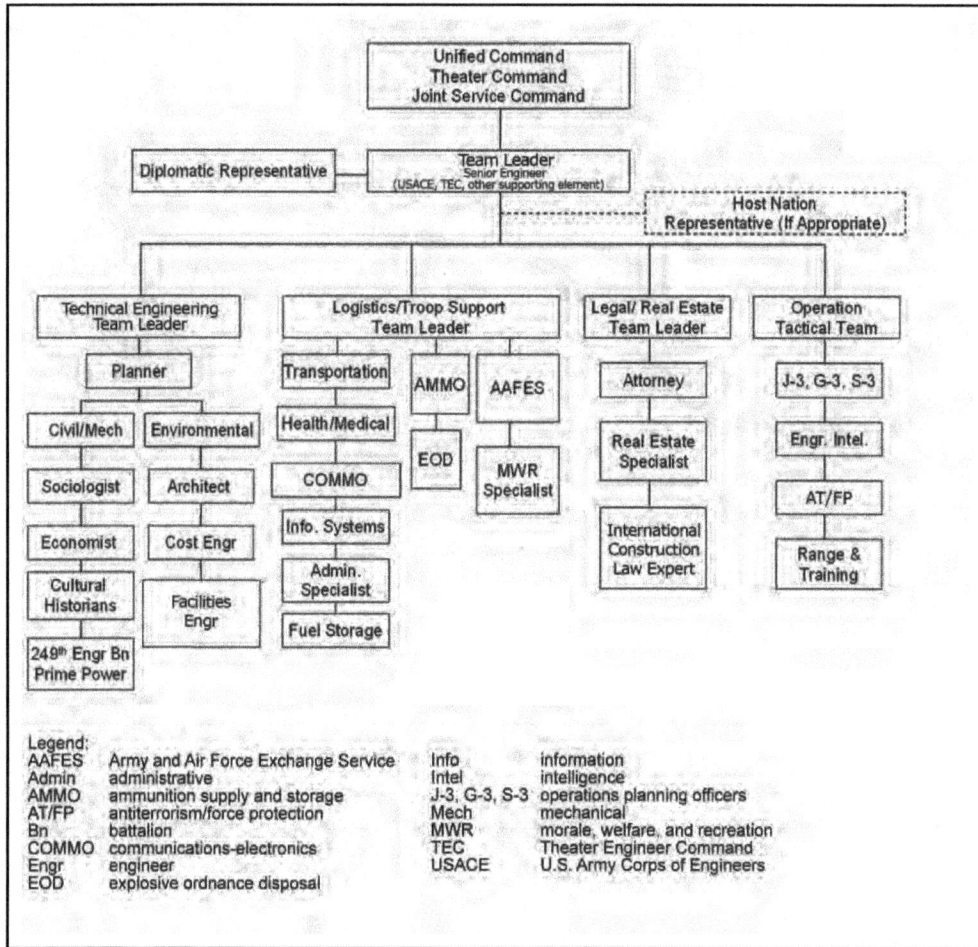

Figure E-2. Example of a location selection team

LAND USE PLANNING

E-19. This step integrates the physical elements of a base camp (both natural and man-made) with the human activities (military and socio-cultural). It involves calculating, mapping, and planning the allocation of land based on general use categories, mission analysis, functional requirements, functional interrelationships, standards, criteria, and guidelines. A land use plan (shown in figure E-3, page E-6) depicts general locations for land use areas in relation to existing development patterns, forces, and features at the base camp location.

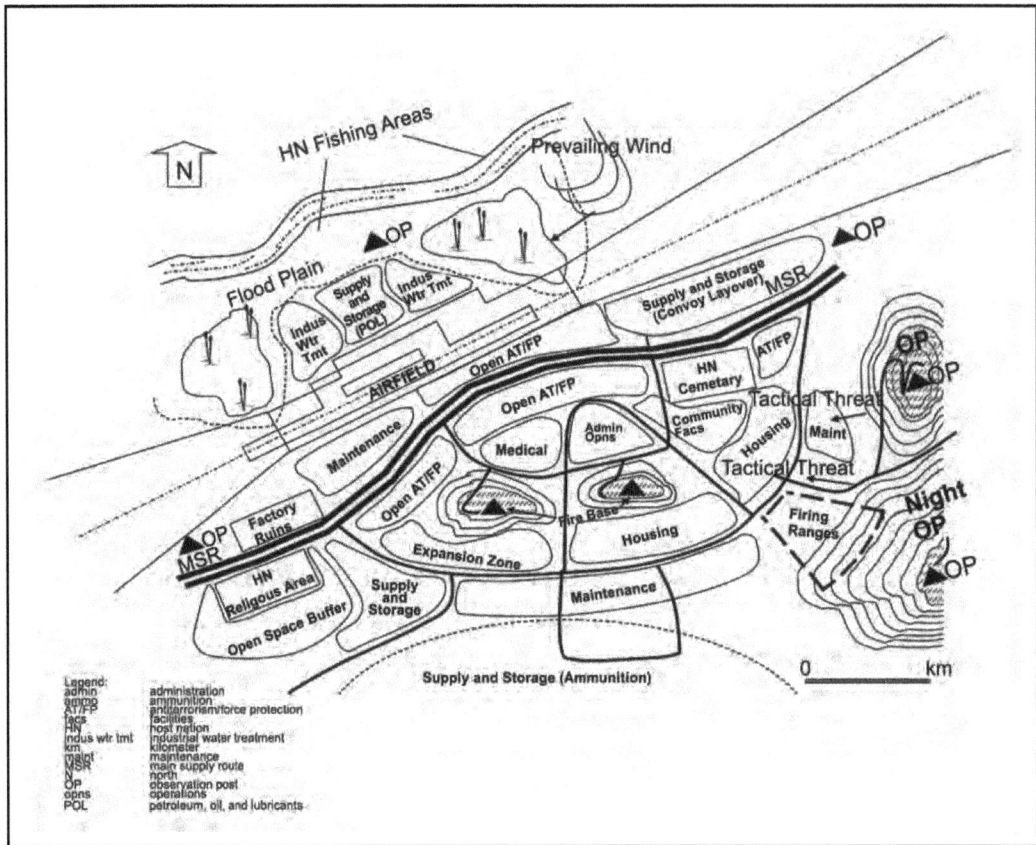

Figure E-3. Example of a land use plan

E-20. This plan serves as the skeleton for the further development of the base camp. The land use pattern accounts for constraints that cannot be overcome, leverages opportunities that exist, accommodates existing requirements, and facilitates future expansion. The major land use categories or functional areas are—

- Life support areas, including housing, dining, and showers.
- Administration.
- Maintenance and equipment storage.
- Logistics.
- Buffer zones.
- Airfields.
- Medical considerations.
- Ammunition storage.
- Training.
- Recreation.

FACILITY REQUIREMENTS DEVELOPMENT

E-21. This step refines the initial estimate of facility requirements developed during preliminary planning. Facility requirements are determined by coordination between the base camp planning team and the prospective base camp users (supported unit). These requirements are compiled into a list of the existing and proposed facilities and infrastructure that must be present on the base camp to support the mission and are approved by the commander. The facilities requirements development process includes the following eight tasks:

- **Task 1.** Inventory existing assets to determine what space, buildings, and supporting infrastructure are available to support operations.
- **Task 2.** Analyze the mission.
- **Task 3.** Determine allowances based on base camp life span and theater guidance.
- **Task 4.** Coordinate with the customer.
- **Task 5.** Determine specific requirements versus initial allowances.
- **Task 6.** Document existing and required facilities into a tabulation of existing and required facilities.
- **Task 7.** Analyze shortfalls (short-term and long-term) and excesses.
- **Task 8.** Recommend the best COA.

GENERAL SITE PLANNING

E-22. This step begins after final site approval has been made and facility requirements have been determined. Base camp site planning is essentially a compromise among survivability measures, existing terrain and facilities, customer requirements and desires, and site planning principles—with the objective of organizing requirements and site conditions into a documented plan that best supports the base camp's mission. This is accomplished by producing a written record of the general site planning process, a base camp development site plan that portrays the physical layout of the required facilities and infrastructure, and an action plan that establishes the priority and the sequence of base camp development. The base camp development site plan contains to-scale, plan-view drawings (referred to as footprints) of the proposed buildings and site improvements (such as roads, hardstands, and parking areas) identified in the tabulation of existing and required facilities produced during the facility requirements development processes described above. An example of a base camp development site plan is shown in figure E-4, page E-8.

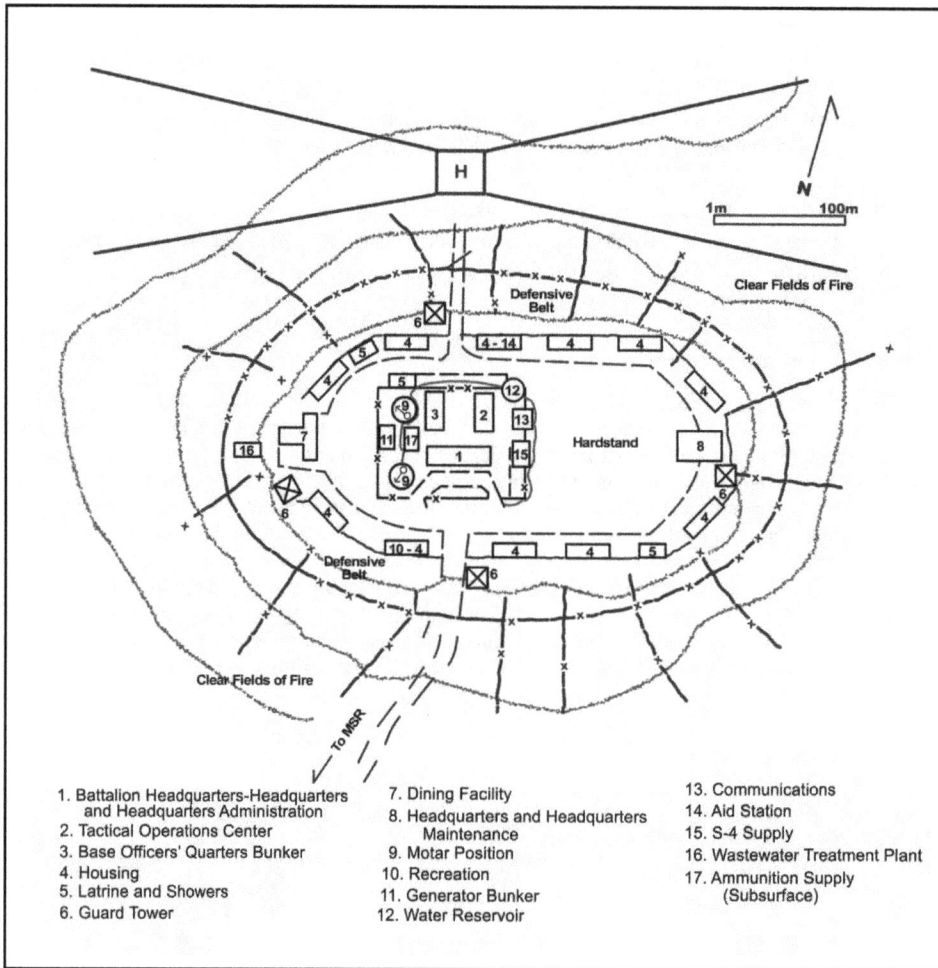

Figure E-4. Example of a base camp development site plan

E-23. During this step, operational, functional, aesthetic, environmental, and health and safety issues are addressed in detail. An important aspect throughout this step is ensuring operational efficiency by analyzing time-distance relationships among the various base camp functions. A final determination is also made on the facility types, construction standards, and the anticipated camp population. The base camp development site plan is developed by—

- Assembling and reviewing reference documents (such as existing facility maps and special studies) that provide detailed information about the base camp location.
- Retrieving the requirements from the tabulation of existing and required facilities produced during the facility requirements development process.
- Obtaining or preparing footprints.
- Placing the footprints on the base camp development site plan in the proper land use zones as shown in figure E-5.

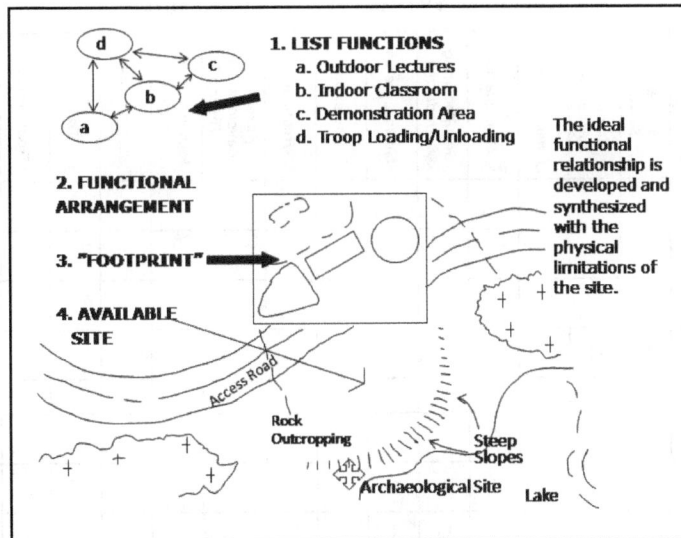

Figure E-5. Formulating a base camp development site plan

E-24. The largest areas and facilities (such as airfields and firing ranges) and those requiring exact positioning (such as petroleum, oil, and lubricants (POL) storage areas and wastewater treatment facilities) are normally sited first. Having a land use bubble diagram or affinity matrix (see table E-2, page E-10) visible during this step, while also continually referring to the land use plan, will aid planners in maintaining the functional relationships of facilities as they are arranged. When positioning footprints of proposed buildings and facilities on the base camp development site plan, planners consider the following:

- Common areas provide equitable access to all users.
- Site access is supported by roadways and parking areas.
- Vehicular and pedestrian traffic patterns are arranged to avoid conflict.
- Buildings are related in groups and are compatible (affinity relationships) with adjacent land uses.
- Existing utility lines are maximized to avoid additional development cost.
- Buildings and facilities are located on well-drained sites and are not in major drainage courses.
- Prevailing winds, solar orientation, and microclimatic conditions are considered to conserve energy and provide comfort to facility users.
- Survivability, environmental, and safety measures are observed (such as standoff distances, building separation requirements [see FM 3-34.400], and safety zones).

Table E-2. Example of an affinity matrix

Land Use Categories Evaluated	Administration	Commercial Services	Community Facilities	Family Housing	Maintenance	Manufacturing & Production	Medical, Dental	Operations	Recreation	Research, Development, Testing	Research Land, Buffer	Supply Storage	Training	Troop Housing	Utilities	Water Areas	Wetlands
Administration																	
Commercial Services	C																
Community Facilities	C	C															
Family Housing	I	N	C														
Maintenance	I	I	I	I													
Manufacturing & Production	I	I	I	I	C												
Medical, Dental	N	C	N	N	I	I											
Operations	I	I	I	I	C	C	I										
Recreation	C	C	C	C	I	I	C	I									
Research, Development, Testing	N	C	I	I	C	C	N	I	N								
Research Land, Buffer	C	C	C	C	C	C	C	C	C	C							
Supply Storage	N	I	I	I	C	C	I	I	N	N	C						
Training	I	I	I	I	I	N	I	I	N	I	C	N					
Troop Housing	N	C	C	I	I	I	N	I	C	I	C	I	I				
Utilities	N	N	N	I	C	C	I	N	N	N	C	C	I	I			
Water Areas	C	C	C	C	N	N	N	N	C	I	C	I	I	C	I		
Wetlands	I	I	I	I	I	I	I	I	C	I	C	I	I	I	I	C	

Legend:
C Compatible
N Neutral
I Incompatible

PROGRAM, DESIGN, AND CONSTRUCTION

E-25. Programming centers on determining and obtaining funding from the various funding options that are available, depending on the situation.

E-26. Design includes completing facility and infrastructure designs. TCMS is the Army's principal tool for base camp design. It is an automated military engineering construction planning and execution support system that delivers engineering and construction information for use in-theater. Whenever possible, planners should incorporate existing designs (from previous operations), existing structures, and available prefabricated or pre-engineered units to the fullest extent possible.

E-27. There is no single correct design to a base camp. There are an infinite number of designs that are equally efficient and functional. In practice, construction and design are determined by balancing any two of the following priorities—cost, quality, or time—but not all three. For example, if the customer wants something quick and inexpensive, the degree of quality is often a lower priority. Whenever possible however, designs should be configured for multiple purposes, to accommodate future changes in mission priorities and requirements.

E-28. The ability to begin construction hinges on the timely acquisition of labor and materials. Ideally, using local materials and labor saves time and reduces costs. When local material is not available, planners must provide adequate lead time to accommodate logistical requirements by developing initial estimates for base camp construction as early in the planning phase as possible. As with any construction effort, delays should be expected and planned for. The preliminary estimates should include the following:

- Real estate required, in area (square feet or meters).
- Equipment hours required for construction for each type of equipment.
- Man-hours required for construction, by construction skill.
- Materiel requirements, in short tons.

MAINTAIN AND UPDATE PLANS

E-29. Base camp planners must maintain and update plans for site layout and designs, while continuing to plan for camp improvements and expansion. The operation of the base camp should work hand in hand with the tactical requirements. A director of public works, EFD, or other like organization is typically used to manage base camp operations. Mayor cells, base camp planning boards, and other like boards and cells are established to manage master planning for short-term and long-term improvements, reductions, and expansion. All future planning relies on current and accurate base camp development site plans.

CLEANUP, CLOSURE, AND ARCHIVE

E-30. Base camp cleanup and closure procedures present many challenges. A wide range of U.S. and HN laws, regulations, policies, and procedures can apply. In those cases where U.S. policies are more stringent than those of the HN, the U.S. policies will usually govern. Though they do not have the force of law within the theater of operations, the ethical and practical intent and the spirit of many U.S. laws strongly influence base camp cleanup and closure operations. See FM 3-34.5 for more information.

E-31. Cleanup and closure requirements must be considered during initial planning to minimize liability and avoid costly remediation or restoration efforts when turning over base camps to third parties or returning lands and facilities back to the HN. These requirements may be defined in a land use agreement or a status of forces agreement. As a minimum, a base camp cleanup and closure plan includes the following:

- Condition of property.
- Disposition of facilities.
- Environmental cleanup standards.
- Procedures for EH removal.
- Procedures for site mapping of land areas, buildings and structures, and infrastructure, to include a real property inventory or building information schedule.
- Procedures for records archival, to capture before, during, and after activities.
- Procedures for executing base camp closure, including phasing plans, schedules, inspection checklists, and specific task assignments for realistically achieving the desired land and facility conditions.
- Methods of determining and or adjudicating liability claims.
- Documentation of uncompleted actions with the appropriate justifications.
- Procedures for record archival that captures before, during, and after activities and can assist in adjudicating liability claims.

This page intentionally left blank.

Appendix F

Tailored Engineer Force Packages

This appendix provides illustrative engineer force packages at each higher echelon. Since there is no set force structure for these echelons or for the operational themes in which they will be involved, the packages shown should not be considered authoritative. These illustrations primarily serve to provide planners with a framework for considering the types and organization of units that may be tailored to meet the CCDR's actual needs.

THEATER ARMY ENGINEER FORCE PACKAGES

F-1.   The tailored engineer force supporting the theater army echelon will typically address both specific operational and broader support requirements. The TEC is the engineer headquarters designed for operational command of engineer capabilities at EAC level and often will provide C2 for an operationally configured theater army headquarters. When the full TEC is tailored for the operation, it is capable of also addressing the broader support required by the ASCC's ADCON, ASOS, and CUL responsibilities. In cases where the TEC is not deployed in full, or at all, the ASCC may consider an alternative organization to control engineer support requirements. Table F-1 provides considerations at the theater echelon for scenarios in which an engineer brigade and MEB may be required.

Table F-1. Considerations for brigade-level headquarters in theater scenarios

Maneuver Enhancement Brigade	Engineer Brigade
The maneuver enhancement brigade is primarily designed to provide support to the division but is capable of being employed to provide support to higher-echelon organizations as well.	In major combat operations with a theater engineer command tailored in support of a joint force land component, one or more brigade headquarters may be required to extend the theater engineer command's span of control.
The maneuver enhancement brigade may be required to establish or support a theater-level Joint Security Coordination Center.	A theater engineer command deployable command post or the engineer brigade headquarters may be required to support a theater echelon joint task force in crisis response or contingency operations.
The maneuver enhancement brigade has the ability to control an area of operation, such as an aerial port of debarkation or seaport of debarkation during early-entry operations.	When a theater army headquarters is not operationally engaged, but only providing administrative control, Army support to other Services, and common-user logistics functions for a separate joint force commander, an adequate engineer controlling headquarters (theater engineer command, brigade, or battalion) may also be required to support those functions.

F-2.   The theater army headquarters will have an assigned LNO from USACE. This LNO provides access through reachback to additional technical support. The LNO may also assist in coordination with the DOD-designated CCA for the AOR or selected JOA. Additional FFE support may be tailored through FESTs supporting the theater army headquarters, the TEC, or both.

F-3.   Specific capabilities required at each subordinate echelon will vary widely based on mission variables. As baseline and specialized elements are tailored to meet identified and anticipated requirements, adequate consideration must also be given to the control of these capabilities. The engineer brigade headquarters controls functionally focused engineer operations and includes a span of control adequate to support either corps or division echelons. The MEB controls multifunctional maneuver support and support area operations and includes a span of control that typically supports a division echelon but may also support a corps echelon as well.

TAILORED FOR MAJOR COMBAT OPERATIONS

F-4.   When the CCDR acts as the JFC during major combat operations, the theater army may provide the land component commander and headquarters. In that case, it exercises OPCON over land forces deployed to a JOA. Figure F-1 shows a theater army echelon engineer force organized under the control of the TEC.

F-5.   In this illustration, the full TEC is tailored for the operation and is capable of addressing the specific operational requirements and broader support required by the ASCC's ADCON, ASOS, and CUL responsibilities. An EFD or FEST (typically a FEST–M) is tailored to support the TEC and may serve as a base for a provisional USACE district or division if required during the operation. A FEST–A may be required to support the theater army echelon engineer staff. Specific capabilities tailored for the subordinate corps and division echelons are not included in this illustration but are shown separately in subsequent paragraphs and figures.

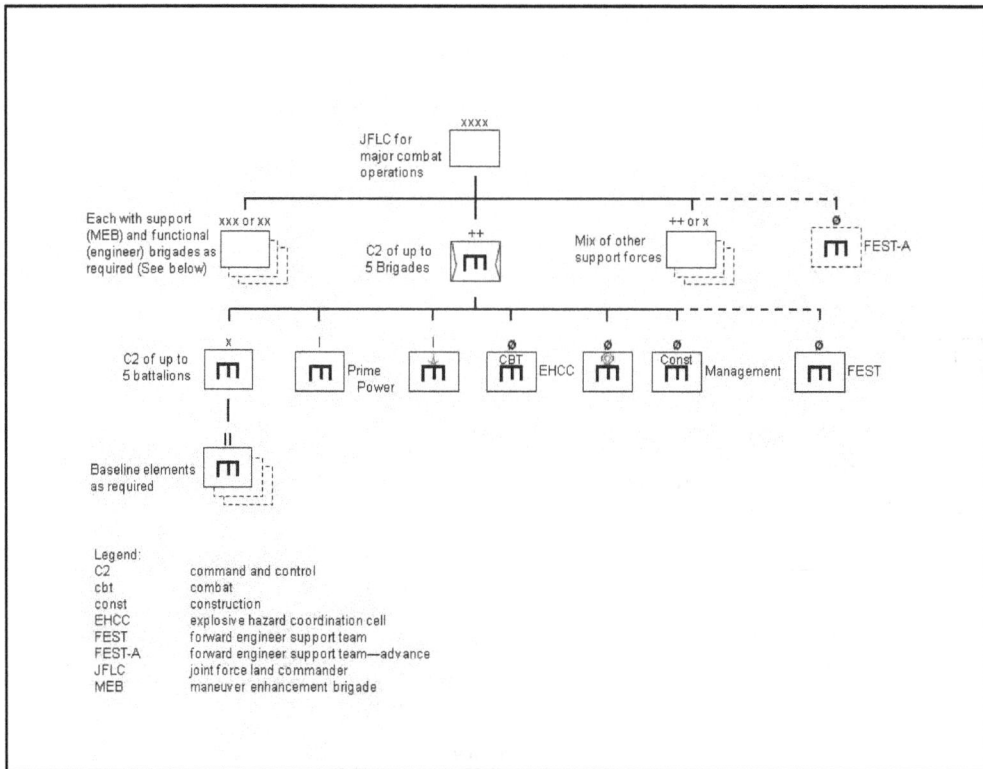

Figure F-1. Notional theater engineer force package

TAILORED FOR A CONTINGENCY

F-6.   When required, the theater army can provide a headquarters able to command and control a JTF for contingencies with other Service augmentation. A significant consideration for this operational configuration is the designation of the JTF ENCOORD. The theater army echelon ENCOORD may remain with theater army main CP while a designated alternate supports the deployed JTF CP as ENCOORD. Figure F-2 shows a theater army echelon JTF engineer force organized under the control of either the TEC's DCP or an engineer brigade headquarters.

F-7.   In this illustration, either the DCP from the TEC or an engineer brigade headquarters is tailored for the operation and capable of addressing the specific operational requirements. An EFD or FEST is tailored to support the TEC or engineer brigade headquarters and a FEST–A may be required to support the JTF engineer staff. Specific capabilities tailored for the subordinate division and brigade echelons are not included in this illustration but are shown separately in subsequent paragraphs and figures.

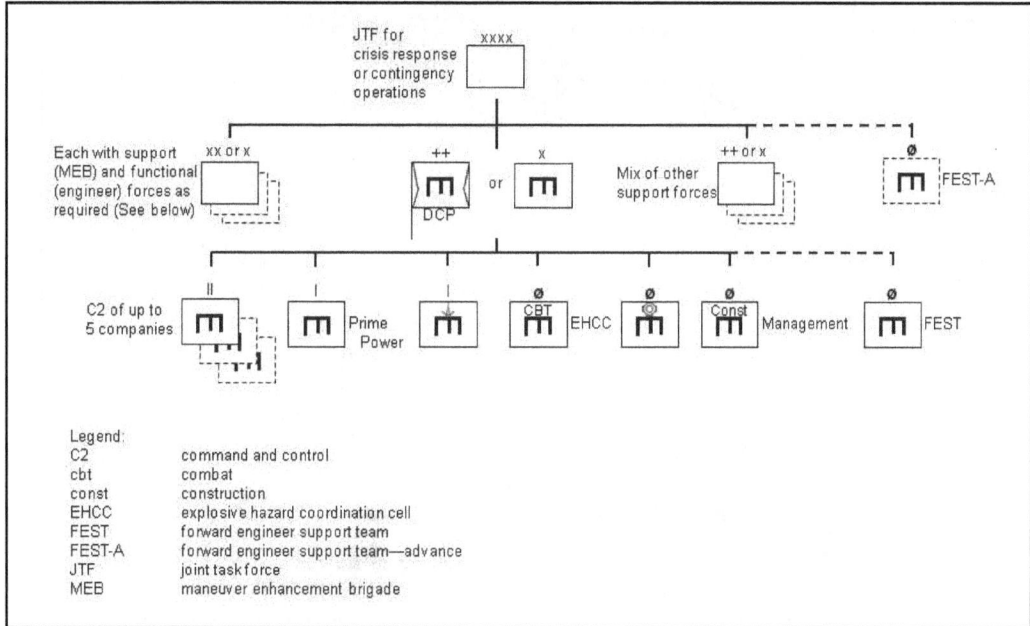

Figure F-2. Notional theater JTF engineer force package

TAILORED FOR SUPPORT TO ARMY, JOINT, INTERAGENCY, AND MULTINATIONAL FORCES

F-8.   The theater army headquarters continues to perform AOR-wide functions in addition to its operational responsibilities. These functions include RSOI, logistics over-the-shore operations, and security coordination. Figure F-3, page F-4, shows cases in which the theater army headquarters performs both operational and support functions or supports a separate JFC.

F-9.   If the theater army headquarters functions as an operational headquarters while continuing to perform its AOR-wide functions, the tailored engineer force will typically also address both sets of requirements. Both the TEC and engineer brigade are capable of controlling operational and other support requirements, but the engineer brigade headquarters is better suited for a limited span of control. When the theater army headquarters is not operationally engaged, but is only providing ADCON, ASOS, and CUL functions for a separate JFC, an engineer force package with an adequate controlling headquarters may still be needed.

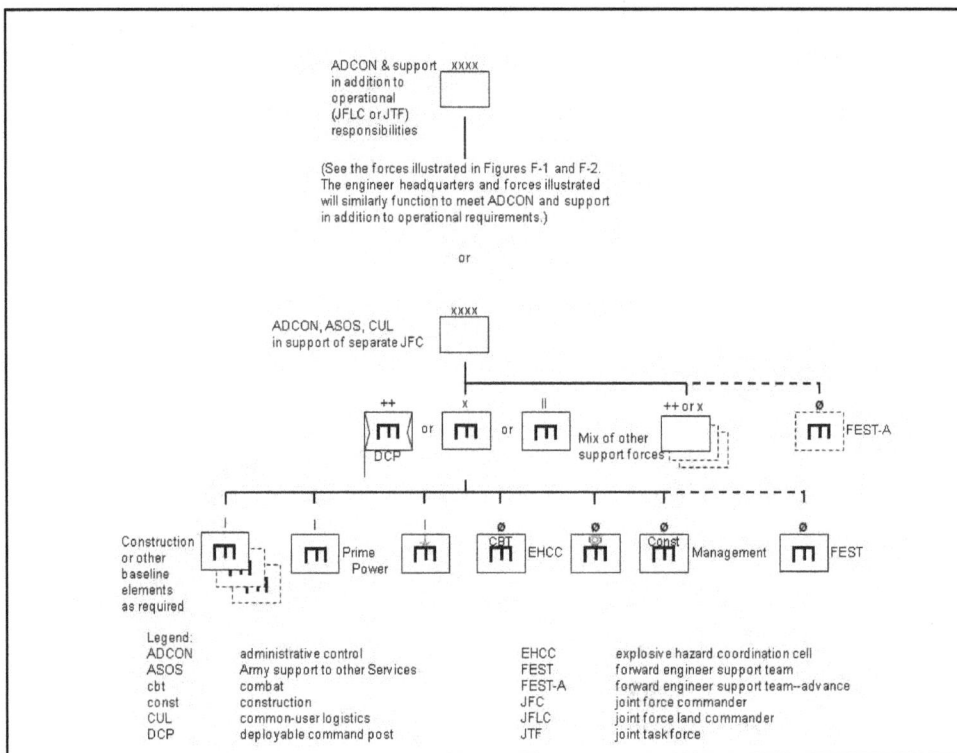

Figure F-3. Notional ASCC engineer force package

CORPS ENGINEER FORCE PACKAGES

F-10. The tailored engineer force supporting the corps echelon will typically focus more specifically on operational requirements. The engineer brigade is capable of providing effective C2 of engineer operations for most contingencies in which the corps headquarters is required and is the most likely headquarters to be tailored for a corps echelon engineer headquarters. Most operations or contingencies requiring the deployment of the corps headquarters in one of its configurations will also require an engineer brigade headquarters element. Additional engineer brigades and MEBs may be required in support of the corps and its subordinate divisions. Table F-2 provides considerations at the corps echelon for scenarios in which an engineer brigade and MEB may be required.

Table F-2. Considerations for brigade-level headquarters in corps scenarios

Maneuver Enhancement Brigade	Engineer Brigade
The maneuver enhancement brigade is primarily designed to provide support to the division but is capable of being employed to provide support to higher-echelon organizations as well.	Most operations or contingencies requiring the corps headquarters in one of their operational configurations will also require at least one engineer brigade headquarters.
Most civil support operations with a significant consequence management component will require at least one maneuver enhancement brigade.	Engineer brigades are well designed to integrate and synchronize engineer capabilities across the corps area of operation.
In combat operations, the maneuver enhancement brigade should be considered when a command and control capability is needed to control terrain and provide protection for key corps assets in a support area. When given an area of operation, maneuver enhancement brigades have limited ability to integrate and synchronize engineer capability across the force.	

F-11. The corps headquarters may receive an LNO from USACE. This LNO provides access through reachback to additional technical support. The LNO may also assist in coordination with the DOD-designated CCA for the selected JOA. Additional FFE support may be tailored through FESTs or EFDs supporting the corps headquarters, the engineer brigade, or both.

F-12. Specific capabilities required at subordinate echelons will vary widely based on mission variables. As baseline and specialized elements are tailored to meet identified and anticipated requirements, adequate consideration must also be given to the control of these capabilities. The engineer brigade headquarters controls functionally focused engineer operations and includes a span of control adequate to support either corps or division echelons. The MEB controls multifunctional maneuver support operations and also includes a span of control adequate to support either corps or division echelons.

TAILORED FOR MAJOR COMBAT OPERATIONS

F-13. When required, a corps may become an intermediate tactical headquarters under the land component command, with OPCON of multiple divisions (including multinational or Marine Corps formations) or other large tactical formations. Figure F-4, page F-6, shows a corps echelon engineer force organized under the control of the engineer brigade headquarters.

F-14. In this illustration, the full brigade headquarters is tailored for the operation and is capable of addressing the identified and anticipated operational requirements. An EFD or FEST is tailored to support the brigade and a FEST–A may be required to support the corps echelon engineer staff. Specific capabilities tailored for the subordinate division and brigade echelons are not included in this illustration but are shown separately in subsequent paragraphs and figures.

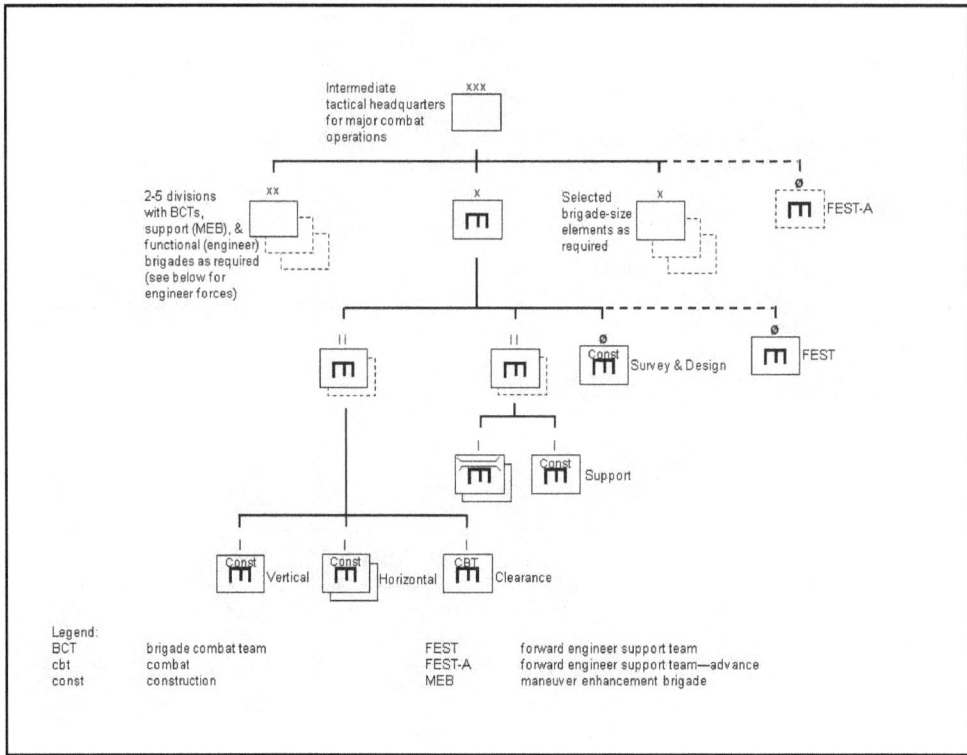

Figure F-4. Notional corps engineer force package

TAILORED FOR CONTINGENCY OR PROTRACTED OPERATIONS

F-15. The corps can rapidly transition to either a JTF or land component command headquarters for contingency or protracted operations. Of note in this operational configuration is the designation of the JTF ENCOORD. The corps ENCOORD transitions to become the JTF ENCOORD and will not have additional responsibilities associated with the Army forces. Figure F-5 shows a corps echelon JTF engineer force organized under the control of either the TEC's DCP or an engineer brigade headquarters.

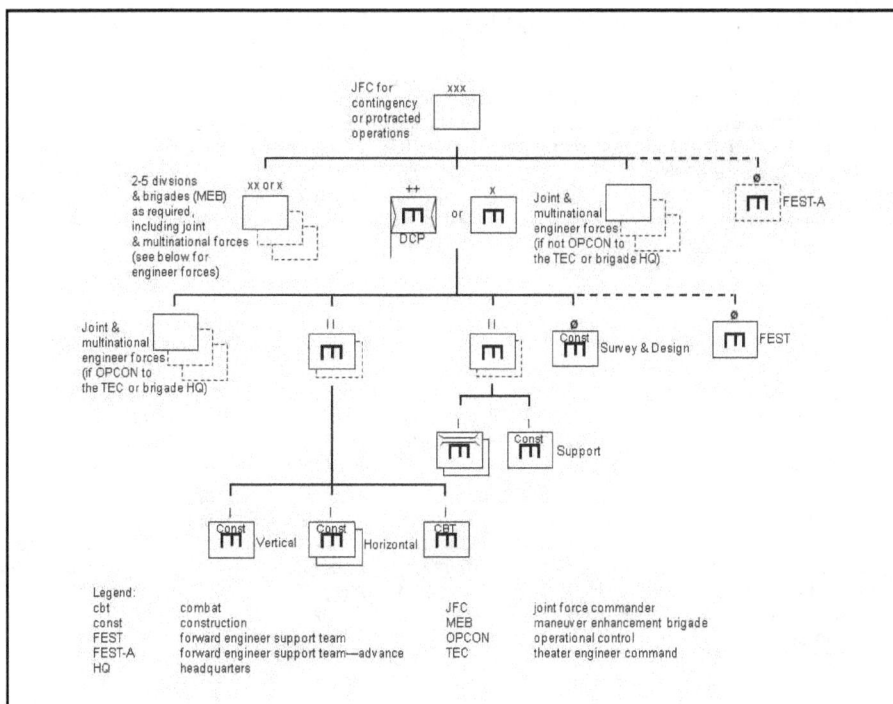

Figure F-5. Notional corps JFC engineer force package

F-16. In this illustration, either the DCP from the TEC or an engineer brigade headquarters is tailored for the operation and capable of addressing the specific operational requirements. Either is capable of controlling joint and multinational engineer forces, or these forces may operate directly under JTF control. An EFD or FEST is tailored to support the TEC or engineer brigade headquarters, and a FEST–A may be required to support the JTF engineer staff. Specific capabilities tailored for the subordinate division and brigade echelons are not included in this illustration but are rather shown separately in subsequent paragraphs and figures.

DIVISION ENGINEER FORCE PACKAGES

F-17. Typically, at least one MEB will be required in operations or contingencies requiring deployment of the division headquarters in one of its configurations. In some cases, the division may need an additional functional engineer brigade, based on mission requirements. The tailored engineer force supporting the division echelon will typically focus primarily on support for the tactical-level requirements of subordinate brigades. Table F-3, page F-8, provides considerations at the division echelon for scenarios in which an engineer brigade and MEB may be required.

Table F-3. Considerations for brigade-level headquarters in division scenarios

MEB	Engineer Brigade
A division involved in major combat operations should be supported by all five types of support brigades, including the maneuver enhancement brigade. In combat operations the maneuver enhancement brigade is specifically designed to control the division support area to provide for the collective protection of the units in the support area and to enable movement within the support area through the establishment of movement corridors.	A division acting as the primary tactical echelon headquarters in major combat operations will require an engineer brigade headquarters when the engineer functional requirements exceed the limited capabilities of the maneuver enhancement brigade. This will likely be the case if the maneuver enhancement brigade is assigned an area of operation to control.
With adequate resources, a maneuver enhancement brigade can conduct stability tasks in an area of operation while simultaneously supporting offensive or defensive operations being conducted by its higher headquarters.	A division will significantly benefit from the engineer brigade's functional span of control in most stability or civil support operations. During stability operations, the division may need an engineer brigade to integrate and synchronize engineer capabilities if the maneuver enhancement brigade is assigned its own area of operation in which to conduct stability operations.
When given an area of operation to control (either the support area or an area of operation requiring stability operations), the maneuver enhancement brigade has limited ability to integrate and synchronize engineer capability across the force.	When the division is configured as joint force commander for smaller contingency operations, one or more engineer brigades may be required based on the mission variables.

F-18. In some cases, the division headquarters may receive an LNO from USACE. This LNO provides access through reachback to additional technical support. The LNO may also assist in coordination with the DOD-designated CCA for the selected JOA. Additional FFE support may be tailored through FESTs or EFDs supporting the division headquarters, the engineer brigade, or both.

F-19. Specific capabilities required at subordinate echelons will vary widely based on mission variables. As baseline and specialized elements are tailored to meet identified and anticipated requirements, adequate consideration must also be given to the control of these capabilities. Whenever two or more engineer modules are task-organized in support of a BCT, MEB, engineer brigade, or other unit, an engineer battalion headquarters may be required for the C2 and sustainment of those modules.

TAILORED FOR MAJOR COMBAT OPERATIONS

F-20. Divisions are the Army's primary tactical warfighting headquarters. Their principal task is directing subordinate brigade operations. Figure F-6 shows engineer capacity under the MEB and each BCT. Additional engineer capacity at the division echelon engineer force may be organized under the control of the engineer brigade headquarters. All the engineer forces shown are in addition to the packages shown at higher echelons in previous figures.

F-21. In this illustration, an MEB supports the division while each BCT is tailored with augmenting combat engineer capability. An engineer brigade headquarters is tailored to address identified and anticipated division-level requirements above and beyond the capabilities of the BCTs and MEB. An EFD or FEST is tailored to support the engineer brigade, and a FEST–A may be required to support the division echelon engineer staff. Specific capabilities tailored for the subordinate BCTs are included in this illustration but will vary based on mission variables.

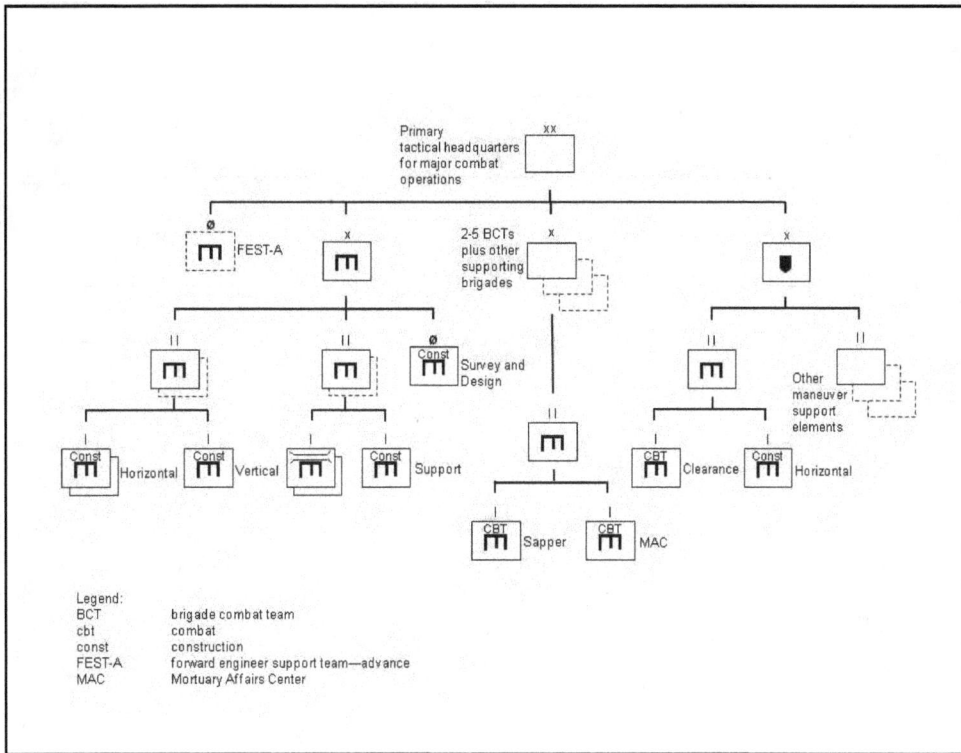

Figure F-6. Notional division engineer force package

TAILORED FOR A SMALLER-SCALE CONTINGENCY

F-22. With appropriate joint augmentation, a division can be the JTF or land component command headquarters for small contingencies. Figure F-7, page F-10, shows a division echelon JTF engineer force organized under the control of an engineer brigade headquarters.

F-23. In this illustration, an engineer brigade headquarters is tailored for the operation and is also capable of controlling joint and multinational engineer forces, or these forces may operate directly under JTF control. Additional engineer capability is shown under the MEB and each BCT. An EFD or FEST is tailored to support the engineer brigade headquarters and a FEST–A may be required to support the JTF engineer staff. Specific capabilities tailored for the subordinate BCTs are included in this illustration but will vary based on mission variables.

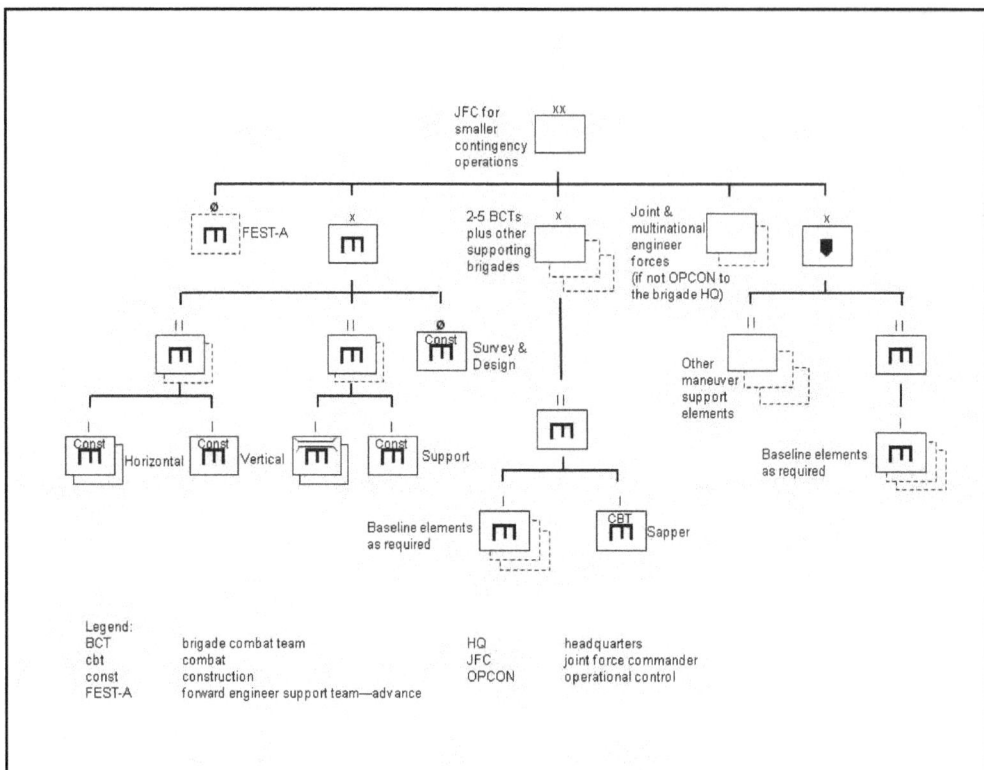

Figure F-7. Notional division JFC engineer force package

Source Notes

These are the sources used, quoted, or paraphrased in this publication. They are listed by page number. Where material appears in a paragraph, both page and paragraph numbers are listed.

1-1   "Make no mistake...": Colonel Jerry C. Meyer and Brigadier General Gregg F. Martin, "Join the Campaign: Engineer Leader Technical Competency," *Engineer, The Professional Bulletin of Army Engineers*, January–March 2008, 4.

2-1   "The (7th Engineer) Brigade units...": Colonel Samuel C. Raines, 7th Engineer Brigade Command Report—Operations Desert Shield and Desert Storm, 9 April 1991.

3-1   "Combined arms operations are familiar...": FM 3-0, *Operations* (27 February 2008), 4-7.

4-1   "Initially, the Central Command (CENTCOM) Commander...": Lieutenant General (Retired) Robert B. Flowers.

5-1   "In the early morning hours of 24 August 1992...": "Hurricane Andrew: The 20th Engineer Brigade Perspective," Major Robert M. Ralston and Lieutenant Colonel Douglas L. Horn, 1 October 1992.

6-1   "...[Y]ou may fly over a land forever...": T.R. Fehrenbach, *This Kind of War* (Dulles, VA: Brassey's, 2001), 290.

7-1   "Faced with such demands...": Engineers of the Southwest Pacific 1941-1945, Volume 8. Critque.

This page intentionally left blank.

Glossary

The glossary lists acronyms, abbreviations, and terms with Army or joint definitions, and other selected terms. Where Army and joint definitions are different, (Army) follows the term. Terms or acronyms for which ATTP 3-34.23 is the proponent manual (the authority) are marked with an asterisk (*).

SECTION I–ACRONYMS AND ABBREVIATIONS

Acronym/Term	Definition
AAFES	Army and Air Force Exchange Service
ACR	armored cavalry regiment
ADC	area damage control
ADCON	administrative control
admin	administrative
AFCAP	Air Force contract augmentation program
AFCESA	Air Force Civil Engineer Support Agency
AFSB	Army field Service brigade
AIF	anti-Iraqi forces
AJP	Allied joint publication
AL	Alabama
ALT	acquisition, logistics, and technology
AMD	air and missile defense
ammo	ammunition
AO	area of operations
AOR	area of responsibility
APO	Army post office
APOD	aerial port of debarkation
ARFOR	Army forces
ARNG	Army National Guard
ARNGUS	Army National Guard of the United States
ASCC	Army Service component command
ASCOPE	areas, structures, capabilities, organizations, people, events
ASOS	Army support to other Services
ASP	ammunition supply point
AT/FP	antiterrorism/force protection
ATHP	ammunition transfer and holding points
ATP	Allied tactical publication
attn	attention
BCT	brigade combat team
BDE	brigade
BFSB	battlefield surveillance brigade
BLST	brigade logistics support team
bn	battalion

Acronym/Term	Definition
BPT	be prepared to
BSTB	brigade special troops battalion
C2	command and control
CA	civil affairs
CAB	combat aviation brigade
CACOM	civil affairs command
CBRN	chemical, biological, radiological, and nuclear
cbt	combat
CCA	contract construction agent
CCDR	combatant commander
CCIR	Commander's critical information requirements
CEERD	Center for Energy-Environment Research and Development
CENTCOM	Central Command
CERP	Commander's Emergency Response Program
CJCSM	Chairman of the Joint Chiefs of Staff manual
CJTF–7	Coalition Joint Task Force–7
CM	countermobility
CMD	command
CMOC	civil-military operations center
CO	company
COA	course of action
COCOM	combatant command
COL	colonel
CONPLAN	concept plan
const	construction
CONUS	continental United States
COP	common operational picture
CP	command post
CPM	critical path method
CPT	captain
CRM	composite risk management
CSA	Chief of Staff, United States Army
CSR	controlled supply rate
CUL	common-user logistics
DA	Department of the Army
DAC	disaster assistance centers
DC	District of Columbia
DCP	deployable command post
DCST	Defense Logistics Agency contingency support team
DHS	Department of Homeland Security
DIVENG	division engineer
DLA	Defense Logistics Agency
DMC	distribution management center

Acronym/Term	Definition
DOD	Department of Defense
DOS	Department of State
DRMS	Defense Reutilization and Marketing Service
DRU	direct reporting unit
DS	direct support
DSN	defense switched network
DTSS	digital topographic support system
EAB	echelons above brigade
EAC	echelons above corps
EAD	echelons above division
EFD	engineer facility detachment
EH	explosive hazard
EHAT	explosive hazard awareness training
EHCC	explosive hazard coordination cell
e-mail	electronic mail
EN	engineer
ENCOM	engineer command
ENCOORD	engineer coordinator
ENG	engineer
ENGR	engineer
EOD	explosive ordnance disposal
ERC	exercise-related construction
ERDC	Engineer Research and Development Center
ESC	expeditionary sustainment command
ESP	engineer support plan
FACE	forward aviation combat engineering
FACS	facilities
FASCAM	family of scatterable mines
Feb	February
FEMA	Federal Emergency Management Agency
FEST	forward engineer support team
FEST–A	forward engineer support team—advance
FEST–M	forward engineer support team—main
FFE	field force engineering
FHA	foreign humanitarian assistance
FM	field manual
FMI	field manual–interim
FMT	field maintenance team
FOB	forward operating base
FORSCOM	United States Army Forces Command
FRAGO	fragmentary order
FSC	forward support company

Acronym/Term	Definition
G-1	assistant chief of staff, personnel
G-2	assistant chief of staff, intelligence
G-3	assistant chief of staff, operations
G-4	assistant chief of staff, logistics
G-6	assistant chief of staff, information management
G-7	assistant chief of staff, information engagement
G-9	assistant chief of staff, civil affairs operations
GCC	geographic combatant commander
GCSS	Global Combat Support System
GEN	general
GEO	geospatial
GEOINT	geospatial intelligence
GI&S	geospatial information and services
GPC	geospatial planning cell
GRP	group
GS	general support
GSR	general support reinforcing
HBCT	heavy brigade combat team
HCA	humanitarian and civic assistance
HHC	headquarters and headquarters company
HMMWV	high-mobility multipurpose wheeled vehicle
HN	host nation
HQ	headquarters
HR	human resources
HRC	Human Resources Command
HSS	health service support
HTML	hypertext markup language
http	hypertext transfer protocol
IA	Iraqi army
IBCT	infantry brigade combat team
ID	infantry division
IDN	initial distribution number
IED	improvised explosive device
IGO	intergovernmental organization
INTEL	intelligence
IP	Iraqi police
IPB	intelligence preparation of the battlefield
I/R	internment/resettlement
ISB	intermediate staging base
ISF	Iraqi security forces
ISR	intelligence, surveillance, and reconnaissance
J-2	intelligence directorate of a joint staff

Acronym/Term	Definition
J-3	operations directorate of a joint staff
J-4	logistics directorate of a joint staff
J-7	doctrine and training directorate of a joint staff
J-8	force structure, resources, and assessment of a joint staff
JCMEB	joint civil-military engineering board
JEMB	joint environmental management board
JFAC	joint force air component
JFACC	joint force air component command
JFC	joint force commander
JFLC	joint force land component
JFLCC	joint force land component command
JFMC	joint force maritime component
JFSOC	joint force special operations component
JFUB	joint facilities utilization board
JMD	joint manning document
JOA	joint operations area
JOPES	Joint Operation Planning and Execution System
JP	joint publication
JTF	joint task force
LAP	logistic assistance program
LMTV	light to medium tactical truck
LNO	liaison officer
LOC	line of communications
LOGCAP	logistics civil augmentation program
LSC	life-support centers
LSE	logistics support element
LZ	landing zone
M	mobility
MAC	Mortuary Affairs Center
MAGTF	Marine air-ground task force
MAINT	maintenance
MANSCEN	Maneuver Support Center
MCB	movement control battalion
M/CM/S	mobility/countermobility/survivability
MCO	major combat operations
MCRP	Marine Corps reference publication
MCT	movement control team
MCWP	Marine Corps warfighting publication
MDMP	military decisionmaking process
MEAPO	Middle East Area Project Office
MEB	maneuver enhancement brigade
MECH	mechanical

Acronym/Term	Definition
MEDCOM	medical command
MEDEVAC	medical evacuation
MEF	Marine expeditionary force
METT–TC	mission, enemy, terrain and weather, troops and support available, time available, civil considerations
MG	major general
MI	military intelligence
MICLIC	mine-clearing line charge
mil	military
MILCON	military construction
MKT	mobile kitchen trailer
MNC–I	Multinational Corps–Iraq
MND–N	Multinational Division–North
MOE	measure of effectiveness
MOP	measure of performance
MP	military police
mph	miles per hour
MS	Mississippi
MSR	main supply route
MTF	medical treatment facility
MTOE	modified table of organization and equipment
MU	mobile unit
MVR	maneuver
MWR	morale, welfare, and recreation
NATO	North Atlantic Treaty Organization
NAVFAC	Naval Facilities Engineering Command
NCO	noncommissioned officer
NGA	National Geospatial–Intelligence Agency
NGO	nongovernmental organization
NIMS	National Incident Management System
NIPRNET	Nonsecure Internet Protocol Router Network
NLT	no later than
NRF	National Response Framework
O-6	colonel
O&M	operations and maintenance
OBSTINTEL	obstacle intelligence
OCE	Office of the Chief of Engineers
OCP	operational command post
OE	operational environment
OIF	Operation Iraqi Freedom
OP	observation post
OPCON	operational control
OPLAN	operation plan

Acronym/Term	Definition
OPORD	operation order
opns	operations
PEO	program executive officer
PMESII–PT	political, economic, social, information, infrastructure, physical environment, time
pp	page
POC	point of contact
POL	petroleum, oil, and lubricants
PRT	provincial reconstruction team
R	reinforcing
RCEM	regional contingency engineering management
RFI	request for information
RI	relevant information
RSOI	reception, staging, onward movement, and integration
RSR	required supply rate
S	survivability
S-1	human resources staff officer
S-2	intelligence staff officer
S-3	operations staff officer
S-4	logistics staff officer
S-5	civilian affairs/public affairs staff officer at the battalion/brigade level
S-6	communications and information management staff officer
S-9	facilities management staff officer
SCATMINE	scatterable mine
SCR	Stryker cavalry regiment
SECDEF	Secretary of Defense
SIPRNET	SECRET Internet Protocol Router Network
SITEMP	situational template
SJA	staff judge advocate
SJFHQ-(CE)	standing joint force headquarters (corps element)
SOP	standing operating procedure
SPO	support officer, operations
SPOD	seaport of debarkation
STANAG	standardization agreement
STB	special troops battalion
SUST	sustainment
TAA	tactical assembly area
TACON	tactical control
TBP	to be published
TCEM	theater contingency engineer management
TCF	tactical combat force
TCMS	Theater Construction Management System
TDA	table of distribution and allowances

Acronym/Term	Definition
TEC	theater engineer command
TF	task force
TPFDD	time-phased force and deployment data
TRADOC	United States Army Training and Doctrine Command
TSA	theater storage area
TSC	theater sustainment command
TTP	tactics, techniques, and procedures
UFC	unified facilities criteria
UN	United Nations
UNAAF	Unified Action Armed Forces
U.S.	United States
USACE	United States Army Corps of Engineers
USAES	United States Army Engineer School
USAF	United States Air Force
USAFRICOM	United States Africa Command
USAID	United States Agency for International Development
USAMC	United States Army Materiel Command
USAR	United States Army Reserve
USARAF	United States Army, Africa (Combatant Command, GEO)
USARCENT	United States Army, Central Command
USAREUR	United States Army, European Command
USARNORTH	United States Army North
USARPAC	United States Army, Pacific Command
USARSO	United States Army, Southern Command
USCENTCOM	United States Central Command
USEUCOM	United States European Command
USJFCOM	United States Joint Forces Command
USMC	United States Marine Corps
USNORTHCOM	United States Northern Command
USPACOM	United States Pacific Command
USSOUTHCOM	United States Southern Command
UXO	unexploded explosive ordnance
WARNO	warning order
WG	working group
WIT	weapons intelligence team

References

SOURCES USED

The following sources are either quoted or paraphrased in this publication.

ARMY PUBLICATIONS

DA Forms are available on the APD web site (www.apd.army.mil).

AR 71-9. *Warfighting Capabilities Determination.* 28 December 2009.

DA Form 2028. *Recommended Changes to Publications and Blank Forms.*

FM 1-01. *Generating Force Support for Operations.* 2 April 2008.

FM 2-0. *Intelligence.* 23 March 2010.

FM 3-0. *Operations.* 27 February 2008.

FM 3-07. *Stability Operations.* 6 October 2008.

FM 3-24. *Counterinsurgency.* 15 December 2006.

FM 3-34. *Engineer Operations.* 2 April 2009.

FM 3-34.2. *Combined Arms Breaching Operations.* 31 August 2000.

FM 3-34.22. *Engineer Operations: Brigade Combat Team and Below.* 11 February 2009.

FM 3-34.230. *Topographic Operations.* 3 August 2000.

FM 3-34.400 (5-104). *General Engineering.* 9 December 2008.

FM 3-37. *Protection.* 30 September 2009.

FM 3-39.40. *Internment and Resettlement Operations.* 12 February 2010.

FM 3-90. *Tactics.* 4 July 2001.

FM 3-90.31. *Maneuver Enhancement Brigade Operations.* 26 February 2009.

FM 3-90.61. *The Brigade Special Troops Battalion.* 22 December 2006.

FM 3-100.21 (100-21). *Contractors on the Battlefield.* 3 January 2003.

FM 4-0 (100-10). *Sustainment.* 30 April 2009.

FM 4-01.30. *Movement Control.* 1 September 2003.

FM 4-02. *Force Health Protection in a Global Environment.* 13 February 2003.

FM 5-0. *The Operations Process.* 26 March 2010.

FM 5-19. *Composite Risk Management.* 21 August 2006.

FM 5-102. *Countermobility.* 14 March 1985.

FM 5-103. *Survivability.* 10 June 1985.

FM 5-412. *Project Management.* 13 June 1994.

FM 6-0. *Mission Command: Command and Control of Army Forces.* 11 August 2003.

FM 20-3. *Camouflage, Concealment, and Decoys.* 30 August 1999.

FM 90-7. *Combined Arms Obstacle Integration.* 29 September 1994.

FMI 4-93.2. *The Sustainment Brigade.* 4 February 2009.

FMI 4-93.41. *Army Field Support Brigade Tactics, Techniques, and Procedures.* 22 February 2007.

USEUCOM Red Book. *Base Camp Facility Standards*. 1 February 2004.
  http://www.dcsengr.hqusareur.army.mil/Red_Book.pdf

USCENTCOM Sand Book. *Construction and Base Camp Development in the USCENTCOM Area of Responsibility*. 17 December 2007.
  https://acquisition.army.mil/asfi/upload/W91CRB10R0059/Attachment_17_Sand_Book.pdf

JOINT PUBLICATIONS

CJCSM 3122.01A. *Joint Operation Planning and Execution System (JOPES) Volume I (Planning Policies and Procedures)*. 29 September 2006.

CJCSM 3122.03C. *Joint Operation Planning and Execution System (JOPES) Volume II, Planning Formats and Guidance*. 17 August 2007.

JP 1. *Doctrine for the Armed Forces of the United States*. 2 May 2007.

JP 1-0. *Personnel Support to Joint Operations*. 16 October 2006.

JP 1-02. *Department of Defense Dictionary of Military and Associated Terms*. 12 April 2001.

JP 2-03. *Geospatial Intelligence Support to Joint Operations*. 22 March 2007.

JP 3-0. *Joint Operations*, 17 September 2006.

JP 3-08. *Interagency, Intergovernmental Organization and Nongovernmental Organization Coordination During Joint Operations, Vol. I and II*. 17 March 2006.

JP 3-10. *Joint Security Operations in Theater*. 3 February 2010.

JP 3-15. *Barriers, Obstacles, and Mine Warfare for Joint Operations*. 26 April 2007.

JP 3-28. *Civil Support*. 14 September 2007.

JP 3-31. *Command and Control for Joint Land Operations*. 23 March 2004.

JP 3-33. *Joint Task Force Headquarters*. 16 February 2007.

JP 3-34. *Joint Engineer Operations*. 12 February 2007.

JP 3-35. *Deployment and Redeployment Operations*. 7 May 2007.

JP 4-07. *Joint Tactics, Techniques, and Procedures for Common-User Logistics During Joint Operations*. 11 June 2001.

JP 4-08. *Joint Doctrine for Logistic Support of Multinational Operations*. 25 September 2002.

JP 5-0. *Joint Operation Planning*. 26 December 2006.

MULTI-SERVICE PUBLICATIONS

FM 1-02/MCRP 5-12A. *Operational Terms and Graphics*. 21 September 2004.

FM 3-34.170/MCRP 3-17.4 (5-170). *Engineer Reconnaissance*. 25 March 2008.

FM 3-34.5/MCRP 4-11B. *Environmental Considerations*. 16 February 2010.

OTHER PUBLICATIONS

Arms Export Control Act of 1976, 22 October 1968.

ATP-52(B). *Land Force Combat Engineer Doctrine*. 18 December 2008.
  https://nsa.nato.int

DOD 7000.14-R. *Department of Defense Financial Management Regulation*. September 2008.

DOD Directive 4270.5. *Military Construction*. 12 February 2005.

DOD Directive 5100.46. *Foreign Disaster Relief*. 4 December 1975.

Eckstein, (Colonel) Jeffrey R. *Engineer*, "Modular Engineer Structure in Divisions," *The Professional Bulletin of Army Engineers*, January-March 2008, 61.

Engineers of the Southwest Pacific 1941-1945, Volume 8. Critque.

Foreign Assistance Act of 1961, Section 607A.

STANAG 2394 E, Edition 3, *Land Force Combat Engineer Doctrine – ATP-52(B)*. 18 December 2008.
https://nsa.nato.int

Title 10, United States Code 401. *Humanitarian and Civic Assistance Provided in Conjunction with Military Operations.*

Title 10, United States Code 2350j. *Burden Sharing Contributions by Designated Countries and Regional Organizations.*

Title 10, United States Code 2551. *Equipment and Barracks National Veterans' Organizations.*

Title 22, United States Code 2318. *Special Authority.*

Title 31, United States Code 1535. *Agency Agreements.*

DOCUMENTS NEEDED
These documents must be available to the intended users of this publication.

None

READINGS RECOMMENDED
These sources contain relevant supplemental information.

FM 1. *The Army.* 14 June 2005.

FM 3-28.1. *Multi-service Tactics, Techniques and Procedures for Civil Support (CS) Operations.* 3 December 2007.

This page intentionally left blank.

Index

This page intentionally left blank.

ATTP 3-34.23 (FM 5-71-100, 5-100-15, 5-116)
8 July 2010

By order of the Secretary of the Army:

GEORGE W. CASEY, JR.
General, United States Army
Chief of Staff

Official:

JOYCE E. MORROW
Administrative Assistant to the
Secretary of the Army
1019602

DISTRIBUTION:

Active Army, Army National Guard, and United States Army Reserve: To be distributed in accordance with the initial distribution number (IDN) 110451, requirements for ATTP 3-34.23.